Plumbers and Visionaries

Further praise for Plumbers and Visionaries

Plumbers and Visionaries

Securities Settlement and Europe's Financial Market

Peter Norman

John Wiley & Sons, Ltd

Published by   John Wiley & Sons Ltd, The Atrium, Southern Gate, Chichester,
West Sussex PO19 8SQ, England

Telephone   (+44) 1243 779777

Email (for orders and customer service enquiries): cs-books@wiley.co.uk
Visit our Home Page on www.wiley.com

Other Wiley Editorial Offices

John Wiley & Sons Inc., 111 River Street, Hoboken, NJ 07030, USA

Jossey-Bass, 989 Market Street, San Francisco, CA 94103-1741, USA

Wiley-VCH Verlag GmbH, Boschstr. 12, D-69469 Weinheim, Germany

John Wiley & Sons Australia Ltd, 42 McDougall Street, Milton, Queensland 4064, Australia

John Wiley & Sons (Asia) Pte Ltd, 2 Clementi Loop #02-01, Jin Xing Distripark, Singapore 129809

John Wiley & Sons Canada Ltd, 6045 Freemont Blvd, Mississauga, ONT, L5R 4J3, Canada

Wiley also publishes its books in a variety of electronic formats. Some content that appears
in print may not be available in electronic books.

Anniversary Logo Design: Richard J. Pacifico

British Library Cataloguing in Publication Data

A catalogue record for this book is available from the British Library

ISBN 978-0-470-72425-5 (HB)

Typeset in 10/12pt Times by Aptara Inc., New Delhi, India
Printed and bound in Great Britain by Antony Rowe Ltd, Chippenham, Wiltshire, UK
This book is printed on acid-free paper responsibly manufactured from sustainable forestry
in which at least two trees are planted for each one used for paper production.

Contents

List of Tables and Figures

TABLES

FIGURES

Preface

The origins of this book can be traced to a lunch in the City late in 2004. Over coffee, Chris Tupker, then the chairman of Euroclear, suggested it would be a service to posterity if somebody could record the reminiscences of the pioneers who helped create the modern securities settlement industry in Europe.

Nothing happened immediately. But shortly afterwards, Deutsche Börse made its approach to take over the London Stock Exchange and a more ambitious project began to form.

Europe's exchanges and post-trade infrastructures appeared to be entering an end-game of restructuring and consolidation in a fast changing regulatory environment which would be governed by new rules expected from the European Commission in Brussels. The time seemed ripe to start a broader history of the European securities settlement industry, incorporating the memories of the founding fathers but also focusing on the difficulties and challenges of cross-border transactions, which had by this time been identified as hampering Europe's economic growth.

Three years on and the eventual shape of Europe's post-trade infrastructure is still undetermined despite much change in the meantime. But the book, *Plumbers and Visionaries: Securities settlement and Europe's financial market*, is complete.

Plumbers and Visionaries is the story of a financial sector that has grown hugely in importance in the 40 years since Euroclear was created to deal with a settlement crisis that threatened to smother the international capital market in its infancy.

The book follows the development of securities settlement across Europe's frontiers from the free-wheeling days of the Eurobond market in the 1960s through the growing integration of the European Union to the highly regulated and efficient multi-trillion euro business it is today. It is the story of a sector strongly influenced by developments in the US that has nonetheless developed in a uniquely European way.

Securities settlement may appear to be an abstruse subject. The first chapter of this book seeks to explain why it has a wider significance than may at first be apparent. With this in mind, I have tried to write a book that reaches beyond the specialist to the reader with a more general interest in economics, finance, business and the political economy of Europe.

This book has been made possible by the support of Euroclear plc, which helped finance its research. The story of Euroclear forms part of this book. But throughout, the relationship between company and author has been one at arm's length. The book is not an official history of Euroclear or any other company in the sector.

I am indebted to many people who have helped with the research of this book. Written sources on the securities settlement industry are few and far between, reflecting the tendency of fast growing, IT-based companies to consign archives to the skip each time they move office.

My thanks go to members of the settlement, regulatory, policy making and media communities who gave freely of their time and, with good humour, dealt with questions that must sometimes have appeared tedious and often naïve. They include: Walter Allwicher, Marc Bayle, John Berrigan, Luc Bomans, Benoit Bourtembourg, Bruce Brackenridge, Rolf-E Breuer, Massimo Capuano, Diana Chan, Alastair Clark, Ignace Combes, Clifford Dammers, Godfried De Vidts, Martine Dinne, Diana Dijmarescu, Oliver Drewes, Philippe Duvieusart, Bill Ellington, Pierre Francotte, The Financial Times Library, Werner Frey, Jean-Paul Frising, Ambassador Evan Galbraith, Matthias Ganz, Alberto Giovannini, Jean-Michel Godeffroy, David Green, Sean Greenaway, Judith Hardt, Gerd Häusler, Walter Imthurn, Pierre Jaans, Piia-Noora Kauppi, Pen Kent, Tom Ketchum, Fritz Klein, Walter Koller, John Langton, Sir Andrew Large, Olivier Lefebvre, André Lussi, André Lutgen, Michael March, Jacques-Philippe Marson, Tim May, Joël Mérère, Paul Mousel, Mario Nava, John Nordstrom, Michael Patterson, Tom Perna, Denis Peters, Agnès Petiau, Albert Petersen, Patrick Poncelet, Herschel Post, André Roelants, Stanley Ross, Bruno Rossignol, Iain Saville, René Schmitter, Stephan Schuster, Werner Seifert, John Serocold, Hugh Simpson, Ian Steers, Peter Sucaet, Paul Symons, Brian Taylor, Jeffrey Tessler, Yolande Theiss, Jean-Francois Théodore, Martin Thomas, Bernie Till, Gertrude Tumpel-Gugerell, A. Chris Tupker, Charles D'Ursel, Gérard Van Nieuwenhove, Rüdiger Von Rosen, Sir David Walker, Sir Nigel Wicks, David Wright, Eddy Wymeersch, Stanislas Yassukovich, Carlos Zeyen.

There would be no book without Chris Tupker's inspiration and encouragement. I also owe special thanks to Pierre Francotte, chief executive of Euroclear SA/NV, and Martine Dinne, the recently retired CEO of Euroclear Bank, who took the time and trouble to read parts of the text and made helpful suggestions.

At no time did they, or anyone else at Euroclear, seek to influence this work. The judgements and any errors in the pages that follow are mine.

Part I
New Problems. New Solutions

1
Settling Securities Across Borders

1.1 TURNOVER IN THE TRILLIONS

By any standards, 450 trillion is a big number. Forty five followed by 13 zeros defies easy comprehension.

Put a euro sign in front of that 450 000 000 000 000 and you have nearly 40 times the annual output of goods and services of all 27 members of the European Union as measured by gross domestic product. Divide the €450 trillion into €1 coins and imagine them piled up, one on top of the other: the column of coins would stretch 1.05 billion kilometres into space – a distance seven times greater than that between Earth and the Sun. Shared out, €450 trillion would be €920 000 for every man, woman and child in the EU.

This almost unfathomable sum is the annual turnover of a group of companies, headquartered in an anonymous office block in Brussels. Euroclear, the company in question, and the other members of the Euroclear group, settled securities transactions with a value of €452 trillion in 2006. Euroclear is not a household name. Stop any passer-by and ask them to describe what the company does. Unless you are in the immediate vicinity of that office building at lunchtime, it is a fair bet that no one will know.

Yet without Euroclear and companies like it, the world economy as we know it could not exist. As the biggest company of its type in Europe, Euroclear is one of a number of companies around the globe providing vital infrastructure services for the world's financial markets.

The world's securities markets have been enjoying a golden age. Impersonal, unsentimental and transmitted as bits and bytes by the latest information technology, footloose funds flash round the world at the speed of light seeking the best possible return. At the centre of the markets are mighty commercial and investment banks with financial power that dwarfs many a nation's economy. We all depend on these markets: the businessman seeking finance to expand; the pensioner looking for a better return on meagre savings; the young family wanting to move to a new house and the government that borrows to cover its budget deficit.

Securities will change hands many times to fit the needs of these very different customers. The security might be an equity share in a company, a bond issued by a government or corporation or a share in a collective investment, such as a unit trust or mutual fund. It may be transformed, diced and sliced into a completely different financial instrument – a derivative – to redistribute risk or boost yield. The place where the security is traded may be a registered securities exchange, such as the stock exchanges located in London, Paris and Frankfurt, an 'over-the-counter' market such as that for international bonds where dealers trade using telephones or trading screens, or the trading book of a big investment bank.

Central to any securities market is the transfer of ownership of the security from seller to buyer in return for payment. That is where the idea of an exchange comes from. But if language followed logic, the world's securities exchanges would no longer glory in that name. Securities are listed on exchanges, they may be traded on exchanges. But the actual exchange of the securities is handled by the various specialised 'post-trade' services which are commonly lumped together under the heading of clearing and settlement.

Companies like Euroclear provide the 'settlement' and related services that follow the trade of a security and enable the markets to work. Clearing and settlement are often regarded as the 'plumbing' of securities markets: a series of electronic 'pipes' linking customers with electronic 'storage tanks' which keep customers' securities accounts. Although this end of the securities business is unglamorous and unheeded unless things go wrong, it is of existential importance for the markets.

No matter how sophisticated or speedy the platform on which securities are traded, the market in question cannot serve its purpose without an apparatus that actually completes the transfer of securities from seller to buyer and ensures payment flows in the other direction from buyer to seller. All trading venues have a vital interest in a settlement infrastructure that is fast, efficient and as cost effective as possible and that can meet demands for additional services that can enhance the profitability of those companies that use them.

Just as exchanges and the instruments that they trade have grown more technologically advanced and complex over the past half century, so too have the companies that handle post-trade arrangements.

For much of this period, however, Europe's post-trade service providers were neglected by policy makers so that the sector remains ill adjusted to the needs of the European Union's single market and a globalised world.

The sector is fragmented, posing a major challenge for executives and politicians alike. Its activities – and its efforts to overcome barriers to greater efficiency in Europe – are the subject of this book.

So too is the story of Euroclear, which has grown to be a €450 trillion business in 40 years despite the imperfections of Europe's still incomplete single market.

Securities have always been traded across national frontiers in Europe, historically in small volumes and at a price. Unremarked at the time, 21 July 1967 marked a turning point.

The day was Belgian national day. King Baudouin, the Belgian monarch, would have been inspecting his troops in the Rue de la Loi near the centre of Brussels. Not everybody was taking that Friday off, however. A few hundred metres away, in a building of Morgan Guaranty, the US bank, bankers and technicians were launching a securities settlement service to try to overcome a paperwork crisis that threatened to throttle a still young international capital market: the Eurobond market.

That pilot scheme became Euroclear[1] the following year. That it should grow into a business with a turnover of €450 trillion in four decades reflects the dynamic forces that have shaped capital markets and the securities settlement industry in the intervening years.

The first is technology. The calendar was still BC – 'before computers' – when the Eurobond market was created in 1963. True, the integrated circuit was invented in 1959. But a few years would pass before its potential was recognised. In 1965, Gordon Moore, co-founder of US chip maker Intel, observed that the number of transistors per square inch on integrated circuits had doubled every year since 1959 and the trend would continue. In 1975 Moore revised his prediction to a doubling every two years. Moore's law – in synthesis, the rule of thumb that computer power doubles every 18 months or so – has proved an uncannily appropriate predictive tool for the growth of Euroclear's business ever since.

---

[1] The service was in fact called Euro-clear, with a hyphen. The hyphen was part of Euroclear's name and used in the company logo from its foundation in 1968 until 1990. To avoid confusion, this book will refer to the company throughout as Euroclear except when citing in full the company name as used before the rebranding of 1990.

Technology was a necessary but not sufficient condition to unleash the next important force: financial innovation. The growing power of computers and the rapid development of information technology enabled the replacement of physical securities held in the form of paper certificates by electronic records stored in computer memories. Once free of their vaults, securities settlement providers could expand the services they offered in scale, scope and speed in line with the power of computers. But it required financial expertise to develop ever more elaborate financial instruments and additional post-trade services, such as securities lending and borrowing in the 1970s. Financial innovation in turn helped clients make money and capital markets to grow.

That such inventiveness could flourish reflects another factor: liberalisation and the spread of market forces. The Eurobond market that spawned Euroclear was a reaction to national financial restrictions in the US. The UK's 'Big Bang' liberalisation of the London Stock Exchange in 1986, the fall of the Berlin Wall in 1989, the ensuing collapse of Communism in Russia and eastern Europe, the entry of China and India into the world economy were all milestones in a process of liberalisation that fuelled the growth of financial markets and the activities of financial infrastructure providers.

Liberalisation both thrives on and feeds the exchange of ideas. This has been especially true for financial markets and their infrastructure providers. Ideas flowed back and forth, notably across the Atlantic. The expertise that created Euroclear in the late 1960s contributed to the establishment in 1973 of the Depository Trust Company in New York to immobilise equity and bond certificates and transfer title of ownership by book entry. An influx of US investment banks into Europe after Britain's Big Bang raised demands and expectations for improvements in securities settlement arrangements.

The gradual consolidation of equity settlement in the US that culminated in November 1999 with the foundation of The Depository Trust & Clearing Corporation (DTCC) as a low cost, user-governed, regulated monopoly serving a continent became for many in Europe a model of how the industry in the EU should develop.

As it happened, Europe has not followed the US example. The development of the US post-trade infrastructure for equities originated in a decision of Congress in the mid-1970s, before liberalisation and free market economics became global mega-trends. Instead, post-trade infrastructures have developed far more haphazardly in Europe, reflecting the way European integration – a hugely important overarching force – impinged upon the post-trade sector, but only after considerable delay.

Although half a century has passed since the foundation of the European Common Market and a decade and half since European Union leaders agreed in Maastricht to create a European single currency, the task of creating a deep, liquid and efficient EU-wide capital market has yet to be completed. For financial infrastructure providers, integration came late to the party, long after technological advance, financial innovation and market liberalisation had wrought changes in structures that served national markets in Europe.

Europe's fragmented post-trade infrastructure developed along national lines before the introduction of the euro and was shaped in each country by national regulations and historical traditions. Developments in the industry during the 1990s accentuated national specificities. Vertically integrated structures linking activities along the value chain from trading to clearing and settlement developed in most member states because this was judged the best way of securing fast and efficient straight-through processing of securities transactions. Also in vogue was demutualisation which turned securities exchanges and infrastructure providers into for-profit businesses. Although most at that stage still worked in the interests of their users, the link between user and owner was eroded in the 21st century when some of the demutualised exchanges obtained stock exchange listings.

In general, the post-trade tasks of clearing and settlement operate efficiently and at low cost within each EU member state. Complications start once securities trade across borders. Barriers are created by different tax systems, legal systems, market practices and business models among service providers. These factors, combined with vested interests at all levels of the securities business, increase the cost of clearing and settling securities across Europe's internal political borders to several times the cost of a domestic trade. The EU's fragmented financial infrastructure amounts to a significant impediment to the creation of a competitive, continent-wide capital market for Europe.

However, it would be wrong to be too harsh on the architects of Europe's single market or the euro for failing to notice the importance of clearing and settlement. Throughout most of history Europe's infrastructure providers have toiled in obscurity so that post-trade activities in Europe have evolved in an almost tribal environment, where the members of the tribe are a coterie of experts versed in the intricacies of securities markets.

Until around the start of this century, the experts, with their specialisations in computer and information technology, the law, accountancy and local procedures, practices and conventions, were distant from the preoccupations of politics and mainstream business.

Nowadays, the systems they design, build and manage set constraints and create opportunities for generating revenues in the front offices of securities firms the world over. The settlement business has become increasingly IT intensive over the years, with sharply rising investment needs and risks. Securities settlement is more than ever a business subject to economies of scale and scope: the bigger the capacity and the more comprehensive the market coverage, the lower the cost of providing the service should be – so long as the settlement provider can attract the right amount of business, ensure that the IT works and is properly regulated.

Even so, the activities of the financial infrastructure experts are often little known to the top management of the financial conglomerates that depend on the efficient execution of post-trade functions and which sometimes own the businesses that carry them out.

At the level of the expert, post-trade activities offer a world of comradeship and competition that sometimes spills over into personal antagonism. Post-trade issues have a tendency to split those who work in the sector into rival sects. To an outsider, disputes over competing business philosophies such as 'vertical' versus 'horizontal' integration seem arcane. (A vertical silo is where the activities of securities trading, clearing and settlement are integrated often in one company; horizontal integration is where the trading activity is separately controlled from the clearing and settlement activities but where one or all of these activities are integrated with those of other providers according to function.) As with religious wars throughout history, such schisms among infrastructure providers can be a cloak for vested interests.

Securities settlement is a world where everybody in the business knows everybody else. But, despite its tight-knit character, it is also a world with no common language for telling the outside world what it does. There is no standardised terminology covering post-trade activities. Different words mean different things to different people. That makes it difficult for outsiders, such as policy makers, to master the intricacies of the trade. In so far as practitioners have interacted with a growing EU public policy agenda on clearing and settlement, the result has often been perplexity on both sides.

Nonetheless, since the start of this century the business of cross-border settlement in Europe has moved from being a matter of concern to the small number of financial professionals and their clients to a vital public policy issue in the development of the EU's single market. The growing integration of the EU, the introduction of the euro, the increasing sophistication of financial markets, globalisation and the mind boggling scale of the transactions settled have all helped propel the economics of cross-border securities trades out of the 'back offices' of banks and brokerages to the centre-stage of EU politics.

Clearing and settlement have climbed up the priority list of EU policy makers, occupying finance ministers, central bankers and dedicated officials in the European Commission's directorates general for the internal market and competition.

The reasons were highlighted by Alberto Giovannini, an Italian financial expert who has helped devise a strategy to overcome Europe's post-trade fragmentation, in the second of two reports he prepared for the European Commission. Writing in 2003,[2] Giovannini noted how:

> Clearing and settlement are at the core of any financial system; inefficiencies in these processes have serious consequences. When clearing and settlement are too costly or complex, financial transactions are discouraged. In the context of the EU, the result is that national markets have remained isolated: resources are not pooled efficiently, the allocation of economic resources across time and space is sub-optimal, the techniques that allow the trading of risk are too expensive and financial asset prices fail to convey all information that is available to market participants.

Giovannini composed his report four years after the launch of the euro and 11 years after Europe was supposed to have created a single market for goods and services. He concluded that 'the EU financial market cannot be considered an integrated entity but remains a juxtaposition of domestic markets'.

To a considerable extent, this state of affairs still applies today. It means trading securities across national frontiers in the European Union carries extra cost. The precise amount of these extra costs and the factors that cause them are a matter of debate among practitioners and academics. Much attention has focused on the fees charged by individual post-trade infrastructure providers. Although these have fallen in recent years and often account for only a small proportion of the overall cost of a trade, their impact can be considerable when trading volumes are increasing rapidly. There are structural problems too. Compared with domestic transactions, cross-border securities transactions in Europe usually involve far more intermediaries along the value chain from trading, through clearing to settlement, so adding to costs. The overall complexity of completing securities transactions among different jurisdictions and traditions necessitates bigger and more labour intensive back office operations. These factors make the whole value chain expensive and put Europe's financial market at a competitive disadvantage compared with the US: a comparable, continent-sized economic area.

This handicap is important. The more sophisticated the world's big economies become, the more persuasive is the proposition that their financial systems should be based on markets, where financial assets are pooled and traded in response to decisions taken by millions of anonymous savers and investors. For some years, this arm's length system has been hailed as one reason for the consistently superior performance of the US economy compared with that of Europe.

As the European economy has grown in scale and scope with the enlargement of the EU and the introduction of the euro, so too have the reasons for it to move more towards a financial system based on securities markets. Family-based finance may be the only option available in a less developed economy. Bank-based finance might have advantages in a smaller scale or more developed economy where the bank can know its clients and when to support them. But

---

[2] Giovannini Group: 'Second report on EU clearing and settlement arrangements', Brussels, April 2003.

above a certain size, deep and liquid securities markets – provided they are clean, transparent and well organised – are the more efficient means of mobilising the surplus funds of savers and channelling these to investors at prices that mark the equilibrium between supply and demand. They can also be more efficient in transmitting messages to and from savers and users of capital about the efficiency of the allocation of capital in an economy.

Europe's fragmented financial infrastructure means the cost of capital is higher than it need be. Bankers argue that integrated financial markets pool risk more efficiently. The more risk is pooled, the less volatile should be the prices of financial instruments. The less the volatility, the less the need for banks and other intermediaries to retain capital. The less capital they require, the cheaper their services should be.

Sub-optimal arrangements for completing securities trades across borders also hinder the development of a pool of liquidity in Europe comparable to that in the US. The cost of trading securities falls in an inverse relationship to the size and depth of the pool of liquidity in a financial market. The lower the cost of trading a given security, the lower the cost of capital that security represents.

Cheaper capital is obviously of interest to companies. It is one of the factors that can help them compete in today's highly competitive globalised world. It is also of huge importance to the average citizen. The lower the cost of capital, the better the company profits that should accrue to pension funds or mutual funds and the lower the cost of borrowing when necessary.

The specific savings to be gained on any transaction from more efficient financial infrastructures may be tiny – measured in terms of fee reductions of a few hundredths of a percentage point. But such savings mount up in a world where investors' holdings of assets across borders amount to roughly $60 000 billion or about 120% of annual global output.[3]

The good news is that work is in progress to overcome the fragmentation of clearing and settlement in the EU. A host of actors from the private and public sectors – including Euroclear – are engaged in building the single market for clearing and settlement in Europe.

- The European Commission is overseeing an industry code of conduct to increase competition and lower costs along the value chain from trading to settlement.
- More controversially, the European Central Bank is consulting with the industry on its own plans for a settlement platform.
- Euroclear is building a 'domestic market for Europe' which will cut costs sharply for investors. The group is implementing a 214 point plan to harmonise market practices in the EU member states where it settles domestic securities.

The bad news is that overcoming Europe's fragmentation in clearing and settlement is a slow process. This is:

- partly a problem of the rules having changed in midstream. The coming of the euro was meticulously planned by public authorities in every area except clearing and settlement. Change now means changing long established structures and practices.
- partly a problem inherent in infrastructure investments. These take an inordinately long time to arrange in a European Union of 27 member states. Although benefits can accrue to smaller clusters of countries and markets, they only become wholly effective when the last component of the investment is in place.

---

[3] According to Kenneth Rogoff, former chief economist at the International Monetary Fund, writing in the *Financial Times*, 8 February 2007.

The situation is in some ways analogous to the investments in railway infrastructure in the 19th century. The investments of the Union Pacific and Central Pacific railway companies that built the first US transcontinental railway with one company starting from the east and the other from the west only bore full fruit once the final piece of track was hammered into place in the middle.

Achieving harmonisation and interoperability among existing infrastructures is even more tortuous. In a 2003 report, the Group of 30, a top level think-tank comprising eminent financiers and influential former policy makers from around the world, suggested that the rewards from making clearing and settlement systems better able to interact with each other could be as great as those gained from the national standardisation of railway track gauges in the US in the 19th century.

The G30 report did not mention that it took from 1862 when Congress specified the northern four foot eight and a half inch gauge as standard for US transcontinental railways until 1886 when the southern states finally converted their five foot wide tracks to achieve standardisation: a 24 year delay despite the South having in the meantime lost the Civil War.

This book will start a century later: in the 1960s.

After a guide to the processes and participants in post-trade activities, the story begins with the settlement crisis in the Eurobond market. It describes how Euroclear and later Cedel, its arch-rival, were founded to solve it. The book will follow Euroclear's development as a cross-border settlement provider for a growing range of securities in the context of the European securities settlement market as a whole. It will demonstrate how securities settlement became an issue for public policy after the stock market crash of 1987 and how the problems of cross-border settlement moved rapidly up the European policy agenda after the euro's launch. It is a story of companies and computers, institutions and ideas, markets and managers.

It makes no apology for being an empirical work and for highlighting the sometimes unpredictable role of individuals in shaping Europe's securities settlement industry and its prospects – both for good and ill. Some often larger-than-life characters have toiled in an unglamorous area of the financial world to build an infrastructure on which Europe's economic growth and well-being depends.

If this book has a theme, it is that financial markets and the infrastructure services that support them do not develop according to any grand design or plan. They are the result of a complex interplay between global macro-financial forces, competition between companies, developing technology, national politics and laws and above all the vision and drive of people working away in financial markets.

This book seeks to trace the complex and often messy interplay of these forces in the development of securities settlement, especially in the European Union over the last few decades.

1.2   PROCESS AND PLAYERS

'Clearing and settlement are basic functions in a financial system, but they are also very complex processes.' Alberto Giovannini's observation is both pithy and true.

Defining the functions and the providers of post-trade services is no easy task. When the European Commission produced a working document on definitions of post-trading activities in 2005 with the help of practitioners[4] the preface contained a clutch of disclaimers and the observation that those experts in the group with a banking background disagreed with the approach taken.

Given the lack of a common terminology for the business, the following cannot be a definitive guide to securities settlement and related activities. It is a simplified guide to the processes and players involved in clearing and settlement in the broader context of post-trading functions.[5]

A securities transaction passes through a number of stages once the *trade*, the binding agreement between two counterparties to exchange securities and cash at a future date, has been completed.

The first is *verification*, which is the process of comparing and, if necessary, reconciling discrepancies in the transaction or settlement details. There is some dispute whether verification – which covers issues such as price, quantity and settlement date of the trade – should properly be described as a post-trade activity because it is commonly handled at or close to the point of trade. It is preliminary to rather than part of clearing and settlement.

Clearing comes next. Clearing was defined in the Commission document as 'the process of establishing settlement positions, possibly including the calculation of net positions, and the process of checking that securities, cash or both are available'. Clearing, according to this definition, ensures that all the prerequisites for settlement are in place. It focuses on establishing the respective obligations of the buyer and the seller.

In recent years, however, clearing has come to have other meanings of greater importance than the calculation of who owes what to whom following a trade. Clearing in the modern sense refers to the activity of 'central counterparty clearing' or CCP clearing, which is provided by a central counterparty or CCP, a specialised financial institution that is placed between the buyers and sellers of securities.

The Commission distinguishes between *counterparty clearing* and *central counterparty clearing*.

Counterparty clearing is defined as 'the process by which a third party interposes itself, directly or indirectly, between the transaction counterparties in order to assume their rights and obligations'. In this process, the CCP assumes the credit risk of the participants in the trade, possibly by guaranteeing a transaction.

In central counterparty clearing, the CCP not only assumes the rights and obligations of the counterparties, it also acts 'as the direct or indirect buyer to every seller and the direct or indirect seller to every buyer'.

Central counterparty clearing activities of CCPs are an increasingly important part of financial market infrastructure. By being placed in the middle of a vast number of transactions, a CCP is able to net the gross obligations it incurs. In other words, the CCP offsets the amounts it owes and is owed by market participants and reduces its obligations to (usually small) residual amounts that become single debits or credits between itself and each of its members.

CCPs and netting developed hand-in-hand with derivatives trading from the 1970s onwards. The netting process is of vital importance for these markets where contracts are usually closed out and very rarely settled in the sense of transferring an asset with finality from one investor to another in return for payment.

---

[4] Commission Services Working Document on Definitions of Post-Trading Activities, Working Document/MARKT/SLG/ G2(2005)D15283.

[5] The working document is one of several sources of information consulted by the author for this section.

Central counterparty clearing began to appear in securities markets in Europe in the late 1990s, providing many benefits. CCP clearing simplifies the management of counterparty risks by supplying a single counterparty instead of several. It increases liquidity through netting and cuts settlement costs by reducing the number and value of transactions that have to be settled. It also enables counterparties to remain anonymous to one another.

CCPs assume the risk of default of the counterparties to trades and therefore need to have adequate capital and sophisticated risk management techniques in place. On the other hand, once up and running, they are well placed to exploit economies of scale and scope.

Clearing, as conducted by a CCP, is a separate business to settlement. Although there are some cases – the Deutsche Börse group being one – where clearing forms part of a value chain from trading, through clearing to settlement in what is known as a 'silo', it is a functionally different activity. There is no necessity for clearing to be included with other functions of the securities business in the same business entity.

Unless suitable corporate governance arrangements are in place, a case can be made from a competition policy viewpoint for keeping the CCP separate from both trading and settlement. The CCP acts as a funnel by netting all transactions after the trading level and can be in a dominant position to decide where the netted trades will be settled. At the end of the clearing process, the instructions for the transfer of the securities and the funds to pay for them are transmitted to the settlement organisation.

Unlike central counterparty clearing, the *settlement* of securities transactions has been necessary for the functioning of bond and equity markets for as long as these markets have existed. Securities markets are unthinkable without settlement systems because the transfer of equities and bonds from seller to buyer is only final when delivery and payment have been completed.

In Europe, the vast majority of securities are either immobilised or dematerialised which means, in effect, that they no longer are traded as physical certificates but only as records – nowadays usually in electronic form – in accounts held by the issuer or an approved institution.

An immobilised security is one where the physical certificates have been placed in a vault or depository, often in the form of one 'global' instrument that represents the entire amount of the security issue, so that subsequent transfers can be made by *book entry*. Dematerialisation occurs when the physical securities or documents of title that represent ownership of securities are eliminated so that the securities exist only as accounting records.

According to the Commission, settlement by book entry is 'the act of crediting and debiting the transferee's and transferor's accounts respectively, with the aim of completing a transaction in securities'.

This, however, is a minimalist definition of settlement that does not include the many additional *stock-related activities* that are linked to the security itself and are independent of the completion of the trade. Nor does it deal with the institutions involved or how payment for the securities should be made.

The Commission identifies four main stock-related activities: establishing securities in book entry form; deposit; account providing and asset servicing.

The *establishment of securities in book entry form* is defined as the 'initial representation and subsequent maintenance of securities in book entry form through initial credits and subsequent credits or debits to securities accounts'. The book entry can be established on the basis of information from the issuer or by counting the number of physical securities on deposit in the vault.

Deposit refers to the storage of physical securities on behalf of others. *Account providing* refers to the maintenance of securities accounts for the client, or account holder. *Asset servicing* covers the provision of services for the investor arising from events affecting the security. These events are called *corporate actions* and range from the very simple, such as payment of interest or a dividend, to the very complex, such as put options on a structured product. They could affect, for instance, an investor in equities who could expect to be asked to vote for or against the company's dividend and its board, would be invited to attend the annual meeting, would be informed of approaches from a possible bidder and perhaps asked to subscribe to a new share issue or react to a takeover bid. Asset servicing could also include the *valuation of portfolios*, the *processing of tax reclaims* or *withholding tax* to pay to government authorities.

There are three types of providers of settlement services: the Central Securities Depository or CSD; International Central Securities Depositories or ICSDs and intermediaries – a catch-all term that covers other commercial organisations engaged in settlement activity. These are usually banks, acting as agent banks, and/or global custodians.

The *CSD* is the basic building block of a modern settlement infrastructure. It is a special financial institution created to remove the need to shift securities in physical form from one investor to another.

CSDs have several functions. In some countries, they are the public *notaries* for securities because the names of the account holders on their electronic systems are the definitive record of title. They often provide the simple (non-CCP) clearing services. The CSD is the institution responsible for immobilising securities in its depository so that the buying and selling of securities can be settled on its books by adjusting investors' securities and cash accounts. In some cases, CSDs carry out extra services such as corporate action services.

It is difficult to generalise about CSDs because they are national institutions with differing rules and competences. This reflects the national structure of the securities business in Europe and the way that domestic securities have traditionally been settled on a national basis. Companies that list their shares on a country's stock exchange place their shares in the national CSD. Because each CSD is governed by different national legal requirements covering activities such as corporate actions, they tend to function as monopolies for some services. It is difficult, for example, for a company that has issued shares in one country to move its share to the CSD of another country.

Post-trade services are not a competition-free zone, however. There is some competition among CCPs, between CSDs and CCPs and among CSDs. As this book will make clear, competition is fierce among ICSDs. There is also competition between CSDs and their clients. In some markets, local banks are strong competitors of the CSD for at least some of its services, notably settlement. It is estimated that half the securities settlement in France is handled by banks away from the books of the national CSD in a process known as internalisation of settlement. A study in 2002 suggested that more than half of transactions by non-resident investors in Italy were settled outside the CSD where the security was issued.

Membership of a CSD is generally reserved for banks and other financial institutions that meet strict eligibility criteria. There are some exceptions. In Scandinavia, CSDs provide the registrar function for individual investors in their jurisdiction and so maintain millions of accounts which are operated by a handful of banks. Euroclear UK & Ireland Ltd, the British and Irish CSD,[6] maintains accounts for some 40 000 'personal' members.

---

[6] Euroclear UK & Ireland Ltd has been the legal and operating name of the CSD previously known as CRESTCo since 1 July 2007. In this history, the company is usually referred to by its original name. The CSD's processing system continues to be known as CREST.

When buying or selling securities, the investor interacts with the CSD through an intermediary, such as a bank or stock broker, which is a member of the CSD.

As will be described in some detail in this book, the International Central Securities Depositories or *ICSDs* were set up by banks in the late 1960s to be the CSDs of the stateless Eurobond market, which is now more usually known as the international bond market. Euroclear and Cedel (later Clearstream) have pursued an intense rivalry ever since. The ICSDs diversified into settling domestic bonds and equities from the 1980s onwards and have formed groups with CSDs since the beginning of the 21st century. Euroclear took over the CSDs of France, the UK, Ireland, the Netherlands and Belgium. Cedel first merged with the German settlement company owned by Deutsche Börse and was eventually fully taken over by Deutsche Börse. In Switzerland, SIS SegaInterSettle combines functions of a CSD and ICSD.

By holding securities in the form of electronic information, CSDs and ICSDs hold a stock of financial assets that the securities' owners can allow to be lent and borrowed and used as collateral by market participants. Once this attribute of securities in a CSD or ICSD was linked to the power of modern computers and a sophisticated banking infrastructure, there was a huge increase in the use of securities as collateral, powering a securities repurchase or 'Repo' market worth billions of euros a year.

The two big ICSDs and SIS differ from most CSDs in one important respect: they are banks. For example, Euroclear Bank, the ICSD of the Euroclear group, has a banking licence which allows it to extend credit and make profits from banking activities, although these are strictly linked to securities settlement.

The provision of such value added services creates dilemmas for the settlement business. Is it, or should it be, comprised of utilities serving the market, or a profit making activity, or both? What competitive forces or competition rules should exist to ensure no single settlement provider is ripping off other participants in the securities industry value chain? Are there generally accepted rules of corporate governance that can ensure the business generates enough money to invest but not so much as to act as a tax on the capital markets?

Such tensions are not limited to the post-trade sector, of course. The securities business can be very profitable at all stages of the value chain from trading to settlement, triggering conflicts of interest between users, owners and managers of the systems. Company decisions are variously dictated by market requirements, executive ambition and technical achievements and failures.

The Euroclear group strives to overcome these problems by being user owned and user governed. But in general, the tensions arising from these questions have grown in line with the growth of securities markets in Europe and will reappear frequently in the pages that follow.

For a securities' transaction to settle there must be payment for, as well as delivery of, the security. The payment of funds typically involves a CSD or ICSD and the banking and payment systems. The cash leg in national systems is usually provided by the central bank, which is the source of central bank money, the safest of all means of payment. Where settlement takes place in central bank money, payment moves directly and irrevocably between accounts on the books of the central bank.

There can be no central bank behind the international bond market served by the ICSDs, because this is a stateless market. In this case, the cash leg of settlement is transacted in commercial bank money with payment moving between the accounts of the ICSDs.

But while central bank money provides the safest form of payment in a securities settlement transaction, commercial bank money is often the payment medium of choice for big commercial and investment banks. It can be cheaper and more flexible because it allows transactions to be secured against assets denominated in currencies other than that issued by the central bank in question.

Issues of payment have proved to be neuralgic throughout the history of the securities settlement business because, in aggregate, transactions involve huge sums of money. The fear that failure could put at risk the financial system of a nation or group of nations is never far from the thoughts of supervisors.

The quest for delivery versus (simultaneous) payment in order to mitigate risk became a preoccupation of the industry's executives and policy makers for a decade after the worldwide stock market crash of October 1987. More recently, the sensitivity of some national central banks in the eurozone about the outsourcing of the cash leg of settlement transactions in central bank money to CSDs has prompted the European Central Bank to embark on a project, dubbed Target2-Securities, to build a settlement platform of its own to serve the euro area. Instead of outsourcing, T2S, as it is called, would 'insource' the core securities settlement function of the eurozone CSDs to a platform operated by the ECB.

Commercial enterprises with a speciality in securities settlement form the third group of institutions involved in the business. Grouped together as *intermediaries*, they are, in fact, a heterogeneous bunch. Generally, they are custodian banks which hold securities for their customers and provide value added services such as access to national CSDs or settlement on their own books.

ICSDs also provide such intermediary services. Euroclear and Clearstream have each forged links with about 30 CSDs in addition to those that are members respectively of the Euroclear and Deutsche Börse groups.

Custodian banks exist to overcome the complexities that persist for securities settlement across borders. The settlement of securities is easy to handle in a national framework: securities are held in a CSD, and intermediaries have direct or indirect access to the system for settlement in a single jurisdiction. A cross-border transaction, by contrast, requires the receipt and delivery of securities held in different countries in return for payments passing between different jurisdictions. It means gaining access to a settlement system in another country or ensuring that the different settlement systems can interact.

As mentioned earlier, a cross-border securities transaction usually means a sharp increase in the number of intermediaries involved in its settlement, raising the costs of execution and the risks of the transaction failing. In his 2001 report, Giovannini found that a cross-border equity transaction required as many as 11 intermediaries compared with only five for a corresponding domestic deal and as many as 14 instructions between parties and as many confirmation messages.

It is the job of custodian banks to smooth away these worries – at a price. They divide into two types: the local agent banks and the global custodians. It is easy to confuse the two categories, not least because since the mid-1990s several banks have entered and exited one or the other of the two markets in a wave of corporate restructuring in the sector. There are also some banks, such as Citigroup and BNP Paribas, which are active in both fields through different business lines.

The *agent bank* typically is a local bank with access to the national CSD and whose business it is to provide the non-resident investor with all the services associated with ownership of the security. This route, which gives the foreign investor the benefit of local expertise, has characteristically been used for cross-border equity investments.

Agent banks come in all shapes and sizes. Deutsche Bank provides typical agent bank services in Germany and also, for historic reasons, in some other European and Asian countries where it is a custodian. Deutsche is not, however, a global custodian, having pulled out of that business. A local agent bank can be a one market agent, like Intesa in Italy or Bank of Bangkok in Thailand. It can be a two or three market agent, like Santander in Spain, which serves Spain, Portugal and Latin America but no other market. There are also multi-market agents, serving 10 or more markets such as BNP Paribas, Citigroup, Euroclear Bank and Clearstream Banking Luxembourg.

The agent banks are the true beneficiaries of Europe's fragmented markets and never more so than when they are able to settle a transaction on their own books. While access to the local CSD is at the heart of the agent bank's business, it will, whenever possible, settle trades on its own books through a process known as settlement internalisation. This can take place when two counterparties in a trade are already on the bank's books so that the transaction is settled without using the CSD.

A *global custodian* is a large globally active bank, such as State Street or The Bank of New York Mellon[7] of the US which can cover many markets. A global custodian provides more sophisticated value added services via a single access point for investors to national CSDs through a network of local agents including ICSDs, and in rare cases, such as Citibank, through its own subsidiaries or branches.

A global custodian would typically be able to hold a range of assets such as bonds, equities, mutual funds and derivatives on behalf of customers in perhaps more than 100 markets. There has been a process of concentration among global custodians over the past decade as the companies involved have reacted to market pressures for economies of scale and the need to make substantial investment in information technology to support their networks.

There is a hierarchy of services offered by the various types of custodian. The global custodians offer the high margin, sophisticated, upmarket services such as portfolio valuation for pension funds, corporations and insurance companies in the largest number of markets. The agent banks provide settlement, custody, sometimes collateral management, but also financing services in the form of credits and securities lending. The CSDs and ICSDs offer basic services for financial intermediaries, such as no-frills settlement, custody and some collateral management.

Whereas the agent banks will lend clients' securities with the specific aim of making money for them in what is known as *Street Lending,* the securities lending and borrowing programmes of the ICSDs exist to increase settlement efficiency and prevent transactions failing. Says Pierre Francotte, chief executive of Euroclear: 'We match supply with a very specific demand, which is only to settle the securities. We do not have a lending desk, a Street Lending desk, offering securities to the market.[8]'

But there is also overlap among the custodian banks and ICSDs. A global custodian, for example, will offer basic services such as safe keeping of securities to foster other client relationships. While it is the ICSDs' job to provide commoditised services to the market, there is a tendency for the scope of such services to go up-market and include activities that only a few years before were among the high margin offerings of the global custodians. This, according to Francotte, is a natural business trend.

Things that the global custodians were doing 10 years ago have become commoditised. They used to make margins of 30% or 40% and then everybody copied what they were doing, and they make

---

[7] The Bank of New York Mellon was formed in July 2007 through the merger of The Bank of New York Co. Inc. and Mellon Financial Corp. The references to The Bank of New York elsewhere in this book refer to BoNY before the merger.

[8] Conversation with the author, 24 November 2006.

margins of perhaps 10% on these services now. That's when they push it to Euroclear. Proxy voting is an example. When I arrived at Euroclear in the early 1990s, proxy voting was the most sophisticated thing. Within five years, people were saying, why doesn't CREST [the UK CSD in the Euroclear group] do it? And now CREST does it. That's a cycle of things being very exciting, making a lot of money at the beginning, becoming commoditised, and being put into the CSDs.

In this crowded and competitive world, the global custodians and ICSDs appear to have achieved a *modus vivendi*. Relations are far less harmonious between the agent banks and the ICSDs because their activities overlap far more. Since Euroclear's acquisition of national CSDs, Citibank and BNP Paribas – in their roles as agent banks – have emerged as Euroclear's bitterest rivals. All three companies are competing for the same kinds of business – and especially the settlement of equity trades. Euroclear's plan of a 'domestic market for Europe' based on harmonised market practices and a single settlement platform threatens to disintermediate the agent banks' services for cross-border transactions.

Disintermediation, overlapping activities and the blurring of distinctions are inevitable consequences of financial change and innovation. One side effect has been an increase in the difficulties of defining and describing the market for securities settlement.

The words clearing and settlement are often uttered in the same breath as if they are a single activity. As this guide makes clear, they are not. They are different functions in the post-trade process.

The confounding of the two activities dates back at least to the 1960s. Then, at the beginning of our story, post-trade activities were less complex. The business known as securities settlement was often called clearing or clearance because clearing in the sense of 'who owes what to whom' was invariably the stage before settling a securities transaction. When in 1968, Morgan Guaranty of New York set up its business to secure safe settlement of securities traded on the recently established Eurobond market, nobody thought it odd that it should be called Euroclear.

Habits persist. Nearly 30 years later, when Deutsche Börse, the German stock market operator, consolidated Germany's securities settlement activities in one company, it chose the name Deutsche Börse Clearing. When in January 2000, the newly merged business of Deutsche Börse Clearing and Cedel, the Luxembourg-based settlement system for international securities and cross-border transactions in domestic securities, was rebranded, it was launched under the name of Clearstream International.

Words such as clear, clearance and clearing will recur time and again in the story of the securities settlement industry since the 1960s, often as part of company names. However, the functions of clearing in its modern usage will only appear to any significant degree towards the end of the narrative when CCPs and central counterparty clearing help shape the securities settlement industry as it is today.

2
The Eurobond Market and the New York Settlement Crisis

2.1 AUTOSTRADE SHOWS THE WAY

Our story begins in a bygone age. In Europe, the 1960s are probably best remembered for the Beatles, mini-skirts and the sexual liberation that followed the development of the contraceptive pill. For many people, living in the western part of the continent, they were years of growing wealth and optimism, tinged with fear arising from the nuclear stand-off between the US and the Soviet Union.

The prosperity that blossomed with reconstruction after the Second World War was still in full swing. The German *Wirtschaftswunder*, or economic miracle, brought full employment with low inflation to regions that had been devastated during the defeat of Hitler's Germany two decades before. Even Britain, which opted after the war to give priority to building a welfare state over investment in productive assets, enjoyed sufficient growth for Prime Minister Harold Macmillan to fight and win an election in 1959 with the slogan: 'You've never had it so good'.

But this prosperity applied in only half the continent. The 'iron curtain' separated western Europe from the Communist east. Running north to south, from the Arctic to the Mediterranean Sea, it divided Germany and its pre-war capital, Berlin. Behind frontiers of barbed wire, mine fields and watch towers, the nuclear-armed Soviet Union enforced one party rule and command and control economics in a swathe of satellite countries that had fallen to the Red Army in 1944–45.

Protected by the American nuclear umbrella and US garrisons, the nation states of western Europe built and rebuilt their democracies on the basis of mixed economies that combined, in varying degrees, the rules of the market with systems of welfare and social protection. In 1957, six of them – France, West Germany, Italy, the Netherlands, Belgium and Luxembourg – decided to pool some of their sovereignty and create the European Economic Community in order to pave the way for a common market in goods and services.

The concept of a common market did not stretch to finance, however. The 1960s 'golden age' of full employment and low inflation was a period of financial regulations and controls. The international monetary system, invented in the New Hampshire resort of Bretton Woods in 1944, relied on virtually fixed exchange rates that were pegged to the dollar and supported by restrictions on capital flows. Each European country developed its own rules for banking, finance and financial infrastructure behind national boundaries. Those individuals who mastered the art of circumventing the controls discovered that it was an age of loopholes that the affluent were quick to exploit.

Even those who prospered in this divided Europe were sometimes prey to fear. The Second World War was still fresh in the memories of policy makers and investors. The ensuing 'cold war' between the West and the Soviet bloc threw up its fair share of crises, as in 1961 when the communist East German regime built a wall around West Berlin to stop the flight of its own citizens to the more prosperous west. The balance of nuclear deterrence between east and west meant confrontation fell short of open hostility. But for investors of a nervous disposition, the spectre of Soviet forces sweeping westwards across the north German plain towards the Rhine or south west through the Fulda gap to Frankfurt and on to France was never far away.

Meanwhile, the US, the guarantor of western Europe's security, became embroiled in an increasingly hot war in Vietnam in east Asia. American military personnel were sent to South Vietnam in the late 1950s to help the regime resist a Communist insurgency. The war escalated during the administration of President John F. Kennedy and more sharply after his assassination in November 1963. The outflow of dollars from the US put its balance of payments and the Bretton Woods system under growing strain. Many of these dollars found their way to Europe where they added to a pool of dollar liquidity, started by the US-led Marshall Plan for rebuilding Europe after the Second World War and fuelled by the large scale US presence on the European continent.

By the early 1960s, some banks began to see opportunities in the growth of dollar holdings outside the US. In February 1961, Evan Galbraith, a 32-year-old lawyer, joined Morgan Guaranty Trust Co. of New York as a vice president when the bank was seeking to enter the underwriting business proscribed for US deposit banks by the Glass-Steagall Act of 1933. 'I did a certain amount of legal research and came up with a view that the act probably didn't apply outside the United States,' he recalled.[1] The research was submitted to the Federal Reserve which agreed with Galbraith.

In 1962, Morgan Guaranty set up a Paris-based subsidiary – Morgan et Cie SA – to carry out underwriting business. Galbraith moved to Paris as a director. Very soon afterwards, in February 1963, Morgan et Cie did a large underwriting through an international syndicate for a public offering of shares in the German mail order and retail company Neckermann Versand.

According to Galbraith, the Neckermann offering became 'the kind of model for what became the Eurobond market'. It revealed 'an interest in European securities of a worldwide nature' and encouraged Morgan et Cie to search for borrowers so it could underwrite debt instruments of good quality outside the US. The foundations were being laid for an international capital market in Europe that would grow spectacularly.

The launch of the Eurobond market is commonly traced to two events in July 1963. On 1 July, a group of bankers met in the London offices of merchant bankers SG Warburg & Co. and agreed to subscribe to a $15 million bond issue by Autostrade, an Italian motorway financier guaranteed by IRI, Italy's state owned industrial and financial holding company. The $5\frac{1}{2}$%, 15-year bond was novel because it was an internationally syndicated and traded, tax-free, bearer security designed to tap the pool of dollars outside the US. The Autostrade bond is generally recognised as the first Eurobond.

Just over two weeks later, President Kennedy supplied the ideal conditions for the fledgling international bond market to thrive. In a speech to Congress on 18 July, he proposed an Interest Equalisation Tax to deter foreign issuers of securities from tapping the domestic US capital market. US purchases of foreign securities would be taxed with the aim of stemming the outflow of dollars from the US. The IET, which was approved by Congress the following year with retroactive effect to the president's announcement, imposed a 15% tax on the cost of foreign shares bought by US citizens and a graduated tax on foreign bonds of between 2.75% for those with a maturity of less than $3\frac{1}{2}$ years and 15% on long dated bonds. IET effectively closed the US bond market to foreign borrowers by raising the cost of their borrowing in the US by about

---

[1] Conversation with the author, 30 September 2005.

one percentage point. In future, non-US borrowers were faced either with borrowing on their domestic bond markets or, following the example of Autostrade, tapping the growing number of dollars that were slopping round Europe.

The Autostrade bond was a simple 'plain vanilla' issue. But it had characteristics that would apply to all subsequent Eurobonds, no matter how complex they became. The bond was denominated in a currency different to the country of the borrower; issued in bearer form, which meant it could be held anonymously; placed outside the borrower's country; syndicated by an international banking consortium; and listed on a European stock exchange while principal and interest were tax free.

The portability, anonymity and its dollar denomination gave the Autostrade bond undeniable appeal for the growing numbers of quietly affluent European investors. A pessimist would see it as something to pop in a briefcase while fleeing ahead of invading Russians. Others, immortalised in Eurobond market lore as 'the Belgian dentist', might consider it an ideal vehicle for avoiding the attentions of the local tax man.

The Belgian dentist stood as proxy for many individual European investors who, for the first time after decades of depression, war and post-war reconstruction, were able to put aside some money as savings. These people found themselves living in mixed economies, where income tax rates were high by historic standards. Although the beneficial owners of Eurobonds were usually supposed to declare the income from the bonds for tax purposes in their country of residence, many did not. Instead, they would frequently keep their money in another country, taking advantage of strict banking secrecy rules which many continental European countries saw as an important civil liberty after years of dictatorship or occupation.

That said, it is unlikely that the Eurobond market would have been so successful[2] had it not been planted in territory that had already become used to an earlier type of dollar bond.

This was the foreign dollar bond market. The methods of settlement it used were adopted for many Eurobonds with results that initially bordered on disaster before prompting the creation of a cross-border securities settlement capacity in Europe.

2.2 FOREIGN DOLLAR BONDS AND THEIR SETTLEMENT

The foreign dollar bond market was a market in debt instruments, issued primarily by sovereign governments. It began between the world wars, following the emergence of the US from the First World War as the world's leading creditor nation in place of Britain. It survived through the Second World War and grew thereafter, reflecting the supremacy of the dollar in the post-war economy and the US as the home of the world's most developed capital market. The bonds were almost entirely issued in New York and quoted on the New York Stock Exchange. They were documented under New York law and consisted of bearer obligations with coupons attached.

Foreign dollar bonds could be cashed in centres such as New York, Amsterdam, London and Paris. In the years of tension and uncertainty that accompanied the shift from world war to cold war, they became the debt instrument of choice of those cross-border investors, characterised by the Belgian dentist. They also attracted some institutional investors, including shipping companies and reinsurance companies based in Bermuda. Foreign dollar bonds were a safe

---

[2] The Euromarkets could pose hazards for the unwary or the unlucky, however. In January 1967, a failed euro-equity sale prompted Morgan Guaranty to scale back its activities sharply. It sold two thirds of Morgan et Cie to Morgan Stanley, which took over running the Paris operation in time to profit from the booming market in Eurobonds.

investment thanks to high quality issuers, which included Commonwealth governments such as Australia, French government agencies such as Crédit Foncier and Scandinavian borrowers, such as the Kingdom of Norway or the City of Oslo.

Because they were New York listed, the secondary market for these bonds was largely in New York. Generally they were bought and sold over the counter in a market maintained by relatively few New York houses and one or two Canadian firms.

According to Stanislas Yassukovich,[3] who in the early 1960s was beginning a distinguished international banking career in the Zurich office of White Weld, the leading US bond trader in Europe, it became increasingly apparent that the main holders of these bonds were non-Americans and included a great many continental Europeans with accounts in Switzerland and Luxembourg. A large float of any particular issue would therefore be owned outside the US.

However, handling the bonds was a business jealously guarded by US banks. Foreign dollar bonds would have a US investment bank as lead manager and be underwritten by a syndicate of US banks. Custody arrangements would often be maintained with US banks. Thus the Belgian dentist might have an account with a Swiss bank, where the dollar was his safe-haven currency. He would instruct the Swiss bank to buy dollar bonds. The Swiss bank would send an order to its New York correspondent to buy the bonds, which would be held in a US custody account with a US bank.

It soon dawned on a small group of European-based companies, including White Weld, that there was business to be made by offering a dealing service for investors in the European morning, before New York opened in the afternoon. According to Yassukovich, this activity began in the 1950s, probably as early as 1953–54. Other participants in the market were Dominion Securities, a Canadian house; Strauss Turnbull & Co., a London stock broker, whose partner Julius Strauss traded foreign dollar bonds before the war; Deutsche Bank through its office in Mannheim; Kredietbank SA Luxembourgeoise; Stockholms Enskilda Bank; Banca Commerciale Italiana in Milan and Paribas in Paris. These banks and brokerages would be among the stalwarts of the Eurobond market.

But while there was some dealing activity in Europe, the transactions had still to be settled in the US. Instructions would be sent to a New York counterparty which would in turn instruct the custodian banks to handle the settlement. The payment instructions would be made and the dollars would be transferred or perhaps sold for Swiss francs. 'It was a cumbersome and very physical process, literally done by hand,' Yassukovich recalls. The foreign dollar bonds were 'not within the New York securities clearing system because these obligations were odd and out of the mainstream', not least because interest was accrued on a 360-day basis rather than 365 days.

This settlement infrastructure was adopted for the many of the new fangled Eurobonds and it was not long before it was causing trouble.

2.3   FROM AUTOSTRADE TO THE NEW YORK SETTLEMENT CRISIS

The Autostrade bond was followed by a steady stream of new issues of varying types. Contrasting with the exponential expansion of later years, a handful of Eurobonds were issued in 1963, rising to just over 40 a year in 1964 and 1965.

---

[3] Conversation with author, 26 July 2005.

The dollar-denominated Autostrade issue was followed by an international issue by the City of Copenhagen in Swiss francs. This turned out to be both the first and the last EuroSwiss franc bond, because of objections from the Swiss National Bank. In November 1963, Morgan and Galbraith arranged a $15 million convertible bond for Takeda Chemical of Japan, initiating a wave of convertible debenture issues by Japanese companies.

By 1965 bonds were being denominated in D-marks, which soon became the second most important currency in the market. The D-mark sector was less free-wheeling than other parts of the Eurobond market. From late 1968, it was controlled through a series of gentlemen's agreements between the Bundesbank and Germany's issuing banks which regulated the flow of new issues and steered German banks into the role of lead manager.

In the mid-1960s, the US administration took new steps to curb the outflow of dollars. In February 1965, President Lyndon Johnson announced a Voluntary Restraint Program which set voluntary limits on outflows for direct investment abroad by US corporations. At the same time, US commercial banks were discouraged from making loans of more than a year to international borrowers, including subsidiaries of US companies. Three years later, in January 1968, Johnson imposed mandatory restrictions on US foreign investment and created an Office of Foreign Direct Investments to enforce the rules.

In reaction, US multinational companies scrambled to borrow outside the US. Peter Shearlock and William Ellington[4] have reported that more than 70 US companies turned to the Eurobond market in the 12 months following the January 1968 restrictions and 40 more came in 1969. More than half the issues were convertibles. Altogether US corporate borrowers raised 'a fraction under $5 billion between 1965 and 1970'.

This increase in issuance spawned a fast growing secondary market. It was not long before this surge of activity was matched by problems at the settlement level. The boom in US issues put a big strain on New York as the centre for settling dollar Eurobonds when it was already buckling under the weight of domestic securities business.

For Eurobond traders in Europe the rise in volume of so-called 'New York delivery' bonds was accompanied by a sharp increase in the number of 'DKs' or 'don't know' notifications received from correspondents in New York when they failed to match delivery and payment instructions.

DKs put capital at risk because the prevailing practice in the secondary market was to pay on value date, in expectation that delivery either had taken or would take place. This reliance on honest dealing may have worked in national financial centres. But it came under strain when the participants were separated by the Atlantic Ocean and when intercontinental telecommunications were both erratic and expensive. Adding to the problem, securities settlement was a low grade job in the New York of the 1960s. The back office was generally tucked away behind steel bars and known disparagingly as the 'cage'.

'You have to remember that in those days, systems were all manual, with armies of low paid, incompetent and seemingly non-English speaking clerks in New York, shuffling huge mountains of paper around,' recalls Stanley Ross, resident managing director of Kidder Peabody Securities in London from 1967. 'Even people holding key positions in New York had no idea what a euro-dollar was, let alone a Eurodollar bond.'[5]

Ross was one of the one of the most experienced Eurobond traders in London. As head of the foreign dealing room at Strauss Turnbull in 1963, he was appointed by Julius Strauss to

---

[4] In the *Eurobond Diaries* published by Euroclear Clearance System SC in 1994.
[5] Conversation with the author, 14 October 2005.

trade the Autostrade issue and so became one of the first people to trade a Eurobond. By the time he joined Kidder, London was becoming the home of the secondary market in Eurodollar bonds. New York, however, remained the centre for their settlement.

Ross's clerks would send a nightly, half speed telex to New York listing the bonds that Schroder, his New York bank, should receive and deliver on his behalf. He remembers seeing occasional replies telling of deliveries in with payments made on his behalf, but never receiving any telexes reporting deliveries out, with corresponding money being received. 'Thus, at a time of increasing interest rates, our overdrafts went straight through the roof, and our profits out the window.'

He flew to New York to investigate the problem. His bank sent him down to the vaults. Ross takes up the story: 'This guy swaggers in, I can see him today. He wore a blue shirt, pens all along his top pocket, was chewing gum and he snarled at me: "Whaddaya want, Mac?" I replied, somewhat loftily, I admit: "I should like to see the delivery accounts of Kidder Peabody Securities London". Eventually, he rolled his way back again – he walked just like John Wayne – and threw this grubby, tattered folder down in front of me. It was soon apparent why our overdraft had gone into the stratosphere, Schroder had simply cut our telexes into little strips, acting on all the Receive ones, and leaving in the folder all the Delivery strips. When I opened the file, hundreds of little delivery instructions flew up in the air and fluttered to the floor. I put my head in my hands and moaned: "Oh my God. Oh my God".'

As Ross groaned, he heard a deep voice behind him say: 'Never mind, Stanley. I am here since six weeks and I've turned a $7 million debit into a $16 million credit'. It was a fellow trader, Wolfgang Kron from Deutsche Bank. He was there with exactly the same problem.

Their experience was not unique. 'There came a day when the bond market settlement stopped, because it was Luxembourg payments and New York delivery,' recalled Ian Steers, who headed the Eurobond operation of Wood Gundy, a Canadian house and one of the leading broker-dealers of the 1960s. Steers, who was chairman of Euroclear for four years from June 1980, was called by his chairman. 'Mr Gundy rang me up and said: "Do you realise you have the whole capital of the firm tied up in unsettled transactions." And other firms were the same. Business stopped, you couldn't buy and sell because you couldn't get delivery, and you hadn't got any collateral, because the stock had gone.'[6]

The paper jam proved the undoing of some companies. In 1968, Weeden & Co., an aggressive US brokerage, discovered a fail position of more than $50 million – three times its capital and a huge amount of money by the standards of the time.[7]

Walter Imthurn traded Eurobonds for Weeden in London, where the office was a branch of the US company and so had to meet US capital adequacy requirements. 'In New York, you had a 20 for one capital requirement meaning you had to carry 20 times your net exposure as capital,' Imthurn recalled.[8] 'At Weeden, my fails to deliver were in the millions all of a sudden, because I couldn't get the bonds.' Weeden was forced to withdraw temporarily from the Eurobond market in 1969 to conserve capital.

After his visit to the New York vault, Ross went back to Kidder's offices. He urged the company 'to sue Schroder for negligence and refuse to pay their iniquitous interest charges'. The top brass at Kidder treated the incident as a joke and directed him to pay the charge and absorb the interest losses into his London profit and loss account.

---

[6] Conversation with the author, 24 November 2005.
[7] According to Stanley Ross's rough and ready calculations, Weeden's fail position 'equates today to a billion dollars of funds gridlocked with just one small firm'.
[8] In conversation with the author, 30 August 2005.

Traders like Ross were not the only victims of the paperwork crisis. In an unregulated market, customers were sometimes cheated by banks which cynically exploited the inefficiencies of the settlement infrastructure for their own ends. It was not unknown for merchant banks deliberately to hold on to bonds they had already been paid for, even deliver them on to some other counterparty, and collect funds a second time while twice pocketing the interest.

According to Ross, many of the early buyers – the Swiss banks and their Belgian dentist clientele, who were responsible for about 90% of the market's buying power – might not see their bonds for a year or even two years after having paid for them on the value date, which was probably two weeks after purchase. When delivered, the bonds would often be minus the intervening coupons. Missing coupons were a particular problem with convertibles, on which interest was paid half yearly. By holding on to bonds, money and coupons, some banks accumulated millions of dollars, which in reality were owed to their trading counterparties or investors. The more prudent transgressors would keep the funds in an escrow account for some years, after which they would be written into their profit and loss account.

Ross and other Eurobond professionals realised that the paperwork log jam with its attendant malpractices would eventually kill the market. In the second half of the 1960s, there emerged, in reaction, a professional body for the Eurobond market and the first steps were taken towards a clearing and settlement system.

2.4   THE AIBD

The Association of International Bond Dealers has many parents. Some credit the idea to Walter Imthurn who was an early advocate of a social organisation along the lines of bond dealers' associations in North America to help traders in the still young Eurobond market to get to know each other better.

By 1968, however, the New York paper jam that was to overwhelm Imthurn at Weeden became such a problem that thoughts of creating a professional association to regulate the market gained in purpose and urgency.

On 28 October 1968, 19 senior bond dealers met in the offices of NM Rothschild & Sons in the City of London. Among those present were Imthurn and Ross. The meeting elected a steering committee drawn from some of the most active houses. It comprised Walter Koller of White Weld in Zurich, Rolf Hallberg of Stockholms Enskilda Bank, Paul Sherwood of Strauss Turnbull, Armin Mattle of Bondtrade, and Richard Weguelin of Eurotrading. The latter two institutions were specialist consortium houses set up by groups of commercial and investment banks to pool resources for trading in the new market.

The steering committee invited applications to join the association and fixed 18 April 1969 for the first meeting of the AIBD in the Great Eastern Hotel next to London's Liverpool Street railway station. Members were invited to pay a subscription of $150 for the year ending 31 December 1968, sent an admittance card and advised that those attending would have to pay £2 for luncheon. The subscription fee and bill for lunch are reminders that the Eurobond market pre-dates the great inflation of the 1970s.

The steering committee drafted the association's articles. Koller was in charge of printing the articles and the invitations to the meeting and mailing them from Zurich. The AIBD's objectives combined the social and the practical. They were: 'a. To promote friendly relations between member firms and between representatives. b. To provide a basis for joint examination, discussion and elimination of mutual technical problems. c. To maintain a close liaison with the international bond issuing houses'.

Membership was open to 'banks, bankers, members of recognised stock exchanges, members of other securities dealers associations or affiliates of such, who actively contribute to the functioning of the international bond markets.' International bonds were defined as 'Euro-dollar and multiple currency securities'.[9]

The AIBD's first meeting in the Great Eastern Hotel was – like the Eurobond market itself – an overwhelmingly male affair. There was, according to Stanley Ross, only one woman representative present, a certain Mademoiselle Courtine. The agenda was dominated by the New York paper jam. Koller was also chairman of the AIBD's Committee for New York and European Settlements and, as such, was despatched on 20 April to New York to try to resolve the problem.

'White Weld was the prima donna. So I went to New York and organised a meeting with all the New York clearing banks. I asked people from about 20 banks to White Weld, among them Morgan, Citibank and Chase,' Koller recalls. According to his own account of the meeting, he asked: 'Gentlemen, what are we doing wrong in Europe to explain this problem. I didn't accuse them. I asked: Can you tell us.'

He was told that people in New York didn't understand the instructions they were receiving. There were language problems – with Finnish company names causing particular difficulty. Koller conceded that there were defects on the European side. He promised to 'go back to Europe and tell them that all instructions must be given very precisely, with delivery versus payment etc., and if anything goes wrong, you must call us back, or telex us to say what is wrong'.

Koller's diplomatic approach extracted an important concession in return. He got the New York banks to agree to a discrepancy form which obliged them to explain non-delivery. 'That way, things were better but not perfect. It forced the New York banks to justify their DKs – to say there was a lack of money or securities or wrong instructions.' In this way, the AIBD was able to bring some order to the settlement chaos.

Its other achievement was to create a legislative framework for the market that would stand the test of time. Koller and Mattle – both Swiss-Germans – were responsible for drafting many of the AIBD's rules. They worked without a secretariat, legal department or formal headquarters. 'The AIBD's rules at that time were very simple,' Koller recalled.[10] 'There were just a few. I had been in New York and because I was a registered member of the NYSE, and had passed the exams, I took the NASD book and took over a lot of that but tailored it to the international market. I did it together with Armin Mattle. His English was better.'

In Ross's view, Koller and Mattle were 'the two people who did most to bring about that gigantic transition from the sheer chaos that existed when we began, to the superb efficiency the industry enjoyed after a dozen or so years. They undoubtedly bore the greatest burdens and made the very greatest contributions. They just never stopped. They worked at it morning till night, week in, week out, year in, year out.'

Other rules were the work of the Market Practices Committee led by Ross, the committee's first chairman. The committee drew on prevailing trading practices and common sense to produce the AIBD's first trading rules, the first yield book and the first register of members. It defined standards without which the market would have fragmented.

The AIBD members, representing 200 financial institutions, agreed almost all the rules drafted by the association's executive committee at an extraordinary general meeting of the

---

[9] Reproduced in Ian M. Kerr's *History of the Eurobond Market: The first 21 years*, Euromoney Publications, London, 1984.
[10] Conversation with the author, 9 August 2005.

AIBD in Geneva in November 1969. Their achievement, according to Ross, was 'to standardise the wide variety of payment and delivery methods that were, at best, leading to constant misunderstandings and confusion, and, at worst, to deliberate abuses of haphazard settlement procedures'.[11]

Looking back at those early days after an interval of 10 years,[12] Ross noted in a 1979 monograph that the AIBD rules permitted the market to maintain its growth without a constant need to legislate on an ad-hoc basis for new situations and contingencies. The rules were rarely challenged by the association's members. 'We simply gave the market the regulation it needed. But, it is important to note, no more and no less than it needed.'

The AIBD's rule makers recognised that participants in the Eurobond market were accustomed to considerable individual freedom of action. The market was highly competitive, classless, buccaneering and flamboyant. The last two attributes were never more apparent than at the annual meetings of the AIBD, when the association's members turned from the business in hand to the social agenda.

In many ways Ross exemplified the spirit of the early Eurobond market. From a working class London background (his father was a bus conductor), he left school at 15 to work in a nearby factory. After military service in the Royal Air Force, he joined Strauss Turnbull in the City where Julius Strauss gave him the opportunity to trade. There he rose to head the foreign dealing room. In 1967, he started Kidder Peabody's Eurobond trading operation in London, which quickly became one of the main profit centres of the US-based firm.

Ross's world was one in which people worked hard and played hard. There was the favourite table at the Savoy Grill and a succession of fast cars: from a Jaguar XK 140 in the late 1950s, when still a young trader, to the custom built Porsche 928's of later years. Rather than rely on a conventional means of transport to get to the 1970 AIBD meeting in Copenhagen, Ross flew there as passenger cum navigator through driving rain in a colleague's small Cessna aircraft. A year later, he sailed his own 12 ton sloop across a storm-tossed English Channel and up the Seine to the AIBD annual meeting in Paris.

For 20 years, the annual meetings of the AIBD reflected the highs and lows of a burgeoning business sector in which years of boom far outnumbered periods of bust. Copenhagen, Geneva, Vienna, Amsterdam – one by one the great cities of Europe succumbed to conspicuous consumption and outright hedonism as the AIBD's members hit town. When the annual caravan of Eurobond professionals pitched up in Nice in 1984, the health of the market could be measured by the size of yachts in the harbour that had been hired by the Eurobond trading houses.

But all good things come to an end. By the late 1980s, the international bond business had become commoditised and lost much of its panache. In the course of the 1990s the 'must attend' annual social event for securities settlement providers became SIBOS, the trade fair organised by the SWIFT financial communications system.

2.5   SETTLEMENT SERVICES IN LUXEMBOURG

Only US dollar denominated Eurobonds were caught in the New York settlement jam. This helped Luxembourg, the EEC's smallest member state, to emerge as a service centre for the new international capital market.

---

[11] 'Eurobonds – the changing face of the secondary market' by Stanley Ross, 1971.
[12] 'AIBD rules and regulations' by Stanley Ross, March 1979.

The Grand Duchy's wealth, which was considerable, was rooted in the iron and steel industry which had boomed in the late 19th century after metallurgical advances permitted the exploitation of local deposits of iron ore. But it was more the invasion and occupation by Germany twice in the first half of the 20th century that prepared the ground for Luxembourg's development as a significant Euromarket centre.

Before the First World War, the Grand Duchy was a member of the Zollverein, the German imperial customs union and German competed with French and the local language Letzeburgesch to be the country's main language. Angered and shocked after being invaded and occupied by Germany in that war, Luxembourg formed an economic and monetary union with Belgium and adopted French as its formal language.

Multilingual Luxembourg therefore had economic and cultural ties with all three of its neighbours. The experience of invasion and occupation in the two world wars taught its citizens the value of privacy and banking secrecy. A law of 1929 made Luxembourg a fiscally advantageous location for establishing holding companies. Its economic union with Belgium did not extend to tax matters.

Luxembourg therefore became a stopping off place for tourists in pursuit of cheap wine, cigarettes and petrol. Some visitors were Belgian dentists, or similar professionals from other countries close to the Grand Duchy, who could see the attractions of holding one or more bank accounts in a separate tax jurisdiction of a currency union.

The Belgian dentist, often with his wife, mistress or daughter, could be seen most week days on the train – known colloquially as the 'Coupon Express' – which would leave Brussels at around 9.30 am and convey its briefcase-carrying clientele in well-upholstered comfort to Luxembourg City in time for lunch. After an ample meal and some post-prandial business in one of the many bank branches in the town, the same passengers could usually be seen taking the evening train back to Brussels.

One feature of the monetary union with Belgium was that Luxembourg had no central bank until the conversion of the Luxembourg franc to the euro in 1999. D-mark deposits in Luxembourg therefore could escape the German Bundesbank's minimum reserve requirements, which forced German-based banks to deposit a certain percentage of their deposits in non-interest bearing accounts with the central bank in Frankfurt. Luxembourg became an 'offshore' centre for dozens of German banks from the late 1960s, after the post-Second World War antipathy to Germany had died down and the monetary turbulence of the 1970s caused the Bundesbank to use its minimum reserves as an increasingly draconian instrument against speculative flows into the D-mark.

The Luxembourg banks developed ties with London banks in the early 1960s, because of the imposition of stamp tax of between 1% and 2% on securities in London. To circumvent this, London banks would issue temporary scrip certificates, which had a status similar to an allotment letter and which would be exchangeable for bonds in physical form in Luxembourg up to six months later. Many of these bonds were deposited by foreign banks with their Luxembourg correspondents, which acted as custodians.

Also important were the banks' links to the big Swiss banks, which, as the major takers of Eurobonds, would have one or several accounts in the Grand Duchy. Adding to its financial fire power, Luxembourg was the home of triple-A rated EEC institutions such as the European Coal and Steel Community and the European Investment Bank which had recourse to the international capital market for funds.

The local financial sector had developed some useful skills. There are some who say Kredietbank SA Luxembourgeoise should be credited with launching the first Eurobond in January

1961 when it arranged an offering for SACOR, a Portuguese entity, worth $5 million. The bond was certainly more complicated than the 1963 Autostrade issue: it was denominated in European units of account (EUA), an artificial cocktail of seven currencies, which allowed the investor to be paid in any one of its components consisting of Belgian francs, D-marks, Dutch guilders, French francs, Luxembourg francs, Swiss francs and sterling.

Luxembourg was unbureaucratic. The Autostrade bond was listed in Luxembourg because the local stock exchange could handle the formalities faster than the London Stock Exchange and did not require a prospectus. Luxembourg thereafter became the prime listing location for Eurobonds.

Partly because of their placing power with the Belgian dentist and his ilk, the big local banks – Banque Internationale à Luxembourg, Banque Générale du Luxembourg and Kredietbank Luxembourgeoise – were invited to take part in the syndication of Eurobonds and also took on the roles of listing and paying agent.

Taken together, these attributes made Luxembourg a prime candidate for settling securities. In the 1960s, the big three banks, together with Crédit Industriel d'Alsace et de Lorraine and Ste Générale Alsacienne de Banque, developed a basic service for the settlement of secondary market transactions in addition to providing paying agency services.

Philippe Duvieusart was second in command at Kredietbank Luxembourgeoise from 1965 to early 1973. He remembers Luxembourg having 'the central role' in European settlement in the mid-1960s. 'There were no formal rules for this, but the fact was that European settlements were operated in Luxembourg.'[13]

The Luxembourg banks built up a thriving business settling bonds. The operations were physical and involved trundling the bonds between the various banks in armoured cars. There was no delivery versus payment and the service was expensive, not least because the movements had to be insured. But John Langton, later vice chairman of the AIBD and for many years the chief executive and secretary general of ISMA,[14] its successor organisation, remembers how, when he worked for Strauss Turnbull in London in the 1960s, 'we used four or five Luxembourg banks because Luxembourg got the first listing, in 1963 of Autostrade, and all the transactions cleared between them'.[15]

But this cosy existence was not to last. Duvieusart and his colleagues at Kredietbank got wind of plans by Morgan Guaranty to launch a securities settlement system in Brussels and tried unsuccessfully to rally support among Kredietbank's shareholders and friendly banks for action to deal with the threat. Some were unconcerned as long as it was just a project. Others were reluctant to invest the necessary effort and finance to launch a competing system when there was no guarantee that the Eurobond market would prove a lasting phenomenon. 'We made some soundings within our group and externally,' he recalls. 'But we didn't feel there was sufficient interest to compete with the Morgan Guaranty project.'

Thus it was that Morgan Guaranty stole a march on Luxembourg in setting up the first proper settlement infrastructure for the Eurobond market.

---

[13] Conversation with the author, 29 September 2005.

[14] The AIBD changed its name to the International Securities Market Association (ISMA) on 1 January 1992, reflecting product diversification in the international capital markets. ISMA merged with the International Primary Market Association (IPMA) with effect from 1 July 2005 to form the International Capital Market Association (ICMA).

[15] Conversation with the author, 30 August 2005.

3

The ICSDs – Euroclear and Cedel

3.1 CLOSINGS IN BRUSSELS

One of the distinctive rituals of the early Eurobond market was the closing. This was where bonds were authenticated and the lead manager would pay the proceeds of the new issue to the borrower, who in turn would deliver the securities – in temporary or definitive form – to the lead manager. In the market's early days, Paris was the centre for bond issuance which was why Morgan et Cie was founded there. But French tax law put a damper on Paris as a centre for closings. The stamp tax ruled out London. A search was launched for alternatives.

Among their many activities, the Luxembourg banks had built up a niche business closing primary market issues. They had several advantages. Most Eurobonds after Autostrade were listed on the Luxembourg stock exchange and the Grand Duchy was, as noted earlier, a place of light regulation and convenient tax rules. But Luxembourg was awkward to reach, especially from Paris. Moreover, its cuisine, while nourishing and robust because it was heavily dependent on locally sourced game from the Ardennes, was perhaps not the most refined that the European continent could offer.

The quality of food was important because a closing would usually involve a small ceremony and a slap-up lunch for the issuers, bankers and underwriters of the issue. According to Herschel Post, who was posted to Brussels as Morgan Guaranty's commercial manager with responsibility for Euroclear from 1974 to 1978, 'Morgan charged $25 000 for doing a closing and providing a lunch.'[1] Post suspected that the lunch cost more than the activity involved in the closing.

In 1965, John Cattier, in charge of administration at White Weld in Zurich, approached James Chandler, head of the securities department at Morgan Guaranty in Brussels, to see whether it would be possible to have closings in Brussels. The Belgian capital had good transport links with Switzerland, was easier to reach from Paris than Luxembourg and had better hotels and food. Morgan had been established in Brussels since 1919 and was the New York paying agent for a large number of outstanding bonds. Morgan Guaranty's offices at 27 avenue des Arts were on top of a very large vault.

Chandler checked with legal counsel and regulatory authorities in Brussels and found they had no objections. Morgan's lawyer, a certain Mr Ferrier, persuaded the Belgian tax authorities that closings should not be subject to Belgian stock exchange turnover tax. He successfully argued that Morgan did not want to do stock exchange transactions, but simply execute contracts to deliver securities against payment.

Thus towards the end of September 1965, Morgan Guaranty's Brussels office played host to the first of many closings. It was for a $20 million, 15-year borrowing by Cynamid International Development Corp., a financing subsidiary of American Cynamid Co.

While Eurobond trading was generally a classless activity, there was a distinct 'upstairs-downstairs' quality about the business of closings. Count Charles d'Ursel, head of Morgan

---

[1] Conversation with author, 21 July 2005.

Guaranty's Brussels branch, remembers how 'the closings took place in the board room of the bank on the second floor. We had on the table, the pile of bonds, pieces of paper, authenticated and signed. The lead underwriter was around with his lawyer, and the telephone line was open to New York. And when the man in New York said the money had been paid by the lead underwriter into the account at the bank in favour of the issuer, we physically handed over the pile of bonds.'[2]

Down below, in the vault, was a squad of bank officials and clerks, some of whom were Morgan pensioners rehired for the occasion. Gérard Van Nieuwenhove, who joined Morgan in Brussels as an auditor in 1965 and moved to the securities department the following year, remembers his first closing was for a bond issued by Phillips Petroleum. 'There was a little ceremony, and then the allocation of the bonds to investors. We had a 12 column sheet and we put on it A to B, B to C etc., all by hand, and we moved the securities, physically, from the vaults to A, B, C, D, whatever. People in the vaults were packaging the bonds – often in bundles of 25 – and sending them to Switzerland, London and New York by post.'[3]

At that time, Eurobonds were not fungible which meant the clerks had to take special care to ensure investors received the right bonds with the correct serial numbers. This made for extra work in the event of a trade on the margins of the closing. 'Say Strauss or White Weld was selling, then you had to go back to each package and take out the bonds with the specific numbers and move them to somebody else, either physically or within the vault,' Van Nieuwenhove recalls.

The staff at Morgan Brussels soon discovered that few people wanted to take the bonds out of the building after the closings. D'Ursel remembers that after handing over the pile of bonds to the lead underwriter, he would often be told to keep them because they had already been sold to a second tier of underwriters. 'And it would turn out that the second tier had also already sold the bonds. So in the first few days, we kept the bonds in our vault and kept track of who owned them.'

At this point, someone – d'Ursel thinks it was Cattier of White Weld again – spoke to Chandler and suggested that Morgan Guaranty should hold onto the bonds until maturity. 'Jim came to me, as his boss, and said, why don't we do it? It might be interesting. And I wrote to New York, and said, we think this could be good business.'

According to d'Ursel, there was no immediate reply from New York. However, he and Chandler took up the idea and spent much of 1966 discussing with White Weld and others how such a system for securities might work. At the beginning of 1967, d'Ursel asked Chandler and Marcel Deleebeeck, head of operations at Morgan Guaranty in Brussels, to carry out a detailed study of what the market wanted and how to execute it. While Chandler spoke with traders and potential depositaries, Deleebeeck assembled a small working group to produce plans for a system that would be able to deal with dollar denominated securities from September 1967.

D'Ursel wrote to Morgan in New York and asked for permission to go ahead with the plan. His answer came in the form of a visit in June 1967 by John M. Meyer Jr, at that time president, or the second highest ranking officer after chairman of Morgan Guaranty Trust Co. in New York.

D'Ursel took Meyer to the Cercle Gaullois, the exclusive dining club opposite the Belgian prime minister's office in downtown Brussels. Meyer told him that Barclays was thinking of a similar operation. 'He said we should start right away and not leave it until October. I went to

[2] Conversation with the author, 29 September 2005.
[3] Conversation with the author, 3 October 2005.

the telephone in the Cercle Gaullois and called Marcel Deleebeeck and asked him if he thought we could start keeping the bonds for all their life straightaway. He said let's try it.'

Meyer put his considerable authority behind the scheme. According to Bruce Brackenridge, who later worked closely with him when Morgan sold Euroclear to its users: 'Meyer, who had trained as an investment banker and had closely followed the development of the Euro-bond market, knew that the market was having great difficulties with physical deliveries and settlements.'[4]

The system – for dollar securities only – was launched on Belgian national day, 21 July 1967. Settlements were known as 'clearances'. Participants had to open a securities account and a cash account with Morgan Guaranty so that transactions could be carried out. The physical movement of securities around the vault was replaced by a book entry system which allowed delivery versus payment and eliminated, at a stroke, much of the risk of the physical settlement with payment on value date.

Kansallis Osake Pankki, a Finnish bank, was the first to apply to join. According to Van Nieuwenhove's[5] account of the period, there were 17 participants at the start and the system handled just 10% of total clearances. The first depositary banks were lined up to hold securities for the system outside Brussels. These included Kas Associatie in Amsterdam and Morgan Vonwiller in Milan as well as Morgan branches in western Europe. Given the Luxembourg government's interest in promoting the Grand Duchy as a financial centre, it was something of a coup for Morgan to secure the state owned savings bank, the Caisse d'Épargne de l' État, as its depository in Luxembourg.

Although the service was little more than a pilot scheme, it attracted important members of the London broker-dealer community, including Wood Gundy, Kidder Peabody and Samuel Montagu. This progress encouraged Morgan to think of a bigger and better operation.

3.2   THE CREATION OF EUROCLEAR

The new service was not without its critics. The system ran on IBM punch card technology similar to that used by Morgan in New York and there were problems keeping track of Eurobond serial numbers.

Van Nieuwenhove remembers that in May 1968 he submitted a report to d'Ursel saying the clearing service was a mess: 'I told him there was no order.' D'Ursel decided that Hal Jackson, the comptroller of Morgan Brussels, and Deleebeeck should reorganise the service. In the meantime, Van Nieuwenhove sent another report, 'saying it was more than a mess. I put on paper that it didn't work at all.' At this point, d'Ursel told Van Nieuwenhove that, as he was so critical, he could join the group trying to find a solution to the problem.

So Van Nieuwenhove joined Deleebeeck and Jackson. They worked non-stop from May 1968 to December on what was to become Euroclear. 'Initially, we said we needed a month to organise the clearing service. Then it went from one month to three months and after three months, we needed another three months, because we couldn't make everything run properly,' Van Nieuwenhove recalls. 'During the six months to December, we would be in the office at 8.30am, go on until any time between 8pm and midnight, Saturdays and Sundays included, without a vacation.' Recalling the student uprising that nearly brought revolution to France that year, Van Nieuwenhove joked: 'We only found out about the Paris Spring of May 68 six months later.'

---

[4] Conversation with author, 13 December 2005.
[5] 'The Euroclear story' by Gérard Van Nieuwenhove, monograph written in 1992.

Morgan, however, began recruiting for the new operation. By July it had built up a staff of 40. Learning from the pilot scheme and drawing lessons from the worsening New York settlement crisis, the technicians around Deleebeeck devised improvements in the service to be offered. One important innovation was the idea of 'matching' participants' instructions and then automatically selecting trades chronologically for clearance. This procedure dramatically reduced the number of fails and was to develop into the system known as 'chaining', which would be at the core of Euroclear's settlement processing.

An early and difficult question was whether bonds placed in the system should always be identifiable by their serial numbers and therefore unfungible. The lack of fungibility of early Eurobonds caused problems both for Morgan's Brussels office and Morgan Guaranty in New York. Initially, Morgan in New York was the main depository for bonds cleared in Brussels. These would often go astray, particularly when the Brussels office sent instructions for bonds en-route to New York to be delivered to a bank in London or Switzerland. There was always a risk of officials in New York failing to find the securities with the correct serial numbers and delivering other bonds of a given issue to the bank in question. This would create reconciliation problems and add to the trans-Atlantic paper jam.

According to Van Nieuwenhove, the team building the system quickly realised that the bonds would have to be fungible for it to work efficiently. Fungibility meant participants' accounts were credited with the amount of security deposited for them in the system, without specifying individual certificates by serial number. A participant would always have the right to take out bonds of the same issue and value as those deposited in the system, but not the numbered certificates that formed the original deposit.

Adopting fungibility saved a great deal of time, because there was no need to keep serial numbers for each transaction, and speeded up settlement for the market as a whole. It allowed Morgan to use its international network of depositary banks to deliver bonds to investors, reducing the need to ship securities around the banking system as part of individual transactions. In future, any deficiencies in stocks of a security at a given depository could be made good by bulk shipments, reducing risk, cost and delay.

Fungibility was an up and coming idea. Belgium, for example, adopted fungibility for CIK,[6] a CSD for domestic securities, which was set up in 1967–68. A Belgian law,[7] which defined the rules applicable to fungible securities, gave depositors of such securities rights of co-ownership. Without this law, the holders of fungible bonds in a system such as Morgan's pilot scheme would be at a disadvantage against non-fungible bond holders if ever the bank went bankrupt, because the fungible bonds would form part of the claims against the bank of all creditors instead of being considered as belonging to the bond holder.

Chandler and Jackson ensured that the concept of fungibility was written into the terms and conditions of the service. It was Evan Galbraith's job to sell it to the financial community in countries where it was not practised. Accompanied by John McDaniels, a lawyer from the Paris office of Davis Polk & Wardwell, Morgan's legal firm, Galbraith set forth around Europe to explain how the new central depository for Eurobonds would work.

'McDaniels and I went around – and this was the better part of the year – trying to get people to come in,' Galbraith explained. 'We were trying to settle the legal problems that arose between transactions between countries, trying to deal with the tax issues (the stamp taxes and

---

[6] A short acronym for a very long name expressed both in French and Flemish: Caisse Interprofessionnelle de Dépôts et de Virements de Titres SA/Interprofessionele Effectendeposito-en GiroKas NV. CIK was approved by Royal Decree on 1 April 1968.

[7] Belgian Royal Decree No. 62 of 10 November 1967.

other things) to enable it to be done, and trying to explain to people who didn't understand the idea of settlement that you would have your securities deposited in a central location, and that you would just simply move entries around on the books rather than physically shove securities around. Client privacy would be maintained.' It took an effort. 'It was clearly the most difficult thing I think I ever did,' Galbraith said later.[8]

Jim Chandler, an Englishman who had settled in Brussels after the war, was also heavily involved in marketing the service. John Langton remembers Chandler 'looking every inch the perfect English gentleman' as he went about establishing the Morgan settlement system.

At the end of November, Meyer telephoned from New York. Deleebeeck said his team needed another month. But Meyer, who had heard reports that other banks were preparing similar systems, answered: 'It will start on 2nd December and that's it.'

Euroclear (with a hyphen) was launched with more than 50 banks and dealers signed up to the service. During 1969, the number of participants increased to nearly 150.

There were four sections on the operational side of the business: input, processing, reconciliation and payment. According to Agnès Petiau, an early recruit, input was considered the most important activity. It was certainly the area with the greatest risk of human error because it consisted of feeding into the system all the instructions received from clients by telex or messenger – the two means of communication that were available at the time.

The operation grew quickly. According to Van Nieuwenhove, Euroclear handled around 800 operations a day at the start. Petiau[9] can remember him ordering champagne for the staff when completed instructions first topped 1000 in a day. It soon moved into separate premises around the corner from the bank branch. Euroclear hired a significant number of young female staff. A cohort of young female employees came from just one school in the Belgian town of Tubize because their teacher was friendly with a member of Morgan's personnel department. An early recruit (but not from Tubize) was school leaver Martine Patureau, whose first job in 1969 was matching and settlement as an employee in the operations department. As Martine Dinne, she would rise through the ranks to become chief executive of Euroclear Bank.

Rapid growth and separate premises helped generate a strong *esprit de corps* among the Euroclear's youthful staff. 'People were devoted. Initially, everybody felt it was growing, it was giving opportunities of promotion, of salary increases,' Gérard Van Nieuwenhove remembers. 'That even created some problems with the bank, because we had young people gaining promotion unlike those who had refused to come to Euroclear. People would work on Sundays if necessary, without demanding overtime immediately. That applied from Jim Chandler at the top, down to telex operators at the bottom.'

Euroclear got off to a good start because the broker-dealers that supported the pilot project were strong backers. Ross remembers telling Chandler: 'I want to do anything that gets us out of the clutches of New York: they simply don't understand the business and certainly have no clue as to how it should be settled.' The Morgan staff in Belgium, building up Euroclear, consulted dealers like Ross about how they should conduct their business. The result was a system aimed to suit their needs. 'Euroclear was a great design, simplicity itself. DvP: delivery versus payment,' Ross recalls.

---

[8] Conversation with the author, 30 September 2005.

[9] 'Histoires d'Euroclear', Agnès Petiau's personal recollections of Euroclear, November 2003.

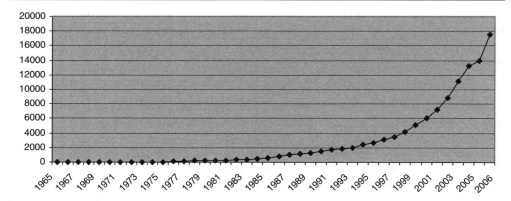

Figure 3.1   Growth in the international bond market (amount outstanding in US$ billion). *Source:* BIS –
Adapted from International Bonds and Notes by Residence of Issuer. www.bis.org

Kidder Peabody was the first major trading firm to make a ruling that anyone wanting to deal
with it would have to be a member of Euroclear. 'I got earfuls from the Luxembourg banks,
saying why do you support this.' Ross says: 'I think that in taking such a stand, what I did for
Euroclear was absolutely amazing', adding, only half in jest: 'But not only did they not thank
me, they didn't even send me a life time crate of pink champagne every year, which has been
a continuing source of irritation with each passing year.'

The new service was advertised in September 1968 in the *Financial Times*, *The Times* (of
London) and the *International Herald Tribune* as 'a way to unjam the Eurobond market'.

It would succeed well beyond the dreams of its founders. Euroclear came at just the right
time to prevent the Eurobond market seizing up. 'It made a huge difference as soon as it was
up and running,' says Stanislas Yassukovich. 'It helped to generate significant increases in
volume.'

The international capital market embarked on years of exponential growth. As Figure 3.1
shows, the $1.6 billion of international bonds and notes outstanding at the end of 1968 grew
more than 10 000 times to $16 267 billion – more than $16.2 trillion – by the third quarter of
2006, according to Bank for International Settlements figures.[10]

Also unexpected at first was how Euroclear would prove to be a money spinner for Morgan.
The requirement for participants to open cash accounts and the institution of delivery versus
payment meant a sudden boom in deposits with Morgan in Brussels. 'This came as a surprise
to us in Brussels,' Charles d'Ursel recalls. 'This business was creating huge cash deposits with
our little office in Brussels. As a result Euroclear became very profitable because we paid
perhaps a small rate of interest on the sight deposits. We knew this money wouldn't go away,
and we invested it and we made quite a bit of money out of it.'

'They made a fortune out of it,' remembers Galbraith, who quit Morgan shortly after Euroclear's launch to become director and chairman of Bankers Trust International in London in
1969. 'One of the reasons I left Morgan Guaranty was because of the miserable bonus they
paid me after I was instrumental in setting up this cash cow for them.'

---

[10] www.bis.org.

3.3   ESTABLISHING CEDEL IN LUXEMBOURG

The founding of Euroclear in December 1968 was unwelcome news in Luxembourg. 'It was a shock,' remembers Philippe Duvieusart, who was in charge of Euromarkets and international financial operations at Kredietbank SA Luxembourgeoise.

At the time, Duvieusart and his Kredietbank colleagues were completing plans to ease the problems caused by the settlement jam in New York, where the Luxembourg banks experienced difficulties every bit as bad as those suffered by Stanley Ross and Walter Koller. 'Very soon, an incredible situation developed. We had to send people – we were dealing mainly with Chase in New York – to get reconciliation of accounts. There was a backlog sometimes of one year. It was incredible in terms of disorder but also of risk that we took,' Duvieusart recalls.

'In February 1969, we in Kredietbank Luxembourgeoise took an initiative and decided – after consultation with some major banks, the leading one being Union Bank of Switzerland – that we would start settlement in Europe for all new issues of dollar denominated bonds and stop having physical delivery of new dollar Eurobonds in New York.' The market followed this initiative. It was a step forward.

Morgan's decision to set up Euroclear helped concentrate minds further among the top managers of the Luxembourg banks who had been reluctant to act earlier on reports of developments in Brussels.

Once again, Duvieusart, Constant Franssens, his boss, and a team from Kredietbank set about sounding out banks in Luxembourg and abroad about a possible response to Morgan's action. This time, they won the support of the Luxembourg banking community and a group of big foreign banks, comprising UBS, Banque Nationale de Paris, Barclays, Dresdner Bank, Westdeutsche Landesbank, Algemene Bank Nederland and Banca Commerciale d'Italiana. In the course of 1969, they set up a study group to decide in broad terms the sort of institution they wanted.

Reflecting a widespread suspicion that Morgan was using Euroclear to gain an insight into the business secrets of its rivals, they decided that no individual participant should have an advantage over the others in terms of operations or information. The new organisation would be international, independent, neutral and open to all securities market professionals. It would operate according to the motto: 'From the market, for the market.'

The study group then commissioned a feasibility study from a Luxembourg consultancy, Fiduciaire Generale de Luxembourg, where René Schmitter and Raymond Flammant took charge.

According to Duvieusart, 69 banks put up $1000 each for the study. On 18 January 1970, Fiduciaire was entrusted with defining the objectives and scope of the new venture which would be called Cedel. The title was an acronym of the French Centrale de Livraison de Valeurs Mobilières. It also stood for Centre of Delivery (of securities) – an English translation of the French name, which never caught on.

Things then moved very rapidly. Schmitter recalls scrutinising Morgan's operation in Brussels and contacting CSDs, where they existed in Europe. These included the Frankfurt Kassenverein in Germany and Sicovam in France. Georg Bruns, general counsel of the Frankfurt Stock Exchange and manager of the Frankfurt Kassenverein, was drafted in as a special consultant to the project. On 2 April, Fiduciaire produced a paper of questions and proposals to enable the study group to clarify outstanding issues. Cedel itself was launched by 71 banks from 11 countries on 28 September 1970. Its starting capital was $1.15 million.

Kredietbank and Duvieusart opted to play a less prominent role from this point. Kredietbank proposed that Edmond Israel, a rising star at Banque Internationale à Luxembourg, the Grand Duchy's oldest bank, be elected Cedel's first chairman. Schmitter was appointed secretary to the board and executive committee.

Franssens had earlier met Israel at a lunch and interested him in Kredietbank's ideas for a Luxembourg-based settlement system. Israel became a vigorous promoter of Cedel who devoted his considerable energy and much time to the project. Always a great talker, he never missed an opportunity to spread the news of Luxembourg's rival to Euroclear. The chairman's role was non-executive and supposed to be held on a rotating basis for three years. 'Somehow this did not work out,' Israel recalled later.[11] 'The large banking groups preferred someone from a small country like Luxembourg to be at the helm of this institution.' Israel would be Cedel chairman for 20 years.

Cedel, like Euroclear, required users to open securities and cash accounts and settled transactions by book entry. But Cedel differed from Euroclear in some important respects.

The two systems operated at different times: Cedel during the day on settlement date and Euroclear overnight, during the night before settlement date. The contrasting cycles meant Euroclear's clients would be able to know that their settlements were done and the status of their cash positions when they arrived in their offices in the morning. This was very important for the broker-dealer community which operated on a fairly thin capital base.

There was no single bank behind Cedel to give it or its users financial support. In one sense this was a strength, because Cedel could promote itself using the slogan 'from the market, for the market'. But it was to prove a disadvantage when users came to expect credit to help fund their operations. Cedel was competing with a 'triple A' bank in Morgan Guaranty. Although participants could access credit lines provided by a consortium of banks, led by Citibank, the operation was inevitably more burdensome than that operated by Morgan.

However, Cedel had been able to learn from some of the deficiencies of Euroclear as perceived by the market. It offered services that Euroclear could not, because it invested in modern computer equipment – unlike Euroclear. These included settlement services for non-dollar denominated securities and settlement of non-fungible as well as fungible instruments.

Euroclear's focus on settling dollar denominated bonds was a weakness when European currencies were used increasingly for Eurobond issues. The D-mark, in particular, was an important currency for issues in the late 1960s when there were strong flows of speculative funds from France and the US into Germany.

Cedel's ability to settle non-fungible bonds was important because fungibility was not yet the rule in Europe. Indeed, it was only several months after Cedel's launch that Luxembourg brought its law into line with that of Belgium and facilitated fungibility. In its work for the bankers' study group, Fiduciaire made clear that Cedel would have to cope with non-fungible securities.

Cedel gave the securities in the system specific certificate numbers that followed them from issue to maturity and guaranteed delivery of the same numbers. In this way, Cedel made its system especially attractive to German and Italian banks which were obliged by law to tell clients the serial numbers of bonds held on their behalf. It also offered greater security to private investors in case of loss or theft. In 1971, Cedel concluded a cooperation agreement with the Deutscher Auslandskassenverein (AKV), a recently created specialist institution for

---

[11] Quoted from *In Love with Life: An American dream of a Luxembourger* by Edmond Israel, published by Sacred Heart University Press, Fairfield, Connecticut, in 2006.

settling foreign securities in Germany. This agreement facilitated German bank participation in Cedel by affiliating German banks, with accounts at the AKV, to Cedel.

The securities, once settled, were allocated by issue to designated custodians from among Cedel's participants around the world. This made them easier to locate and retrieve than securities held by Euroclear's depositories, where bonds of the same issue might be held in four of five different vaults. It was only in 1977 that Euroclear introduced the specialised depository that centralised and immobilised each issue of securities at a single depository rather than at several places around the world.

Cedel therefore proved an attractive alternative to Euroclear for banks in particular. Whereas Euroclear rapidly built up a following among traders and broker-dealers on the 'sell side', Cedel's support was concentrated on the 'buy side' among banks, and especially those with a strong customer base among private investors and asset managers.

3.4   CEDEL'S SUCCESS

Cedel was an immediate success. The Luxembourg-based settlement system attracted supporters from a broad range of financial institutions, extending well beyond the continental 'buy side' banks. It made a profit in its first year and claimed a market share that was bigger than Euroclear. It also exercised downward pressure on settlement fees.

Some of Cedel's early supporters were Morgan's traditional competitors from the Anglo-Saxon banking world which were instinctively inclined to support a rival system to Euroclear. This was especially true of banks such as Citibank, Chase and Barclays, which were in the custody business.

But it soon became apparent that the differences between the two organisations extended beyond normal commercial rivalry. Stanley Ross witnessed the hostility between Euroclear and Luxembourg bankers in November 1969 at the extraordinary general meeting of the AIBD in Geneva. In a review of 25 years of AIBD meetings, written in May 1993,[12] Ross noted when the bond dealers held their annual meeting in Copenhagen in 1970 'most of the action was devoted to keeping the clearing systems from each others' throats'.

Herschel Post, who joined Euroclear in 1974 as head of commercial operations, has argued that the roots of this divide lay partly in the difference between the sell and buy sides of the market. 'You have a cultural difference that still is reflected in the Anglo-Saxon trading community and the continental European buying community. The big difference had always been traders versus custodians. Basically, the European institutions were representing the investors, and the London participants in Euroclear were the people who were selling securities to those investors. So you might say it is a sell side versus buy side cultural split'.

But this divergence of interests – which in many respects were complementary – can hardly explain the visceral rivalry that was to build up between Euroclear and Cedel over the 30 years following the foundation of the two ICSDs.

Some have traced the bad feeling back to different motives behind the creation of the two companies. According to this version, Euroclear was created to deal with the practical problem of a market in crisis and sought answers in efficiency, and gradually in automation. Cedel was the answer to a second order problem of European banks not wishing to see a new financial activity monopolised by a US institution.

---

[12] 'From where I stood', recollections of 25 AIBD meetings, by Stanley D. L. Ross.

This view is shared in part by Stanislas Yassukovich, who believes the gulf between the two settlement systems has several deep-seated causes. 'It's philosophical, it's cultural. It's based on the respective histories of financial intermediation in the two different worlds. It's based on different legal systems, between common law and prescribed Napoleonic systems,' he suggests.

Yassukovich argues that the international capital market, as it developed in Europe, was always sharply divided between what he calls the Anglo-Saxon and the continental model. 'And Cedel was formed against the risk that Euroclear, which was clearly an Anglo Saxon model, might become so dominant and powerful that it might form a victory for the Anglo Saxon branch of the Euromarkets: meaning the American and British houses ranged against the Benelux, German and Swiss houses.'

Certainly there was a strong, consciously European attitude among many of Cedel's early backers who privately took the view that anything Anglo-Saxon, British or American had to be opposed. This was probably exacerbated by a current of anti-Americanism at the time that was fuelled by US involvement in the Vietnam war and concern about US economic power. In 1967, Jean-Jacques Servan Schreiber, a French media magnate, had enjoyed huge success with the book *Le Défi Américain* – the American challenge – which warned that Europe faced relative economic decline because of the spread of US goods, ideas and services. The book achieved record sales for a political essay in France and became an international best seller.

Whatever the reasons, continental banks were drawn to Cedel. Banks from France, Germany, Italy, Luxembourg and the Netherlands were prominent among its early backers. The case of Switzerland was somewhat different. There banks divided along ancient fault lines, reflecting their domestic priorities and rivalries. UBS was a major supporter of Cedel from the beginning. Crédit Suisse and Swiss Bank Corporation, which had stronger business interests in the securities markets, backed Euroclear.

Cedel's early success had repercussions in Brussels. Gérard Van Nieuwenhove, by this time in charge of operations at Euroclear, had to cut staff. Numbers declined from 125 to 66 through natural wastage and redeployment in other parts of Morgan.

For the market, the arrival of a second settlement provider brought some clear benefits. 'Competition is always important,' says Walter Koller. 'Back then and still today, I'm very pleased that two systems emerged because otherwise Euroclear could have kept up its prices.' Evan Galbraith, by this time running Bankers Trust International in London, remembers that 'my view at the time was the more the merrier. Morgan Guaranty was making a monopoly fortune on their deposit system and they had to share some of that. A lot of people wanted competition.'

According to Yassukovich, it was 'healthy' for the market to have two settlement organisations. 'The clearing charges of Euroclear had to come down. The launching of Cedel also increased pressure on Morgan Guaranty to mutualise Euroclear, because Cedel was originally conceived as a mutual, owned by several big continental users, which made Morgan Guaranty look a bit isolated as single owner of this utility.'

But the market would have benefited more had the two settlement organisations been able to work together more constructively. There was a need for business to flow efficiently between Euroclear's 'sell side' traders and Cedel's 'buy side' bankers, which was impeded by commercial rivalry between the two organisations. Writing early in 1972, Stanley Ross[13] welcomed the creation of Cedel as a competitor to Euroclear, but he observed: 'Unfortunately the degree of cooperation between the two systems has, to say the least, been fragile.' For the market's

---

[13] Eurobond market report in *Money Management*, February 1972.

sake, Ross urged Euroclear and Cedel to make 'watertight, same-day payment against delivery facilities' within and between the systems a 'number one priority'. It would be many years before his wish was granted.

3.5 THE WIDER SETTLEMENT PICTURE

Euroclear and Cedel represented a significant innovation in Europe's financial infrastructure. They provided a home for Eurobonds, which were homeless securities, when nearly all financial activity in Europe was defined by national laws, applying in national currency areas, behind international frontiers.

The ICSDs were independent of all national stock exchanges and created at a time when not all European countries had central securities depositories or CSDs. Where national CSDs did exist there were wide variations in their structure, service offering and quality. However, they invariably formed part of a coherent domestic financial infrastructure. Their activities were often defined by law and they were closely associated with their national central banks which would supply the cash leg of the securities transactions that were settled on the books of the CSD.

The idea of the CSD, on which the ICSDs were based, was not new. The Wiener Giro- und Cassenverein of Vienna became the first institution in the world that could be described as a CSD as long ago as 1872. Similar bodies were established shortly afterwards in Bismarck's Germany and known as Kassenverein. The early German CSDs were founded by banks and were incorporated as a special form of bank: a Wertpapiersammelbank.[14] This restriction applies to this day in Germany.

The main reasons for holding securities in a central location in the late 19th century were to ensure safekeeping and to be better able to control fraud, by checking their authenticity. In 1937, the various regional Kassenvereine[15] in Germany were regulated by a Securities Deposit Act.[16] This established the legal basis for the safe custody and administration of securities by banks using book entries. It provided protection to owners of securities, in particular by ensuring they did not lose their proprietary rights in the event of financial problems at the depository bank.

The Frankfurt Kassenverein, which provided some of the know-how for Cedel, was one of several CSDs refounded in western Germany after the Second World War. Established in 1949, a year after the creation of the D-mark, the Frankfurt Kassenverein was set up by local banks to support the Frankfurt stock exchange. Germany's banks set up other Kassenvereine, to serve bourses in Berlin, Düsseldorf, Hamburg, Hanover, Munich and Stuttgart, reflecting the decentralised, federal structure of West Germany's political and financial systems.

In 1970–71, the German banks created the Deutscher Auslandskassenverein (AKV) in Frankfurt to settle foreign securities that were traded away from the official stock exchange floors. The AKV became a mini-ICSD handling D-mark denominated Eurobonds. The AKV's 1971 cooperation agreement with Cedel linked its users to the cross-border settlement services of Cedel.

One of the by-products of France's defeat by Germany in the Second World War was the creation, in 1941, of a German-style CSD. Probably the main reason the Vichy government set up the Caisse Centrale de Dépôts et de Virement de Titres (CCDVT) was to gain an insight

---

[14] Literally translated as 'a bank for collecting securities'.
[15] The plural of Kassenverein.
[16] The 1937 Act still provides – at the time of writing – the legal basis for Germany's securities settlement system.

into, and therefore control over, the wealth of French investors who traditionally held their securities in bearer form. The Vichy regime introduced book entry accounts for securities and initially insisted on their being deposited in CCDVT. Another characteristic of CCDVT was that the securities in the system were fungible.

CCDVT was dissolved after the war. But the CSD did not die in France. In 1945, the Banque de France was given the task of managing by book entry the Treasury notes and bills held by French financial institutions. In 1949, leading banks and brokerages set up a new company, Sicovam,[17] to take over where CCDVT left off and 'facilitate the circulation of shares among member institutions via book entry transfers'.[18]

Sicovam proved to be a technical and economic success. It cut costs for its users, which thereafter promoted it vigorously. Sicovam also built up a reputation for reliability as it progressed from manual through electromagnetic to computer processing and steadily expanded the type of securities it handled.

Advances in technology and growth in financial services activity resulted in several initiatives to introduce securities depositories with book entry from the mid-1960s. In 1965, the Oesterreichische Kontrollbank, owned by the major Austrian banks, was established as a Wertpapiersammelbank to provide CSD services. Four years later the law was changed to allow collective safekeeping of securities. As already noted, CIK in Belgium was set up around the same time with rules that allowed fungibility.

Switzerland phased out the paper settlement of securities in 1970 when the country's banks established SEGA,[19] a securities depository based in Basel. In SEGA's early years, however, the delivery of securities was separated from the process of paying for them, which was handled by the Swiss banks' system for clearing payments. Delivery versus payment for securities made its first appearance in Switzerland in 1982 and was implemented by SEGA in 1983–84.

In Sweden, VPC[20] was set up as the country's CSD in 1971 to handle matching, clearing and settlement services relating to securities traded on the Stockholm Stock Exchange.

Payments arrangements were one feature that distinguished the ICSDs from the national CSDs that were emerging in Europe. A downside of being independent of national structures, such as stock exchanges and banking systems, was that the cash leg of settlement transactions conducted by ICSDs had to be settled in commercial bank money. National CSDs were set up with accounts at their national central banks and could settle transactions in central bank money, the payments medium with the highest level of security for users.

There were well-established post-trade practices but no CSD in Britain when Euroclear and Cedel were founded. The law in Britain (as in the US) required securities to be registered. A paper-based infrastructure for settling securities operated among the firms and individuals serving the stock exchange during two-week account periods for the settling of bargains. Although there was a phased introduction of computerised processes in the 1960s and 1970s, it was 1979 before the London Stock Exchange launched Talisman,[21] a batch processing system which functioned in part as a CSD. Talisman dematerialised securities for jobbers – the forerunners of market makers – in trading accounts. The Central Gilts Office (CGO), an electronic book entry transfer system for settling the stock side of transactions in UK

---

[17] Société Interprofessionnelle pour la COmpensation des VAleurs Mobilières.

[18] Order of 4 August 1949, quoted in 'Sicovam, a history of France's depository institution' by Nathalie Chabrolles and Hervé Juvin, Éditions Les Djinns, 1992.

[19] Schweizerische Effekten-Giro AG.

[20] Värdepapperscentralen AB.

[21] Talisman stood for Transfer Accounting and Lodgement for Investors, Stock MANagement for Jobbers.

government gilt-edged securities, followed in 1986. The CGO, which was developed with the stock exchange, was owned and operated by the Bank of England.

The US meanwhile had started down the route that would leave it – at the end of the 20th century – with a consolidated post-trade infrastructure in the form of The Depository Trust & Clearing Corporation (DTCC), which many in Europe envied. There was a false start in 1913 when the New York Stock Exchange considered setting up a CSD modelled on the Vienna Cassenverein only for the project to be stillborn. Nearly half a century later, in 1961, the NYSE teamed up with several leading custodian banks to run a one-year 'pilot operation for central handling of securities'. Starting with 15 securities, 31 member companies made deliveries among themselves by book entry without any physical movement of certificates.

The following year, work began on the monumental task of changing legislation to prepare for a centralised service of all issues listed on the NYSE. New legislation was required in virtually every US state to amend article 8 of the Uniform Commercial Code so that the transfer of ownership or pledge of securities by depository book entry could replace delivery of physical certificates. This took until 1970 to complete.

By the late 1960s, the paper jam in New York, which was threatening the nascent Eurobond market, was crippling the NYSE. Share trading was reaching 16 million a day, a huge volume for the time, pushing the market's paper and labour intensive settlement structures to their limits. To cope with the backlog, exchanges closed one day a week and shortened trading hours on other days.

In 1968, however, the NYSE established the Central Certificate Service to immobilise share certificates, marking a first step towards a depository system for the US. Morgan had a big 'thought leadership' role in the process through John M. Meyer Jr, who was chairman of Morgan Guaranty from 1969 to 1971 and also chair of JP Morgan & Co., the holding company created in April 1969 for Morgan Guaranty and other Morgan units. Also in 1968, a US Treasury regulation authorised the first book entry procedures to eliminate US government securities in paper form. Thereafter, US government bonds were issued and transferred electronically on the records of Federal Reserve Banks.

Meyer, who was instrumental in creating the Brussels pilot scheme for Euroclear in 1967, was well qualified to take the lead in promoting reform of securities settlement infrastructures in the US. Already chairman of the New York Clearing House Committee, he took charge in February 1970 of the US Banking and Securities Industry Committee (BASIC) which was set up to resolve what by now had become known as the 'paperwork crisis'.

It was no easy task. In a slim volume of reminiscences, which Meyer[22] wrote with two colleagues from Morgan Guaranty, he noted dryly that: 'One of BASIC's first goals and major breakthroughs was successfully persuading security dealers, brokers, trade associations, banks, and stock exchanges to talk with each other and to work together.'

BASIC's efforts were crowned with success in 1973 when The Depository Trust Company was set up by the NYSE, the American Stock Exchange and the National Association of Securities Dealers (NASD) as a limited-purpose New York State bank to immobilise stock and bond certificates and transfer title by book entry. Meyer not only contributed his extensive knowledge of US markets and infrastructure to establishing the DTC. Through him, the committee also drew on the experiences of Euroclear to create a CSD for the leading financial centre in the US.

---

[22] Some comments about the Morgan Bank by Longstreet Hinton, John M. Meyer Jr and Thomas Rodd, published by Morgan Guaranty Trust Co., 1979.

4

Euroclear Fights Back

4.1 THE SALE OF EUROCLEAR TO ITS USERS

Euroclear continued to grow after Cedel's launch.[1] But it was clear by 1971 that the Luxembourg settlement system posed a threat to Euroclear's business. Criticism of US ownership of Euroclear and the counter-attraction of Cedel's mutual structure forced Morgan Guaranty to react.

Early in 1972, Bruce Brackenridge, the head of Morgan Guaranty International Finance Corp., was given the job of sorting out Euroclear's future. He was told to set up a separate Euroclear company and then sell it to the Euroclear participants with Morgan keeping only a small ownership. Brackenridge had just moved to New York to take responsibility for the bank's foreign equity investments after working for Morgan in Germany. He was familiar with Europe, having moved to Germany from London, where he was based between 1964 and 1968.

Brackenridge began to explore options, in consultation with friendly banks. He worked closely with Davis Polk, Morgan's lawyers in New York, where Bruce Nichols and Dick Grandquist played important roles. 'A lot of the credit should go to the late J. Wallace (Wally) Hopkins at Davis Polk's Paris office,' he adds.

Brackenridge also had powerful support from John M. Meyer Jr, who stepped down from chairing Morgan Guaranty and JP Morgan & Co. in 1971, and Jack Bochow, Morgan's senior international credit officer. Morgan was anxious that Euroclear should have at least a modest profit, and to this end put a big effort into controlling costs. What emerged from the discussions was a structure of considerable ingenuity, designed, Brackenridge says, 'to avoid virtually all taxes'. It was a non-resident English company, with its domicile in Switzerland and a contract with the Belgian branch of an American bank.

By mid-April 1972, Morgan and Davis Polk had worked out a general concept for selling Euroclear to its users which would also entail the newly mutualised company contracting out its settlement operation to Morgan Guaranty's Brussels branch. Later that month, when speaking to the annual meeting of the AIBD in Geneva, Chandler gave the first public hint that Euroclear might be turned into a separate company, with Morgan as a minority shareholder.

By the end of May, Morgan and Davis Polk had drafted the details and a timetable for incorporating Euroclear and selling it to the institutions that used it. As the new company would be non-resident in the UK for tax purposes, it could not hold board meetings in Britain. It would be taxed in Switzerland.

On 28 June, Morgan Guaranty International Finance published an offer of shares divided into 'A' and 'B' shares to balance out the interests of the system's bank and trader users. The traders were to have no more than 30% of the shares issued and be able to elect at least one quarter of the company's directors.

---

[1] An operating statement prepared in November 1972 by Price Waterhouse for the board of Morgan Guaranty showed fee income for business years ending 30 November rising from $569 000 in 1969 to $998 000 in 1970 and $1.97 million in 1971. A $15 000 loss before taxes and other charges in 1969 was followed by income of $59 000 in 1970 and $304 000 in 1971.

Ownership of Euroclear was not open to all. Applicants for shares had to be approved and restrictions were placed on the onward sale of the shares that obliged potential vendors to notify the directors and sell stock through them. The maximum holding of any single shareholder, including Morgan Guaranty, was initially set at 5%.

On 7 July, Euro-clear Clearance System Ltd was incorporated. Its address was the London office of Slaughter & May, Morgan's UK solicitors. The company's objective was described as being to 'own and operate or cause to be operated a clearing service for securities of all kinds'. Whereas the US offer of shares said Euroclear was engaged in the 'settlement of transactions', there was no mention of settlement or settling securities among the 16 objectives of the company listed in paragraph 3 of the UK certificate of incorporation. The mixing up of the terms clearing and settlement would continue for some years yet.

These documents provide a snapshot of Euroclear's operations three and a half years after its launch. It had 116 full time staff and during an average week in the first five months of 1972 settled securities with a nominal value of $212.1 million, up from the $165.5 million weekly average of the same period of 1971. The number of users had risen to 376 from 74 when operations started. The system handled more than 1365 issues of internationally traded securities, which were held in depositories in Brussels, Amsterdam, Basel, Frankfurt, Hong Kong, London, Luxembourg, Milan, New York, Paris, Tokyo, Toronto and Zurich. The securities were denominated in dollars, D-marks, Dutch guilders, French francs and pounds sterling. The addition of non-dollar currencies in 1972 was a sign that Euroclear was responding to the competitive challenge posed by Cedel.

The Euroclear system would continue to be run by Morgan staff members whose salaries and pensions were paid by the US bank. The operating agreement with Morgan specified that Euroclear would reimburse the bank's costs of providing the settlement and custody services, plus a fee of 5% of such costs or a minimum of $50 000 a year. It also paid a royalty of $1500 to use the Euroclear trade mark. The documents made no mention of the money that Morgan would make from operating the customers' cash accounts, which would prove to be the major source of the bank's income from the venture.

During the summer, Brackenridge and a small team criss-crossed the world selling the offer with support from Meyer, who, according to Brackenridge, 'made some of the critical phone calls'. The sales process was not easy. There were strong anti-Morgan and anti-US feelings among many European banks. However, Morgan's 'triple A' status proved a significant factor in garnering support. 'Euroclear would not have sold if it were not backed by a triple A bank,' Brackenridge says.

Euro-clear Clearance System's first board meeting took place on 30 August 1972, in New York, with a temporary board of four Morgan Guaranty officials, chaired by Brackenridge. Less than a month later, a press release was issued announcing that 20 000 shares in the new company had been allocated to 118 financial institutions in 20 countries at a par value of $125 each. The issue was oversubscribed with a maximum allocation of 650 shares to any one shareholder, representing 3.25% of the issued capital of $2.5 million.

On 30 November, the Euroclear system was sold by Morgan Guaranty to Morgan Guaranty International Finance Corp. for $1.7 million. The following day, on 1 December, Euroclear's shares were placed with its users for $2.5 million. MGIFC took $1.75 million in payment for the Euroclear system, leaving the remaining proceeds of the share sale with the new company as working capital.

When the sale was completed, 15 875 'A' shares were allocated to the banks and 4125 'B' shares went to financial institutions and traders active in the secondary market. By the end of

December 1972, ECS had 125 shareholders of which 91 held 'A' shares and 34 'B' shares. A further 4000 unclassified shares were not issued and held in reserve.

The biggest single shareholders were banks, each of which paid \$81 250 for 650 'A' shares. These were Morgan Guaranty International Finance Corp., Sté Générale de Banque of Brussels, Sté Générale of Paris, Deutsche Bank of Frankfurt, Amsterdam Rotterdam Bank, Skandinaviska Enskilda Banken (SEB) of Sweden,[2] Swiss Bank Corp and Crédit Suisse. The biggest holders of the traders' 'B' shares, with 300 each, were Kidder Peabody, Wood Gundy and Orion Bank, a consortium bank that specialised in the Eurobond market.

The big shareholders dominated Euroclear's 14 strong board and a seven strong executive committee drawn from board members. Both bodies met for the first time at the Dolder Grand Hotel above Zurich on 7 December 1972.

The banks supplied 10 board members of whom five sat on the executive committee. Rolf Hallberg of SEB was elected ECS chairman with effect from 1 December 1972 in place of Morgan's Brackenridge, who remained a member of the board and executive committee. Hallberg was also chairman of the AIBD – a position he held until the association's annual meeting in Vienna in May 1973.

The three other banking representatives on the board and executive committee were Georges Streichenberg of Swiss Bank Corp., who took over as chairman from Hallberg on 11 June 1976 and held the post until 6 June 1980, Etienne Bairiot of Sté Générale de Banque and Ernst Studer of Crédit Suisse. Representing the traders on both bodies were John Cattier of White Weld and Wood Gundy's Ian Steers, who followed Streichenberg as chairman of Euroclear between 6 June 1980 and 22 June 1984.

Five other banks were represented on Euroclear's first board: Société Générale of Paris, the Caisse d'Epargne de l'État of Luxembourg, Amsterdam-Rotterdam Bank, Deutsche Bank and Pictet & Cie, the Geneva-based private bank. The other two traders were Merrill Lynch, represented by Alfred G. Lutz, and Stanley Ross, representing Kidder Peabody. 'In a way,' Ross says now, 'I guess this might have been Euroclear thanking me for all I had done in helping their operation get under way.'

Ross resigned from the board on 2 March 1973 to concentrate on trading. It was a move he bitterly regretted later. 'I was stupid, I really was stupid,' Ross admits. 'How could I have been so dumb to walk out on that? But I did genuinely feel that my job was to make money for my firm Kidder, not to spend time continuing to help Morgan Guaranty. It seemed to me that once they had the mechanics sorted out, it was not a business for me because I was, at heart, a trader.'

4.2 DIFFICULT DAYS

ECS shares were to become an extremely lucrative investment. The pool of shareholders became a rather exclusive club. And a seat on the Euroclear board became a very desirable perk. But none of that was obvious in the years immediately following the sale of ECS to its users.

The sale did nothing to ease the competitive challenge of Cedel, which had put Euroclear on the back foot. It was only after Cedel's foundation that Euroclear invested in a proper computer and hired a manager – Alfred (Freddy) Jamar, a former ship's captain – to take charge of it. An

---

[2] Skandinaviska Enskilda Banken (SEB) was created in 1972 through the merger of Stockholms Enskilda Bank and Skandinaviska Banken of Sweden. Hallberg came from the Stockholms Enskilda Bank part of the merged entity.

IBM 360.25 was installed in January 1971. It used a cumbersome program, as Herschel Post discovered when he arrived at Euroclear as commercial manager at the beginning of 1974. 'It was written in a language called assembler, which was particularly problematic because when you modified one element of a programme, you essentially had to rewrite the whole programme,' he remembers. 'The system wasn't appropriately documented. There was one person in IT who really understood it and he came to work on a motorcycle. So I think there was a feeling the whole thing wasn't very stable.'

A great deal of paper was still being moved around the globe with inevitable glitches. In an article to mark Euroclear's 25th anniversary, Martine Dinne remembered when 'bonds that were supposed to be delivered to Astaire & Co. in London ended up at the Fred Astaire Dancing School in New York, because of a bad instruction'.[3] Charles d'Ursel remembers how a bag containing bearer bonds destined for foreign parts fell off a motorbike between Morgan's office and Brussels airport. In another case, a bundle of missing bonds was traced to the offices of Euroclean, a Brussels industrial cleaning company.

Euroclear was little known outside the Eurobond market. The system kept its light under a bushel during the first two years following its creation, unlike Cedel, which bombarded news organisations in Brussels with publicity about every additional participant. According to Gérard Van Nieuwenhove, Euroclear's first meeting with the Brussels press corps did not take place until the spring of 1971.

In 1973, Cedel had some $5.5 billion of securities in its system against $3 billion in Euroclear, suggesting that the Luxembourg-based settlement system had about 65% of the market. Cedel was also capable of aggressive manoeuvring. In January 1973, it did a deal with the European Investment Bank over the issue of an 800 million Luxembourg franc global bond issue. Under the terms of the EIB deal, none of the issue could leave the Cedel system to be settled in Euroclear until individual bearer bonds had been issued – a process that took several weeks.

The rivalry between the two systems played out against a dramatic deterioration in global business conditions. The Bretton Woods system of semi-fixed exchange rates, which had been under strain for some years, finally collapsed in March 1973 as most European countries and Japan adopted floating exchange rates. The resulting sharp devaluation of the dollar against European currencies[4] threw Euroclear's finances into disarray because its revenues were denominated in the US currency and its costs were mainly in Belgian francs.

Worse was to follow. The falling dollar, high inflation in the industrialised countries and the Yom Kippur War of October 1973 between Israel and Egypt prompted OPEC, the Organisation of Petroleum Exporting Countries, to increase sharply the price of oil and cut supplies, precipitating the first oil crisis of the 1970s. The industrial world experienced its worst recession since the Second World War and had to get used to a new concept: 'stagflation', a hitherto unforeseen combination of economic stagnation and inflation.

Britain, which had joined the EEC in 1973 in the hope of boosting its economy, succumbed early in 1974 to power shortages, a three-day working week and political turmoil as the Conservative government of Edward Heath emerged as the loser in a confrontation with the country's coal miners. In the US, the long running Watergate scandal came to a grisly end in August 1974 when Richard Nixon became the first US president to resign from office.

---

[3] 'Euroclear turns 25', in *Euroclear Review*, Winter-Spring 1994.
[4] The Deutsche Mark, for example, gained in value by 41% against the dollar and 23% against all other currencies between the end of 1972 and 9 July 1973.

Confidence in international financial markets buckled as the leading industrialised economies were floored by a lethal cocktail of currency turmoil, soaring inflation, sharply rising interest rates and a collapse in economic growth.

The deterioration in business conditions proved too much for some banks. Franklin National Bank, the 20th biggest bank in the US, collapsed in May 1974, its demise hastened by fraud on the part of Michele Sindona, a Sicilian financier. On 26 June, the spotlight turned to Germany, when Bankhaus I.D. Herstatt, a prominent Cologne-based private bank, went under after massive and misguided currency speculation. The Herstatt collapse sent shockwaves around the world: not so much because of the errors of its founder and chief executive Iwan D. Herstatt, a fun loving pillar of Cologne's pre-Lenten carnival, as the clumsy action of the German authorities in shutting the bank at the end of the German banking day while markets in the US and elsewhere were still trading.

The timing of the Herstatt closure meant the Deutsche Mark leg of some of its foreign exchange contracts for value on the day of closure had been settled while the dollar legs of those contracts had not been finally paid. The bank's unfortunate counterparties were unable to recover the funds owing to them. The bank's closure therefore risked further defaults which, if left unchecked, could ultimately threaten the financial system.

The Herstatt bank closure and resulting crisis was a striking example of the risks created by growing financial interdependence among the leading economies in the 1970s. It gave rise to the concept of 'principal risk' – that is the risk of loss of the full value of an asset delivered. Although the Herstatt bank closure followed foreign exchange losses, the mechanics of principal risk could apply equally well to cross-border securities settlement transactions. This insight would underpin pressure for the institution of delivery versus payment (DvP) in such transactions for many years after.

One immediate consequence of the Herstatt closure was a 'flight to quality' by investors. The market for syndicated euroloans, which in the first half of 1974 were a major channel for recycling the rapidly growing current account balance of payments surpluses of the oil producers to the deficit countries of the industrialised and developing world, seized up. The number of new issues in the Eurobond market slumped to around 80 in 1974 from more than 200 in 1972 and prices for existing issues tumbled. The value of new issues in 1974 fell below $2 billion, around a third of issuance in 1972 and at a level not seen since 1967.

The Euromarkets recovered somewhat towards the end of the year after the central banks of the Group of 10 industrialised countries and Switzerland made clear that they would act as lenders of last resort to the euro-banks if necessary. But by then, some consortium banks had quit the market while maturities for new bond issues had shrunk from around 12 years before the crisis to between five and seven years.

Herschel Post arrived in Brussels at the end of 1973 to take up the post of commercial director in January 1974. As he arrived, Cedel cut its settlement charge by about a third from $3.50 per transaction to $2.25.

'Euroclear had been making small amounts of money and on the day I started in January 1974, Cedel announced an enormous tariff cut,' Post recalls. 'From that point, Euroclear immediately started losing money. A lot of people began to wonder why we had two clearing systems and a substantial amount of pressure began to arise for a merger between Euroclear and Cedel.'

The damage showed up in the annual report of Euro-clear Clearance System Ltd for the business year to 30 November 1974 which disclosed an after tax loss of $29 765. Euroclear was forced to reduce some of its fees from 1 May 1974 in reaction to Cedel's initiative.

However, the loss also prompted Morgan Guaranty to take action to deal with the competition of Cedel. The ECS report for 1974 noted that: 'In conjunction with the reduction in fees a supplementary agreement was reached with Morgan Guaranty Trust Co. of New York to undertake a joint effort to increase the efficiency of the system.'

4.3   COMMITMENT TO INVESTMENT

Morgan's decision to invest in Euroclear appeared brave at the time. On 1 January 1974, the US cut to zero the Interest Equalisation Tax – the levy that had given such a boost to the Eurobond market a decade before. This action, followed by the final abolition of the tax in June, prompted some to fear that the entire Eurobond market could move back to New York.

There were some in Morgan's New York office who would have welcomed such a development. Not everyone shared the enthusiasm of Brackenridge and Meyer for Euroclear.

Some executives wondered why such an eminent bank was involved with such a humdrum business as securities settlement in Europe, and one that required subsidising to boot. Post remembers Alec Vagliano, the head of Morgan's international banking division who sent him to Brussels, telling a press conference in the mid-1970s that if Morgan were to start over again it would not create Euroclear. Suggestions had surfaced earlier in the Euroclear and Morgan boards that Euroclear and Cedel should merge. Talks were held in the small south Belgian town of Marche en Famenne. However, they came to nothing.

Three people played a vital role in pulling Euroclear out of this mire: Robert Wilmers, who was posted as deputy general manager to Morgan's Brussels office between 1973 and 1978; Herschel Post, the commercial director; and Albert Petersen, a Belgian technical expert who steered Euroclear into a period of technical advance. Both Post and Petersen would become members of the Euroclear board long after they left Morgan while Wilmers would acquire a bank in Buffalo, New York, and make a fortune.

Both Wilmers and Post worked for New York's Democrat mayor Robert Lindsay before joining Morgan in Brussels. Wilmers had worked in the finance department. Post was deputy administrator for parks and cultural affairs.

Bob Wilmers is remembered by contemporaries for his penetrating blue eyes, colourful ties, loud braces, a Mickey Mouse watch and his decision – viewed as the height of eccentricity by Belgian colleagues at the time – to ship an antique Volkswagen Beetle (a 1955 model with a divided rear window) by container from the US to Brussels.[5]

Appearances were deceptive. Wilmers was the first of several young, fast-track bankers sent by Morgan Guaranty in New York to manage Euroclear. His approach towards his responsibilities was anything but eccentric. He had a clear mandate to invest in the operation and modernise it and this he proceeded to do with determination.

Post was quieter. Colleagues remember a self-deprecating, cerebral sense of humour. Charged with selling Euroclear's services, he focused on diversifying its offering and tailoring Euroclear's services to the needs of the market. Increasingly, this meant making Euroclear attractive to the broker-dealer community, which was now concentrated in London.

As a result, the system announced during 1975 that it could settle Eurobonds denominated in Canadian dollars, handle South African gold mining shares and facilitate arbitrage trading in a limited number of Dutch, French and German equities. Post's marketing of Euroclear

---

[5] As reported by Agnès Petiau in 'Histoires d'Euroclear'.

also took him to the Arab world and the Far East where he and Sean McSharry, his successor, secured agreement in 1978 for the acceptance of 'Samurais' – yen denominated foreign bonds issued in Tokyo – into the system.

'When Herschel Post came aboard as head of the commercial department in 1974, the environment really changed,' Martine Dinne recalled.[6] Euroclear was moving 'from a factory-style environment to a client-oriented one'. Dinne was by now 'part of a small, new client support group, which had been created to respond to the growing number of questions from participants and to show the market that we were serious about meeting its needs'.

Having decided to upgrade the operations of both Euroclear and the bank branch, Wilmers called in Arthur Andersen, the consulting firm, to help. There was no Euroclear operations centre at the time. Everything was embedded in the Morgan Guaranty branch. There were a few departments operating some activities specific to Euroclear's settlements, but the technology, accounting, cash management, foreign exchange and personnel were intertwined.

The Arthur Andersen manager appointed to the project was Petersen, who worked on the consultancy's payroll in Morgan Guaranty's Brussels branch for about a year and a half to improve the banking side and the operations shared with Euroclear. Computer staff numbers grew rapidly from six in 1970 to 70 in 1973, according to Gérard Van Nieuwenhove. Even so, it soon became clear that the job was much bigger than Wilmers and Andersen had anticipated.

According to Petersen, the infrastructure, in terms of technology and human resources, of Morgan Guaranty's Brussels office was 'extremely stressed and underdeveloped.'[7] He found a lot of tabulating equipment and the small IBM 360 computer barely coping with what, in absolute terms, were small volumes of business.

'Euroclear hadn't really been designed as a settlement system,' he says. 'It had basically happened. Different people in different departments tried to deal with one new client request at a time. So it did not have a very solid infrastructure. They had a lot of people of goodwill, who were trying to make it work.'

The Euroclear staff could hardly keep up with the daily demands of processing and telexing communications to clients worldwide. And any problem created serious delays. As a result, Wilmers reviewed progress with Arthur Andersen's representatives and concluded that Euroclear would only be put right by a long-term programme and increased resources. He turned to Petersen and offered him a job. Petersen accepted and joined Morgan Guaranty in 1975. During that year, the agreement with Morgan Guaranty to help improve the Euroclear system was extended for two years to 30 November 1977.

For Petersen rebuilding the systems and processing capacity of Euroclear and the Morgan Guaranty branch in Brussels involved creating an environment in which systems could be developed to meet Euroclear's needs. It meant recruiting and training people, developing methods of working, plans and programmes and managing expectations.

It was a case of learning by doing. 'There were a lot of people in Brussels, who had been doing a lot of things manually at small volume levels and they provided a certain amount of background. We talked a lot to participants in the system. We talked to a lot of technology manufacturers. And we had to go gradually, because we didn't have the manpower or knowledge or resources to go faster. We had to do things step by step in an organised way and learn to become reasonable with our expectations, so that we could accelerate later, which happened.'

---

[6] Interview with *Euroclear Review* – Winter-Spring 1994.
[7] Conversation with the author, 13 December 2005.

As Petersen got down to upgrading the infrastructure, business took off, making his job more difficult. Wilmers had asked Herschel Post to promote the service, Petersen recalls. 'Post did a brilliant job and with some rejuvenation of the Eurobond market, the volume of activity in Brussels turned round all of a sudden. Volume was very small compared with today, but it was doubling every three months or so.'

Petersen's operation became a breeding ground for talent. Ignace Combes, appointed deputy chief executive of Euroclear Bank in 2002 and of Euroclear SA/NV after the corporate restructuring of 1 January 2005, started with Euroclear as a Morgan Guaranty trainee in the systems department in 1976. Luc Bomans, Euroclear general manager from 1994 to 2000, was hired by Petersen as a project leader in the IT division in 1978.

Petersen's first priority was to supply the functions, such as an effective multi-currency settlement system and multi-currency credit lines, that Euroclear lacked. But he also had to ensure that the settlement system worked day in and day out.

He found processes of mind-boggling complexity were used to inform Euroclear's users about the settlement of their securities operations. 'A computer would process the settlement overnight and produce all the financial activities related to that. When everything was done, it would print the reports on paper and punch cards. These cards would be taken by an operator, and would be brought onto a machine that had been created by IBM. That machine would read the cards and would produce telex tapes. These telex tapes would be taken by an operator to the telex room and be put into a telex machine and telexes would be sent to clients worldwide, to tell them about the settlement that had happened overnight in their cash positions and securities positions.'

The process created an enormous bottleneck. There were two special machines to do the processing. One of these broke down about a month after Petersen joined Morgan Guaranty. 'They couldn't repair it, they didn't have parts for it,' Petersen recalls. The defective machine was supposed to be a backup but had been used for processing to cope with volumes doubling every three months. Euroclear took its problem to IBM. 'This went up to the highest level at Morgan and IBM, and they basically recreated the parts for us.'

At the core of Euroclear's overnight processing was a set of programmes, called the 'chaining'. A proprietary system based on the pioneering work of Freddy Jamar, the chaining positioned the day's securities transactions, verifying that the seller had the securities to sell and the buyer the cash or credit to trade.

The chaining linked transactions to each other to maximise settlement in a given day. There was a capacity to chain back, or settle a transaction that was failed using cash or securities that came available from another transaction that settled – perhaps a few seconds later. Chaining therefore 'was a very complex programme,' Petersen commented. 'And that programme was extremely difficult to change. We supported it for many, many years until we could have the infrastructure to replace it.'

The persons responsible for rewriting the chaining were George Piette and Ignace Combes, who was appointed project leader for the development of the new securities settlement system in 1979. 'We wrote the system to be launched in 1981,' Combes recalls.[8] 'There were two major improvements. It was multi-currency and it had a dynamic positioning of transactions, including the valuation of when you sold securities, when you bought securities and the collateral value of the securities in order to minimise the amount of credit you needed from Morgan Guaranty.'

---

[8] Conversation with the author, 28 September 2005.

Minimising credit requirements through the chaining process was an important part of Euroclear's strategy for securing the support of the broker-dealer community. 'It is very important for brokers to minimise the use of credit or maximise their securities positions, to do much more turnover,' Combes explained. 'Because generally speaking, they have low capital but do a lot of volume and therefore need to make sure settlement is happening very efficiently.'

Petersen's programme of recruiting, training and systems development took around five years to complete. By the end, the entire Euroclear system was rewritten. The company was equipped with a very sturdy system and data processing operation capable of handling day-to-day activities and short-term and long-term priorities. 'We introduced new technologies, and also a lot of new functionalities in order to operate with increasingly high volumes and increasing demand for specific functions. That was the first envelope of what I had to do.'

In 1978 and 1979, he hit critical mass. 'Everything accelerated enormously, because by then we had a very sound infrastructure and a pretty big systems development department and a very sound operation.' There followed three major developments: Euclid, Euroclear's information and communications system; automated securities lending and borrowing and the electronic Bridge with Cedel. Combined with its overnight settlement system, these innovations allowed Euroclear to develop economies of scale.

4.4   EUCLID

Euroclear soon found that telex communications could not cope with putting instructions into a daily settlement system with increasing volumes, significant peaks and troughs in volumes and clients distributed worldwide.

It concluded that there had to be an input and information flow straight to the system from the customer. The result was Euclid, a revolutionary development that ran on a time sharing system. Euroclear convinced most participants to link to it and provide it with data through a telecommunication and data processing system, eliminating the need for armies of people standing by for incoming transactions which they would put into the system over a number of hours. This was well before the Internet and sophisticated telecommunications.

Euclid was a significant investment for the time. The 1979 and 1980 annual reports of Euro-clear Clearance System Ltd tell of the company assuming the cost of 'developing an advanced communication time-sharing system' to the tune of $189 288 in 1978, $580 712 in 1979 and $371 938 in 1980. These amounts compared with profit after taxation of $412 353 in 1978, $775 214 the following year and $719 179 in 1980. The time sharing system worked, on a real-time basis, to authenticate and validate all the transactions that were submitted so that clients would know immediately that their transactions were good, valid and accepted. Euroclear then took the transactions at different times during the day and input them into a settlement system.

'It was a pretty sophisticated system for the time,' Petersen remembers. 'We were extremely successful with it. But its early development was not very easy, because we had very little knowledge. We had a conceptual idea, if you like. And that's when I hired Luc Bomans. That was his first project and he made all the difference.'

Euclid marked a first step towards straight through processing. It was also an early example of outsourcing. General Electric provided a very large data processing capacity that could be accessed from terminals. Euroclear developed applications programs that were operated by GE. Euclid used GE's telecommunications network, which had entry points around the world so that the costs of users were relatively low. It meant Morgan Guaranty did not have to create an international telecommunications network or invest in and manage telecommunications computers.

By 1982, some 81% of securities instructions were transmitted to Euroclear by Euclid. Very quickly, and to the surprise of many, participants used Euclid and asked for more. Euroclear started to distribute reports and information through Euclid in response, creating a two-way flow of information between the system and participants.

Euclid was a major development that helped Euroclear cope with very rapid growth in volumes. It eliminated the uncertainty about being able to meet deadlines for putting valid data into the system. Over the years, Euroclear has added greatly to Euclid's functions. It has migrated from time sharing to a PC-based, and Internet-based, and telecommunications-based system.

4.5 SECURITIES LENDING AND BORROWING

The second big innovation of the Petersen regime was computerised securities lending and borrowing. A programme of securities lending and borrowing was one of Herschel Post's innovations to promote the activities of Euroclear with the broker-dealers. But when introduced in 1975, it was a manual process. Participants who received telexes in the morning, telling them that their transactions had failed, would contact Euroclear and say: 'I was supposed to deliver a security, but I didn't have it, can I borrow it?'

Euroclear would then call potential lenders, and, acting as a middleman, would ask them if they would lend to the particular participant. In that way a contract was established between the lender and the borrower and administered by Euroclear. Morgan Guaranty provided a guarantee that both sides would receive their securities or their cash and that their collateral would be administered correctly.

Post's innovation took off relatively quickly, but without automation. Initially there was neither time nor resources to make computerisation a priority. But in 1978–79 – when Euroclear's systems and data processing capacity was reaching critical mass – Paul Caron,[9] general manager of Morgan's Brussels branch between 1978 and 1982, asked Petersen to step back and create a small product development department to accelerate innovation for Euroclear.

A small team set about harnessing the know-how of Euroclear's staff to devise an automated system for securities lending and borrowing. They analysed the transactions and information in the system to determine what was settling and not settling on the day. They studied the causes of fails and the parties involved. They concluded that even though the manual borrowing and lending system was a big help for the market, there was significantly greater potential to be tapped.

Petersen 'was probably the first one to understand that really what was going to drive the development of the international bond market was the greater or lesser degree of efficiency in the market makers,' Herschel Post said.[10] 'He observed that something less than 50% of all trades settled in the first go-around through the settlement process. And the reason for this was that trades formed a lumpy stream. You have some big trades, some very small. And often your big trades get caught because the other side to that stream is a lot of little trades. What you are generally doing is settling securities in a chain – a sequential stream – and if you got

---

[9] And therefore responsible for Euroclear.
[10] In a conversation with the author, 21 July 2005.

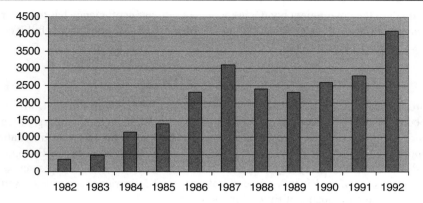

Figure 4.1 Euroclear – securities lending and borrowing (US$ million). *Source:* Euroclear annual reports

blocked at some point – either through lack of cash or lack of securities – that trade was then sent back to the back of the queue; to start again, on another day.'

In 1982, Combes became product manager of the securities lending and borrowing project. Benefiting from his systems development knowledge, the team came up with a system that automatically analysed the backlog of transactions that were about to fail or had failed and the availability of securities with potential lenders. It automatically created borrowings and lending that matched the availability of securities, based on a series of criteria that the participants selected ahead of time. They would tell Euroclear how aggressive or passive they wanted to be in their borrowing and lending.

The system not only arranged automatic borrowing and lending, it also automatically reversed it. When a borrower had securities available, the system would reimburse the loan. As soon as a lender had need of his securities, it would substitute a new lender. It was arranged to ensure nobody received preferential treatment. The system, therefore, managed collateral, credit, lending and borrowing, and potential lending. The impact on Euroclear's business was immediate. After its launch in June 1983, Euroclear was able to cut staff numbers in the borrowing and lending department substantially.

More important, there was a sharp expansion of liquidity in the market. The volume of lending leaped overnight. The average daily value of securities loaned jumped to nearly $600 million in the June to November period of 1983 from around $400 million in the preceding six months. The value of securities loaned in 1983 as a whole averaged $487 million a day against $351 million in 1982. As Figure 4.1 shows, the average daily value of securities loaned by Euroclear exceeded $1 billion in 1984 and continued to grow rapidly until 1987.

Post recalls that prior to Petersen's analysis, the only reason for borrowing securities was to avoid problems in the event of serious delay of perhaps a week, a month or longer in delivering securities that had been sold. 'But if you looked at securities borrowing and lending as a tool for speeding up efficiency of the settlement process, then you began to borrow for intra-day periods and the use of borrowing shot through the roof. You were in a new world for the international bond business which was maximising the number of trades you could do because maximising the number of trades depends upon high levels of settlement efficiency.'

The automation of securities borrowing and lending was to have a profound effect on the market for government bonds. As Ignace Combes observed, the increased liquidity 'was critical to the growth of the government bond market, where settlement efficiency has to be very high. People are not necessarily making a lot of money on those transactions. If you fail it costs you money, so you can't afford to fail.'

4.6 THE BRIDGE

The third innovation under Petersen was the electronic Bridge with Cedel. Until 1980, the Bridge between the two systems was just that: the Pont Adolphe in Luxembourg which linked Cedel's depositories such as Kredietbank SA Luxembourgeois and Banque Internationale à Luxembourg in the old city centre with Euroclear's depository, the Caisse d'Épargne on the other side of the valley. Every day armoured cars or messengers with leather satchels would cross the deep gorge of the River Petrusse to make physical deliveries of securities in settlement of trades between participants of Euroclear and Cedel.

It was a system fraught with risk and extremely costly. Deliveries across the Bridge were plagued by delays – not least because until 1977, Euroclear's decentralised network of depositories meant the securities often had to be brought from far away for delivery in Luxembourg.

After a lot of pressure from the participants of both systems, the two ICSDs finally agreed to open cash and securities accounts with each other and carry out securities transactions between the two systems by book entry transfers. The Bridge was a reciprocal link between the two systems over which, in principle, all securities eligible for deposit with the two systems would be eligible for Bridge delivery.

But it had a defining characteristic that over the years was to be a source of great advantage to Euroclear's customers and an increasingly serious cause of friction with Cedel.

Euroclear's overnight settlement process took place during the night before settlement date while Cedel's day time settlement cycle took place on the settlement date. Because of this difference in their operating timings, Euroclear participants could settle back-to-back transactions with Euroclear or Cedel counterparties on a same day basis, while a Cedel participant would lose a day in their settlement of transactions with a Euroclear participant. This translated into a loss of one day in cash or collateral availability.

The financial disadvantage caused to Cedel and its clients by the Bridge was not a big issue in the early days and was more than offset by the advantages the electronic Bridge offered all parties by eliminating risk, uncertainty and fails. But Cedel acted swiftly to compensate its customers: an act of good public relations in the early years of the Bridge when volumes were low, but which proved extremely costly as settlement volumes exploded in the late 1980s and early 1990s.

Cedel developed a lending and borrowing programme, using a pool of lendable securities supplied by its customers to be able to deliver earlier to Euroclear. It also subsidised customers directly. The costs of 'backvaluing' participants' cash receipts by one day and waiving securities borrowing charges rose from about $1 million a year to $35 million by the end of the 1980s and $65 million by 1992.[11]

The Bridge became a *cause célèbre* in the international bond market. Both the sell-side traders and buy-side banks were united in wanting an efficient system like the Bridge. But they did not want the subsidy cost borne by Cedel and, therefore, by Cedel's owners. The AIBD came out publicly against the way the Bridge was operating in the late 1980s declaring

---

[11] Figure for 1992 quoted in 'Cross-border securities settlements', Bank for International Settlements, March 1995.

it unacceptable. But, despite a generally bad press on the issue, Euroclear was extremely reluctant to negotiate its competitive advantage away.

Ultimately Euroclear agreed to negotiations that resulted in a revised Bridge agreement, which took effect in 1993. But Martine Dinne, who led the negotiations in the early 1990s, was determined to preserve the competitive position of Euroclear and its customers as far as possible. 'Why,' she still asks 'should we give a competitor at the time an edge to become more competitive? We were fighting in our customers' interests.'[12]

The three big innovations initiated by Petersen transformed Euroclear's potential. By the time he left Euroclear in August 1983, the company had forged ahead of its rival Cedel in terms of product design, delivery and technology and was handling some 60% of securities settlement in the international bond market.

4.7 PROSPERING IN DIFFICULT TIMES

The transformation in fortunes was not all down to Euroclear. Despite many ups and downs, the turbulent years between the first oil crisis of 1973–74 and the second of 1979–80 produced, on balance, a positive outcome for the Eurobond market and the ICSDs created to serve it.

After the dark days of 1974, Euroclear, in particular, benefited from periods of recovery in financial markets and in the global economy thanks to the strong position it had built up with the broker-dealer community. The 1970s were prone to boom and bust, with periods in which business conditions changed rapidly. Euroclear's core clients, the traders, made money from volatility and from 1974 onwards there was plenty of that in the international capital market.

The bleak business conditions which preoccupied Herschel Post after his arrival at Euroclear in 1974 improved with remarkable speed. By May 1975 short-term dollar interest rates had halved to 6.5% from 13% the previous August. The falling rates triggered a phenomenal rally in bonds and a surge in new issuance from late 1974, albeit for bonds with shorter maturities than the 10- to 20-year bonds common in the market's first decade. The good times, marked by record levels of new bond issues, rolled until 1977 when adverse pressures again began to accumulate in the global economy.

The underlying economic position of the industrialised world was weak. Currencies remained volatile with the system of floating exchange rates under constant strain in the years following the collapse of Bretton Woods. The dollar, the world's leading trading and investment currency, was subject to wild fluctuations. The resignation of Richard Nixon over Watergate in August 1974 ushered in several years of weak US leadership in which the dollar was frequently subject to speculative selling pressure. This was particularly the case during the presidency of Jimmy Carter, a one-term Democrat, on whose watch a new conflagration burst out in the Middle East in the shape of the Islamic revolution in Iran.

Inflation was a recurrent problem, moving at times into double digits in some industrialised countries and causing havoc for public finances and investment intentions. Financial crises were never far away and affected even the most prestigious of banks, as Crédit Suisse found to its cost in 1977 when an overenthusiastic manager at its Chiasso branch close to the Italian border was found to have diverted more than two billion Swiss Francs of deposits into an illicit and financially unsound empire of companies in Italy.

In continental Europe, France, Germany, the Benelux countries and Denmark tried to shield their exporters from the worst of the currency fluctuations through a joint float of their

---

[12] Conversation with the author, 15 November 2005.

currencies. This so-called 'snake' was sustained by currency intervention and subject to occasional crises, temporary collapses and 'realignments' where one or other of the lesser currencies would be effectively devalued against the D-mark.

But the snake was at the beginning of a long journey that would fundamentally change Europe's financial and economic landscape. In 1978 the EEC's leaders felt sufficiently confident to put the snake on a more permanent footing. The European Monetary System began operating in March 1979 with the aim of boosting the European Communities' growth and employment, primarily by limiting fluctuations among its members' currencies through an 'exchange rate mechanism'. The EMS was launched without UK participation in the ERM and, like the snake, was prone to speculative attack and realignments. But it helped prepare the way for the euro, the European Union's single currency, at the end of the 20th century.

Of more immediate significance for the Euromarkets was the massive shift in financial power to the oil producing countries that followed the Yom Kippur war. In particular, the thinly populated Arab oil producers of the Middle East began to accumulate large dollar surpluses that had to be invested. For the rest of the decade, policy makers and financiers were preoccupied by the petrodollar surpluses which were accumulated by the OPEC nations and then recycled to finance the balance of payments deficits of developing and industrialised countries.

The petrodollar years saw huge fluctuations from feast to famine in the balance of payments positions of the industrialised, developing and oil exporting countries. In 1974, the current account surplus of the oil producers reached a hitherto unimaginable $57 billion only to fall to $29 billion by 1977 and $5 billion the following year as the newly rich countries spent more of their surplus on the products of the industrialised west.

In 1979, the pendulum swung back again after an increase in OPEC prices on 1 January that was followed a few months later by the toppling of the Shah of Iran. As oil prices doubled over the 12 months to the end of 1979, the OPEC surpluses soared once more to some $62 billion in 1979 and a record $115 billion the following year.

Hailed at the time as a cunning solution to a vexatious problem, recycling would come back to haunt economic policy makers and the financial world in the 1980s. To a large degree, the oil surpluses were recycled to deficit countries through the Euromarkets. The Middle East became a Klondike for ambitious young executives, among them Andrew Large, then of the consortium bank Orion, and later, as Sir Andrew Large, chairman of Euroclear between 1998 and 2000. But much of the money that flowed back to borrowers in the industrialised and developing countries was intermediated by the banks as syndicated Eurocredits rather than bonds.

The syndicated loans market quickly shook off the decline in confidence that followed the Herstatt bank collapse. The banks operating in the syndicated Eurocredit market were free of restrictions such as minimum reserve requirements or credit controls and their business boomed accordingly. The volume of newly contracted middle- and long-term Eurocredits increased from around $21 billion in 1973 to $28.5 billion in 1974. After falling to $20.6 billion in 1975, the volume increased every year until 1981 when it reached $146 billion.

The growth was not unproblematical, however. Syndicated Euroloans were generally roll-over credits where the borrower would obtain funds for an extended period. The banking syndicate providing the funds would refinance the transaction through short-term borrowings of six months, effecting the transformation of maturities by means of a floating interest rate at a given margin over one of the main benchmarks, such as the London interbank offered rate (LIBOR) for Eurodollars.

For a while, all went well. There was a widespread perception that sovereign borrowers could not go bust[13] and banks were happy to take the credit risk. There were some good addresses among the early borrowers. The UK, although generally regarded in the 1970s as the 'sick man' of Europe, was unlikely to default. It borrowed $1.2 billion in the spring of 1974 and the Banque de France $1 billion shortly afterwards.

But gradually, the underpinnings of the market weakened. The quality of borrowers declined. Competition among banks increased. Margins shrank, not least because of the aggressive business practices of Japanese banks which were seeking market share after being allowed to operate on the Euromarkets for the first time in 1972.

While the industrialised countries of the OECD reported a surplus of around $9 billion in 1978, largely because of the export successes of Germany, Japan and Switzerland, some developing and newly industrialising countries were taking advantage of Euromarkets awash with liquidity to borrow beyond their means.

Monetary authorities, such as the German Bundesbank, started to complain about 'over-recycling'. An especially worrying trend was the way less creditworthy sovereign borrowers eschewed financial support, with conditions attached, from official bodies such as the International Monetary Fund and World Bank. Instead, they arranged bank loans with no strings attached at rates in 1978 which were just 50 basis points, or half of one percentage point, over LIBOR. The syndicated loans market – and the banks that created it – had clearly forgotten the lessons of 1974.

The market for syndicated loans put the Eurobond market in the shade during the heyday of petrodollar recycling. But apart from a decline in 1978, the volume of new bond issues grew year by year after the 1974 slump, quadrupling in value in 1975 compared with the low base of 1974 and doubling again in 1976.

The changing requirements of the market place were met by a growing diversity of currencies, instruments and issuers. Most important for its future and settlement providers such as Euroclear and Cedel, the Eurobond market was able to play a role in recycling the petrodollars while avoiding the general slippage in quality that afflicted the syndicated loans market.

The EEC produced one innovative response to the problem of petrodollar recycling in 1976 when it raised loans and medium term credits in the Euromarkets worth a total of $1.3 billion. On the strength of a common guarantee system set up by EEC members at the beginning of 1975, the Community raised $300 million and DM500 million in Eurobonds with maturities of six to seven years and $800 million by direct placements with international bank consortia. The proceeds were passed on to Italy and Ireland.

Borrowers from the industrialised OECD countries and supranational entities such as the World Bank and the European Investment Bank dominated Eurobond issuance in the later 1970s. True, developing countries made a relatively strong appearance in 1977 with new Eurobond issues worth nearly $3 billion. But this total was small compared with developing country borrowings of $17.6 billion through medium-term Eurocredits, of which $11.3 billion went to non-oil exporting developing countries.

A time bomb was being primed. The 1979 Islamic revolution in Iran that toppled the Shah triggered a second international oil crisis that brought the twin evils of inflation and recession

---

[13] Immortalised by the observation of Walter Wriston, Citicorp chairman, that people and companies may go bankrupt but 'countries don't go out of business'.

for the global economy in its wake. Christmas 1979 brought the 1970s to an appropriately bleak end when Soviet troops invaded Afghanistan and the western industrial powers, led by the US, were powerless to halt the action.

In the US, however, there was one man who was determined to take inflation by the throat. Paul Volcker, appointed chairman of the Federal Reserve Board in early August 1979, faced a sharply declining dollar and double digit inflation that autumn. The situation was so grave that it required a radical response. Volcker took the unusual step of issuing a statement on a Saturday – 6 October. This shifted the emphasis of the Fed's monetary policy from setting interest rates to targeting money supply, triggering a sharp rise in interest rates and a collapse in the dollar sector of the Eurobond market. US prime rates rose to 15.75% in November 1979 against a background of US inflation running at 13% and oil at $40 a barrel.

Volcker's action triggered a revolution in the bond market. It caused interest rates to swing wildly and their gyrations up or down prompted inverse movements in bond prices. Bonds were transformed from being instruments favoured by the cautious investor into tools for speculation, rapid trading and the creation of vast profits and losses in Wall Street and beyond. Volcker's move turned bond traders into the 'masters of the universe' immortalised in Tom Wolfe's 1980s novel, *Bonfire of the Vanities*. Investment banks such as Salomon Brothers grew rapidly into the ultra-profitable, aggressive, money-making machines, wickedly described in *Liar's Poker* by Michael Lewis.

The shift in Fed policy did not have an immediate impact on the volumes of new Eurobonds and Eurocredits. Indeed, 1981 was a strong year for new Eurobond issuance and a banner year for syndicated Euroloans, where volumes were boosted by heavy borrowing by US corporations to finance a takeover spree. But non-oil developing countries were also making heavy use of syndicated credits to finance current account balance of payments deficits swollen by the second oil shock. In the forefront of the borrowers were Mexico, which took in a hefty $10.5 billion in 1981, Brazil ($7 billion), South Korea and Argentina. The time bomb was about to explode.

Between 1979 and 1982, interest rates more than doubled worldwide, bringing a dramatic increase in the cost of syndicated Eurocredits. At the same time, the dollar exchange rate strengthened, making the dollars needed to service or repay loans more expensive. The recession that hit industrialised countries following the oil crisis and the Fed tightening of monetary policy crippled the markets for the exports of developing countries. These in turn saw the prices of their export commodities fall to their lowest levels since the Great Depression.

The developing and industrialising oil importers were hit by a quadruple whammy. The first countries to feel the strain were special cases. In Poland, a crackdown by the Communist government against the Solidarity trade union and civil rights movement in December 1981 forced Warsaw to seek debt rescheduling. Argentina's April 1982 invasion of the Falkland Islands, a British territory in the South Atlantic, led to economic sanctions and cut Argentina off from further foreign borrowing. Worryingly, these cases proved contagious as banks responded by reducing loans to countries that were neighbours or deemed to be in similar circumstances. Then came the big one: in August 1982, Jesus Silva Herzog, the Mexican finance minister, announced his country would not be able to meet payments due on $80 billion of foreign debt. The international debt crisis had arrived.

One by one the heavy borrowers of the 1970s defaulted on their debts. The market for syndicated Euroloans dried up. The results were devastating in country after country. Latin America – which had grown at nearly twice the US rate between 1960 and 1980 – entered a 'lost decade' of hardship. The banks that had so assiduously recycled the OPEC petrodollars to the oil importing nations of the industrialising and developing world suffered heavy losses.

But it is an ill wind that blows nobody any good. The volatility in the bond markets boosted the fortunes of traders worldwide. The debt crisis sharply reduced the availability of bank finance and gave a huge boost to securitisation. And where securities are traded, there has to be securities settlement. Euroclear – and to a lesser extent Cedel – were about to embark on years of rapid growth.

Part II
Winds of Change

5

New Markets, New Tensions

5.1 CAVIAR AND CHAMPAGNE

When Euroclear marked its 10th anniversary as a user owned company on 1 December 1982, there were abundant signs that the investments of the previous years were paying off.

The statement of chairman Ian Steers that accompanied the profit and loss account for the 1982 business year was a succession of superlatives. Turnover of securities settled through the Euroclear system rose a record 110% to $509 billion in the 12 months to 30 November. The nominal value of securities held in the system reached $92 billion at the end of the business year compared with $58 billion 12 months before, and went on to top $100 billion on 11 February 1983. There was an 8% increase in the number of participants to 1265 while the number of issues accepted in the system increased by more than a fifth to 7826.

Euroclear's upbeat tone 10 years after the sale of shares to its users followed several years of steady growth and profitability. The ECS shareholders received a first dividend of 5% for the year to 30 November 1976, which cost $125 000 of that year's after-tax profit of $194 826. Four years later, the accounts for the year to 30 November 1980 reported the first rebate to users (an unspecified sum comprising 20% of the clearance fees charged during the year) as well as an 8% dividend costing $250 000, which was paid from $719 179 profit after taxation.

The 10 years since 1972 saw a steady enhancement of Euroclear's functions in response to market needs. New currencies were added. After adapting the system for Eurobonds denominated in D-marks, Dutch guilders, French francs and pounds sterling in 1972, Euroclear included Canadian dollar bonds in 1975 and yen Samurai bonds in 1978. Two currency units – the IMF's special drawing right or SDR and the EEC's European Currency Unit or ECU – were made eligible for the settlement of securities operations in 1981. In that year too, Euroclear introduced a new procedure for distributing new issues which allowed primary market transactions to be settled within the system.

Increased earnings allowed Euroclear to announce refunds of fees and other charges to users of $4.8 million for the anniversary year of 1982. That left a somewhat lower after tax profit of $2.32 million, down from $2.48 million the previous year, but still more than enough to pay the $600 000 required for a 1982 dividend that was increased by half to 24% from 16% for 1981.

Steers, who took over from Swiss banker Georges Streichenberg in June 1980, was Euroclear's third chairman. Coming from Wood Gundy, a Canadian brokerage that was an important player in the early Eurobond market, Steers was the first Euroclear chairman with a trader's background. It was no coincidence that during his chairmanship, the company began to shake off some of its reticence.

The company's communications with the outside world were few and far between in its early years. The ECS annual reports – with the exception of that for 1975, which highlighted some new services – contained no more than the bare necessities.

The Euroclear report for the business year to 30 November 1981 struck a different note, however. It was the first to contain a chairman's statement. Signed by Steers, this set a successful year of rising profits and expanding services in the context of in-house technical innovations such as Euclid and geopolitical developments such as that year's sharp rise in the dollar which greatly boosted Euroclear's earnings.

Steers sought to create a 'separate ethos' for Euroclear and set about achieving this goal in a characteristically convivial manner. He launched the Euroclear cocktail party which became a fixture of the joint annual meetings of the IMF and World Bank each autumn. 'It became quite a famous institution,' he recalls. 'I argued that there were hundreds of parties at the World Bank and we needed to show that we were not just a back room institution. It was so that top management would recognise that if they had a need, Euroclear had the team and they would have seen them in Washington. These parties gradually gave us an image which was slightly in competition with Morgan's image.

We always had the Euroclear party on the first Sunday [of the IMF/World Bank meetings] before all the other parties, so it gave people something to talk about. We always provided caviar and champagne, and it became a very popular thing.'

Morgan Guaranty was also persuaded of the merits of giving Euroclear a more distinct identity. Tom Fox, the third Morgan-appointed fast-track general manager to be sent to Euroclear from the US, arrived in Brussels in 1982. Shortly afterwards, Euroclear was disentangled from Morgan's Brussels branch and set up as a separate entity.

The Euroclear Operations Centre was part of a strategy by Fox to boost efficiency and strengthen the system's contact with its users. Euroclear had its own dedicated staff – by now 329 – although they remained Morgan Guaranty employees. The only full-time employee of Euro-clear Clearance System plc (ECSplc) was Jim Chandler, executive secretary since 1981.

Albert Petersen recalls how users visiting Brussels could now see what Euroclear was about. 'They could see the building, the number of employees, employees who were talking 100% Euroclear, who were identifying themselves with the participants and with the market.' It was a step down the road that would lead much later to the termination of the Morgan Guaranty operating contract and the creation of Euroclear Bank.

By 1982, Euroclear could boast that its system accepted internationally traded securities that were straight or convertible, in bearer or registered form, with fixed or floating rates and denominated in 20 different currencies.

Admittedly, the business was still almost entirely concerned with the settlement of Eurobond-type securities. But there had been a significant shift among Euroclear's clientele. The buy to hold private investor – characterised as the Belgian dentist – was of fast diminishing importance. The broker-dealers, which in the 1970s were often fairly small companies with a weak capital base, were not only established among Euroclear's most important clients but were gaining financial muscle.

The relationship between Euroclear and its broker-dealer users was mutually beneficial, not least because of the credit facilities available through Morgan Guaranty. 'The main thing – which was also a very useful facility, especially for the dealers with very small capital – was that we could buy and sell, and we could go over,' Steers recalls. 'So if I didn't have the money, or the bonds weren't there, we were never at risk for credit. There was a credit line available, and we used it all the time. You didn't have to top it up all the time. It was a tremendous oiling of the market. And without it, we traders couldn't have got bigger and bigger, which we did – off the back of Euroclear.'

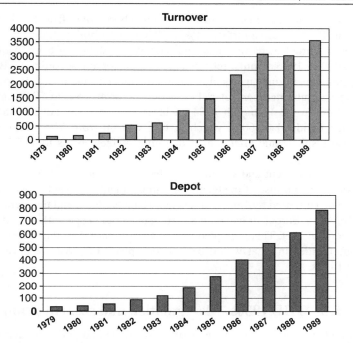

Figure 5.1   Euroclear – growth in the 1980s (US$ billion). *Source:* Euroclear annual reports

Euroclear's technology and business model was designed to attract the brokers and custodian banks and keep them on its books. The chaining, Euclid and the Bridge with Cedel were tailored to their needs while securities lending and borrowing locked both categories of client – the custodians as the lenders of securities and the broker-dealers as the borrowers – into Euroclear's embrace.

As Eurobond issuance increased from the later 1970s, so too did the business of under-writers, broker-dealers and Euroclear itself. Bigger issues meant more trading between sell side operators and insofar as these deals went through the Euroclear system, its volumes and profits grew exponentially.

In the 12 months to 30 November 1983, the nominal value of securities held in the Euroclear system increased by 31% to $120.5 billion: six times the 1978 total of around $20 billion. The nominal value of its 'depot' or depository of securities continued to soar: by 51% to $182 billion in 1984,[1] by a further 50.5% to $274 billion in 1985 and by 46% to $402 billion in 1986.

Securities transactions, which averaged around 5000 a day in 1978, doubled in the period to 1982, before doubling again to around 22 500 a day in 1986. Annual turnover, which in 1978 was less than $100 billion, rose 10-fold to $1029 billion – more than $1 trillion – in 1984 and then more than doubled to $2336 billion ($2.3 trillion) in 1986.

Much of this activity – summarised in Figure 5.1 – was powered by securities lending and borrowing. The average daily value of securities loaned nearly tripled in just two years after

---

[1] Figures for 1984 were flattered somewhat by Euroclear opting for a 13-month accounting period to bring its business year into line with the calendar year from 1 January 1985.

Euroclear introduced automated securities lending and borrowing: from $487 million in 1983 to $1.4 billion in 1985. It rose a further 64% in 1986 to $2.3 billion.

The number of Euroclear participants rose each year – doubling from just under 1000 in 1979 to over 2000 in 1986. Profits, rebates and dividends grew accordingly. By 1985, when Fox ceased being general manager and became a member of the board, Euroclear appeared to be suffering an embarrassment of riches. After-tax profit rose to $9.86 million in 1985 from $7.68 million in the 13-month 1984 business year. It easily covered the $1.5 million cost of the 1985 dividend of 60%, which in turn was up from 52% or $1.3 million paid for 1984. These results came after a near doubling of fee rebates to $15.56 million from $7.87 million.

In response, Euroclear cut and simplified its fees on 1 January 1986 and backdated them from 1 January 1985. Because of the technical improvements initiated under Albert Petersen, the commercial drive started by Bob Wilmers and Herschel Post, and the increased efficiency achieved by Tom Fox, Euroclear had built a system that could cope with all that was thrown at it by the Eurobond market. This prompted its managers to turn their thoughts to other markets and other opportunities in what would be a second phase of proactive development in the middle to late 1980s.

5.2   THE 1980s – deregulation and securitisation

The 1980s provided a very favourable economic, financial and political environment for securities trading and Europe's ICSDs. The securities settlement industry benefited from a surge in securitisation which was bolstered both by bad news – in the form of the international debt crisis – and by good, as governments adopted policies of economic liberalisation and deregulation.

The debt crisis showed how dangerous the syndicated loans business could be for internationally active banks. Reporting at the beginning of 1984, Wilfried Guth, one of two managing board 'spokesmen'[2] of Deutsche Bank, calculated that no fewer than 52 nations were either rescheduling their debts or experiencing difficulties maintaining existing payment schedules.

Guth was speaking from a relatively comfortable position as German banks and their foreign subsidiaries supplied only about 10% of all problem debts and just 6% of Latin American bank borrowings compared with US banks' 40% exposure south of the Rio Grande. But the impact on Deutsche Bank was severe, nonetheless. For two years running, Deutsche Bank's Luxembourg subsidiary – its main Euromarket bank at the time – had to retain record profits to cushion itself against bad debts until loan loss provisions added up to about DM1.5 billion or roughly half the subsidiary's DM3.2 billion exposure to countries involved in rescheduling.

It was little wonder that international bank lending declined. Net 'voluntary' lending by banks to non-oil developing countries fell to just $2 billion in first nine months of 1983. The US switched from being an exporter to an importer of capital in the second and third quarters of the same year. The Bank for International Settlements in Basel reported a drop in international bank lending in the third quarter of 1984 – the first such fall since the Herstatt crisis 10 years before.

By contrast, securities issuance grew. In 1983, the volume of new Eurobond issues exceeded issues of Eurocredits as banks switched from syndicating international loans. Some banks took

---

[2] In effect, one of two joint chief executives.

to borrowing on the international bond market to strengthen their own balance sheets. Deutsche Bank came to the market in August 1984 with a convertible DM Eurobond while Dresdner Bank issued two DM bonds with warrants attached. In that year, National Westminster Finance BV floated the first perpetual floating rate note.

Securitisation was boosted by financial innovation which in turn blossomed in the free-wheeling environment of the Euromarkets. The swap market flourished, enabling issuers to tap whichever currency offered the best conditions. New instruments proliferated and markets for them grew – and sometimes shrank – with impressive speed. In the early 1980s, for example, there was the surge in the issuance of short-term Euromarket paper, which Euroclear was initially reluctant to handle.

The growth of securitisation was underpinned by political change. Right wing governments were elected in the UK in 1979 and in the US in 1980 and a centre-right coalition took power in western Germany in 1982. In particular, the UK under prime minister Margaret Thatcher and the US following the election of president Ronald Reagan cut income taxes and implemented policies to deregulate, which had an immediate effect on financial markets.

In October 1979, Britain's newly elected Conservative government abruptly abolished exchange controls. The move, which ended 40 years of measures first introduced to shore up the British economy in the Second World War, exposed the UK economy overnight to the harsh discipline of competitive market forces.

Coinciding with Britain's transformation into a significant oil producer, the measure pushed up the value of sterling. It turned the UK back into a large international investor and unleashed a pent-up demand for foreign assets by investment institutions. Less obviously, the abolition reinforced the international culture of Britain's financial services industry, ensuring that London would remain one of the main international financial centres.

Thanks to the diversification of portfolios, the City – by now well established as the home of the secondary market for international bonds – gained a head start over other centres in trading international equities. As international financial markets became more global, additional activities converged on London, creating a virtuous circle of deregulation, innovation and expansion. The renewed expansion of London as a financial centre boosted the fortunes of the broker-dealer community and attracted large scale inward investment by US banks and brokerages. These trends were of huge benefit to Euroclear.

Deregulation was also high on the US agenda. According to an OECD report of January 1984, the US enacted no fewer than 22 regulatory changes that affected financial instruments between mid-1978 and October 1983. Using annual summit meetings of the Group of Seven leading industrialised nations as their bully pulpit, the UK and US spread the word on the merits of rolling back the state and liberalising markets.

Market-based economic policies, pioneered in the UK and US, became the new orthodoxy of institutions such as the IMF and the OECD. In Britain, Thatcher's government implemented, as well as advocated, radical policies. It liberalised labour markets and broke the power of the country's trade unions, notably by defeating the powerful miners' union in a protracted and bitter strike in 1984–85.

Thatcher's radicalism applied also to financial markets. In October 1986, 'Big Bang' at the London Stock Exchange abolished the system of fixed commissions on share deals paid by investors. The deregulation, which followed a competition enquiry and a deal in 1983 between the government and the exchange, also lifted restrictions on the foreign ownership of UK stockbrokers. The elimination of the distinction between jobbers, who made markets on their own account, and brokers who acted as agents, opened up the City to the big US investment banks. A wave of investment in new techniques, new technology and expensive acquisitions and hirings followed. The old-established City firms would lose out to the newcomers. But the City was confirmed as Europe's premier financial centre and the largest wholesale financial market in the EEC.

The intertwining of the City and the Eurobond market was made clear when the AIBD was designated an 'international securities self-regulating organisation' as part of the structure of self-regulation created for London financial markets after Big Bang.

The UK authorities had only recently woken up to the huge international market in their midst. Peter Shearlock and Bill Ellington have recounted[3] how Professor Jim Gower, when preparing his review of investor protection in the UK in the early 1980s, left until late any contact with UK Association of New York Stock Exchange Member Firms. This was because he considered them the 'odds and sods': companies that appeared marginal to the main markets of UK equities and government gilt edged stock. Gower was shocked to be told that their main theatre of activity – the Eurobond market – had grown 10-fold in a decade and was much larger than the market for UK government gilt edged securities.

The AIBD's regulatory obligations (and those of its successor organisations ISMA and more recently ICMA) were relatively light. But its newfound status highlighted another development: how the international bond market was gradually being brought out of the regulation-free zone, in which it was created and grew, and more into the financial mainstream.

The distinction between Eurobonds and domestic bonds in the leading economies was becoming blurred. Changes in national tax policies started the trend. In July 1984, President Reagan signed a tax bill removing the 20% withholding tax from bond interest paid to non-residents. Later that year, Germany and France repealed the 25% withholding taxes imposed on domestic bonds held by non-residents.[4]

It was not long before the blurring of international and domestic bonds reached into the back office. In 1989, the World Bank offered a $1.5 billion 'global' 10-year bond with Deutsche Bank Capital Markets of London and Salomon Brothers as lead managers. Not only was the bond listed on stock exchanges in the US, Europe and Asia but clearing and settlement was possible through a choice of national and international agencies comprising Euroclear, Cedel, the Deutscher Kassenverein and either the Federal Reserve Book entry system (FRB) or DTC in the US. The issuer benefited from greater placing power in markets which until then had been separated by different settlement systems.

As a result of the deregulation of national bond markets and the convergence of market rules, the Eurobond market, which Euroclear and Cedel were created to serve, no longer looked particularly special by the end of the 1980s. As investors turned to more liquid domestic bonds, the market for international bonds became more mature and commoditised.

Financial liberalisation proved contagious. France signalled its Gallic 'Petit Bang' in 1984. This eliminated the trading monopoly of its stockbrokers. By an Act of 22 January 1988, they were allowed to sell equity stakes to banks and insurance companies to enable them to bolster their capital and competitiveness and pay for new technology.

---

[3] In their introduction to the *Eurobond Diaries* published by Euroclear Clearance System Sté Coopérative, 1994.

[4] This was a temporary repeal in Germany's case, underlining the deep ambivalence of the Bundesbank, Helmut Kohl's centre-right government and Germany's judicial authorities towards financial liberalisation. Germany announced plans for a 10% withholding tax on interest payments from domestic bonds in October 1987. This was introduced in 1989 but had to be abolished seven months later after huge capital outflows. Following a Constitutional Court ruling, a 30% withholding tax was introduced in 1993 that applied to interest income from bonds above certain individual thresholds. It too triggered a massive capital outflow – swelling the popularity of Luxembourg-based mutual funds.

In May 1985, Germany, a grudging reformer, allowed foreign owned banks to lead-manage D-mark bonds. The authorities were goaded into action by the decision of Deutsche Bank late in 1984 to shift its non-DM Eurobond issuing business to London from Frankfurt.

Only one financial centre appeared to miss out on the excitement. The internationalisation of London and the difficulties experienced by continental banks in the Eurocredit market posed problems for Luxembourg. After a 12-fold growth of banking business volumes between 1972 and 1981, its international business stagnated in the early 1980s.

Luxembourg's lack of a strong domestic capital market made it a less attractive base for the US investment banks that were expanding in London and elsewhere. Bonds issued in Luxembourg francs were popular only with Belgian-based investors. Turnover on the Luxembourg stock exchange was small, even though some 80% of Eurobonds – representing more than 10 000 issues – were listed there.

It is true that by 1985, the Grand Duchy was developing new business areas, notably as an investment centre for private clients – many of whom sought the same advantages as the 1960's Belgian dentist. But over time, this policy would create tensions in Luxembourg's relationships with its much bigger neighbours: France and Germany. Meanwhile events such as the February 1985 decision of the Swiss Volksbank to close its Luxembourg subsidiary in favour of its London operations hinted at relative decline.

When barriers fall, ideas spread. Governments in France, Belgium, Italy and Britain took steps to encourage individual equity investment. The number of equity investors in France more than doubled to 4 million by 1985 from 1.7 million in 1978, after the Loi Monory, named after the country's finance minister, allowed a small amount of equity investment (up to FF5000) to be tax deductible. In Britain, Chancellor of the Exchequer Nigel Lawson's 1986 budget halved stamp tax on share transactions to 0.5% and introduced personal equity plans, allowing individuals to shield modest annual investments in equities from income tax on dividends and capital gains tax. A relaxation of controls in Switzerland enabled some pension funds to invest up to 30% of assets in equities from 1 January 1985.

Privatisation – a British invention – freed industries and services from the dead hand of the state. Of particular importance for financial services in the UK was the privatisation of British Telecom and the approval of a competing service, Mercury. The disappearance of long delays in providing customers with telecommunications lines and equipment and the lifting of bureaucratic restrictions on data transmission strengthened London's position as a financial centre compared with European rivals, such as Frankfurt.

Privatisation brought ownership of securities to new categories of investor around the globe. In the US, the spread of defined contribution pension funds in the wake of the Employment Retirement Securities Act (ERISA) of 1974 built up a pool of capital, some of which was invested abroad. In 1986, purchases and sales of foreign stocks by US investors' reached a record $102 billion. However, this total was dwarfed by record foreign investor activity in the US that year of $277.6 billion.[5]

By the mid-1980s, Europe was in the midst of an equities boom, fuelled in part by falling oil prices and declining bond yields – especially in Germany. The 1980s saw well-known German companies – Porsche, the sports car makers; Nixdorf, the computer manufacturer and Henkel, maker of 'Persil' washing powder – become publicly quoted for the first time. Shortly before Christmas 1985, Deutsche Bank sold a 10% holding in German car and truck maker

---

[5] SEC figures quoted by the US General Accounting Office in its January 1988 report, 'Preliminary observations on the October 1987 crash'.

Daimler Benz, formerly held by the Flick Group, raising DM3.8 billion in just one day. This was a dramatic transaction by the standards of the time. The Deutsche Bank's executive board member responsible for capital markets was Rolf-Ernst Breuer, who in June 1984 took over as chairman of Euroclear from Ian Steers.

The lift-off in stock market activity stimulated cross-border equity investment in Europe, albeit from a low base. The UK brokerage Phillips and Drew[6] estimated that foreign investors were behind 65% of stock exchange transactions in Zurich, Geneva and Basel in 1985. US and UK pension funds put a net DM3.7 billion into German shares in 1984 and DM9.5 billion in the first 10 months of 1985 at a time when German domestic investors were selling.

The resilience of the Euromarkets and the apparent upsurge in cross-border equity investment did not mean all was well with the global economy, however. Financial innovation, securitisation and the internationalisation of markets were pushing senior bankers and regulators into uncharted territory. In 1985, the BIS voiced concern about some of the new instruments and how banks were investing heavily in international capital market issues. In September that year, the Bank of England warned about the risks of banks taking business off balance sheet through the use of new instruments and securitisation.

The persistence of serious payments imbalances and the tendency of floating currencies to 'overshoot' valuation levels consistent with purchasing power in their home economies caused concern among financial officials and regulators.

The value of the dollar was a constant preoccupation for markets and policy makers. The greenback was the superstar of the foreign exchanges for the first half of the 1980s as Paul Volcker at the Fed maintained a tight monetary policy to offset the Reagan administration's lax fiscal policies. There followed a period from September 1985 to February 1987 in which the major industrialised powers tried first to manage an orderly decline in the dollar's value against the other leading currencies and then a stabilisation of its exchange rate.[7]

In the event, the strain showed most dramatically on the world's equity markets. Early in October 1987 the US and Germany disagreed publicly over interest rate policy, prompting fears that efforts to stabilise currencies were breaking down. On 14 October, the US announced an unexpectedly large trade deficit, causing the dollar to fall and bond yields to rise. That day, legislation was filed in Congress to terminate tax benefits in the financing of corporate takeovers.

Arbitrageurs started to sell takeover stocks and share prices began to slide. In the seven days following 14 October, the Dow Jones Industrial Average fell by 31%. This included the Dow's largest one-day fall in history on 19 October 1987, when it tumbled 508 points, or 23%, amid record trading volumes. The broader-based Standard & Poor's 500 index slumped 22% that day. World stock markets fell in line.

A huge shock at the time, 'Black Monday' appeared to leave few lasting scars on the global economy. The international capital markets recovered quickly. In its *Financial Market Trends* of June 1988, the OECD reported that international capital market borrowing jumped to a record $118.2 billion in first three months of 1988 – up $24 billion from $94.3 billion in the first quarter of 1987.

Eurobond issuance slumped in the final quarter of 1987 but recovered by $23.5 billion to $54.1 billion in the first quarter of 1988. In the three months to the end of April 1988 new bond issues were running at an annual rate of $250 billion. Syndicated credits also came back

---

[6] A leading City firm, long since absorbed by UBS,
[7] Book-ended by the Plaza and Louvre Accords. These international agreements were reached between the finance ministers and central bankers of the leading industrial countries and named respectively after the Plaza Hotel in New York and the Louvre in Paris, which in 1987 housed part of the French finance ministry as well as the world famous museum.

into favour, becoming, the OECD said, 'the primary source of long-term finance for corporate borrowers' by early 1988. Such loans were running at an annual rate of $130 billion in the six months to the end of April 1988, which, according to the OECD, was 'by far the largest total ever recorded'.

Remarkably, the 1987 crash provoked few lasting calls for controls or restrictions on capital markets. Instead, the OECD hailed the 'inherent overall resilience of the market'. The following year's BIS annual report reflected the view that financial markets had coped well with the crisis. While admitting that destabilising capital flows could reach 'vast proportions', the central bankers' bank sought a solution in more stable economic policies and better policy coordination.

But the crash did draw the attention of regulators and policy makers to the state of post-trade infrastructure, especially at the level of counterparty clearing houses, or CCPs, in the US, of which there were now several serving derivatives and options markets.

In a May 1990 report assessing the risks attached to clearing and settlement, the US General Accounting Office found that the unprecedented price falls and trading volumes on October 1987 caused trade processing problems at CCPs and exchanges. Some CCPs were unable to determine their clearing members' financial risk and exposure in other markets. Some members of CCPs had insufficient funding to meet their obligations and had to increase their borrowings from banks. Some banks, CCPs and their members did not make necessary payments to each other within normal timeframes.[8] The GAO identified the processing of information about trades, the risk management procedures used by the CCPs, and payments to and from clearing organisations as three broad areas of concern.

According to a later IMF study,[9] the complexity and fragmentation of the clearing systems for US equities, futures and options 'created delay and confusion over payments of margin calls triggered by stock price falls, raising concern over the solvency of securities brokers and the ability of exchange clearing houses to make payments'. Banks reacted swiftly by limiting lending to brokers. The resulting lack of liquidity and worries that investors would be forced to sell more investments to meet margin calls helped push prices lower and increased a flight of funds to quality in the form of cash and high quality bonds.

One problem was the way settlement arrangements differed across different products and markets, with, for example, equities on exchanges settling five days after trading (a so-called T + 5 settlement) compared with same-day settlement for stock index futures. In consequence, investors who were hedged across the different markets could still face large cash demands.[10] This need for cash in turn threatened gridlock in the payments systems and the stock and futures markets.

Disaster was averted in October 1987 after the Federal Reserve made clear it would provide sufficient liquidity for the US financial system and the authorities put pressure on large commercial banks to lend to firms heavily exposed to equities. But rather than easing financial stress, the clearing houses or CCPs in the US appeared to have added to it. In the acute conditions of the 1987 crash, insufficient coordination among the components of the US clearing and settlement infrastructure stoked up systemic risk.

These insights were not immediately apparent. They emerged as a result of a number of reports that were commissioned in the aftermath of the dramatic events of October 1987. In

---

[8] 'GAO report to congressional committees: clearance and settlement reform', April 1990.

[9] 'Global financial stability report', September 2003. Chapter III Appendix: Case Studies.

[10] Explained in 'Systemic risk and the financial system', a background paper by Darryll Hendricks, John Kambhu and Patricia Mosser of May 2006, commissioned by the Federal Reserve Bank of New York.

connection with clearing and settlement, the awareness grew that 'time equals risk'. The need to reduce settlement cycles helped shape corporate and public policies on post-trade issues in Europe, as well as the US, during the following decade.

5.3   DIVERSIFICATION AT EUROCLEAR

Euroclear's reaction to the challenges of the 1980s was to diversify. It had done so before. Euroclear responded to the shock of Cedel's successful launch in the early 1970s and the changes in the Eurobond market that followed the first oil crisis by including new currencies in its settlement system and offering a limited service for internationally traded equities.

It was only from the mid-1980s, however, that new services devised by Euroclear coincided sufficiently with market developments to start a real and lasting change in its core business. Euroclear's still recent technical innovations of chaining with multicurrency capability and its automated securities lending and borrowing programme underpinned this second phase of adaptation and development in which the company began to diversify away from the dollar and greatly expand the types of financial instrument that it settled.

The first significant diversification was into handling short-term Euro-commercial paper (ECP) and Euro certificates of deposit (ECD) by book entry. These instruments were based on long established US models.

ECDs first appeared as dollar denominated investments at the end of the 1960s. Often issued by banks, they were bearer certificates, usually with a minimum face value of $1 million or $5 million although sometimes lower, with a fixed interest rate, aimed at the institutional or high net worth investor. ECP first became established in the early 1980s. Generally with a minimum face value of $500 000, or the equivalent in other currencies, it too was targeted at institutions or high net worth individuals. ECP differed from ECDs by having no coupon and was instead offered at a discount to nominal value. Thanks to the steady liberalisation of European capital markets, ECDs and ECP were increasingly available in non-dollar currencies from the mid-1980s onwards.

Euroclear thought long and hard before diversifying into short-term Euromarket investments. 'Originally, we didn't think that was a business of ours because the securities have a very short maturity, involve a lot of paperwork and risk, and because there are lots of flows and not a lot of custody revenue,' Martine Dinne recalls. 'So we had an intense debate internally, asking whether this was the business for us. But I'm glad we did it, because it is a big business today.'

Overcoming initial reluctance, Euroclear introduced a same-day issuance against payment service for the Euro-commercial paper market in 1985. The following year, the system accepted a significant amount of Euro-commercial paper denominated in non-dollar currencies. It also appointed First Chicago of London, which was established as a clearer of short-term Euromarket paper, as a depository. Looking back on developments in the Euroclear annual report for 1986 from the perspective of April 1987, Rolf E. Breuer, Euroclear's chairman, reported 'an explosive growth' in the handling of short-term paper with Euroclear claiming a market share comparable to that in its other markets.

There would be no such quick win in equities, the other significant area of diversification in 1985–86. Euroclear was no stranger to equities. It had accepted international depositary receipts in its early years. During 1975, the system announced it would handle South African gold mining shares and facilitate arbitrage trading in a limited number of Dutch, French and German equities.

Breuer was keen for Euroclear to build up its settlement of international equities. He had joined the Euroclear board in 1974 and took over from Steers as chairman 10 years later. 'It always came to my mind, in my very early Euroclear days, that as successful as we were in bonds, we had the real thing to offer when it came to international equities. Of course, it's a different animal, it is more cumbersome because of all the corporate actions. But it was my view that the international equity market was on an upward wave and we would see more and more of it in the years to come. The need for one single very efficient clearing and settlement agent for international equities was immanent, because it was extremely expensive to do cross-border equity transactions.'

Euroclear started studying the equity markets seriously in 1984 and began development work in 1985. In April 1986 – at about the same time as Cedel – it introduced an extensive range of services for internationally traded equities, including delivery against payment in home markets and 'comprehensive custody and servicing facilities'. Available initially in Belgium, the Netherlands, Sweden, Switzerland and West Germany, the service was expanded to 10 countries within a year and used for some equity offerings. But despite forging a link with Sicovam, the French CSD, and extending Euroclear's depository network to Sweden, Italy and Austria, the international equity business failed to take off as hoped.

Euroclear's equity settlement business lacked critical mass in a market where agent banks were well established and where national stock exchanges passed data for settlement only to their local CSD. For the cross-border investor, settling through Euroclear or Cedel only made sense if it was cheaper than settling through a local agent. That was only possible if trades took place within the books of the ICSD. This problem would dog Euroclear for years. Settling equities was, Breuer admits, 'one thing where we were never successful enough'.

Government bonds or 'govys' were a more hopeful area. The introduction of Japanese Samurai bonds into the system in the later 1970s was a first step towards integrating domestically traded instruments into international markets. The annual report for 1986 mentioned that the Euroclear system accepted Australian treasury bonds and Danish domestic bonds – as well as Swiss franc private placements and commercial paper. This was the first sign of a fundamental change in Euroclear's activities that really took hold in the 1990s.

In settling government bonds, Euroclear could exploit similarities with its traditional business of settling international bonds. But there were differences too. At that time, Eurobonds, as bearer securities divorced from any tax regime, were relatively easy to settle. In the case of government bonds, a settlement company had to deal with issues such as withholding tax and differing national tax regimes. If the ICSDs wanted to engage in the business, they needed to forge links with national CSDs. This they did. After building its first CSD link to Sicovam of France in 1986, Euroclear established links with the Frankfurt Kassenverein and ultimately with more than 30 CSDs worldwide.

The ICSD's links with local markets varied in sophistication depending on the volume of business they carried and the technical development of the partner. The most actively used, such as Euroclear's link with the Kassenverein, were similar in concept to the Bridge between Euroclear and Cedel.

They enabled international investors to invest in domestic bond markets without penalty and were heavily used. The links greatly increased the scope of book entry settlement that could be 'internalised' by the two ICSDs. Euroclear's broker-dealer clients were able to buy and sell domestic securities against payment without incurring financing costs, contributing to a surge in turnover in the late 1980s and 1990s. Cedel's links, although important, handled fewer transactions, reflecting the Luxembourg's ICSD's smaller business volumes and its greater reliance on buy side clients who used the links to realign positions rather than trade.

The links forged respectively by Euroclear and Cedel with the national CSDs were constantly improved, harnessing the benefits of network economics and the economies of scale. There was, however, another factor that explained their success. The ICSDs were able to provide delivery versus payment across the links because they could offer credit: Euroclear through Morgan and Cedel via its consortium of banks.

'You needed to be a bank because you took exposure,' Martine Dinne explains. 'It was not enough to put two computers together to talk to each other. Because somebody paid first, you needed the capability to absorb risk.' National CSDs did not have this capability, which helps explain why the links they established between themselves were little used.

In 1986, Euroclear underlined its commitment to the exploration of new business opportunities when Peter Culver, who took over as general manager from Tom Fox in 1985, set up what became known as the strategic department.

Started and led by Martine Dinne, it began as 'a sort of study job for a year or two with a very small group of very bright people,' she says. 'I had the job of determining how Euroclear should move forward. This was the beginning of thinking ahead to what new things we should do.' The job became permanent, with added responsibility for product development and product management after Tom Ketchum became general manager in May 1987, following Culver's sudden and untimely death on 11 March that year.

Ketchum arrived in Brussels at short notice and, because of Culver's death, without the usual overlap between Euroclear general managers. His background was in corporate finance and before being sent to Brussels he was responsible for Morgan's business in Asia, outside Japan. He had no prior experience in back office work, apart from that required of all Morgan area managers.

A few months later, financial markets across the world were shaken by the October 1987 equity market crash. The resulting flight to quality saw Euroclear's systems successfully cope with sharply increased settlement volumes as investors moved assets into government bonds, high quality Eurobonds and short-term money market instruments.

In facing these challenges, Ketchum was able to count on an increasingly capable and qualified home grown management team: people like Martine Dinne, Ignace Combes and Luc Bomans. These 'fantastic Belgians', as Rolf-E. Breuer has called them, were products of Morgan training programmes at a time when 'Morgan Guaranty was the prime banking school in the world'.

The training programmes 'created a very strong network of people, who were shaped and formed, both in terms of a better understanding of the banking business and the JP Morgan culture,' recalls Ignace Combes, who was sent to New York for such a programme in the early 1980s. 'Euroclear was always recognised for the quality of its people. It was quite analytical, very methodical in its approach, focusing a lot on teamwork and more of a consensus-driven organisation. But we were very competitive, looking at what was happening in the market, at the opposition and how to improve things. That's a commercial, competitive drive we've always had.'

When Ketchum took over, the effect of diversification was beginning to show up in Euroclear's results. In 1984, two thirds of 8600 different securities in the system were straight Eurobonds. In 1988, straight Eurobonds accounted for only one third of the 27 000 securities in the system. Euroclear was being transformed from a company founded to settle a single dollar-denominated instrument into a supplier of multi-instrument, multi-currency securities settlement services.

From the vantage point of early 1990, the authors of the group's 1989 annual report took the opportunity to look back over 10 years of remarkable growth and change.

The system's membership had risen to 2528 participants in 64 countries from 974 in 1979. Settlement instructions processed through the system reached 7.7 million, 19 times the 400 000 instructions processed in 1979. The value of securities held for participants at the end of 1989 exceeded $782 billion, 27 times the $29 billion held at the end of 1979. More than 35 000 securities were accepted for clearance, settlement and custody in the system.

The value of settled transactions in 1989 was put at $3.4 trillion, 33 times the $102 billion of 1979.[11] Securities borrowing was higher too, with a daily average value in 1989 of $2.3 billion, 23 times the $100 million of 1979. By 1989, the lending and borrowing programme included domestic securities and equities.

The change in the nature of Euroclear's business was almost as impressive. By the end of the 1980s, the system was clearing and settling transactions in a wide range of instruments: Eurobonds, short- and medium-term paper, warrants and convertibles, domestic debt securities of 14 countries, equities of 15 countries, and most recently global bonds. Activity in domestic debt and equity instruments in 1989 was already slightly more than 30% of secondary market turnover in the system. At 45.6%, the share of traditional Eurobonds was less than half of turnover, while other instruments accounted for the remaining 24.3%.

In terms of currencies, the US dollar accounted for just over half of total turnover in 1989 compared with about 80% of all transactions settled at the start of the decade. Euroclear's advantage to participants was that it provided them with a system to match, confirm, clear and settle trades in debt and equity instruments by book entry in any of 27 currencies on a simultaneous delivery versus payments basis. 'In 1980, a participant used the Euroclear system to clear and settle in Eurobonds principally in US dollars. Today the participant can also use the system to settle a purchase of French OATs in Deutsche Marks and settle the immediate onward sale of the same securities in Japanese yen,' the report noted.

The annual report for 1989 was written after a modest rebranding of the company. In 1990 the hyphen that was part of Euroclear's name since its launch in 1968 disappeared.

The simpler name and a revised logo coincided with a more complex age. Markets continued to be turbulent after the October 1987 crash. The equity business, in particular, involved a lot more interaction with other settlement systems via the links with domestic securities markets.

Technology was the great enabler. Euroclear's management team took advantage of rapid advances in communications and data processing technology to improve the efficiency of Euroclear's core settlement processes. They built on a decade of incremental innovations that started with the introduction of delivery versus payment for new issues and ended with a same-day confirmation, matching and reporting service, known as ACE. The added complexity of equities and government bonds forced Euroclear to upgrade its depository, a key source of its revenue. The team set in train a major custody development effort.

Efficient settlement was no longer enough. 'We quickly realised we had to enhance our custody service, offering tax recovery, proxy voting and corporate actions – and that required a large investment,' Martine Dinne recalls. 'The custody platform could be used for all instruments,

---

[11] The value of settled transactions in 1989 was revised upward in later reports to $3.57 trillion. This is the figure used in the illustration of Euroclear turnover in the 1980s on page 65.

however. So we moved, not just across instruments, but also in the nature of services that we were offering.'

Just as the demarcation line between international and domestic securities was becoming blurred, so too was the distinction between Euroclear, national CSDs and agent banks.

5.4   THE BELGIAN COOPERATIVE

Diversification and rapid expansion prompted a need for bigger premises and brought a shake-up in Euroclear's corporate governance. In 1985, the 430 employees in the Euroclear Operations Centre moved to a new and bigger home in central Brussels. The building, at 4 rue de la Régence, was close to the Royal Palace and a stone's throw from the Sablons, two pretty squares renowned for their antique shops and fashionable eateries.

In its publicity material, the company chose to stress the improved efficiency, security and cost effectiveness of the new building's communications and data processing equipment. But the building's inauguration in September 1985, in the presence of international big-wigs and senior Belgian officials, was a prestigious occasion and showed how Euroclear was going up in the world.

This raised the question of the company's relations vis-à-vis Belgium, its host country. The corporate structure devised in 1972 had fulfilled its objective of enabling Euroclear 'to avoid virtually all taxes' outside Switzerland. But was such a policy appropriate now that the focal point of the company's activities was so obviously the Euroclear Operations Centre, which employed a significant number of people in a country that was heavily indebted because of large scale borrowings during the oil crises of the 1970s?

There were other issues too. When Morgan sold shares in Euroclear in 1972, Euro-clear Clearance System could claim that its shareholders were – more or less – its users. By the mid-1980s, however, the controls exercised over the sale of ECS shares meant that while the identity of some shareholders had changed, overall numbers had not. At the end of 1986, there were still around 120 shareholders compared with more than 2000 participants. It was a gap that Cedel, with its claim to be 'from the market, for the market', was only too happy to exploit – even though Cedel had fewer shareholders than ECS.

The board mulled such questions during 1985. It investigated moving Euroclear's headquarters to Zurich and consulted the Swiss federal tax administration about the implications of such a move. In January 1986, Euroclear's lawyers submitted a memorandum suggesting that the group be restructured as a Belgian Cooperative.

The idea was to offer each participant, whether or not an ECS shareholder, a share in the cooperative with the aim of making substantially all the participants members of the Belgian company. The 2000 or so participant shareholders would then hold a minority stake in a new entity Euro-clear Clearance System Société Coopérative. There was no question of the original ECS shareholders ceding control under the new structure. The memo from the lawyers suggested that the participants should have a holding of about 15% leaving Euro-clear Clearance System plc, the holding company for the 120 founding shareholders, with the remaining 85%.

ECSplc would be the owner of Euroclear's growing portfolio of real estate and investments and continue to hold the rights to the Euroclear system which it would license to the cooperative. The cooperative would in turn contract out the running of the system to an operator – which turned out, as before, to be Morgan Guaranty. The cooperative's shareholders delegated their powers to a board of directors, which with 23 members, was deliberately large to reflect a broad cross-section of Euroclear's users. The board took responsibility for the group's strategic direction. As operator, Morgan Guaranty had one seat on the board.

On 25 March 1986, Breuer wrote to ECSplc shareholders to tell them about the cooperative. The board had decided to keep ECSplc as a UK incorporated company with a Swiss domicile and to transfer Euroclear's building and investment portfolio – accumulated from annual profits after dividends and rebates – to a Luxembourg holding company. It proposed to end the distinction between the ECS 'A' and 'B' shares, which would be reclassified as $125 nominal shares of equal rank.

On 18 April 1986, an extraordinary general meeting of ECSplc shareholders at the Savoy Hotel in Zurich approved the creation of the Belgian cooperative and collapsing the two types of ECS share into one. Thereafter, all Euroclear's participants – whether ECS shareholders or not – were invited to subscribe to shares in the cooperative, which was constituted on 21 November 1986.

The lawyers in their memo had pinpointed one disadvantage of the new structure. 'It was recognised that to date the structure of the company has been extremely tax efficient but it was the view of the committee that the time had come where the company should be prepared to bear a normal incidence of taxation both in Belgium and abroad.' That pain was felt immediately. The cooperative paid BF178.7 million ($5.93 million) in income tax for 1987, its first year of operations. This was a big increase on ECSplc's tax bill of $35 900 for 1986.

But there were compensations. The cooperative structure allowed rebates to participants to be treated as a tax deductible expense. It was easier to add new shareholders without the palaver of a capital increase. In particular, a Belgian cooperative structure offered Euroclear a chance to polish up its user-owned credentials.

Although the participants' holdings in Euroclear were 'more symbolic than real', the cooperative was, in Breuer's opinion, 'a very creative idea that worked very nicely'. 'We had meetings of owners, or shareholders, if you will, and rules and regulations, and everybody had a chance – theoretically – to speak up, if they wanted to. It was democracy, and equal rights. I felt it was one of the best ideas that we had.'

The cooperative probably helped ease some of the strains that were building between Euroclear and its users. But it is doubtful whether it did much to resolve underlying tensions between Euroclear's users and Morgan Guaranty. This was a gap that troubled Breuer. 'It became clearer and clearer that over time, we had a problem, or a topic that could develop into a problem: namely, the weight of Morgan Guaranty in the whole set-up, opposed to the users.'

The Euroclear board in its pre-cooperative days was not by nature a troublesome body. Its members went unpaid until 1985, when modest emoluments of $100 000 in total were paid for the first time. Steers remembers it as 'a peculiar board in the sense that a lot of people didn't speak: the Japanese in particular never said anything although they were invited to do so'. But, he adds: 'A lot of my time as chairman, and as board member before, there was a continuous tension.'

The tension focused on one issue: the profits that Morgan was making from operating the system and providing credit to its users. Although Euroclear's annual reports became gradually more informative, they stayed silent about Morgan's profits. The board was kept in the dark too.

'We never knew the figures, and they would never tell us, and we spent a lot of time trying to find out how much they were making out of it. And eventually, it was found out that it was enormous – which we knew or guessed,' recalls Steers.

Steers got an inkling of Euroclear's worth when visiting the chairman and top management of Morgan in New York. 'They took an interest – which alerted people to the fact that Euroclear was a rather valuable piece of Morgan property,' he says. 'On the tariffs of course, there was always discussion about how the rebate should be done. But a lot of the money was made from the depository, where people kept their stock for a charge. . . . Sometimes the Brussels side of Morgan was very cooperative. So, sometimes, was the top man from New York, although at other times, we were viewed with suspicion. We sometimes had to get into Morgan's mind the fact that we owned Euroclear. However, to give Morgan credit, they always sent high-class people to run Euroclear. They were people on their way up.'

'They had golden years, and didn't talk about it,' remembers Breuer. 'Clearing and settlement is not just a utility, it is a business, and it became a very lucrative business. This was not clear in the beginning when Morgan Guaranty started the whole thing, but it was a tremendous business until too many people became aware of what was really happening, and said [to Morgan]: "Hey. You do all the banking business, why's that?" and then tried to share the banking side of the business, which was lucrative.'

Breuer, who was a member of a very small and exclusive tribe of top world bankers, had no difficulties with Morgan on the personal side. 'They were always very gentlemanly. Chairmen of Morgan Guaranty, like Dennis Weatherstone, behaved impeccably.' But like Steers during his chairmanship, Breuer felt Morgan's role as operator of the Euroclear system should not go unchallenged.

Steers says that during his chairmanship he proposed informally that Euroclear should be treated as a genuine cooperative, 'that we should join up with Cedel, that it was a market facility, a utility'. The idea was never taken up by the board. Morgan never openly opposed the idea, according to Steers. But the suggestion 'shattered the Morgan people,' he says. 'Because of the profitability of their lending, it went down like a lead balloon. It was a very unpopular line as far as Morgan was concerned.'

At one point, Breuer raised the question with Morgan of whether the Euroclear board had a choice of operator and toyed with offering the job to Bankers Trust.[12] 'That terrified them,' he remembers, adding with a chuckle: 'at least for a minute.'

Breuer has since said his gambit was 'more an intellectual play' made in the course of negotiating a new operating contract with Morgan. In the end, the Euroclear board decided to stay with Morgan as system operator in return for some changes to the contract. From January 1987, Morgan was compensated for its costs of operating the system less a discount of BF135 million, which would be subject to annual adjustment. The cooperative would keep a cash account with the bank. Termination was subject to three years' notice.

By the late 1980s, ECS was rewarding its shareholders handsomely. In 1987, the annual dividend reached $125 a share, matching the price paid by the company's 125 investors in 1972. But it was also clear that Morgan's role as Euroclear system operator was no longer accepted without question. The rumblings of discontent showed how Euroclear was growing up.

---

[12] This was many years before Deutsche Bank took over Bankers Trust in 1999.

6

After the Crash

The October 1987 crash focused the attention of top policy makers and senior bankers on risks arising from post-trade arrangements for the first time. As a Bank of England report put it later: 'The events of 1987 moved settlement issues out of the back office and into the boardroom.'[1]

During the 1980s, the volume of transactions on the world's securities markets had grown dramatically, reflecting more sophisticated trading strategies, increased computer power and greater volatility of markets.

Many national clearing and settlement systems failed to keep up, leading in some cases to situations reminiscent of the back office crises of the 1960s. Some systems did not settle trades until weeks after they were executed. Following 'Big Bang' in the UK, for example, a huge volume of unsettled equities trades began to build up in back offices during 1987 as a result of larger volumes, the bull market and intense activity stemming from the government's privatisation programme. Although some countries' systems offered delivery versus payment there was no common understanding of what DvP meant.

Numerous studies were initiated, including one by the Group of Thirty, an influential think-tank, which pioneered standards for providers of securities settlement services. It was un-fortunate – although understandable – that the G30, like many of those studying financial infrastructure after the crash, looked at clearing and settlement from a national perspective.

The environment for investors and infrastructure providers in Europe had started to change. Cross-border issues were advancing up the agenda. The European Community committed itself in 1985 to creating an internal market for completion by 1992. Going further – and against the wishes of the UK's Margaret Thatcher – European heads of government at their June 1988 summit in Hanover asked a committee of central bank governors, under the chairmanship of Jacques Delors, the Commission president, to study how to achieve economic and monetary union (EMU) in what by this time was a community of 12 nations.

6.1 STRENGTHENING COOPERATION AND NATIONAL SYSTEMS

Although bodies such as the OECD and the BIS oozed satisfaction about the resilience of the world's financial system a year after the crash, there was no disguising heightened official concern about the state of the global securities industry in its immediate aftermath.

The two-day slump in share prices in the UK on 19 and 20 October prompted the Bank of England to go beyond its established role as a bank supervisor and begin monitoring the capital adequacy of London securities houses. Its main focus was on those firms that were part of banking groups but its surveillance also included the large US investment houses which normally reported only part of their business to the UK stock exchange authorities.

---

[1] 'Task force on securities settlement' – report to the Governor of the Bank of England, June 1993.

The crash concentrated attention on all types of financial risk. The dangers of Herstatt or 'principal' risk were known since 1974. A new preoccupation was 'position risk', otherwise known as market or market price risk, where losses could arise from movements in the prices of securities held for trading purposes. The BIS later disclosed that 'equity price declines of 25% to 35% between trade date and settlement date were not uncommon' during the 1987 stock market crashes.[2] In the UK, concerns were exacerbated by the long two-week stock exchange account period that delayed settlement procedures.

The growing internationalisation of securities trading was another issue. Bank of England officials contacted colleagues in Japan, Hong Kong and in the US Federal Reserve during the fortnight after the crash. One result of these contacts was the realisation that there was no regular forum for international discussions among supervisors of securities markets.

Central bankers from the big industrialised countries met every month at the Bank for International Settlements in Basel and had developed cooperation mechanisms that extended from standard setting to crisis management.

By contrast, cooperation among securities regulators was in the very early stages of development. In 1984, securities regulators from France, the UK, Indonesia and South Korea had joined 11 regulatory agencies from North and South America in a group called IOSCO: The International Organisation of Securities Commissions. IOSCO members agreed in July 1986 to set up a small permanent secretariat in Montreal. The prevailing view among central bankers was that securities regulators did not pay much attention to capital or risk. Instead, their main concerns appeared to be with protecting investors and combating fraud.

In February 1988, Robin Leigh-Pemberton, the governor of the Bank of England urged the creation of a new international group of regulators to monitor and control risks arising from the securities business. His particular concern was that the involvement of banks in the securities sector could pose a general threat to the world financial system. Addressing the Overseas Bankers Club in London, he said central banks must also take an interest in securities regulations dealing with market structure, settlement and margins.

Leigh-Pemberton's mention of settlement was a sign that his officials had been looking at post-trade infrastructure and found it wanting. It was a view shared by many leading figures in the financial world. The G30, made up of eminent financiers and influential former policy makers from around the globe, convened a symposium in London to discuss clearing and settlement practices in the world's main markets. Attended by nearly 100 investors, traders, exchange officials, bankers and regulators, it concluded that the state of clearing and settlement was unacceptable and there should be agreement on a set of practices and standards that could apply in the world's securities markets.

A 12 strong steering committee of top level financiers from eight countries was set up, headed by John Reed, chairman of Citicorp and including Dennis Weatherstone, president of JP Morgan. This mandated an international working committee of senior clearing and settlement experts to produce specific recommendations.

The report was published in March 1989. Pen Kent, the Bank of England's executive director responsible for financial structure, remembers its UK launch at a gathering of top level officials and City grandees in the splendour of the Egyptian Hall of the Mansion House, the official residence of the Lord Mayor of London. Among those present to put their weight behind the report

---

[2] In a 1992 report entitled 'Delivery versus payment in securities settlement systems'. The report recalled that the worldwide collapse of equity prices 'exposed weaknesses' in many settlement arrangements and that 'by far the largest financial risks in securities clearance and settlement occur during the settlement process'.

were Eddie George, the Bank's deputy governor; Gordon Richardson, former Bank governor and G30 chairman; John Reed; and Andrew Hugh Smith, the chairman of the London Stock Exchange. 'I thought: Never has a panoply of such lustre from central banking and finance assembled to talk about the operational side of the plumbing. Something is changing,' Kent says.[3]

The G30 pinpointed a number of deficiencies in the clearing and settlement of securities transactions that added to the risks facing markets and operators. These included different settlement periods for different markets, ranging from same-day settlement to several weeks; a lack of delivery versus payment (DvP), which left one or the other party to a transaction 'unduly exposed'; and the absence of book entry processing for securities settlement in many markets.

The group put forward nine recommendations to make the world's securities markets 'more efficient and potentially the source of less risk'. Risk, it suggested, could be contained 'by shortening the time between trade date and settlement, promoting trade guarantees and assuring the simultaneous exchange of payment and securities'. The promotion of efficiency would come 'by eliminating the movement of physical certificates, encouraging the use of netting systems where appropriate and standardising communications methods and settlement schedules'.

The G30 recommendations were targeted for implementation in 1990 or 1992. Those on trade matching, 'rolling settlement', DvP and securities lending would, if implemented, go a long way to alleviating problems that surfaced in October 1987.

The report also tried to set some standards of good practice. In discussing the proposal for a CSD in each country, the G30 suggested it should be owned by all segments of a nation's securities industry and that it 'should not attempt to maximise its profits'.

The G30 report was hugely influential. Its recommendation on DvP, in particular, was a concrete response to the post-1987 idea that 'time equals risk'. The group's conclusions spurred trade associations, securities firms, their supervisors and central banks into action and spawned a host of reports and recommendations. But while the G30's report was a coherent piece of work, there was one major deficiency as far as the securities settlement industry in Europe was concerned.

The G30 recommendations

(i) Trade matching: all comparisons of trades, between direct market participants such as brokers, broker/dealers and other exchange members should be done by the day after trade date (T + 1) by 1990.

(ii) Indirect market participants, such as institutional investors, should be members of a trade comparison system by 1992.

(iii) Each country should have an effective and fully developed CSD organised and managed to encourage the broadest possible industry participation by 1992.

(iv) Each country should study whether a trade netting system[4] would help reduce risk and promote efficiency. If so, the netting system should be implemented by 1992.

(v) Delivery versus payment (DvP) should be the method for settling all securities transactions with systems in place by 1992.

(vi) Payments associated with the settlement of securities transactions and the servicing of portfolios should be made consistent across all instruments and markets.

---

[3] Conversation with the author, 9 September 2005.
[4] A CCP.

(vii) A 'rolling settlement' system should be adopted by all markets with T + 3 by 1992 and T + 5 by 1990 as an interim target.

(viii) Securities lending and borrowing should be encouraged to help the settlement of securities transactions while regulatory and taxation barriers that inhibited the lending of securities should be removed by 1990.

(ix) By 1992, each country should adopt the standard for securities messages developed by the International Organisation for Standardisation (ISO Standard 7775). They should also adopt the ISIN numbering system for securities issues defined in ISO standard 6166, at least for cross-border transactions.

Although the recommendations set out to deal with problems that had become more acute through the internationalisation of securities markets, they were firmly rooted in national structures. This was particularly the case with the third recommendation that each country should have a CSD. In its introduction to the report, the steering committee said: 'Our recommendations recognise that international compatibility must grow out of established local market customs and practices.' That was easier said than done.

6.2   EUROPEAN CONSIDERATIONS

With its offices in New York and Lord Richardson as its chairman, the G30 might well be suspected of trans-Atlantic bias. But that would be to do it an injustice. The focus of its report on improving and standardising domestic settlement reflected a general view among users of markets that priority should be given to dealing with the inadequacies of national securities processing systems. This was the approach taken in European countries before the 1987 crash.

From the late 1970s – when Euroclear was upgrading its own settlement systems – there were moves in several European countries to modernise their financial infrastructure.

In the Netherlands, a law of 1977 provided for the creation of a CSD, Necigef,[5] which settled virtually all securities listed on the Amsterdam Stock Exchange by book entry. In Italy, the Banca d'Italia and some of Italy's big banks set up Monte Titoli in 1978 as the CSD for listed shares and bonds. Two years later, the Italian central bank took responsibility for managing government securities. Also in 1980, Denmark's VP Securities Services[6] was set up as a private, independent non-profit making CSD to settle all Danish listed securities. According to the Danish national bank, VP became the world's first CSD to dematerialise bonds in 1983.[7] Electronic registration was extended to shares five years later.

Updating a country's financial infrastructure was no trivial task. In France, as will be described later,[8] the process of modernising the infrastructure of the securities markets stretched over two decades from the late 1970s, when a quickening of financial activity exposed back office weaknesses among banks.

In addition to current practice in Europe, there was another reason for the domestic focus of the G30 report. In 1988, the group had agreed a division of labour with the International Federation of Stock Exchanges, known as FIBV[9] by its French initials. The FIBV remit was to

---

[5] Nederlands Centraal Instituut voor Giraal Effectenverkeer BV.
[6] Vaerdipapircentralen.
[7] Payment Systems in Denmark, Danmarks Nationalbank 2005.
[8] See Chapter 9.
[9] Federation Internationale des Bourses de Valeurs. Since renamed the World Federation of Exchanges.

focus on the issues of cross-border securities settlement. It set up a task force of senior figures from depositories and clearing organisations around the world, which first reported in June 1989, shortly after the G30.

The FIBV task force took as its starting point many of the G30's ideas. Building on the recommendation in favour of national CSDs, it concluded that: 'Provided there is a business need and sufficient transaction volume, all national and international central securities depositories (NCSDs and ICSDs) should establish links with each other, based on specific agreements, for as wide a spectrum of services and internationally traded securities as possible.'[10] Much of the FIBV report described models of varying complexity which could be used for the linking of national depositories and clearing houses.

Fine in theory, linking was fraught with difficulties in practice. In particular, the national securities markets in Europe had developed in divergent tax and legal environments. They therefore had different settlement rules, conventions and institutions that made them very difficult and costly to link.

Similar objections applied to a third report, commissioned by the European Commission from Jörg-Ronald Kessler, a former member of the German Kassenverein board and one of the G30's working committee. The Kessler report[11] focused on the need for CSDs in the European Community to cooperate and develop characteristics in common. He suggested they should conclude standardised 'safe custody agreements' to 'enable all variants of cross-border securities transactions to be settled efficiently'.

It was not long before the FIBV began to worry that its recommendations might not suffice to improve cross-border settlement. A delegation visited Lord Richardson in October 1990 to seek his help. Lord Richardson responded cautiously. A follow-up memo noted him as saying that any new initiative would require a great deal of work and he did not want pressure taken off efforts to implement the G30 standards, which, he said, required a 'great heave'.

Hopes for an initiative to promote cross-border clearing and settlement among EEC member states began to fade. In October 1990, the Federation of Stock Exchanges in the European Community had expressed some optimism[12] that bringing domestic settlement systems 'into alignment' in line with the G30 approach would be a starting point for considering improvements to cross-border settlement. By the time the federation was preparing for its general assembly in Athens in May 1991, the tone was far gloomier.[13]

The G30 approach, the European stock exchanges federation concluded, treated settlement 'as a natural monopoly function at the national level' and that 'from the standpoint of the international investor, the present position is far from ideal'. It took the view that there was no chance of a single integrated settlement system for Europe along the lines of that emerging in the US. At the same time, there were numerous disadvantages to relying on networks to and between national CSDs for cross-border trading.

'On the international scale it is impossible to achieve the economies of scale which are obtained, for example, in the securities and derivatives markets of the US. For the international operator, intermediary or investor, risk management is made cumbersome and complex: the benefits of DvP, which within a national market can virtually remove counterparty

---

[10] FIBV Recommendations, June 1989.

[11] 'Study on improvements in the settlement of cross-border securities transactions in the European Economic Community, 1989'.

[12] 'Clearing and settlement in Europe: an outline view', paper prepared for an assembly of the Federation of Stock Exchanges in the European Community in Dublin the following month.

[13] 'Clearing and settlement in Europe. General Assembly, Athens 23rd–24th May,' Federation of Stock Exchanges in the European Community, 1991.

risk, are not available. And the utilisation of stock and money for collateral is made inefficient.'

The European federation highlighted the problem of vested interests exploiting the fragmentation of Europe's post-trade arrangements for their own advantage. Its background paper for the Athens meeting claimed that many proprietary networks in European countries had been created with the intention of obtaining competitive advantage. 'Those who are in the business of providing settlement and custody services make money from the inefficiencies, even though they may in doing so incur unnecessary risk, and it is investors, and particularly institutional investors, who bear the costs of those inefficiencies.'

Without naming them, the federation's report put the spotlight on local agents, usually banks, which had emerged in each European country to handle the settlement of transactions originated on behalf of foreign investors. Throughout the 20th century, they remained the usual channel for settling cross-border equity deals in Europe.

The agent banks had access to the CSD in their country and would offer the foreign investor a full range of services involved in settlement, banking and custody, including tax services and the processing of corporate actions. The expansion of cross-border investment from the 1960s onwards would have been impossible without the expertise of local agents to facilitate communication between foreign banks and national CSDs. But their specialist skills came on terms that were rarely transparent, usually a matter of negotiation between bank and client, and generally beneficial to the profit and loss account of the agent bank in question.

6.3   AMERICAN INFLUENCES

The European federation of stock exchanges was not alone in lamenting the absence of an integrated settlement system for Europe on the lines of that emerging in the US. Two recently established constituencies also took a more continent-wide view of financial infrastructure issues. The US investment banks which invested heavily in London during Big Bang with the aim of using the City as a base for cross-border dealings in Europe wanted lower cross-border settlement costs, because these compared unfavourably with back office costs back home. So too did those big US firms that acted as global custodians.

By the late 1980s, the US post-trade environment was a model for many. Although the reputation of some US clearing systems was dented during the 1987 crash, there was nothing in Europe equivalent to the National Securities Clearing Corporation, a CCP, and The Depository Trust Company, the CSD for equities, which provided financial institutions with efficient, utility-style clearing and settlement services on a continental scale.

The US started creating national clearing and settlement services for securities on a continental scale in the mid-1970s – a few years after The Depository Trust Company (DTC) was set up as a CSD by the New York exchanges.

The DTC initially formed part of a vertical silo with the New York exchanges. This structure was copied in other financial centres such as Boston, Philadelphia and Chicago so that by 1975 there were seven vertical silos in the US. But in that year, Congress – reacting after some delay to the settlement crisis of the 1960s – passed the Securities Acts Amendments to promote a unified market in trading, clearing and settlement.

It put the Securities and Exchange Commission in charge of securing these objectives. The SEC, for its part, decided that competition was highly desirable among brokers and to this end abolished fixed commissions in a manner that was later emulated in the UK's Big Bang. At the same time, the SEC decided that an efficient, robust infrastructure should take precedence in clearing and settlement.

The SEC required CCPs and CSDs to register with it as clearing agencies and proposed regulated free interfaces between regional infrastructures as the way towards a national market system. It actively encouraged and assisted the securities industry to bring about a national system for post-trade services. In the mid 1970s, for example, it published a report highlighting the cost savings that CCP consolidation would bring to the market.

Thus began a period of horizontal consolidation. In 1976–77 the CCPs of the NYSE, American Stock Exchange and NASD merged to form the National Securities Clearing Corp. (NSCC) while the CSDs attached to individual stock exchanges were linked, by opening accounts with each other, to form a national system in which shares were transferred from one owner to another by book entry. Between 1976 and 1997 the CCPs and CSDs of the regional stock exchanges were gradually absorbed by NSCC and DTC respectively to create two single utilities serving the national securities industry.

The system's reach never extended to the markets for financial derivatives which were first developed just as the DTC was being formed.[14] Nor did it settle US government bonds, which were and continue to be the responsibility of the Federal Reserve.

But the US could nonetheless claim to have a continent-wide post-trade infrastructure. In creating it, Congress and the SEC could exploit conditions absent in Europe. There was just one currency, one language and the creation of the DTC showed how variations in state law could be overcome, provided there was sufficient political will. Three other factors combined to help the SEC in its pursuit of a national market system, according to the Securities Industry Association of the US.[15]

- The SEC was a single regulator with strong powers to pursue its goal.
- NSCC and DTC were created when stock exchanges and infrastructure providers were typically not-for-profit entities owned by users, and therefore owned and governed as market utilities. The DTC, for example, did not combine the infrastructure role of the CSD and commercial banking services.
- There was one predominant market centre: New York.

The New York post-trade infrastructure providers benefited from economies of scale that helped them absorb regional CCPs and CSDs, making consolidation at a national level easier. They provided models of service and practice, promoting standardisation across the US. Because so many shares from across the US were listed in New York, the legal changes needed to make NSCC and DTC work were replicated across the nation.

This was not to say the creation of the US system was without controversy. The SEC's regulatory approach had to overcome a legal challenge in the courts. While the banks and brokers supported consolidation, the exchanges resisted merging the CCPs because they provided a significant part of their income. Indeed, the New York exchanges only agreed to the creation of NSCC following a deal which paid them a fee per trade to compensate for the loss of CCP revenues.

By the mid-1980s, however, the national market system had achieved sufficient critical mass for the eventual absorption of the remaining regional infrastructures to be regarded simply as

---

[14] The Chicago Mercantile Exchange invented financial futures in 1972 when it introduced futures contracts on foreign exchange instruments.

[15] Explained in a Background Note on the Organisation in the US Market for Clearing and Settlement: prepared by the Cross-Border Subcommittee of the Securities Industry Association for the European Commission, May 2005.

a matter of time. Throughout the period of consolidation, NSCC and DTC expanded their services and cut costs and fees.

Cross-border settlement in Europe was expensive compared with the national system in the US and this grated with the US banks that settled in London after Big Bang. Unlike many of the old-style City firms which they acquired, the US investment banks that came to London in the 1980s were powerful and aggressive money making institutions.

Thanks to the opportunities for profit generated by financial markets since Paul Volcker's adoption of a quantitative monetary policy in 1979, they were – in contrast to the broker-dealers of the 1960s and 1970s – well capitalised. The London-based US investment banks therefore constituted a powerful lobby for more efficient cross-border securities settlement systems in the business affairs of the ICSDs and in the broader politics of the European post-trade sector in the years that followed.

Ian Steers, who remained a member of the Euroclear board after his stint as chairman, noticed the change. 'There were different forces. The dealers got so big. Salomon hardly existed in 1980. Goldman was nothing in bond market terms. Then suddenly, these huge dealers came on-site. With the Big Bang in the 1980s, you had huge American capital coming in, and playing the game not by the old European standards. The clearing system changed. The bigger users used dramatic things: like saying they were going to move to Cedel. Because they were so big and paying such big bills, there was a big incentive for them to have the costs reduced.'

In pushing for lower fees and easier cross-border settlement in Europe, the US investment banks were joined by a relatively new type of intermediary, the global custodian. Chase Manhattan pioneered the idea of the global custodian in the 1970s to manage the growth of cross-border investment originating in the US. The business model prospered with the diversification of investments by US institutions into Europe.

The global custodian would facilitate settlement for its customers rather than perform settlement functions. Its selling point was to offer its customers a single access point to national CSDs through a network of intermediaries that would usually be local agent banks or ICSDs acting as sub-custodians.

Thanks to their numerous sub-custodians, global custodians such as Chase, State Street or Bank of New York would typically have a greater geographical reach than the two ICSDs. They packaged services with greater added value to a rather different type of customer than the ICSDs or national CSDs, which were in the wholesale market. Global custodians offered safe keeping of securities and asset servicing functions to cross-border investors. Their services would often be tailor-made for customers such as pension funds, insurance companies and mutual funds that sought to access many markets worldwide, and not just in Europe.

They were attractive business partners for the ICSDs. 'We decided from a commercial viewpoint to try to get more business from global custodians so that we could increase the book entry settlement,' Dinne recalls.[16] 'Our objective, in one sentence, was to have more internalisation. To do that, we had to have the broker-dealers, their financing, and the buy side. And if you didn't have the buy side, and they were somewhere else, then you needed to use your links.'

While Euroclear had no qualms about challenging agent banks for settlement business, it took pains not to upset the global custodians. 'We are very careful about competing with

---

[16] Conversation with the author, 24 October 2006.

global custodians, because they are our owners,' says Martine Dinne. 'We are very careful when we introduce a new service to make sure it is commoditised and that our clients – not just custodians, but large clients – feel it is helpful to them, that it is in the industry interest, and that it fulfils an infrastructure role.' A good example, she says, was securities lending and borrowing: 'When we did lending and borrowing we were not competing with street lending: it was complementary.'

Euroclear took account of the business models of the global custodians when deciding its own business future. When Luc Bomans took over as general manager of the Euroclear Operations Centre from John T. Olds in June 1994, he stressed how Euroclear would only develop domestic market links if there was strong demand from its participants to start or improve its service. 'If we can't offer competitive services, it doesn't make a lot of sense to develop them. That's why global custodians cover 40 or 50 markets and we cover 24', he told the company house magazine.[17] This policy continued to apply: at the time of writing, the big global custodians would be present in 80 to 110 markets compared with the 35 markets served by Euroclear.

In truth, the US-owned global custodians, Europe's traditional agent banks and the ICSDs were at once competitors and collaborators. All invested heavily in networks and systems and drew advantages from the inefficiencies of Europe's fragmented settlement infrastructure. But the agent banks had a clear vested interest in the status quo while the ICSDs and the global custodians had complementary business models and could derive advantages from improving Europe's fragmented post-trade infrastructure.

6.4   CENTRAL BANKERS PUSH FOR DvP

It was not just the users who took an ever growing interest in Europe's securities settlement infrastructure. Central bankers, in particular, took a close interest in the G30 report and many became directly involved in efforts to implement its recommendations.

For some central banks, such involvement was a part of their business. The Banque de France, for example, was directly engaged in securities settlement activities. More generally, there was much greater awareness that cross-border financial transactions multiplied risk since the Herstatt bank collapse of 1974. Eleven years after Herstatt, a spectacular mishap in the US settlement environment underlined the huge sums of money at stake when infrastructures failed. During the morning of 21 November 1985, The Bank of New York suffered an IT system failure that meant it was unable to release securities it had sold. It had to arrange crisis borrowings of $30 billion from the Federal Reserve during the day and nearly $24 billion overnight to plug the resulting gap in its balance sheet. The overnight borrowings were 23 times BoNY's equity capital.

In addressing these problems and the lessons of the 1987 crash, the central banks of the main industrial countries had at their command an institution where they could cooperate and coordinate. The Bank for International Settlements, based in Basel where Switzerland borders on France and Germany, was founded in 1930 to administer the reparations imposed on Germany by the victorious allies after the First World War.

Dubbed the central bankers' bank, the BIS had long served as a neutral meeting place for central bankers from the main industrial countries, who would gather in Basel every month.

---

[17] In an interview with the Autumn 1994 edition of *Euroclear Review*.

Its staff developed considerable expertise on cross-border financial issues. The BIS would occasionally grab the headlines as the place where central bankers agreed emergency measures to help a country in distress. That was the case in 1976, when the UK needed financial support from the international community, and at several points in the early stages of the international debt crisis of the 1980s.

The Herstatt bank collapse of 1974 and the international debt crisis turned the attention of central bankers from the Group of Ten[18] financially significant industrialised countries to the state of international banking and payments systems. At the time of the crash, they had just put the finishing touches to a draft accord for minimum capital adequacy standards for internationally active banks. These rules, which were adopted in 1988 and became known as the Basel I accord, were designed to reduce the risks facing the world financial system.

There followed a flurry of activity on the payments front, including two influential reports by G10 experts on netting schemes. The second of these[19] was produced by a group chaired by Alexandre Lamfalussy, the general manager of the BIS and a man who will appear many times as this story unfolds. The Lamfalussy report on netting resulted in six minimum standards for cross-border and multi-currency netting and settlement schemes to ensure that netting systems would be able to complete settlement even if the participant with the highest debit position failed.

In December 1990, the G10 Committee on Payment and Settlement Systems (CPSS) met in Basel to review progress towards implementing the G30 recommendations on securities settlement systems. The committee members decided they needed to know more about delivery versus payment (DvP).

The G30 had called for DvP systems to be in place by 1992 because DvP was seen as the surest way of avoiding 'principal' risk. Analogous to Herstatt risk in foreign exchange dealing, 'principal' risk was the biggest financial risk in the business of securities settlement and arose if a seller of securities delivered, but did not receive payment, or a buyer made a payment but did not receive the promised securities in return.

A CPSS study group on DvP was duly set up and reported in September 1992.[20] It found 'the vast majority' of G10 securities settlement systems claimed to be DvP compliant. But the group's analysis uncovered three main ways of achieving DvP. The difference in methods prompted worries that these might provide different levels of protection, not only against principal risk, but also against credit and liquidity risks in securities settlement.

The three systems of DvP

- Model 1 DvP systems 'that settle transfer instructions for both securities and funds on a trade-by-trade (gross) basis, with final (unconditional) transfer of securities from the seller to the buyer (delivery) occurring at the same time as final transfer of funds from the buyer to the seller (payment)';

---

[18] Confusingly comprising 11 countries: Belgium, Canada, France, Germany, Italy, Japan, the Netherlands, Sweden, Switzerland, UK and US.

[19] 'Report of the Committee on Interbank Netting Schemes of the central banks of the Group of Ten Countries', BIS Basel, November 1990.

[20] 'Delivery versus payment in securities settlement systems', report prepared by the Committee on Payment and Settlement Systems of the central banks of the Group of Ten countries, Bank for International Settlements, Basel, September 1992.

- Model 2 DvP systems 'that settle securities transfer instructions on a gross basis with final transfer of securities from the seller to the buyer (delivery) occurring throughout the processing cycle, but settle funds transfer instructions on a net basis, with the final transfer of funds from the buyer to the seller (payment) occurring at the end of the processing cycle';
- Model 3 DvP systems 'that settle transfer instructions for both securities and funds on a net basis, with final transfers of both securities and funds occurring at the end of the processing cycle'.

The CPSS report was an important piece of analysis. It drew attention to the many types of risk which could affect securities settlement systems. It therefore helped create a climate for increased regulatory involvement with the industry throughout the 1990s, both at the level of the individual settlement providers and at the level of policy making.

The increased vigilance evidently paid off. The securities business had to weather a number of financial crises in the 1990s. Although each differed from the equity market crash of October 1987, they shared one characteristic: new techniques or instruments unleashed unforeseen hazards when in collision with the unexpected.

Bond markets slumped in 1994 after an unexpected rise in US interest rates, which triggered adverse reactions around the globe. Barings, one of the oldest UK investment banks, collapsed in 1995 because of the activities of a rogue trader in Singapore. Emerging markets in Asia and elsewhere suffered meltdown in 1997 and 1998. The 1998 crisis, triggered by Russia defaulting on its debt that summer, led to the collapse of the highly leveraged Long Term Capital Management hedge fund and prompted the Federal Reserve to intervene in support of the financial system. Each crisis produced casualties among the big investment banks and underlined the importance of risk management. None produced problems for the post-trade sector on the scale of 1987.

The CPSS report identified principal risk as the biggest risk facing settlement providers. It had the potential to create systemic problems. In consequence, the report's advice was categorical: it was 'critical' for securities settlement systems 'to create the strongest possible linkage between delivery and payment'.

Other risks included replacement cost risk if a counterparty defaulted before settlement; liquidity risk if a seller did not receive payment when due, because of default or a failed transaction; and credit risks arising from the extension of credits by systems to participants.

In the end, the group found that nearly all systems it studied extended credit to their participants in one form or another, so that the risks inherent in any given system depended more on the controls in place than the model of DvP used.

The report greatly increased the pressure on operators to strengthen their systems and controls and adopt DvP. It gave a spur to the development of real-time settlement solutions. Its three DvP models also became generally accepted categories for policy makers in the future. All three would continue in use, contributing to the fragmentation of the settlement infrastructure in Europe.

That fragmentation was something the CPSS did not address in detail. Its work, like that of the G30, was rooted in national systems. It focused on the settlement of transactions between two direct participants in a single securities settlement system. However, in a coda to the report, the group disclosed that it had 'done some preliminary work' analysing the risks of cross-border transactions and the outlook for DvP between settlement systems.

Like others, the CPSS discovered that cross-border securities deals were full of complexities, resulting in 'inefficiencies and relatively high costs' which appeared to be 'inherent in cross-border settlements'. Although the CPSS report suggested there might be opportunities to improve cross-border linkages, it was a downbeat conclusion for a world in which the verities of more than 40 years had been swept away amid geo-political changes of such magnitude that one academic had proclaimed the 'end of history'.[21]

---

[21] Francis Fukuyama, a US academic, proclaimed 'The End of History', meaning 'the end point of mankind's ideological evolution and the universalisation of Western liberal democracy as the final form of human government', in a 1989 essay and expanded on this thesis in his 1992 book, *The End of History and the Last Man*.

The Coming of the Euro

7.1 A WORLD TRANSFORMED

By the time the G10 central bankers delivered their report on DvP, the Cold War had ended and the European Community had signed a treaty committing member states to economic and monetary union by the end of the century.

These momentous events required a rethink of the post-crash agenda of reform and regulation for the securities settlement industry. Nation-based solutions, as prescribed by the G30 and discussed in the CPSS report on DvP, were fine as far as they went. But they needed updating to be fit for purpose in Europe. As we shall see, the response to this challenge was incomplete.

On 9 November 1989, the East German government removed virtually all restrictions on travel to the West. The fall of the Berlin Wall was a triumph for individual freedoms and the western, democratic way of life. The 25 months that followed saw the toppling of Communist governments in the former Soviet satellites of eastern Europe, the unification of west and east Germany and the collapse of the Soviet Union into Russia and a girdle of independent republics to its south and west.

The end of Communism was a victory for market capitalism and the policies of liberalisation and deregulation that had emerged in the 1980s. The profit motive became the global norm, giving an enormous boost to privatisation and undermining such venerable concepts as mutual ownership. A parallel revolution in information and telecommunications technology made it easier and cheaper to communicate between nations and continents. Investors had more scope to move capital around the world in search of the best returns than at any time since 1914, and could do so much faster. A new era of globalisation had begun.

The reaction of the member states of the European Community to the rolling geo-political revolution of 1989–1991 was to press ahead with ambitious plans for greater integration mooted before the fall of the Berlin Wall. In December 1991, the 12 EC leaders brought several months of difficult negotiation to a close in the southern Dutch town of Maastricht with agreement on the EC's boldest step towards integration since the Treaty of Rome in 1957. Far reaching revisions of the treaty would turn the European Community into the European Union with economic and monetary union (EMU) at its heart.

The coincidence of triumphant capitalism, globalisation, EMU and advances in information and communications technology revolutionised the environment for securities markets and their infrastructure providers. Trading in securities soared in volume and value worldwide. Cross-border activity grew far faster than national economies, aided by the reduction of political barriers and the greater power of computers.

As the 1990s progressed, the interests and concerns of securities markets, settlement providers, regulators and central bankers in Europe increasingly overlapped. They were not identical, however.

Amid soaring trading volumes, regulators and central banks were increasingly preoccupied with the risks that securities settlement could pose for payments systems and financial systems in the broadest sense. The regulators' concerns – together with the rising volume of financial activity – put pressure on infrastructure providers to invest more than before on speeding up and expanding their processing capacity.

What was missing amid the preparations for EMU was any sense that Europe's financial infrastructure should be guided towards continent-wide integration and consolidation along the lines of that in progress in the US since the mid-1970s. The Treaty on European Union, signed in Maastricht in February 1992, did not specifically mention securities settlement systems.[1] Moreover, there was no SEC-type body in place to provide thought leadership as preparations for monetary union got under way.

The 1992 single market programme was heavily focused on goods markets. Financial liberalisation was patchy. Efforts in the early 1990s to liberalise and integrate financial markets were obstructed by the protectionist behaviour of member states in the EU's Council of Ministers.

The Investment Services Directive, an EU law which took effect in 1993, was an unsatisfactory compromise. The negotiations leading to agreement on the ISD were characterised by the determination of member states' governments to defend national financial sectors and interests. Some pan-European rules were agreed, including a provision for regulated markets to offer remote access to investment firms from other EU member states. But the directive was also full of loopholes while its implementation – set for 1996 – was slow.

The priority of EU policy makers in the 1990s was to set the rules for EMU and make sure member states would meet the conditions necessary to join it. In this, the European Commission acted mainly as a cheer-leader for EMU and facilitator of the eventual handover to the single currency from national currencies.

True, the European Central Bank and the European Monetary Institute, its forerunner, became increasingly involved with securities settlement from the moment the EMI began operating on 1 January 1994. But securities settlement was only one part of their agenda and was refracted through the twin prisms of averting risk to the financial sector and ensuring the availability of collateral for the operation of monetary policy.

7.2   BEYOND G30

There was by this time no lack of thought about the issues surrounding cross-border settlement. In June 1993, the Euroclear Operations Centre sought to stimulate debate and action with a special study: 'Cross-border clearance, settlement, and custody: beyond the G30 recommendations',[2] which showed how to adapt the G30's prescriptions to a multi-currency, multi-time zone environment with the aim of maximising cross-border efficiency.

Initiated two years earlier by Rolf-E. Breuer and Dennis Weatherstone, the chairman of JP Morgan, the study was a response to the rapid growth of cross-border securities trading since the 1987 crash. The aggregate volume of cross-border transactions in domestic, foreign and international securities settled by Euroclear and Cedel increased sharply from $4.6 trillion in 1987 to $14.4 trillion in 1992.

The 'Beyond G30' report and its recommendations marked a rare incursion into the world of public affairs for Euroclear. But it was no coincidence that it was published during the term as general manager of John T. Olds, a Morgan high-flyer with an interest in strategy and a great knowledge of capital markets. The report also reflected Euroclear's frustration at the slow implementation of the G30 recommendations. It would be 1 June 1995, for example, before

---

[1] Nor does its most recent version, which incorporates amendments agreed in the Treaties of Amsterdam and Nice and which has been in force since 1 February 2003.

[2] Published by Morgan Guaranty Trust Co., Brussels Office, as operator of the Euroclear System.

the Eurobond market adopted T + 3 while in some national markets – notably the UK equities market – three-day settlement would be still further delayed.

The report focused on the 'friction costs of cross-border clearance, settlement and custody'. It identified as a special problem 'pipeline liquidity risk' or the likelihood that cross-border settlement was made more expensive and complex by a lack of coordination in processing cycles among CSDs and payments systems. These costs, the study estimated, could amount to $25 million a year in interest expenses or foregone interest income for an active trader with an average net daily volume of $500 million.

Like the original G30 report, the EOC publication concluded with nine recommendations, but aimed this time at reducing the extra frictional costs of cross-border investment. Three were addressed to CSDs with the goal of harmonising processing cycles, matching rules and their levels of custody services. Reflecting work under way in the strategic unit of Euroclear, headed by Martine Dinne, the CSDs were urged to increase the number of processing cycles and 'if cost-justified, move to provide real-time processing of transactions'. The report suggested national payment systems should synchronise their processing cycles with CSDs and also, 'if cost justified, provide real-time processing with payment finality on a continuous basis throughout each value day'.

The remaining five recommendations urged changes on national governments and markets. Each country was urged to modernise its securities ownership and transfer laws to secure investors' property rights over securities held by service providers such as CSDs, ICSDs, brokers, local custodians and global custodians; to modernise securities pledging laws in order to facilitate collateral activities, and to streamline procedures for reclaiming withholding taxes.

'Beyond G30' also pondered five settlement models for international securities markets. Some ideas were revolutionary. 'Worldclear' would be a single global CSD for all wholesale participants while 'Global Hub' was a slightly less ambitious idea in which national CSDs and ICSDs would maintain cash and securities accounts at a single, global CSD. The third option – for a single, global 'Central Processing Unit' – would have the CPU perform the computer processing functions for each CSD and ICSD, leaving the CSDs and ICSDs to provide all safekeeping, clearance and settlement functions. The fourth option was a system of bilateral links between CSDs and ICSDs that would later be known as the Spaghetti model. The fifth was the status quo by which cross-border settlement was effected through a multiplicity of CSDs, ICSDs, global custodians and agent banks. This multiple-access model, as Euroclear called it, would be improved by implementing the nine 'Beyond G30' recommendations.

In the end, the report concluded that building on existing structures was the only way forward: the alternatives to an improved multiple-access model were too costly. Euroclear's view, reaffirmed in its 1993 annual report, was that the 'Beyond G30' recommendations were 'technologically practicable'. Indeed, the company complained that the potential of technology in the securities settlement industry far outstripped 'the ability, and sometimes the willingness, to use it'. Citing 'incompatible standards' and 'vested interests', it noted that only four of the nine recommendations hinged on technological improvements. 'The rest of the recommendations require initiatives by the legal community and really involve catching up with technological realities'.

The legal issues were taken up in more detail by Davis Polk & Wardwell, Euroclear's lawyers. In 'Modernising securities ownership, transfer and pledging laws',[3] Randall D. Guynn, a London-based partner of Davis Polk, called for international reform to bring securities laws

---

[3] Published by the Capital Markets Forum of the International Bar Association, 1996.

up to date. Guynn's widely publicised study noted that most legal systems were still geared to holding securities in certificate form and unsuited to paperless securities that changed ownership by book entry and were held by intermediaries.

By the time Guynn's discussion document was published, Euroclear and Cedel were settling nearly $30 trillion worth of cross-border transactions a year. Guynn warned that 'the exploding growth in the value and velocity of global financial transactions' no longer permitted a purely local legal focus. Indeed, the rising costs and risks of legal uncertainty in international securities trading meant 'the old wineskins of existing laws need to be replaced by modern bottles that will not burst'.

Guynn drew inspiration from the securities laws of Belgium and Luxembourg to call for international harmonisation of securities ownership and transfer laws. Enunciating four principles, he urged:

- a rewriting of property rights so that an investor's interest in securities held by intermediaries would be a new type of interest in a pro-rata pool of securities rather than a traceable property right in individual securities;
- the pool of securities would in turn be protected against the claims of the intermediary's general creditors;
- to avoid a conflict of laws, the governing law of any securities transaction should be determined by agreement among the parties involved. In the absence of such agreement, the governing law should be the law of the country in which the account with the intermediary is held, or failing that, the intermediary's home jurisdiction; and
- a simplification of the laws on pledging interests in securities to facilitate their use as collateral.

Both Guynn's paper and the earlier 'Beyond G30' report highlighted and clarified complex problems that imposed barriers to cross-border securities settlement. By stressing the need to overcome divergent laws and standards, both documents pointed out an important means of moving towards a single settlement market for Europe. The two studies brought into the public domain ideas that would resurface in later years, notably in the Hague Convention, the December 2002 draft multilateral treaty for determining the ownership of securities held in electronic form. But neither paper triggered speedy official action.

7.3   THE EMI AND LAMFALUSSY

The absence of any direct reference to securities settlement in the Maastricht Treaty showed how post-trade matters were slow to attract the attention of EU policy makers. They only began to surface in the public domain some months later, after publication of the CPSS report on DvP in September 1992.

Payment systems, on the other hand, were covered in the treaty. Article 105 specified the promotion and smooth operation of payment systems as one of the 'basic tasks' to be carried out by the planned European System of Central Banks. The statutes of the ESCB, which were annexed to the treaty as a protocol,[4] empowered the future European Central Bank to 'make regulations, to ensure efficient and sound clearing and payment systems within the Community and with other countries'.

---

[4] In article 22 of the Statute of the ECSB and ECB. By virtue of being attached to the Treaty in a protocol, the statutes have the same weight as Treaty articles in EU law.

Payments would be one way in which securities settlement were brought into the orbit of the ECB. The conduct of monetary policy, once EMU was up and running, was another. To carry out the ESCB's monetary policy, the ECB and national central banks were empowered to engage in open market and credit operations. These could include repurchase agreements, or repos, and lending 'based on adequate collateral'.[5] The bank's statutes authorised the ECB and the national central banks (which together constituted the ESCB), to 'open accounts for credit institutions, public entities and other market participants and accept assets, including book entry securities, as collateral'.[6]

However, the extent to which securities settlement would become an issue for the European monetary authorities only became clear after the European Monetary Institute – the body created by the Maastricht Treaty to help prepare the EU for EMU – began operating from headquarters in Frankfurt in 1994 under a dynamic president: Alexandre Lamfalussy.

The EMI was charged with preparing the ground for EMU in what was officially called the 'second' or transitional stage of the project. This would run from 1 January 1994 until the participating currencies were locked together and monetary policy was handled by the planned European Central Bank. According to the treaty, this third stage could start as early as 1997. It had to begin by 1 January 1999 at the latest and this soon became the generally accepted starting date for the single currency. The treaty required the EMI to 'specify the regulatory, organisational and logistical framework necessary for the ESCB to perform its tasks' in stage three of EMU no later than the end of 1996.

Although he was initially reluctant to take on the job, Lamfalussy proved an inspired choice to head the EMI. A sprightly-looking 64 year old at the time of his appointment, Lamfalussy was a Belgian citizen of Hungarian extraction who had fled to the west at the end of the 1940s. He had studied economics at the University of Louvain, Belgium's premier university for economic studies, until 1953. After a spell as a research student at Nuffield College, Oxford, he returned to Belgium where he combined the careers of an academic and banker. Wearing his banking hat, Lamfalussy was in Warburg's London office on that July day in 1963 to sign the subscription agreement for the Autostrade issue on behalf of Banque de Bruxelles, which co-managed the issue. He rose to become chairman of the bank's executive board. In 1976, shortly after Banque de Bruxelles merged with another Belgian bank, Lamfalussy moved to the Bank for International Settlements in Basel as economic adviser and head of the monetary and economic department. He became BIS general manager in 1985.

Lamfalussy's CV, therefore, straddled the worlds of economics and finance, making him a rarity among EU officials. His accent-free English was always precise, testifying to a rigorous academic hinterland. Famously discreet, he was equally a member of the international central bankers' club. Colleagues applauded his ability to accommodate and bring together diverse positions in a debate. But that did not prevent him from putting forward trenchant views. He saw to it that the annual reports of the BIS were provocative as well as informative. He had a good nose for identifying problems and proposing solutions well ahead of the herd, as his work on netting at the BIS testified.

His professional life at the BIS had turned him into a firm believer in international monetary cooperation. His background – as a refugee from Communism who had prospered in one of the most federally inclined of the EU states – made him a persistent advocate of greater European integration.

---

[5] In article 18 of the Statute.
[6] In article 17 of the Statute.

Lamfalussy was one of four outside experts appointed to the Delors committee of central bank governors, which in 1988 and 1989 drew up the blueprint for the EMU that would be the basis of the Maastricht Treaty. He could claim to be the father of the EMI, having proposed to the Delors committee that the EC central banks should set up a joint subsidiary for the transition phase of EMU that would centralise some of their operations and perform some of their functions. The EMI never acquired the extensive powers that Lamfalussy suggested. But he turned it into a powerful institution, nonetheless.

The EMI acted first on payments, where its priority was the promotion of a real time gross settlement system. RTGS systems were developed first by the US Federal Reserve System to eliminate intraday balances between banks and so sharply reduce systemic risk. In May 1995, the EMI Council announced plans for TARGET,[7] an RTGS system for the eurozone, to begin operating at the start of stage three of EMU. TARGET's mission was to link national RTGS systems, then in development, to promote more efficient cross-border payments and help the execution of monetary policy in the single currency area.

In November 1995, the EMI published its broad strategy for the changeover to the single currency. The first sign of the EMI linking its interest in payments to securities settlement systems came in April 1996 with the publication of a 'blue book' entitled 'Payment systems in the European Union'. The first blue book was produced by the Committee of Governors of the Central Banks of the Member States of the EC in September 1992 to provide a descriptive guide to payments systems in the EU member states. The second edition from the EMI boasted 'more detailed descriptions of the domestic and European securities settlement systems, reflecting the growing links which exist between payment and securities, such as the development of delivery versus payment mechanisms and the increasing use of collateralisation in payment systems.'

Meeting its treaty obligation, the EMI detailed the operational framework of the single monetary policy in stage three in January 1997.[8] The document made clear that the key instrument of monetary policy would be the repo. The repo was a sale and repurchase agreement, where one party would sell a security to another and simultaneously agree to buy it back at a later date. Through what were known as 'reverse transactions' the central bank would buy or sell assets under repurchase agreements or conduct credit operations against eligible assets as collateral. The bank's repo operations would be used to set the ECB's short-term interest rate for the single currency area and be the means for harnessing collateral to produce liquidity.

A repo-based monetary policy required effective settlement of securities transactions. The EMI therefore defined the minimum conditions required of settlement systems for the operation of monetary policy and to support the integration of the money market in the single currency area. It also detailed, in a single list, the assets to be used for monetary operations and collateralising intraday credits.

The following month, in February 1997, the EMI reported on the securities settlement systems in stage three in greater detail.[9] Like others, it commented on the fragmented nature of the business in Europe. Although all systems in the EU could settle securities by some form of DvP, it noted that 'major differences' existed as regards 'participants in the systems, settlement procedures (and, in particular, the frequency of settlement processing), risk management measures (and, in particular, the approach taken to delivery versus payment mechanisms),

---

[7] Trans-European Automated Real-Time Gross settlement Express Transfer system.
[8] 'The single monetary policy in stage three – specification of the operational framework', EMI, 1997.
[9] 'EU securities settlement systems. Issues related to stage three of EMU', EMI, February 1997.

legal aspects, and the involvement of the central bank'. It added: 'Links between domestic and international systems are even more heterogeneous.'

The EMI would have liked better links between domestic securities settlement systems to help the future European Central Bank run its monetary policy. But it also recognised that a network of linkages between CSDs might require considerable time to develop. Its response to this dilemma was to draw up alternative plans to ensure that eligible collateral would be available across borders to operate monetary policy in the single currency area. It devised the Correspondent Central Banking Model (CCBM) to enable counterparties of participating central banks to borrow from their local central bank using collateral based in another country. The central bank in the other country would be the correspondent and act as the custodian of the central bank lending the funds.

Originally considered a temporary solution, the CCBM became the most important instrument for channelling cross-border collateral to the ECB in first five years of EMU. Although a technical success, critics have charged that the CCBM model has maintained the fragmentation of the European settlement industry. A March 2001 report from the Brussels-based Centre for European Policy Studies[10] found that CCBM 'obliges banks to go through the local CSD, via its central bank, to mobilise collateral. Remote access to other countries' CSDs for monetary policy operations is at present not permitted, thereby restraining competition between CSDs.'

7.4   THE GROWTH OF REPO ACTIVITY

The EMI's choice of a repo-based monetary policy for the ECB took advantage of a financial instrument that was a relatively recent innovation in Europe.

The repo had a long history in the US, where investment banks, lacking a deposit base, developed the market to finance their bond portfolios. The first repo activity in Europe emerged in the late 1980s[11] as broker-dealers sought a cheaper means of covering their short positions and financing their long inventory than conventional bank loans or the securities lending and borrowing services offered by Euroclear and Cedel. The 1987 stock market crash – when brokers found their unsecured bank loans cut – strengthened the case for borrowing against collateral.

Just as DvP eliminated principal risk, the repo protected against counterparty risk, caused when a party to a contract was either unable or unwilling to complete the deal. This had become an increasingly important issue with the changing nature of financial markets. Markets grew so fast and so international as a result of computer developments and deregulation that it was unrealistic to expect operators to know all their counterparties. The UK's Big Bang, for example, meant the end of the convivial City lunch. In the more competitive world of the late 1980s and early 1990s operators preferred exposure that was collateralised, because in this way they were only exposed to market risk. In these circumstances, supervisors and regulators saw the repo market as a welcome development for the stability of the system.

The repo had other attractions. Repos boosted liquidity. In most markets, professional investors could make money on their holdings, without being exposed to fiscal constraints,

---

[10] 'EU securities market regulation: adapting to the needs of a single capital market', report of a CEPS Task Force, March 2001.
[11] According to *The European Repo Market: Its Past Present and Future*, published by Clearstream, 2005.

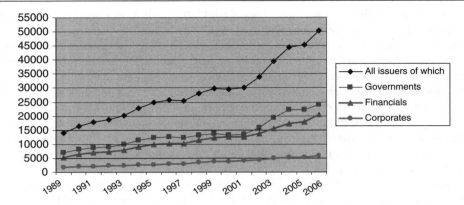

Figure 7.1   The market in domestic debt securities. (amount outstanding in US$ billion). *Source*: BIS adapted from domestic debt securities statistic. www.bis.org

because repo transactions did not represent a divestiture of holdings and so did not have the same tax consequences as the sale of a security.

The repo market gained wider acceptance after November 1992 when ISMA in conjunction with the Public Securities Association (PSA) of the US introduced a Global Master Repurchase Agreement (GMRA) to standardise repo documentation across fragmented financial markets. The standardised documentation virtually eliminated the need for an extensive legal process each time an investor traded with a new counterparty.

The repo market was able to build on a fast growing pool of collateral. According to the Bank for International Settlements the total of international bonds and notes outstanding grew from a meagre $100 million in 1966, when the BIS statistics began, to $1266 billion at the end of 1989, just after the fall of the Berlin Wall. The stock grew to $1746 billion two years later, and more than $5000 billion, or $5 trillion, as the 1990s drew to a close. As Figure 7.1 shows, the growth in the stock of domestic debt securities tracked by the BIS was slower but more substantial: up from $14 135 billion in 1989 to $17 861 billion in 1991 and $29 600 billion by the end of 1999.

The market grew rapidly, helped by changes in the way some countries structured their debt. France, for example, issued more standardised products, and adopted a more systematic issuance as part of its financial market reform programme.

As a settlement-intensive business that hinged on the efficient use of collateral, repo generated business opportunities for the two ICSDs. In September 1992, Cedel took the business in Europe to a new stage when it arranged a triparty repo with SBC Warburg and the European Bank for Reconstruction and Development. This $50 million financing deal, in which the settlement company provided the collateral and undertook to administer it, was the first triparty trade outside the US. Euroclear followed suit a few months later.

At Euroclear, the triparty repo business played to its traditionally strong position with the broker-dealer community and helped attract the custodian banks on to Euroclear's books. As with securities lending and borrowing a decade earlier, Euroclear was able to leverage the strengths of its operating system. The broker-dealers would use triparty repo to borrow against securities and finance their positions. The custodians would be the providers of the cash. As with securities lending and borrowing, Euroclear took no principal risk. Instead it stood in the middle of the deal and, for a fee, made sure that the securities offered as collateral corresponded with requirements.

'By having a very efficient collateral management service, our clients were able to leverage their balance sheets,' says Ignace Combes. 'If a broker-dealer buys a security, he needs to finance that position. And typically, they don't have a lot of capital. What they started to do more and more was to repo out the securities that they bought and then use the cash to purchase that security. With a very efficient system like same-day settlement and tri-party collateral management and so on, all of that helped to really boom the market.' In 1994 multi-currency repo transactions accounted for about one third of Euroclear's record turnover of $21.9 trillion.[12]

Euroclear's operating system handled the complexities, as Combes explains:[13] 'In a tri-party service, a neutral party holds the securities and also does a valuation. If the exposure between the two parties grows, we call on more securities; if it is reduced, we give back collateral. If the company that has repo'd the security wants to sell it to someone else, we substitute another automatically because we know all the settlement transactions in the system. We would know the company trying to sell that particular security. We would know as well if they didn't have a position in their books; that it was locked up in another tri-party account. We have all that information, so what do we do? We say to the company, you have other securities: let's swap – all instantly and automatically. The company does not have to intervene. By providing all that support and automation, we prevent that company failing on a transaction and help further to grow the market.'

Triparty repo was a flexible product. It allowed the seller and buyer to define terms of deals in a broad range of maturities and currencies, while providing for easy substitution of different securities. It made repos more secure and less time consuming for the investor.

Boosted by globalisation and technological advance, repo activity fuelled rapid growth in cross-border securities trading. No one knows exactly by how much, although in a 1995 study[14] of cross-border settlement, the BIS noted that cross-border trading in bonds and equities 'far exceeded growth of GDP over the last two decades and especially during the last few years'.

Drawing on national balance of payments statistics for the Group of Seven leading industrialised countries, the central bankers' bank estimated that by 1993, cross-border trading (defined as gross purchases and sales of securities between residents and non-residents) amounted to 134.9% of GDP for the US: up from 92.1% in 1990, 36.4% in 1985 and just 2.8% in 1970. For Germany the comparable figures were 169.6% in 1993, compared with 61.1% in 1990, 33.9% in 1985 and 3.3% in 1970. Britain – according to the BIS, the most important centre for cross-border trading – stopped gathering the relevant statistics in 1991. In that year, however, cross-border trading of bonds and equities amounted to a phenomenal 1016% of UK GDP, compared with 689% in 1990 and 366% in 1985.

The cross-border trade in securities was booming. The problem in Europe was that the infrastructures were too fragmented to exploit fully the economics of networks and scale. The priority given to delivering the euro did not extend to official support for reshaping securities settlement.

---

[12] According to the 1994 report of ECS Société Coopérative.

[13] In conversation with the author, 28 September 2005.

[14] 'Cross-Border Securities Settlements,' report prepared by the Committee on Payment and Settlement Systems of the central banks of the Group of Ten Countries. Bank for International Settlements, Basel, March 1995.

7.5   THE ECB AND SECURITIES SETTLEMENT

The securities settlement industry was influenced by two streams of decision making in the years up to the third stage of EMU. Like every other business in the EU, it had to take account of decisions taken at the highest level by EU leaders when they held their regular summit meetings in the forum known as the European Council and also by the 'Ecofin' council of economics and finance ministers.

Thus in December 1995, EU leaders at a summit in Madrid agreed the new currency would be called the euro, adopted the EMI's strategy for conversion to it, and confirmed 1 January 1999 as the starting date for stage three, when the currencies of the participating member states would be irrevocably locked. The decision by the leaders on which countries would join EMU would be made 'as soon as possible in 1998'. Similarly the ECB and the European System of Central Banks would 'have to be created early enough' to be able to start functioning at the beginning of 1999.[15]

National banknotes and coins would continue to be used for three years from 1999, with euro notes and coins starting to circulate from 1 January 2002. The substitution of the euro for national currencies would not alter the continuity of contracts and would not change the nominal interest rate paid on fixed interest loans and securities. From 1 January 1999, the public debt of the participating states would be issued in euro. From 1 July 2002 at the latest, debt denominated in the former national currencies would be redeemed in euro only.

In December 1996, at a meeting in Dublin, EU leaders reached agreement on the main elements of the stability and growth pact, setting rules to underpin fiscal discipline in the participating states. In September 1997, the EU's finance ministers agreed that the bilateral conversion rates between the participating currencies and the euro should be fixed in advance of stage three, when the qualifying countries were chosen in May 1998.

In October 1997, Gordon Brown, British chancellor of the exchequer in the recently elected Labour government of Tony Blair, announced that the UK was unlikely to join EMU before the next general election, which would not have to be held until May 2002 at the latest. He also made UK entry dependent on the economy meeting five tests.

It was at an EU summit in Brussels in May 1998 that Blair, as holder of the EU's six-month presidency, announced that 11 members would launch EMU at the start of 1999. Belgium, Germany, Spain, France, Ireland, Italy, Luxembourg, the Netherlands, Austria, Portugal and Finland would embark on an unprecedented experiment of pooling a huge part of their sovereignty in the absence of significant progress towards political union.

That summit on 2–3 May also witnessed a tremendous row between France and the other member states over who should be president of the ECB. The row ended with an unwritten compromise that the job should go to Wim Duisenberg, the former Dutch central bank president who had taken over from Lamfalussy at the EMI on 1 July 1997, provided Duisenberg would make way for the Frenchman Jean-Claude Trichet before the end of his eight-year term. The origins and content of the deal were unedifying reminders of how national priorities and jealousies still dominated politics in EU member states. Duisenberg and the other members of the ECB executive board were appointed towards the end of May by the leaders of the 11 euro area countries. They took office on 1 June 1998: the day the newly created ECB replaced the EMI.

---

[15] The conclusions of the Madrid European Council are, with other significant documents concerning the introduction of the euro, usefully included in 'Economic and Monetary Union: compilation of community legislation published by the European Commission', June 1999.

The other preparations were practical and these took place at levels far removed from the political stratosphere. Securities experts from governments, central banks, the banking communities of the member states and the infrastructure providers put in thousands of man hours, drafting reports and opinions for countless meetings so the switch to the euro as a 'virtual currency' on 1 January 1999 could go without a hitch.

Basic issues – such as whether and how to deal with the redenomination of securities in euro – involved a host of technical and legal problems. How should conversion rates to the euro be expressed in terms of decimal points? What should be the approach to rounding? Should securities be 'renominalised' to produce units in round numbers? Should there be a different approach to bonds that matured during the transitional period to 1 January 2002, when national notes and coins would continue to circulate, and afterwards, when they had disappeared?

Securing timely and effective agreement on such contractual issues was of crucial importance to determine the IT investments and legal changes needed for the successful launch of the euro at company level.

The detailed preparation for the 1 January 1999 EMU deadline included only a few specific initiatives to help the securities settlement industry adapt to the single currency.

Building on the work of the EMI, the newly created central bank published an assessment in September 1998 of 29 securities settlement systems to determine whether they met standards – devised by the EMI – for participating in the credit operations of the European System of Central Banks. All did, although only two – France's Relit à Grande Vitesse and Sweden's VPC system – met the ECB's ideal requirements of offering intraday DvP on a real-time basis, with payment in central bank money in accordance with TARGET operating times.

Ironically, in the light of decisions taken by the ECB eight years later, both RGV and VPC were integrated settlement systems which owed their efficiency in large measure to the decisions of the French and Swedish central banks to outsource the cash leg of the settlement transactions using central bank money to the French and Swedish CSDs.

It was this system, approved at the time by Jean-Claude Trichet when governor of the Banque de France, that proved unacceptable a few years later to some of the more powerful national central banks in the European System of Central Banks. A serious split developed in the ECB governing council over Euroclear's plans to use an integrated settlement system with 'insourced' central bank money as part of its 'domestic market for Europe' in the first decade of the 21st century. Opposition to Euroclear's plans from the German, Italian and Spanish central banks was so strong that the ECB resorted to a radical plan for a settlement infrastructure of its own, known as Target2-Securities, or T2S, which will be discussed in greater detail later.

The controversies over T2S were in the distant future when the standards were introduced. Although designed to protect the ECB and the national central banks of the ESCB, they set sensible benchmarks and so contributed to the efficiency of the settlement market.

The ECB standards

The nine standards cover four areas of risk – legal, custody, settlement and operational risk.

(i) All securities settlement systems and their links must have a sound legal base ensuring settlement of payment and securities transfers is final and the rights of national central banks (NCBs) and the ECB are protected.

(ii) Systems must use central bank money for DvP of ESCB credit operations.

(iii) Systems and the links between them must have safeguards against custody risk.

(iv) NCBs shall not use systems or links that are not regulated and/or controlled by competent authorities.

(vi) Systems must be transparent, giving NCBs 'timely, orderly and reliable information about potential risks'.

(vi) Systems must have risk management procedures to cope with participant defaults.

(vii) Systems must provide intraday finality for certain ESCB operations and by 2002 allow the option of intraday DvP settlement in central bank money.

(viii) Operating hours and opening days of systems must comply with national central banks rules for TARGET.

(ix) All systems must ensure operational reliability of technical systems and have back-up facilities capable of completing daily processing requirements.

Another practical step was the settlement finality directive, adopted by the Commission in May 1998 and which entered into force in December 1999. This established EU-wide rules for dealing with the insolvency of a participant in a payment or a securities settlement system. Designed to reduce systemic risk, the settlement finality directive defined the moment of the opening of insolvency proceedings for all member states and ring-fenced collateral security from insolvency proceedings.

Otherwise, the European Commission approach to clearing and settlement in the run-up to EMU was one of neglect. In October 1998, the Commission produced a document, 'Financial Services: Building a Framework for Action' which outlined how 'a coherent programme of action' was needed to help deliver an optimally functioning financial market for Europe. It contained no specific suggestions on improving the market for cross-border securities settlement.

By May 1999, this preliminary document had developed into the Financial Services Action Plan,[16] a sweeping agenda for creating a single European market for financial services. The FSAP consisted of more than 40 initiatives. The only proposals relating to securities settlement concerned the control of systemic risk where the Commission urged implementation of the settlement finality directive that it had proposed and a new law to provide legal certainty for the cross-border use of collateral.

Some months after EMU's launch in January 1999, Tommaso Padoa-Schioppa, an ECB board member, touched on the paradox of a securities settlement system that was closely entwined with the monetary policy of the European Central Bank but underdeveloped for the economic activities of the EU. He was better qualified than most to comment on the eccentricities of the EU's approach: in previous professional incarnations, he had been a financial regulator in Italy and a senior Commission official.

Addressing an audience at SIBOS in Munich in September 1999, Padoa-Schioppa observed how the growing use of DvP for securities transactions changed the way banks operated, with profound implications for the ECB's conduct of monetary policy.

'Banks include the payment flows stemming from securities settlement in their intraday liquidity management,' he noted. 'If these funds are not delivered, or not delivered on time, payment settlement systems could become gridlocked. Moreover since the liquidity in RTGS systems depends on intraday credit that central banks only grant against collateral, RTGS

---

[16] 'Financial services: implementing the framework for financial markets – action plan,' Com (1999) 232, 11.05.99.

systems would be blocked if securities were not delivered to the central bank on time. This would in turn seriously hamper the implementation of monetary policy.'

At the same time, he added, the fragmentation of the securities industry meant that 'even today, it is not easier for a euro area bank to settle trades in "Bunds" than it is to settle trades in "gilts", although the first are denominated in euro and the second are not.'

The way EMU was prepared meant the eurozone member states embarked on the great experiment of a single currency with a securities settlement infrastructure that would support the monetary policy of the European Central Bank. But it was too fragmented to meet the challenges facing securities markets in both the European single market and the single currency area. The EU launched EMU without a policy on securities settlement and with no sign of any in preparation.

Why was this? Launching the single currency without a hitch was, of course, the overriding priority. But the Commission's documents of 1998 and 1999 outlining future EU financial services policy provide other clues.

The two communications focused on trading. They appeared to believe financial integration was 'within reach'[17] and suggested that the post-trade sector could be left to market forces. The Commission's 1999 FSAP paper gave no hint that clearing and settlement would become a challenge for policy makers. 'Profound changes in the organisation of the EU financial marketplaces are already visible, notably in the relationship between different exchanges and in the consolidation of payment and securities settlement systems,' it said. 'These hold out the prospect of cheaper and more flexible financing arrangements for corporate borrowers, including innovative start-up companies.'

Impressed by manoeuvrings among securities exchanges and infrastructure providers, the European Commission put its faith in the market to bring integration and consolidation of payments and securities settlement systems.

Market forces, however, are moulded by the decisions of companies and individuals, which are sometimes wise, sometimes foolish and rarely predictable. As the following chapters will show, private sector decisions would drive Europe's securities settlement industry in often unexpected ways in the years up to the launch of EMU and beyond.

---

[17] The 1998 document included the headline 'Integrated wholesale markets are within reach'.

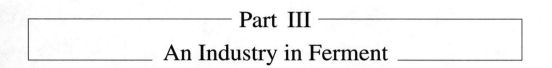

Part III

An Industry in Ferment

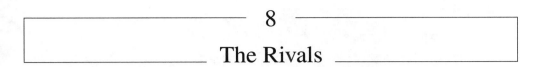

8

The Rivals

The prospect of a single currency for some, if not all, of the leading EU economies and capital markets gave a tremendous boost to cross-border securities trading in Europe as the 1990s progressed.

The EU's plan implied the eventual replacement of national bond markets by a continent-wide market. Investors bet on a narrowing of spreads in the national bond markets of putative members of the single currency in anticipation of a 'one size fits all' central bank interest rate for EMU countries committed to low inflation. These speculative 'convergence plays' boosted turnover in financial markets and the need for cross-border settlement services. These conditions played to the strengths of Europe's two ICSDs, Euroclear and Cedel.

Already, in 1993, domestic debt instruments accounted for 62% of Euroclear's turnover against just 18% for classic Eurobond transactions. The surge in repo-based trading that began around 1994 boosted further the rapid growth of cross-border trading in domestic government bonds.

Users reacted by demanding improved efficiency, lower costs and straight-through processing from bargain to settlement of securities transactions. At the same time, regulators put pressure on settlement and other infrastructure providers to reduce risk.

One result was a drive to develop real-time settlement. The need to invest in IT rose accordingly. When ambitions exceeded technical capabilities, technology became a problem for the industry rather than an enabler. In consequence, the 1990s and early 21st century saw a number of costly IT mishaps, from which Euroclear was not immune.

Although still far from glamorous, the securities settlement industry itself acquired a somewhat higher public profile as the 1990s progressed. This encouraged executive ambition, which would be an additional, important force shaping the industry's future.

A new breed of assertive managers took charge of important settlement providers and exchanges. We shall meet some of them, in the context of their organisations, in this and the following chapters.

We turn first to Euroclear and Cedel. The 1990s were years of rapid growth and significant change for both ICSDs. The traditional rivalry between the two organisations reached new heights of antagonism. The sparks that flew between Brussels and Luxembourg were difficult to reconcile with the popular view that the job of post-trade infrastructure executives was merely to assure efficient plumbing for financial markets.

8.1 EUROCLEAR AND THE BOOM IN DOMESTIC MARKETS

Euroclear was well placed to deal with the profound changes that followed the 1987 crash and the fall of the Berlin Wall. The company's confidence had grown in line with the expansion of its business in the 1980s. Platform improvements and the diversification of settlement services away from traditional Eurobonds put it in a strong position to handle the rapid growth of cross-border trading in domestic government bonds that was such a feature of the 1990s. It saw

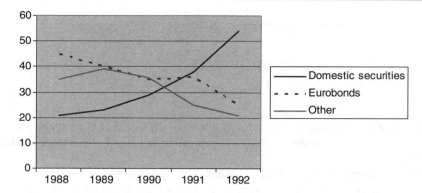

Figure 8.1 Euroclear turnover by instrument (% of total turnover). *Source*: Euroclear annual report 1992

itself as a leading player in securities settlement with a capacity to think and plan strategically. Testifying to the growth of its business, the company relocated to new purpose built premises towards the end of 1992 that put the Operations Centre under one roof.

If the growth of Euroclear was impressive in the 1980s, the scaling up of its business in response to the demands of financial markets in the 1990s was spectacular. The value of securities transactions settled through the Euroclear system had pushed through the $1 trillion barrier in 1984. In 1990, Euroclear's annual turnover exceeded $4 trillion. In the first half of the decade, its business volume about doubled every 18 to 24 months.

Turnover jumped by 71% to nearly $10 trillion in 1992. In that year too, settlement of domestic securities, comprising both bonds and equities, increased by 145%. As highlighted in Figure 8.1, domestic securities accounted for more than 50% of turnover for the first time. Also, for the first time since the system's launch, the US dollar was displaced as the most used settlement currency. Against a background of crisis that autumn in the European Monetary System, the greenback's share of Euroclear turnover fell in 1992 to 22%: below that of the Deutsche Mark at 28%.

The following year – Euroclear's 25th year of operations – yielded a similar performance. The value of securities settled rose by 77% to more than $17 trillion in 1993 from $9.78 trillion in 1992. The number of transactions handled increased by about 30% to more than 40 000 per working day. The value of securities held for participants at the end of 1993 reached $1.47 trillion, up 21% on the previous year.

The upsurge in domestic securities business prompted a mushrooming of links to local CSDs. By 1990 the Euroclear system had links to 16 domestic markets to facilitate cross-border settlement. Two years later, the system was providing DvP settlement for domestic securities from 21 markets.

Euroclear was also gaining market share against Cedel. One indicator was the size of the Euroclear depository, which was more than double that of Cedel at the beginning of the 1990s. In 1995, the same BIS committee that reported on DvP developments in 1992 produced a study of cross-border securities settlement.[1] It found that the combined average daily settlement volumes at Euroclear and Cedel reached the equivalent of $112 billion in 1994 after growing

---

[1] 'Cross-border securities settlements', CPSS, Basel, March 1995.

'over the last few years at a compound annual rate of around 50%'. Euroclear accounted for about three quarters of the total in 1993 and 1994, compared with about two thirds in the later 1980s.

The growth of market share reflected a favourable client mix. According to Ignace Combes: 'We had a situation in the 1990s when most, if not all, of the broker-dealers were on the books of Euroclear and 50% of global custodians – and that figure has since grown. It was very difficult for Cedel to fight against.'[2]

Following Albert Petersen's rebuilding of the system in the 1970s and early 1980s and the subsequent diversification away from Eurobonds, Euroclear embarked, in the early to mid-1990s, on a third major wave of system development to meet the changing needs of its markets. 'We needed to make the system far more sophisticated and further expand in terms of new instruments,' Combes says.[3] 'We moved to daylight and real-time settlement, so that same-day repos and same-day financing could be done as well as collateral management and the tri-party service.'

The moves reflected strategic planning as far back as the mid-1980s. 'Management decided then that we needed to step back and think: should we change the way we operate and change our processing approach to cope with this new environment?' Martine Dinne remembers.

The strategy group created in 1986 and headed by Dinne was put to analysing the implications for Euroclear of its rapid growth, its diversification away from Eurobonds and its increased interaction with domestic markets. It studied the Bridge with Cedel, the links to domestic markets and Euroclear's practice of overnight processing. 'The mission of my team was: should we continue to have our settlement in the night, preceding the settlement date, because that was the way we were operating? Or should we move it to the end of the day, or should we move to real time, or should we move to multiple-batch?'[4] Dinne says.

The system of chaining and multi-currency settlement introduced in 1981 had been improved and made more scalable by steadily reducing the time required to process settlements. Dinne's team decided Euroclear should move from single batch processing to multiple-batch and eventually to real-time settlement.

It was an ambitious programme. 'It had to be done step-by-step, because the technologists were not ready to deliver this vision,' Dinne recalls. But the group's conclusions provided a yardstick against which improvements to the system and the needs of clients – notably the broker-dealers and global custodians – could be measured.

There followed a period of further incremental development of the Euroclear system in which the views of the clients played an increasingly important role to the benefit of both sides. In the late 1980s, both the global custodians and US investment banks put pressure on Euroclear managers to make their system more user-friendly. Service enhancements came thick and fast. The 1990 annual report listed no fewer than 27. There were even more the following year.

One important innovation was the integration of securities lending and borrowing in the settlement process. Introduced in June 1991, this eliminated the risk for borrowers of over- or underborrowing and increased the yield on the lenders' portfolios.

'Integrated stock lending and borrowing made settlements more efficient,' Ignace Combes points out. 'If customers had a lot of fails, they were not able to leverage their balance sheets.

[2] Conversation with the author, 24 October 2006.
[3] Conversation with the author, 24 November 2006.
[4] In conversation with the author, 24 October 2006.

They would need to have capital to set against fails and that would have hampered growth of their business.'

The same year saw the launch of DACE – Deadlines and Corporate Events reporting – which gave holders of securities standardised and detailed notice of forthcoming deadlines and corporate events. The income reporting facility in Euclid 90 was improved, enhancing the cash management possibilities of Euroclear customers.

Participants benefited directly from the innovations through rebates and reduced fees. In 1992, for example, improvements to what had become a PC-based Euclid communications system yielded a 40% cut in communications costs for users that adopted the new infrastructure. Euroclear doubled its rebates to users to $12 million for that year from $6 million the year before.

Client focus and implementation of system improvements were priorities during Ketchum's years at Euroclear, a point noted by his successor John T. Olds. A few months after taking over as general manager on 1 September 1991, Olds observed: 'Great strides have been taken to make the system easier to use. I think we've become much more responsive. Even before the crash of 1987, and dramatically thereafter, our focus was on the cost of doing business. In many ways, participants' cost controls sent us back to the drawing board. The result was the most comprehensive series of system changes in our 23-year history.'[5]

The systems changes mentioned by Olds helped Euroclear towards a long standing goal. Combes recalls how: 'For Euroclear, the whole game was to internalise. Why was that important? First, because of risk: if two counterparties are on the books of the same entity, you have immediate settlement. It's less risky, with a lower number of fails and better service – especially if you have broker-dealers and custodians. You can do borrowing and lending of securities within the same system. The bigger and more internalisation you had, the stronger and better the franchise became.'

By 1994, internal settlements at Euroclear accounted for 68% of average daily turnover of $84.7 billion, according to the 1995 BIS study, well ahead of Cedel where the proportion was 46.5% of $27.1 billion. The remainder of the two ICSDs' turnover was settled over the Bridge between Euroclear and Cedel and through links they forged with local CSDs. Euroclear's receipts and deliveries through local market links accounted for 23% of its average daily turnover in 1994 while at Cedel the proportion was 24% of its smaller business volume. By 1996, more than 25 important domestic markets were linked to the Euroclear system. In 10 of these[6] more than 95% of transactions were settled on a DvP basis.

It was the growing importance of such 'cross-system' settlements that triggered Euroclear's adoption of multiple-batch processing during Olds' term of office. 'People wanted overnight settlement for cash management purposes,' Dinne explains. 'But they also wanted an additional chance to settle during the day.' Daytime settlement was required for repos or the reimbursement of loans while additional settlement cycles were a precondition for improving links to other settlement systems, such as Cedel or the Deutscher Kassenverein (DKV), the German CSD.[7]

During 1993, Euroclear introduced an additional night-time settlement cycle and followed up with a daylight processing cycle towards the end of the year. Multiple-batch settlement was a central feature of a new Bridge agreement with Cedel that entered into force that year.

---

[5] *Euroclear Review*, Spring 1992.
[6] Denmark, France, Germany, Italy, the Netherlands, New Zealand, Portugal, Spain, Sweden and ECU denominated.
[7] Created in 1989 from the consolidation of Germany's regional CSDs; described in Chapter 9.2.

This came after difficult negotiations, handled for Euroclear by Dinne and her team, which are described later in this chapter.

Euroclear's adoption of multiple-batch processing greatly improved the efficiency of settlement with the Kassenverein when combined with DKV's introduction in 1993 of a same-day processing cycle. These innovations gave a huge boost to the repo business in Bunds, as German government bonds were known, because they enabled the settlement of so-called back-to-back transactions. Back-to-back trades allowed dealers to receive and redeliver the same securities on the same-day, with the possibility of a same-day turnaround across the link so long as they met the conditions of the two settlement organisations.

Bundesbank reserve requirements turned London into the centre for Bund repo and derivatives activity even though German government bonds were held in custody by DKV. Euroclear's link with DKV assumed special importance after Deutsche Bank moved its Bund business to London in the early 1990s and at the same time shifted its Bund settlement to Euroclear because most of its counterparties were Euroclear customers. Volumes over the link between the German CSD and Euroclear soared to reach the equivalent of $15.6 billion transactions a day in 1994, according to BIS figures. This amount matched the value of average daily transactions over the much longer established Bridge between Euroclear and Cedel and compared with average daily turnover in D-mark securities worth $23.5 billion and $36.4 billion at DKV and Euroclear respectively.

Multiple batch processing was quickly followed by plans for real-time settlement as the next step in the development of Euroclear's system. On 20 June 1994, Luc Bomans became general manager of the Euroclear Operations Centre (EOC) in succession to John Olds with a clear mandate to develop a new real-time platform.

Bomans was the first non-American to head EOC, and the first with a non-banking background. A civil engineer by training, he had been recruited by Albert Petersen some 15 years before and had won his spurs as the architect of Euclid.

He was a big man from the Dutch speaking part of Belgium where people pride themselves on straight talking and the ability to take tough decisions. His six years running Euroclear gave him plenty of scope to display both characteristics. The appointment of a securities settlement expert, who had risen through the ranks, guaranteed Bomans a good deal of support and respect among Euroclear's staffers and tears were shed when he unexpectedly took early retirement after ill health in the summer of 2000. Bomans expected loyalty and discretion from those around him and returned these qualities with interest. But he was also capable of strong dislikes and undiplomatic enough not to hide them, as both André Lussi of Cedel and Sir Andrew Large, who became Euroclear chairman in succession to Rolf-E. Breuer on 20 April 1998, discovered.

Bomans' aim was for Euroclear to retain its leadership of cross-border settlement when systems in important countries such as France and Germany were consolidating with the goal of becoming more competitive in the European market. The differences in technology and practice among the national CSDs meant Euroclear would have to develop an extremely flexible system to be able to keep up its links and tap into the burgeoning liquidity of all manner of domestic securities markets.

He arrived with two core insights as to what would drive the Euroclear system. In his debut interview with the *Euroclear Review*,[8] he underlined that: 'First, the market continues to ask for shorter settlement cycles.' Second, Euroclear's participants needed 'more and more

---

[8] Autumn 1994.

information about their assets to manage them efficiently'. Bomans argued that Euroclear's clients wanted to control their assets as long as possible. 'Thus settlement cycles will continue to shrink which, sooner or later, calls for continuous intraday settlement.'

There were other pressures pushing Bomans towards real-time settlement. Central banks and regulators favoured ever shorter settlement delays to minimise risk. Another factor was a creeping uncertainty in financial markets about the long-term commitment of Morgan Guaranty to Euroclear. This fed an undercurrent of discontent among many of the settlement providers with which Euroclear had links about Euroclear's insistence that its partners should be the first to deliver securities in any transaction. Euroclear had always been able to brush aside complaints about this cornerstone of its business policy by pointing to the strong ratings accorded to Morgan Guaranty as operator of the system. But this argument looked less persuasive after Morgan began to sell its other securities processing interests in the middle of the 1990s. 'The others were playing on this risk,' Bomans says.[9] 'The only way to cope with that was to have a system whereby any time we had a transaction, we could settle it.'

During 1995, Bomans' first full year, the Euroclear board gave the go-ahead to real-time settlement. In his report for that year to the owners of the Euroclear cooperative,[10] Breuer announced that the project would reduce participants' financing costs and increase the return on their assets. Real-time settlement would be rolled out in several phases, with the first to be launched early in 1998.

The real-time settlement project was called 'Next'. It was seen as strengthening 'the role of the Euroclear system as the gateway for cross-border securities services' in Europe.[11] But getting there proved an unsettling experience. Euroclear, which was proud of its technical record and prowess, found it was overstretched for the first time since the dark days of the early 1970s.

Bomans calculated that there was sufficient time to develop and introduce the new system before the start of the single currency. He was to be proven wrong. 'The problem was that we took the advice of consultants and used the wrong technology. We ended up with a huge performance problem,' Bomans says.[12] 'The idea was good – to create a flexible system, an event driven system, open to different transactions, coming at different times, from different ruling environments.' But the developers of Next made the mistake of applying that sophisticated system, suited to cross-system equity trades, to the more straightforward book entry settlements which accounted for 80% of the transactions processed daily by Euroclear.

The pressures on Euroclear showed to some extent in its research and development spending, which more than doubled from $17.3 million in 1995 to $37.4 million in 1996 (see Figure 8.2). R&D outlays rose further to $50.9 million in 1997 and $53.9 million in 1998, although in these later years the budget also had to cover preparations for the introduction of the euro and action to defuse any problems arising from the Y2K millennium bug.

According to Bomans, 400 people were working on Next. 'In the end, they had a very intelligent real time system that could not process more than 15 000 transactions a day.' This was at a time when Euroclear on peak days was processing more than 100 000 settlement instructions.

The performance of the system was a 'catastrophe,' Bomans says. 'We announced a launching date, but problems grew. As we approached the launch date we scaled down some

---

[9] In conversation with the author, 18 October 2006.
[10] Dated 25 April 1996, in the annual report of Euroclear Clearance System Société Coopérative.
[11] Euroclear Clearance System Société Coopérative annual report for 1998.
[12] Conversation with the author, 30 September 2005.

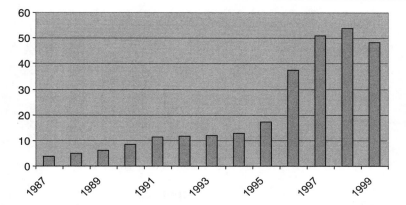

Figure 8.2 Euroclear – research and development expenditure (US$ million). *Source:* Euroclear annual reports

functionalities. Then I learned about the performance of the system. So we had to make the hard decision to stop the investment in summer 1998.' It cost, Bomans says, 'an eight digit dollar figure – between $20 million and $40 million. But we didn't make a loss.'

It was Bomans who forced the decision to delay Next on a reluctant IT department. Euroclear had originally announced in February 1998 that it would launch real-time settlement during the day on 29 June that year. That plan was shelved less than three months later – on 5 May 1998. It was not an easy choice. Delay meant Euroclear had to adapt to the euro's launch on 1 January 1999 using legacy systems.

'We had planned to launch Next before the euro and suddenly we had a problem that would have resulted in two or three months' delay. It therefore conflicted with the euro,' Martine Dinne explains.[13] 'We were planning for the euro with real time already launched. We could do nothing to change the euro date. So a very public crisis emerged: we had to put the euro first and launch the real-time platform a year later. That was very, very visible. Had we not had the euro, we could have had two or three months' delay and nobody would have talked about it.'

'We had systems problems, as often happen with big projects. We had to decide: do we run the risk of not changing our plans and being unable to launch the euro, which would have been ridiculous, or do we change our plan totally and build the euro on the old platform and let real time wait and come later. We chose the second option for very good reasons. There was a meeting here [in the EOC] until midnight. It was a very difficult decision: the people on the project said we were mad, that they were nearly there and only needed two months. But at the best we would have launched the real time one or two months ahead of the euro. Imagine what would have happened if there was another crisis. We would have to say to the market: we made the wrong decision and we are not ready for the euro. We would have lost our business, totally. So it was a risk management decision to say: we play safe, and we'll go public about our problem and the market will be very unhappy. But we play safe.'

The problems with Next were a shock at the time. But the damage was contained. There was a danger of the project losing momentum after the delay. That did not happen. Instead, Euroclear kept the team working on the system. It was quickly proven that what Bomans has described as a more 'traditional' approach would solve the performance problems.

---

[13] As told to the author, 15 November 2005.

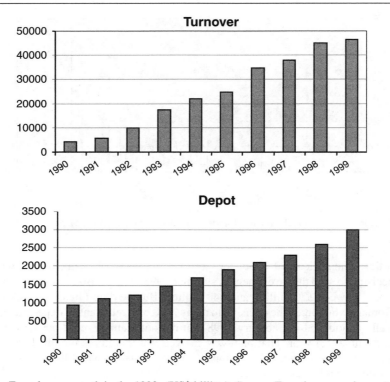

Figure 8.3   Euroclear – growth in the 1990s (US$ billion). *Source:* Euroclear annual reports

Little noticed amid the drama, Euroclear's day-to-day business continued to progress (Figure 8.3). In 1998, the year of postponement, the value of securities trades settled through the Euroclear system reached a new record $44.9 trillion – twice the $21.9 trillion recorded in 1994, when Bomans became general manager. The 'depot', or depository of securities held in the Euroclear system, continued to grow: reaching $2.6 trillion in 1998, up from $1.7 trillion in 1994.

Euroclear was also assembling resources to deal with future challenges. The cooperative's capital and reserves stood at $177 million by the end of 1998, up from $68 million in 1994. At the end of the decade, Euroclear claimed that its share of cross-border settlement business handled by itself and Cedel was 'approaching 80%'.[14]

Of great long-term significance, Euroclear was preparing for a fourth phase of development that would transform the company in the early years of the 21st century. In 1996–97, the company carried out another strategic review – this time to evaluate the prospects and opportunities created by the euro.

The review placed special focus on Euroclear's equities business which continued to disappoint. It concluded that the elimination of currency exposure among the member states would both encourage cross-border investment and permit a much easier diversification of portfolios:

---

[14] According to the 1999 annual report of Euroclear Clearance System Société Coopérative.

trends that should benefit Euroclear. However, it decided Euroclear must take three important steps for success. The company must:

- separate from JP Morgan;
- be able to merge with different entities, such as national CSDs; and
- link with stock exchanges.

The three steps were part of a single strategy. Separation from Morgan was necessary for Euroclear to expand its activities in Europe. 'We wanted to take away the negative connotation of being associated with an American bank,' Combes recalls. 'We could never merge as JP Morgan with local CSDs.'

Merging with CSDs would increase Euroclear's chances of success in cross-border settlement of equities. 'If we wanted to be successful in equities, which were a major part of the business of the national CSDs, we had better merge with them,' Combes adds.

The links with the stock exchanges were necessary if Euroclear, rather than national CSDs, were to handle international trading in equities. 'The equities business was sitting in domestic systems. But if there was more demand for an international approach, the way to get the business into Euroclear was to have feeds from the stock exchanges so that the transactions could be settled directly on Euroclear's books,' Combes adds. 'The only way to do that was to build partnerships with those stock exchanges that were open to the idea.'

Bomans followed up the review with an intensive round of consultations and negotiations that sowed the seeds for the transformation of Euroclear in later years. He initiated discussions with Sicovam, the French CSD, and with the CSDs of Belgium and the Netherlands. With Combes, he took the case for separation from Morgan to the bank's top management in New York.

As we shall see, Euroclear's plans to separate from Morgan were made public on 1 September 1999, a few weeks before real-time settlement was finally launched in a somewhat simplified form at the end of September that year. The delay of more than one year in the real-time project was a consequence of the transition to the euro. The company had to recode and retest the software to be fit for a post-euro environment. Otherwise, the delay would probably have been no more than three or four months, with a maximum of six months.

When Euroclear finally introduced real-time settlement, other companies were experiencing problems with their own plans. Euroclear had learned valuable lessons. Moreover, its system was technically ahead of most other securities settlement systems and ahead of market demand.

'The reason why we and others in the industry were keen on a real-time platform at the time was the expectation that, with the euro, an active same-day repo market would develop, possibly very quickly, within a year or two of the euro's launch. In those circumstances, a real-time platform promised a real advantage,' says Pierre Francotte,[15] who became Euroclear chief executive in succession to Bomans in 2000. 'In fact, the same-day repo market did not develop within the first couple of years and has been developing only progressively since then.'

According to Francotte, the financial impact on Euroclear of the Next delay was 'about 5% of the yearly costs of the company' and therefore 'not material' to the profit and loss account. However, the problems with Next made an impression on the market and on Euroclear's competitors – especially at Cedel in Luxembourg.

---

[15] Comments passed to the author in May 2006.

8.2   LUSSI AND THE REVIVAL OF CEDEL

As the 1980s rolled by, Cedel seemed content to play second fiddle to Euroclear. True, it had almost as many participants – just under 2000 in 1987 – and a similar number of issues accepted for settlement – nearly 20 000. But Euroclear was clearly ahead in terms of turnover and the value of securities deposited in the system, and increasing its market share.

Euroclear had established a technical lead during the late 1970s and early 1980s, although Cedel kept up with the innovations of its rival. As Albert Petersen noted: 'To their credit, they responded every time, and I don't know how they did it. For the participants, Cedel was keeping up with developments, but more in a response mode than initiating.'

To friends and rivals alike, Cedel by the mid-1980s appeared a rather dozy outfit – 'a tool of the bourgeois de Luxe,' as Walter Imthurn joked. It took its slogan – 'founded from the market for the market' – so much to heart that it had more than 40 board members, when its staff numbered fewer than 200. Perhaps indicative of a certain lack of bite were the generally cordial relations between Euroclear managers and their Luxembourg counterparts. Tom Ketchum, who became Euroclear general manager in 1987, remembers Georges Muller, Cedel's managing director, as 'a really nice man: not confrontational but diplomatic'.[16]

The same could not be said of André Lussi, who became Muller's executive vice president in 1988 and stepped into Muller's shoes the following year. Lussi can be a man of great charm. But people rarely fail to add the word abrasive when describing him.

Lussi, a German speaking Swiss, had spent 20 formative years working for UBS, which always played a key role in Cedel's affairs until its merger with Swiss Bank Corp. in the late 1990s. Like many senior officials in that bank, he was also an officer in the Swiss army, where he held the rank of major in the infantry. According to René Schmitter, who had helped create Cedel and was secretary to its board and executive committee, Lussi was 'a little Napoleon' who arrived 'wanting to change everything on the same day' and created a lot of friction in the process.[17] The fact that he was no expert on the securities settlement industry did not ease matters with the long established specialists of Cedel.

Lussi remembers finding himself in charge of a small company of 180 people and $50 million of value. 'It was a cooperative – rather like a milk cooperative up in the Swiss Alps. So I said to myself. There is only one way: the way forward. I have to change this, because if I don't change it, the company will go down the drain.'[18]

According to his own account, Lussi arrived at Cedel with 'a clear view that this was a big business and that securitisation would increase substantially'. He concluded that if settlement was not run as a business, not internationalised, and not run to higher standards, he would be unable to compete against Euroclear and to survive in the market.

He lost no time letting Cedel's board know that change was afoot. André Roelants, who succeeded Lussi as CEO of the Luxembourg settlement system in very troubled circumstances in 2001, was a member of the big Cedel board of the 1980s and remembers Lussi's first appearance before it. 'The first day was already a big shock. The former CEO introduced him very nicely, and Lussi said that the management was an old-style management and that Cedel had to be much more professional, and so on. And at that point, the former CEO left the room, furious. That was Lussi's character.'[19]

---

[16] Conversation with the author, 12 December 2005.
[17] Conversation with the author, 2 March 2006.
[18] Conversation with the author, 1 December 2005.
[19] As told to the author, 15 May 2006.

Changes followed. Lussi replaced Cedel's legal advisers and auditors and secured a new chairman. Edmond Israel, chairman since Cedel's foundation, retired in 1990 and was rewarded with the position of honorary chairman and the creation of the Edmond Israel Foundation to support and promote study and research of capital markets. René Schmitter left in Israel's wake. Cedel's new chairman, Hans Angermueller, came from Citicorp, another long standing supporter of the Luxembourg rival to Euroclear.

In his valedictory message to shareholders,[20] Israel extolled the 'Cedel family spirit' that pervaded 'through all levels of Cedel's structure and organisation'. However, there was little evidence of 'Happy Families' in Lussi's early years. The glossy photographs that now adorned the company's annual reports bore witness to sometimes radical change among the teams of senior managers who were assembled each year to be pictured alongside Cedel's smiling CEO. In 1991 Cedel's bloated board was cut from 41 to 15, including the chairman and chief executive, and Lussi was given greater powers.

Lussi admits he was 'pushy and very demanding'. He says: 'I know about this criticism. I had no alternative because my competitor was JP Morgan. I knew I had to have new governance. I knew I had to have new IT systems. We still had punched cards in '88. We had a room with 10 ladies who were punch card ladies. We had computers, but we still used punch cards – part of those IBM mainframes. If you have time, you can do it nicely and easily. But time was of the essence and JP Morgan was on the other side of the Ardennes. It was an environment where you had to move fast.'

And move fast he did – making Cedel less Luxembourgeois in the process. In 1991, Lussi made English the corporate language. 'Before that, people spoke French and Luxembourgish and a little bit of German. Computers would stop at 12 o'clock when they would go to eat and start again at two o'clock.' He began to hire people of all nationalities. 'In serving an international market, I had to have a cosmopolitan approach. So my second step was a completely changed recruitment policy: Luxembourgers at the end were 15% to 20% of the total and we had 35 nationalities.' Lussi paid well, but demanded loyalty, at all hours of day and night, in return. 'So I pushed, and I said, if you perform I pay you well, you have your freedom. But if you don't perform, and you work against me and the interests of the company you're history.'

He set up an audit committee for Cedel: 'Only a few knew what an audit committee was in Luxembourg,' he claims. 'We had a remuneration committee and an IT committee from the beginning of the '90s. We improved our governance to American standards,' he says. 'Inside Cedel, there were some people I just had to dismiss. I'm against this continental approach, where people say: you owe it to me, you have to keep me. You can't do that and run a business in competition with JP Morgan.'

Lussi made enemies. In May 1992 two dissident senior managers tried to oust him. He survived and set about a new round of dismissals to rid himself of opponents inside the company. 'The approach was not always easy, and I had some failures. I made some mistakes. I went too fast. I didn't allow enough time to make sure there was an understanding between the different cultures,' he admits. 'But at the end, we overcame them. In the end it was a great environment.' He had his supporters, notably among the big international banks. Angermueller 'helped a lot,' says Lussi. 'Some banks switched to my philosophy, and some had difficulties.'

'He had one problem that should not be underestimated,' observed one senior Luxembourg banker. 'He is a German-speaking Swiss, and sometimes when they express

---

[20] In Cedel's annual report for 1989.

themselves – specifically in French – they don't have all the nuances that you can have in your mother tongue. So sometimes, the way he was speaking was a little bit like a Colonel of the Swiss army.'

It was not long before Euroclear felt the effects of the change of management in Luxembourg. Lussi turned his attention to the Bridge and the financial advantage that Euroclear gained by settling overnight ahead of the settlement date.

The 1980 Bridge agreement became a bone of contention between Euroclear and Cedel almost as soon as it was signed. Cedel began compensating its users for the delay in payments as early as 1981 and the cost rose inexorably as volumes increased in the following years. Cedel sought relief, but to no avail. Looking back at his 20 years with Cedel, René Schmitter says 'there was not a single year when there were no discussions [with Euroclear] about the Bridge. But it was always a dialogue of the deaf.'

Euroclear's position was that the Bridge was a mechanical facility for the benefit of dealers in the Euromarkets. It was not a joint venture, not an agreement to share markets or participants, did not imply any commitment of the two companies to develop systems together, and was not intended to give Cedel's users the same access as a Euroclear participant.

Underlying this policy was a wariness regarding Cedel's creditworthiness, because it was neither backed by a bank of Morgan's standing nor particularly profitable. At stake were transfers of securities and cash between the two settlement systems worth billions of dollars a day. Morgan's 'triple A' status ensured that any exposure incurred by Cedel in the course of Bridge transactions could be considered safe. The Euroclear side, by contrast, had at the back of its mind the idea that Cedel could go bankrupt, costing Morgan, as operator of the system, billions of dollars. For that reason, Euroclear ensured that the Bridge operated so that it was never left with a large exposure to Cedel.

Improvements were made to the Bridge during the 1980s but Euroclear was careful to minimise any financial risk from its operations. Successive years saw difficult negotiations about the letters of credit allowed to Cedel for Bridge operations. Set at $70 million in 1983, the volume was grudgingly increased to $120 million in July 1984 and $150 million in July 1986. Once granted, the credit lines were generally handled in a pragmatic manner. But there were occasions when Euroclear took a tough line if traffic across the Bridge exhausted the cash and credit lines in Cedel's account. At times, Euroclear blocked the delivery of its participants' securities to Cedel.

A comparative analysis of Euroclear and Cedel, carried out in 1986, put Cedel's capital base at just $11.4 million. Euroclear's turnover of $1457 billion in 1985 was nearly twice Cedel's $762 billion while the value of securities deposited in the Euroclear system was, at $274 billion, a good two and half times the Cedel total of $106 billion. While Euroclear's net revenues amounted to $54 million, those of Cedel were $16.1 million. Expenses at Euroclear were $30.3 million against $10.4 million at Cedel.

Unfortunately for Lussi, the Bridge was more important to Cedel than Euroclear. In February 1987, for example, Euroclear's receipts from Cedel averaged $911 million a day, or 8% of turnover, a percentage that changed little in the years that followed. Cedel's receipts from Euroclear averaged just over $1 billion or 16% of turnover in 1987. By 1994, according to the BIS, the deliveries received by Cedel from Euroclear averaged $8 billion a day, representing nearly 30% of its total turnover, while Bridge deliveries to Euroclear were only $7.6 billion, or 9% of Euroclear average daily turnover.

On 9 October 1989, Ketchum wrote to Rolf-E. Breuer to tell him that the new management team at Cedel had identified renegotiating the Bridge as a prime objective. Lussi saw the challenge in more dramatic terms. 'I decided I had to solve the Bridge in order to survive. That was the first challenge,' he says.

Lussi divined that his problem was rooted in history. 'I always had to deliver the securities first, because I had daytime processing and they had night-time processing, so I gave them liquidity. It was based on a wrong decision of Cedel at the beginning.' But he took vitriolic exception to the arrangement, which he described as a 'milk machine' that was 'profit-oriented to the nth degree' in favour of Morgan Guaranty.

To the discomfort of Euroclear, Lussi went public with his grievances. 'Relationships between Cedel and Euroclear became more contentious. A lot was on public display, which was unfortunate,' Tom Ketchum says. 'Almost every week and month there was something in the press about the inability of the two companies to agree,' Ignace Combes recalls. Lussi told the May 1990 annual meeting of the AIBD in Amsterdam that the failure to resolve Bridge problems was 'costing the membership' some $35 million a year, prompting Walter Imthurn to observe laconically: 'Well, maybe it's time to burn some bridges.'[21]

Burning bridges was not a solution that Euroclear favoured. Although it agreed to negotiate with Cedel in 1990, Euroclear wanted to keep its competitive position as far as possible.

The task of negotiating with Cedel fell to Martine Dinne and her strategy team because its work had covered many of the issues central to the relationship with Cedel. She proved to be a tough and exceptionally well-informed negotiator.

'We did start negotiating on what we could do to help, without jeopardising the competitiveness of our business and without jeopardising the quality of service for our clients,' she says. 'But there were some things Lussi wanted us to do that would have penalised my clients. He suggested that we both have a subsidy, which he said would be fairer. He said we should not have different processing cycles of day and night. Then he suggested we should settle together, at the same time. But that would have meant a degradation of service for our clients. It was such a technical topic that people were saying poor small Cedel and these bad guys at Euroclear who are making their life difficult. But then to be fair, I was not paid to make their life easier. And I was never going to accept anything that would be worse for my clients for the benefit of his.'

A new Bridge agreement was signed in March 1992, by which time Dinne, Euroclear's 'Queen of the Bridge', was also known as the 'Steel Magnolia' because of her tough negotiating style. Operations under the new agreement were eventually launched in September 1993 when Cedel introduced a new night time processing cycle, as well as its day time cycle. Both systems took to running multiple settlement processing during the night. However, Euroclear again obtained an advantage by limiting itself to two batch deliveries, against Cedel's three, which meant the Brussels-based settlement house was not exposed to the risk of non-payment for a final delivery of securities.

With shorter and more frequent settlement cycles, the new arrangement lowered settlement risks for both operators and sharply reduced Euroclear's credit risk vis-à-vis Cedel. Users of Cedel would in future have the benefit of morning reports on their positions – hitherto an advantage confined to Euroclear clients. The new Bridge promised to reduce the need for securities borrowing. Because both systems agreed automatically to recycle unsettled Bridge instructions, it reduced errors and late deliveries and payments. Above all, the new arrangement all but eliminated the subsidies that Cedel was obliged to give its users through the backvaluing of participants' cash receipts and through borrowing securities for early delivery to Euroclear.

---

[21] Recounted in 'From where I stood: recollections of twenty-five AIBD meetings' by Stanley Ross, May 1993.

For a while, Lussi wanted more. 'The Bridge was a compromise. It was still not perfect,' he recalls. 'But the Cedel board forced me to accept it. It was better than nothing, I could survive, but it was not the solution I envisaged.' His dissatisfaction would nurture a hostile attitude towards Euroclear and Morgan over the rest of the decade.

With the Bridge problem largely solved, Lussi's next big step was to turn Cedel into a bank. The idea sprang mainly from the requirements of the late 1980s Basel agreement on international bank capital adequacy rules, which penalised Cedel with higher risk weightings than Morgan, the operator of Euroclear.

Acquiring a banking licence had always been problematic at Cedel because of concerns among some of its shareholders that Cedel as a bank could compete with them. But Lussi managed to persuade the doubters that Cedel would be better placed to compete internationally. 'It was a money, marketing and security issue. Being a bank enabled us to get a rating and we became a double A-plus rated bank. And this forced my people to be completely different in their approach and to behave like bankers.'

The Luxembourg authorities approved the restructuring of Cedel into a group and a bank in September 1994. Cedel International SA was incorporated in November 1994 and Cedel Bank was granted a licence to start operating from January 1995. Cedel's shareholders approved the changes unanimously in December 1994.

By this time, Lussi was riding high. Cedel's annual report for 1995 – the 25th anniversary year – enthused about a record breaking year 'in almost every way'. Turnover, up 34% on 1994, was approaching $10 trillion. The value of securities deposited, up 18%, exceeded $1 trillion while the addition of 10 000 new securities in the system brought the total to 75 000. Cedel's business was sustained by growth in areas such as domestic government bonds, money market instruments, floating rate notes, emerging market securities and international equities with less reliance on traditional Eurobonds (see Figure 8.4).

In 1994 a new chairman took over who was to become a close ally of Lussi. Robert Douglass, a former vice chairman of Chase Manhattan Corp., was a senior figure at the New York law firm of Milbank, Tweed, Hadley and McCloy. Described by one European business associate as 'a typical, tough, assured East Coast lawyer', Bob Douglass was close to the Rockefellers, having been counsel and later secretary to New York Governor Nelson A. Rockefeller from

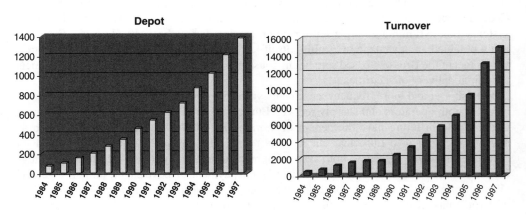

Figure 8.4 Cedel – growth in the 1980s and 1990s (US$ billion). *Source:* Cedel annual reports and media releases

1965 to 1972. His patrician ways were reflected in an interest in ancient Rome – an enthusiasm that he shared with Cedel shareholders in the first two annual reports of his chairmanship.[22] Douglass gave what was still a small, relatively obscure Luxembourg-based company a certain cachet.

For Lussi, Douglass's arrival at Cedel was a boon. Although Douglass was well versed in domestic and international banking he had no particular expertise in the securities settlement. Moreover, he was based in New York which meant that he was rather detached from events in Europe. 'Douglass didn't come from the securities business, didn't have this urgency, wasn't living in the environment where the Euro was coming, with Y2K, and everything in turmoil,' observed one executive from another securities settlement company who had dealings across the table from Douglass.

Lussi therefore had a great deal of freedom which he used freely – for good and ill. Even Martine Dinne, whose relationship with Lussi was bad, admits he made some improvements. 'He did very good things at the start to change Cedel, because it was like a boutique and not very sophisticated and very local. And he changed it into a real professional company, forcing discipline and client focus.'

But, with his chairman based in New York, Lussi found it easy to dominate Cedel and control its pliant board. Meetings of the board would be held away from Cedel's headquarters and often outside Luxembourg – making it difficult for managers, other than Lussi, to communicate with board members. Managers would find their responsibilities usurped or curtailed by an ever growing army of well-paid consultants, hired by Lussi and answering to him.

Lussi was a big fish in the small Luxembourg pond. The Grand Duchy's authorities and business community supported him. But as Lussi's regime progressed, certain incidents caused eyebrows to rise in the more austere corporate culture of Euroclear. Dinne remembers with a shudder attending one ceremony for the Vision for Europe Prize, awarded by the Edmond Israel Foundation. 'He had laser shows with Duisenberg and I said: my God, is that really an infrastructure type of thing.'

There were other tell-tale signs of excess. The Cedel parties at the annual meetings of the AIBD and later ISMA put those of Euroclear in the shade. 'You went to the Cedel party – absolutely. These were big, with a huge budget, well organised,' Walter Imthurn remembers.

'He did a good job but began to believe his own publicity,' one banker observed. As long as business was good, Lussi's position looked secure. 'He had turned Cedel around. Everyone had to admit that.' But Lussi's regime sowed the seeds of its own destruction. He made plenty of enemies, who, in the end, proved stronger than his friends.

---

[22] Douglass's message to shareholders in the 1994 annual report of Cedel International compared the challenges facing the securities settlement industry with those faced by Hannibal crossing the Alps in 218BC. That of 1995 drew parallels with Julius Caesar crossing the River Rubicon 169 years later.

Change at the Exchanges and CSDs

9.1 INVESTMENT AND CONSOLIDATION

While the 1990s saw Euroclear and Cedel locked head to head in fierce competition to capture the market for cross-border settlement, Europe's national securities exchanges and post-trade service providers pursued concerns closer to home.

It was only after a considerable delay that they began to adapt for the approach of the single currency. This was due to the EU's limited success in creating a single market for financial services. The 1993 Investment Services Directive was supposed to create pan-European rules for securities markets in the EU. But compromises during the ISD's adoption had turned it into a piece of legislation reminiscent of the 'curate's egg': it was 'good in parts'.

The ISD set signals for exchanges and national CSDs that both encouraged and discouraged integration at the EU level. It allowed regulated markets to offer remote access to investment firms from other EU member states and many companies took advantage of this 'single passport' provision. On the other hand, it also included a 'concentration rule', which allowed member states to concentrate share trading on regulated markets to the exclusion of telephone trading. Some exchanges such as Italy's were protected by the concentration rule, others such as London's were not.

The ISD gave authorised investment firms remote access to clearing and settlement systems. But CSDs remained unregulated at the European level, enabling member states to maintain restrictions on cross-border access and deterring CSDs from thinking internationally.

Underpinning the ISD was the principle of mutual recognition, by which authorisation by an investment company's national or 'home' supervisor should allow it to trade throughout the EU. But this was undermined by provisions that allowed the foreign or 'host' country to impose its own local conduct of business rules.

The outcome, according to the Commission's 1998 document 'Financial services: building a framework for action' was that 'rigid and unqualified insistence on local trading rules leads to a patchwork of widely differing requirements and makes it difficult for investment service providers to have access to or compete effectively within the framework of other member states' regulated markets'. By allowing host countries to impose more onerous or 'gold-plated' rules, the ISD made life especially difficult for the professional investor and the wholesale client.

It was an environment, however, in which exchanges could thrive, although the incentives thus created propelled them first towards developing their home market. Exchanges such as the Paris and Frankfurt bourses were encouraged to invest heavily in modern electronic trading platforms, which outclassed the London Stock Exchange's SEAQ system and proved far superior to the floor-based trading practices of the US. SEAQ[1] was a screen-based system introduced in preparation for the Big Bang which allowed all transactions on the LSE to be carried out by telephone, replacing the trading floor. For a while in the late 1980s, SEAQ attracted a significant share of European trades in continental blue chip shares.

---

[1] Stock Exchange Automated Quotation System.

New platforms at the exchange level demanded high IT investment and this had several consequences.

- Higher fixed costs provided a spur to economies of scale. As they pursued this goal, some operators – notably Werner Seifert of Deutsche Börse – realised that securities settlement could be recast as a for-profit activity in integrated groups.
- This discovery spurred national vertical consolidation, whereby stock exchanges combined with derivatives exchanges and post-trade service providers. The vertical model, encouraged as it was by the G30 and the European Central Bank's approach to collateral, promised perfect cooperation along the value chain from trading to settlement, leading to efficient straight-through processing in national markets and economies of scale.
- The need for large scale investment helped to encourage demutualisation among stock exchanges: both the Stockholm and Frankfurt exchanges were operating as joint stock companies in 1993.
- More costly systems and increased competition prompted a shake-out and consolidation among regional and global custodians. Morgan Guaranty, the operator of the Euroclear system, was one of the companies cutting back its securities processing business from the middle of the decade onwards.
- The growing cost of investment, against a background of demutualisation and vertical integration, contributed to a decline in the public sector's direct involvement in financial infrastructure. Europe's central banks began quitting the securities settlement business from the late 1990s onwards.

Integration and consolidation at the national level were among strategies for boosting financial centres such as Paris or Frankfurt that aimed to achieve dominance in Europe. They also turned the exchanges into drivers of change in the business of clearing and settlement.

This happened in Germany where the national CSD and the Auslandskassenverein (AKV), the specialised institution that settled foreign securities, were merged and incorporated in the Deutsche Börse group in 1996. It happened in France at the end of the 1990s when SBF, the Paris stock market operator, encouraged the restructuring of post-trade services and pioneered the development of central counterparty clearing for securities.

These strategies were not, however, the best way of preparing for a single market with a single currency. It was only after the business community began to plan seriously for EMU following the decisions of EU leaders at their December 1995 European Council that examples emerged of a different form of integration.

This was the horizontal model, by which companies performing the same functions in the trading to settlement value chain would consolidate across borders to achieve still greater economies of scale. Horizontal integration made only limited progress before the euro's launch. The 1996 merger of the Swiss and German derivatives markets to create Eurex proved the exception rather than the rule.

This was not for want of trying, especially among stock exchanges. As the euro's launch date drew nearer, investors, traders and analysts began to look beyond national frontiers and plan a continent-wide, pan-EU, sectoral approach to the buying and selling of shares.

In response, securities exchanges succumbed to successive bouts of 'alliance fever'. All manner of links and mergers were mooted from 1997 onwards as the exchanges struggled to come to terms with the implications for investors and operators of a single currency affecting at least a core group of EU member states. Most efforts failed to translate talk into action.

Alliance fever did not infect settlement providers to the same degree. There were, to be sure, contacts among CSDs and ICSDs as EMU became inevitable. Some providers drew up blueprints which sought to reconcile vertical and horizontal structures or spread integration and consolidation beyond national boundaries. But none of these ideas got beyond the drawing board. Action came later – after the start of EMU on 1 January 1999.

9.2   SEIFERT IN FRANKFURT – a story of vertical integration

While Lussi was making waves in Luxembourg, another Swiss German was stirring up Germany's stock exchanges. The news in March 1993 that Werner Seifert, a 44-year-old main board director of the Swiss Re insurance group, would take over as chief executive of Deutsche Börse, the Frankfurt-based exchange group, from the end of July came as a surprise to the city's financial community.

Deutsche Börse had been created only a few months before as a joint stock company, largely at the instigation of Rolf-E. Breuer of Deutsche Bank, acting on behalf of Germany's big universal banks. The German exchange group was among the first in Europe to demutualise. The step was intended to give some impetus to the process of modernising Germany's financial sector that got under way in a rather desultory manner in the later 1980s.

Demutualisation did not mean Deutsche Börse was a listed company at this stage. As before, it was owned mainly by German banks, although now as shareholders rather than members of a club. The small regional stock exchanges, which retained their status as independent organisations, held about 10% of the company.

It was Breuer who hired Seifert. At the time, Breuer was the Deutsche Bank managing board member responsible for investment banking and securities business. Already nicknamed 'Herr Finanzplatz'[2] by the German media, he assumed the roles of president of the Frankfurt exchange and supervisory board chairman of Deutsche Börse in 1993. His chairmanship of Euroclear since 1984 bore witness to an above-average interest in financial infrastructure.

Deutsche Börse owned the Frankfurt bourse, Germany's premier stock exchange; Deutsche Termin Börse (DTB), a derivatives exchange; and Deutscher Kassenverein (DKV), the German CSD.

DKV was itself the product of a bank-engineered merger in 1989 of the CSDs that served the Frankfurt stock exchange and the regional bourses of Berlin, Düsseldorf, Hamburg, Hanover, Munich and Stuttgart. As both Deutsche Börse and DKV were owned by banks it was a relatively easy matter for the newly demutualised exchange to become the sole owner of DKV in 1992 and include it in the Deutsche Börse group.

DKV and the Auslandskassenverein (AKV), the specialised German ICSD responsible for the settlement of foreign securities, had close ties with Cedel. These dated back to Cedel's early years when the Frankfurt Kassenverein, the DKV's main constituent company, and the AKV helped establish the Luxembourg-based ICSD.

DKV was a technically advanced system that settled securities on a $T+2$ basis. The Bundesbank provided its payment system. The use of central bank money was made all the

---

[2] 'Mr Financial Centre': an allusion to the prominent role Breuer played in government-supported efforts to boost the financial services sector in Germany in general, and Frankfurt, in particular.

easier because, in Germany's bank-oriented financial system, the DKV's 600 or so participants were banks, except for the two ICSDs and five CSDs.[3]

Seifert's first task was to learn about his new job. He had no background in financial markets. He later said he knew not the slightest thing about the business of exchanges and 'didn't even own a share'[4] when appointed to the job. But he had a quick, logical and powerful mind. He had studied game theory at university and cut his teeth in management as a consultant with McKinsey before moving on to Swiss Re in 1986.

In his trade mark black polo neck shirts, Seifert seemed a breath of fresh air in the somewhat stolid sober suited world of finance in Frankfurt. He was a jazz enthusiast, a virtuoso on the electronic organ, and applied the combination of improvisation and teamwork that characterises jazz music making to much of his working life. He fancied himself as both a lateral and strategic thinker and was much given to brainstorming with a team of enthusiastic, young and loyal managers, many of whom were McKinsey alumni, whom he gathered around him.

Seifert was informal and frank in his dealings with colleagues. In a country where close colleagues of many years' standing would address each other in conversation with old-world formality by their family names and academic titles, he spoke to his board members using their given names to be better able, so it was said, to put his points forcefully.

He did nothing by halves. He smoked a pipe: not just one pipe but three dozen. He collected classic British cars from the 1950s and 1960s, acquiring so many that they have to be stored in a special garage outside Frankfurt. He worked as only a McKinsey alumnus could. Press reports spoke of his waking at 5.30 am, reading three newspapers before arriving early at the office and putting in a 10- to 12-hour day, and then sometimes taking work home.

Some have claimed that Seifert lacks emotional intelligence. He could be charming and friendly. But in negotiations he showed little awareness of the cultural or historical sensitivities of Europe's proud nation states. He often lacked diplomatic finesse. He was poor at handling the media. He did not suffer fools gladly.

He took over an exchange in transition. It was partially modernised under the leadership of Rüdiger von Rosen, the previous CEO, who was booted aside to make way for Seifert. Yet it still had a cosy, inward looking, clubby atmosphere. Seifert faced the challenge of integrating the component parts of Deutsche Börse and establishing common technology and shared services for the group. He needed to update or replace IBIS, the exchange's computerised trading system, which handled only the most liquid shares, and overcome the resistance of brokers and regional exchanges to more screen trading. Although Deutsche Börse had suffered no disaster comparable to the collapse of London's Taurus project in 1993,[5] it had its share of IT problems, including an order routing and quote calculation system that failed to live up to specifications. It had also lost a lot of business to London: notably the Bund futures contract, which was more heavily traded on Liffe, the London futures exchange, than DTB.

Settlement infrastructure was not at the top of Seifert's priorities. But he was to have a profound impact on the business in Europe, largely because of the way he viewed exchanges and the challenges that they faced.

Seifert took some months to study the business. His conclusion,[6] he said later, was that: 'An exchange is nothing special. It is part of the capital market infrastructure. It serves a kind of technological, operations function there. It has to take care of just a few things: first,

---

[3] DTC of New York, Necigef of Amsterdam, OEKB of Vienna, SEGA of Zurich and Sicovam of Paris.
[4] In *Invasion der Heuschrecken* by Werner Seifert with Hans-Joachim Voth, Econ Verlag, Berlin, 2006.
[5] Described in Chapter 9.4.
[6] Conversation with the author, 12 October 2005.

to provide fair, transparent and orderly markets and, second, to provide the market with a straight-through process – to execute every order as fast as possible, as cheap as possible and as secure as possible, from order routing to order matching to clearing and settlement and finally custody. And that's it. It is not a rocket science.'

In consequence, he had no time for those who regarded exchanges as national treasures or totems. 'Our biggest advantage at Deutsche Börse – which was also a disadvantage at times – was that we looked at this business from an industrial perspective. We would like to be remembered as the guys who industrialised the business, which wasn't industrialised before. We never had the embedded exchange view of many in the industry. We looked at it and said, this is a process like many other processes, let's streamline it.'

That meant adopting the best available technology to enable capacity to be scaled upwards with the aim of boosting profits. Seifert realised that an exchange was a fixed cost business and once the initial investment had been made in a system that was 'scalable', every additional customer boosted returns. 'If you take it to the extreme on trading platforms, if you have enough business and you manage it properly, you can transfer top line to bottom line at basically no real marginal cost,' he observed. 'On the other hand, you are broke if transactions are not coming in. You cannot reduce your fixed costs so fast.'

His other significant insight was that exchange operators could profit hugely from vertically integrating exchange trading with clearing, settlement and custody to make a silo. He claimed that customers could also benefit from 'for-profit' operators adopting vertical integration in this way. 'I don't believe in user run utilities,' he said later.

The German financial sector was well primed for the acceptance of the silo structure. The Kassenverein, Rolf-E. Breuer noted, constituted the 'back end' of the country's stock exchanges. 'It was absolutely natural in Germany that the clearing and settlement end of the business was close to, if not belonging to, the front end of the business.'[7]

Deutsche Börse later arranged a test to prove the merits of the silo. 'To assure ourselves that this is at least the right economic perspective and because Deutsche Börse was not comparable with any other animal in this business, we formed a virtual competitor,' Seifert recalls. 'We said who is the best in class? In equity markets, it was the LSE. In derivatives – Liffe. In clearing – LCH. In settlement and custody – Euroclear. So we put together published numbers and simply measured. And the result was clear. Both Deutsche Börse and the virtual competitor were roughly the same in revenue terms, which gives you an idea of how big Deutsche Börse is. Yet Deutsche Börse did all the work, with one third less people, at lower all-in prices and with a higher profitability.'

Having worked out the merits of scale and silos, the next step was to seek more business. 'We saw clearly that Europe would have to grow together and these hurdles to cross-border trading would have to come down. These hurdles are manifold. They start with language and law: how companies incorporate and securities laws. These are all different and they saddle the investors with additional cost. We saw that the business would become more cross-border – more international. Thus, though in terms of transactions we had the largest settlement company in Europe, we wanted to internationalise ourselves.'

He says his interest in Europe transcended the business interests of Deutsche Börse. 'One of the reasons I took the job – and indoctrinated every one at Deutsche Börse – was to say: Europe's biggest chance is its capital market. We are building good products in Europe. But the labour market will not be unlocked so fast. The capital market is a great leverage we have

---

[7] Conversation with the author, 16 December 2005.

against the US, which is our global competitor. To increase capital productivity is the name of the game. Capital productivity is hampered by national barriers in Europe, with a lot of history. We have to harmonise in Europe.'

Thus armed with a business philosophy – and a clutch of paradigms divined from his analysis of the business – Seifert set out to change the status of Deutsche Börse in Germany and Europe. He succeeded dramatically in Germany, drawing heavily on Swiss computer technology and Indian software.

In 1996 Deutsche Börse merged DKV, its CSD, with the Auslandskassenverein, the specialised German ICSD. The combined entity was renamed Deutsche Börse Clearing in 1997. That same year, Deutsche Börse launched the Neue Markt for small capital and entrepreneurial growth stocks and the Xetra trading system to replace IBIS. Costing DM150 million, Xetra enabled remote membership, could be used by other stock exchanges and lowered costs for users.

In September 1998, the Eurex derivatives exchange started trading. Half owned by Deutsche Börse and SWX, the Swiss exchange company, Eurex merged the German and Swiss derivatives exchanges. It replaced DTB and the Swiss Soffex, creating in effect one bourse in two jurisdictions. In its first year, it became the world's second biggest derivatives exchange with 311 members from 14 countries and won back the Bund futures business from Liffe, which had to modernise in response, scrapping its open outcry system in favour of screen trading.

Seifert's endeavours were supported to the hilt by Rolf-E. Breuer. 'We had the greatest backing on earth from our board headed by Rolf Breuer,' Seifert says. 'He was the only guy, at least in Germany and probably including the London City, who separated his hats. He was CEO and chairman of a huge bank, part of this club of 10. But at the exchange he was wildly driving forward.'

However, Eurex notwithstanding, Seifert's record of forging partnerships in Europe was patchy. Initiatives were announced but often not concluded. In June 1997, Deutsche Börse disclosed discussions with the French stock exchange on an electronic link in anticipation of economic and monetary union. Four months later, there were reports of a plan to link the German, French and Swiss derivatives markets, so they could be traded on one computer screen. Neither project reached fruition.

Instead, in July 1998, Deutsche Börse announced plans for a single platform with the London Stock Exchange to trade the top 300 European equities. The news caused consternation in France, where the authorities thought they had a partnership with the Germans. The French finance ministry let it be known that it had only 36 hours' warning of the step. The leadership of the Paris stock exchange responded by trying to inject life into plans for a grand alliance of eight European stock exchanges, which would include London, Paris and Frankfurt.

Seifert takes the view that such chopping and changing was par for the course in the hectic days ahead of EMU. 'Look, in this industry, we have so many approaches between the various parties. And all approaches normally look convincing from the outside. But then politics come in, customers come in, vested interests come in, cultural differences come in and this is why most cooperations, acquisitions or mergers so far have failed.'

This analysis supplies one explanation for the European securities industry's inability to consolidate successfully in the 1990s and early years of the 21st century. It only partly explains why Deutsche Börse was more often than not participating in failed mergers or acquisitions.

9.3   THÉODORE IN PARIS – innovation through IT

Seifert's efforts to forge cross-border deals in Europe brought him into contact with one man more than most: Jean-François Théodore, the head of the Paris stock exchange. In his recent book,[8] Seifert describes Théodore as 'one of his oldest but most endearing opponents in the world of finance'.

Théodore and Seifert would go through many a barren courtship in the dozen or so years before Seifert was finally forced to quit Deutsche Börse in 2005. The two men were always poles apart in terms of personality. But in the 1990s, they appeared to be following similar objectives.

In his book, Seifert speaks warmly of Théodore as 'a genuinely nice person: deft and erudite, ingenious and modest'. While gently mocking his suits of 'crumpled elegance', he has also praised him as an 'old fox' with a remarkable capability for 'adroit tricks'.

It is easy to underestimate Théodore, and many have made that mistake. A quiet man, who speaks English with a pronounced French accent, Théodore can appear almost diffident. He does not strut the stage in the manner of a 'master of the universe'.

On his own turf, he has never needed to. Théodore came to the securities business in 1990 as chairman and chief executive of Société des Bourses Françaises (SBF) from the French finance ministry, the government department that helped bankroll the sector's modernisation in the late 1980s. He arrived with the strengths of training and character – and skills and tricks – that a high flying career in French government bureaucracy can confer.

The son of civil servants and a product of the prestigious École Nationale d'Administration, Théodore was well placed from the time of his graduation to become a member of France's ruling elite. After his move to SBF in 1990, Théodore became *ex-officio* a senior member of France's financial establishment, with close ties to the leaders of the finance ministry, Treasury and Banque de France. These connections were of crucial importance as he guided the SBF and France's post-trade sector in the complex environment of the late 20th and early 21st centuries.

He proved to be an able tactician: a master of delay and calculated vagueness. 'He is extremely apt at managing ambiguity to his advantage – and I say that in a very positive way,' comments one senior executive who has negotiated with Théodore. But he could take important strategic decisions and move boldly and rapidly to secure his objectives – as in October 2001, when he snatched London's Liffe derivatives exchange from under the nose of the London Stock Exchange. These qualities ensured that he would be a great survivor among Europe's securities chiefs.

Rather as Seifert was to do, Théodore took over as head of the stock exchange at a time of transition – although in France, the modernisation of the securities markets and their infrastructure had started much earlier than in Germany.

France's securities markets in the 1970s were both inefficient and expensive. A series of studies urged reform. The most important was produced by a special body – the Pérouse Commission, set up in 1979 to look into 'the modernisation of securities, trading and custody methods'. Its report pointed the way to greater use of securities deposits, book entry and dematerialisation as the elimination of securities in certificate form was known.

Financial modernisation became a policy for governments of both the left and right. Dematerialisation was taken up by the coalition of Socialists and Communists that took power in France after the 1981 presidential election victory of François Mitterrand. Portrayed as a

---

[8] *Invasion der Heuschrecken*, Berlin, 2006.

tax reform, dematerialisation was seen by many as a way of establishing the infrastructure to levy a tax on wealth. Legislation passed in 1982 and 1983 dematerialised all securities issued in France and subject to French law from 3 November 1984. Plans for destroying securities certificates were announced in January 1988 so that after 1989 securities certificates in France had no value, other than as collectors' items. All securities transactions were settled by book entry.

A period of political 'cohabitation' between 1986 and 1988, when a right of centre government took office under Mitterrand, provided a benign climate for France's capital markets. The government of prime minister Jacques Chirac embraced privatisation, boosting activity on financial markets. Computerised trading started on the Paris Bourse in June 1986. The Matif futures exchange was created in the same year and the Monep traded options market followed in September 1987.

Financial sector modernisation enjoyed state support. The finance ministry fixed brokers' fees on condition that a percentage went into a fund to overhaul financial markets and back offices. Even so, there were problems. Technical glitches, especially in the trading and settlement of registered securities, caused trades to be blocked and suspended at times. These difficulties escalated in the turbulent conditions of 1987.

'There were very big problems, especially in France after 1987,' Théodore recalls.[9] 'There were lost securities; difficulties finding the accounts. They were not physically lost because France was in the paperless environment. But settlement was very late. Especially after the crash of 1987, the brokers' back offices were horribly disorganised. There was an accumulation of fails and we had to work a lot to correct this disorder.'

At the same time, however, there were infrastructure improvements under way. In November 1987 Sicovam set up Inter-SVT,[10] a DvP system for primary dealers in the recently liberalised Treasury bond market that ensured trades were settled within 48 hours. In September 1988, the Banque de France set up Saturne[11] to provide DvP for Treasury bills and notes, later extending the system to other negotiable debt securities. Sicovam also began work on a more elaborate DvP system to serve other markets and participants that was known as Relit[12] when introduced in October 1990.

By 1989 Sicovam could claim to have greatly increased the capacity of its system and that it generally met the G30 recommendations. Nonetheless, according to Théodore, 'a complete revamping of the clearing and settlement system' was decided at the end of the 1980s. The idea was 'to build straight through processing, going directly from the exchange to clearing'.

In contrast with Germany, the French decided against any early consolidation of the companies running the nation's exchanges and post-trade services. France had two big market operating companies, each with their own clearing systems. SBF operated the Paris Bourse and Monep. Matif was the derivatives exchange founded in 1986, which also owned the commodities exchanges of Paris, Lille and Le Havre. Securities settlement was in the hands of two entities: Sicovam and Saturne, the latter being part of the Banque de France.

There was no strong pressure to merge these organisations because of the network of institutional and personal links in the French securities business. SBF, for example, held only about 5% of Sicovam. But their business plans could be dovetailed because Théodore chaired both companies from 1993 onwards.

---

[9] As told to the author, 25 July 2006.
[10] So named because it served the Spécialistes en Valeurs du Trésor (SVT).
[11] Système Automatisé de Traitment Unifié des Règlements de Créances.
[12] REglement LIvraison de Titres.

Instead of corporate consolidation, Théodore chose a technical route to straight-through processing. 'IT is the basis of everything. Integration is first IT, supported by highly skilled engineers,' he said later. 'So even if you are not an IT guy yourself, you have to take care of IT.'

The modernisation plans were expensive, costing 700 million French francs. But the project got off to a good start. Relit proved a success. Managed by Sicovam, it provided an order matching system, an order routing system to the exchange, a netting system that provided the services of a central clearing counterparty (CCP) as well as settlement. Relit provided straight-through processing in shorter settlement periods. In March 1992, the DvP deadline in France was cut from T + 5 to T + 3.

Further technical developments followed. It soon became clear that Relit and Saturne had much the same function. When in the mid-1990s, both Sicovam and the Banque de France drew up plans to build new systems, the banks, which were their clients, intervened and suggested they pool their resources.

The banks found a persuasive advocate in Théodore and a ready collaborator in Jean-Claude Trichet, governor of the Banque de France. Théodore convinced Trichet of the merits of creating a single clearing and settlement provider for the benefit of the French financial sector.

The Banque de France, Sicovam and the banks agreed a joint strategy in January 1995. The resulting 'technical consolidation' saw the transfer of the Banque de France's settlement business to Sicovam, with the central bank taking a 40% stake in the CSD in return. As part of the deal, Sicovam initiated development of RGV,[13] a high speed Relit system for large value transactions with real-time settlement that was linked to the central bank's real-time gross settlement system for payments. RGV began operating in February 1998 when it took over some of the operations previously handled by Saturne, which was closed in July that year. Relit, meanwhile, was kept for retail operations.

The decision of the Banque de France to transfer its settlement business to Sicovam was radical. It set a trend followed by other EU central banks, notably those of UK, Italy and Spain, to transfer their securities settlement activities to private sector providers.

Of equal significance was the Banque de France's support for the RGV system. In the jargon of the settlement business, RGV was an integrated system, operating with the DvP 1 model, as defined by the CPSS report of 1992. The cash leg of the settlement process was placed on the same platform as the transfer of securities.

The system was technically very efficient. But it depended on the Banque de France outsourcing to Sicovam the operations of the cash positions in central bank money. Outsourcing was not controversial when Sicovam was part of the French financial establishment and the Banque de France held 40% of the company. But it became extremely contentious inside the ECB after Sicovam became a wholly owned subsidiary of Euroclear a few years later.

Sicovam's integrated system of securities settlement using central bank money was striking testimony to the ability of the French financial establishment to adopt innovation in the design of post-trade infrastructure. Nor was it a one-off development. While RGV was still some way from completion, a further 'technical consolidation' in June 1997 paved the way for the large scale application of central counterparty clearing to French securities markets.

Central counterparty clearers, or CCPs, were not a new concept in financial markets. They were an essential part of the infrastructure for derivatives and options markets where clearing houses – often belonging to the exchanges – would act to close out contracts. As CCPs,

---

[13] Relit à Grande Vitesse.

clearing houses would act as the buyer to every seller and the seller to every buyer and, where exchanges had developed proprietary derivatives contracts, would often warehouse and manage risk exposures over time. Unlike CSDs, clearing houses acting as CCPs assumed and managed risk as principals.

Central counterparty clearing was, however, little known in the European securities business, where the process of clearing traditionally meant no more than the determination of obligations arising from a transaction. That began to change from the mid-1990s with the development of electronic trading platforms[14] which dovetailed well with CCPs. In France, the process received a huge boost in June 1997 when the Paris markets, consisting of the Bourse, Monep and Matif, agreed a technology swap with the Chicago Mercantile Exchange.

The three French markets adopted Clearing 21®, the CME's CCP system, for their CCP operations, enabling a harmonisation of clearing principles and giving market participants common access to all three markets and clearing services. In return, the CME was allowed to adopt the French NSC[15] electronic trading system in use since 1995.

In the course of 1998, ownership of the country's securities infrastructure began to change to reflect the 'technical consolidation' of June 1997. SBF took over Matif. This brought France's oldest CCP, the Banque Centrale de Compensation, into the Paris Bourse group. BCC was created in 1969 to clear contracts traded in the Paris commodity markets and became part of the Matif group when Matif acquired the commodity exchanges. By the time it became an indirect subsidiary of SBF, BCC was trading under the name of Clearnet. As such, it started offering CCP services for over-the-counter cash and repo government bond business in November 1998.

The following year, French financial markets were restructured. All regulated markets were brought together under SBF. In May 1999, the various clearing houses were also merged under the Clearnet banner. After a capital increase, Clearnet became the legally recognised vehicle for clearing trades in regulated markets as designated by the EU's Investment Services Directive. It handled equities and bonds; interest rate and commodities futures and options; equity and index futures and options; OTC traded bonds and repos.

The attractions of CCP clearing for the securities industry were several. CCPs could boost trading activity. They reduced the risks, increased liquidity and boosted the efficiency of securities transactions on exchanges. Among the advantages they provided were post-trade anonymity, which helped protect the interests of traders; the elimination of counterparty risk for market participants and more standardised terms and conditions of contracts traded.

Settlement netting by CCPs promised even greater advantages. CCP netting reduced the flow of transactions to securities settlement systems. This allowed more trades for a given settlement capacity while lowering fees for users. It also reduced the amount of regulatory capital traders needed to support their business activities.

By the end of the 1990s, France had created a thoroughly modern post-trade infrastructure through a deliberate policy of investing in technology. It is true that it looked very much like a silo for trading, clearing and settlement. Looking back, Théodore considers the vertical silo as 'a Darwinian stage in every national evolution of modernisation in the securities business'.

'We were working in response to market pressure and our needs, so that all of us in the 1990s were building vertical silos in each of our countries,' Théodore explains. 'It was the time of

---

[14] According to *Market Protection* (published in 2002 by the London Clearing House), LCH cleared a 'trickle of cash equities' in 1996 that were traded on Tradepoint, a recently established electronic exchange. The staple activity of LCH at the time was the clearing of futures and options traded on Liffe, the London Metal Exchange (LME) and the International Petroleum Exchange (IPE).

[15] Nouveau Système de Cotation.

straight-through processing and it was a vertical silo, because technically speaking, that was the answer to our problems.'

However, the French silo differed in some significant respects from that created by Seifert in Germany. It was open to outside influences: the 1997 technology swap with the CME was intended in part to promote the emergence of international trading and clearing standards. As SBF's relationship with Sicovam demonstrated, Théodore's silo-like structure did not require the common ownership of all its components. It gave considerable prominence to the existence and functions of CCPs, pioneering large scale counterparty clearing systems for equities as well as derivatives.

By the end of the 1990s, SBF and Sicovam were in contact with exchanges and post-trade service companies throughout Europe as the EU's infrastructure providers began searching for ways to bring straight-through processing at the national level into broader networks to handle the challenges of the euro and globalisation.

At this stage, controversy over whether Europe's securities markets should be structured vertically in silos, or horizontally, with separate corporate entities carrying out the various functions of securities trading and post-trade services across Europe's frontiers, lay in the future.

But France's pragmatic IT-based approach meant infrastructure providers could be more flexible in their approach to consolidation once the challenge of securities settlement in Europe shifted from creating straight-through processing at a national level to facilitating cross-border securities trading in a European single currency area. It would be possible to opt for horizontal solutions.

9.4   TAURUS AND CREST – a horizontal system by accident

When Seifert arrived at Deutsche Börse in 1993, he embarked on computerisation with some trepidation. He had good reason to. On 11 March, the day before the announcement of his appointment, the London Stock Exchange said it was scrapping Taurus,[16] a project for a dematerialised settlement system. Taurus foundered, at a cost of around £400 million to the exchange and market participants, because different vested interests in the City failed to agree on what they wanted. That and an absence of effective project leadership turned Taurus into a 'technologist's nightmare'[17] that spiralled out of control.

On the day Taurus was scrapped, the Governor of the Bank of England established a 'Task Force on Securities Settlement' to deal with the LSE's settlement needs as a matter of urgency. Headed by Pen Kent, the Bank's executive director responsible for financial structure, the task force delivered its recommendations speedily at the end of June. It recommended the creation of a new settlement system, called CREST,[18] that would replace Talisman with a service that provided electronic book entry transfer across the market; operated with a short rolling settlement cycle; retained registered stock; reduced movement of paper and provided, mainly for the retail business, the option for shareholders to keep paper certificates.

---

[16] Taurus stood for Transfer and AUtomated Registration of Uncertificated Securities.

[17] According to the *Financial Times* of 19 March 1993.

[18] The name CREST was exceptional in a business where acronyms abound. It stood for nothing in particular, although Kent later recalled that one member of his task force suggested 'Can't Remember Ever Suggesting This'. After CREST's successful launch, the market adopted 'Can't Remember Ever Supporting Taurus'.

Whereas Taurus would have confirmed a silo structure in the UK, the task force's initial report to the Governor indicated another way. The stock exchange, it said, 'does not necessarily see the provision of settlement services as part of its long term role'. The task force therefore proposed that the Bank take charge of the project. Looking further ahead, it recommended exploring whether 'ownership might later be vested in some sort of market consortium'.

So because of the stock exchange's misfortunes, the UK moved towards adopting the horizontal model for post-trade equity market services. The Bank had some experience of building settlement systems. It had created the Central Gilts Office (CGO) in 1986 in a joint project with the stock exchange and, later, the European Settlements Office (ESO), for securities denominated in Ecu, the European Currency Unit. It had a great deal of authority so that the rival vested interests that had helped scupper Taurus were less able to make their objections felt. It was also intervening on the back of a monumental failure that had cost millions of pounds and the career of the stock exchange's chief executive.

Kent took charge of CREST and recruited Iain Saville from inside the Bank as project controller. Saville and Kent took on the respective roles as 'bad cop – good cop', according to Kent.

Kent – a Bank official since 1961 – looked the quintessential Threadneedle Street man. Tall, in his pin-striped suit, he oozed authority in a quietly spoken way. Saville was younger and more abrasive. He was a mathematical physicist by training, had worked at the Bank as a statistical economist in the 1970s, had designed and marketed ESO and, before joining the CREST project, was running the UK's monetary reserves.

A major objective was to keep CREST simple and within the £29 million of finance available. This the project managers did, completing the system for £25 million. The Bank of England kept a firm grip over the project. When in October 1994, CRESTCo was capitalised to finance and manage CREST's development, it had 69 shareholders, representing all sectors of the equity market. The Bank, however, held the only voting shares until CREST's inauguration.

CREST was inaugurated in July 1996 with Saville as chief executive and Kent as chairman. It began settling securities a month later, replacing Talisman completely by April 1997. During CREST's development, the stock exchange had introduced T plus 10 day rolling settlement in July 1994 in place of the traditional fortnightly account period. In June 1995, the market moved to a shorter T plus 5 day rolling settlement cycle. CREST was designed with real-time settlement and irrevocable delivery-versus-payment in mind.

It was only as the project moved forward that the Bank defined its ideas for ownership of the system. By May 1994,[19] it was spelling out its vision of 'a utility service' that 'would be best owned by its users'. It rejected an attempt by the stock exchange to regain control of the system. Instead: 'In the Bank's eyes, ownership should be broadly based and to preclude dominance by any sector or single organisation within the industry.'

'We had gone to some trouble to break up a silo, and that was a well-considered policy choice, arrived at in discussion between the Bank of England, the Treasury and the Securities and Investment Board,'[20] Iain Saville recalls. 'We rather firmly believed we should not embed people's monopolies. At the time there was a competing exchange to the London Stock Exchange and the LSE showed signs of anxiety about that entity having access to settlement

---

[19] According to the May 1994 Bank of England *Quarterly Bulletin*.
[20] The industry's regulator.

on the same terms as its own trading platform. I'm thinking of Tradepoint, which was an electronic order book before the LSE really had one.'[21]

'I came to all this with a strong anti-silo mentality, as did my board and most of my customers: certainly the large investment banks which could absolutely see the point. Also we had rather consciously set CREST up as a principled entity – in essence, a user cooperative with a fixed dividend on its shares. We didn't want to drive a wedge between its owners and users. And we copied from the US DTC a mechanism to relate owners to users.'

Saville's priority in the first years of operation was 'to get a decent functioning system for UK and Irish equities. The notion that one had to worry about other people's securities was a crash course starting in 1998–99.'

9.5   THE SWISS VALUE CHAIN

It was no coincidence that Saville's crash course was to bring him into closer contact with the Swiss than with other European securities settlement providers.

Uniquely in Europe, the UK and Switzerland played host to international financial markets. There were, to be sure, differences between the two. London was both a trading and investing centre. The UK was home to large internationally active pension funds. London was a hub through which US institutional investors channelled their activities elsewhere in Europe and the base of the broker-dealers and big US investment banks that supported Euroclear.

In the case of Switzerland, cross-border financial flows were driven in large part by private investment that entered and left the country. The Swiss banks were therefore big 'buy side' institutions and the proportion of buy side to trading activity in the overall business activity of the larger banks helped determine whether they backed Cedel or Euroclear.

Both the UK and Switzerland had a vital interest in smoothing cross-border investment, whereas elsewhere in Europe – even in Germany and France – markets were overwhelmingly domestic. The international nature of Swiss financial markets encouraged its banks to create Intersettle,[22] a Zurich-based ICSD, in March 1988. Intersettle handled international securities transactions in currencies other than the Swiss franc on a joint platform with SEGA, the domestic CSD founded in 1970 by the Swiss banking community.

By the time of CREST's inauguration, the Swiss had created an impressively up-to-date post-trade infrastructure. The 'Swiss Value Chain' began operating in 1996 and allowed straight-through processing from trading to settlement without depending on common ownership of trading or settlement platforms.

The Swiss Value Chain was the culmination of developments stretching back more than 25 years. Its foundations were laid long before the concentration of the Swiss banking sector into two very large banks[23] and a host of smaller institutions in the final years of the 20th century. The origins of the value chain lay in the 1970s and 1980s, when Swiss banks saw a common economic interest in cooperating to improve the country's financial infrastructure. They were the drivers of change in the country's securities settlement business, drawing heavily on their experience of payments infrastructure to innovate.

SEGA, the Swiss CSD, was quickly accepted by the country's stock exchanges after its foundation in 1970. A cash leg was added in 1982, using central bank money. But delivery of

---

[21] Conversation with the author, 20 September 2005.
[22] Swiss Corporation for International Securities Settlement.
[23] Crédit Suisse and UBS: the latter after a thinly disguised reverse takeover of UBS by Swiss Bank Corp.

the securities still lagged payment by several days, creating a less than ideal situation for the cash managers of the big Swiss banks. As all purpose banks, these sought to benefit from a concentration of liquidity from securities and payments activities.

Their cause was taken up by senior bank managers and in particular by Robert Studer, head of finance at UBS between 1980 and 1988. Studer, who rose to become president of the UBS executive board in 1991 and chairman of the board of directors five years later, had a long standing interest in back office issues. He played a big part in the appointment of Lussi to run Cedel.

At the initiative of the big Swiss banks, work began in 1980 on developing Swiss Interbank Clearing (SIC), a real-time gross settlement (RTGS) system designed for settling interbank payments in Swiss francs in accounts at the Swiss National Bank. SIC, which pre-dated RTGS systems elsewhere in Europe, began operating in 1987.

SEGA meanwhile began developing SECOM, a settlement platform that allowed for simultaneous, final irrevocable delivery. SECOM was launched in October 1993 and linked to SIC in March 1995 to allow final and irrevocable DvP in real time. The Swiss Value Chain was completed in 1996 when SIC's payment and SECOM's securities settlement systems were linked to SWX, the Swiss electronic exchange. SWX's trading platform had replaced the open outcry trading 'rings' in the stock exchanges of Zurich, Basel and Geneva only a few months before.

Thanks to the Swiss Value Chain, SWX's electronic platform could now provide investors with fully automated and integrated trading, clearing and settlement of all securities transactions.

Swiss banks were the indirect owners of Switzerland's payment, settlement and trading activities. Swiss Interbank Clearing AG, the operator of SIC, was a subsidiary of Telekurs, a private sector payments company dominated by the big Swiss banks. SEGA and Intersettle were also owned by the Swiss banking community, but through a completely different company. SWX, while also owned by banks, had a different shareholder register than either SEGA or SIC: it harked back to the clubby ownership structure established for Swiss stock exchanges during the years of floor trading.

In May 1999, there was a consolidation in the Swiss securities settlement industry when SEGA and Intersettle merged to form SIS SegaInterSettle under a new holding company, FSG Swiss Financial Services Group. This merger presaged attempts by SIS, as SIS SegaInterSettle was generally known, to build up business elsewhere in Europe. As before, the value chain came under the control of no single corporate entity.

9.6   DIFFERENT BLUEPRINTS

The coming of the euro presented the EU's securities settlement providers with a dilemma. Consolidation within national markets and technical advances had greatly increased the efficiency of CSDs in the member states. But they were ill suited to a single currency area, where it was generally expected there would be few remaining barriers to cross-border trading. The ICSDs, on the other hand, had plenty of cross-border expertise. But their business was concentrated on Eurobonds and government securities. Despite the best efforts of Euroclear in particular, they had only a small percentage of the market for settling cross-border equity trades.

Jean-François Théodore remembers how 'at the end of the 90s, when the euro was being created, every market player was persuaded that it would be very dangerous to be purely national in Euroland'. The upshot was 'a search – independent of the big game going on about exchanges and trading – for some kind of agreement that would keep the straight-through process, which we still have and which is needed, and yet would include the CSDs, of which Sicovam was the French one, in a more global network'.[24]

The months before the euro's launch witnessed an intensification of contacts across the securities settlement industry and the elaboration, on the part of some providers, of ideas for reconciling vertical integration to the needs of the single currency area.

During 1998, Deutsche Börse Clearing came close to linking with the Austrian and Swiss CSDs. Euroclear and Cedel also had discussions with the SIS during that year. CREST of the UK began to reach out to other settlement providers through the framework of ECSDA, the European CSD association founded in November 1997. In the second half of 1998, Euroclear had fairly detailed talks with Sicovam on platform cooperation. But ahead of the switch to the euro, the talks remained just that. There was neither sufficient ambition nor fear to precipitate any mergers or other steps towards consolidation.

Many users looked with envy across the Atlantic, where the integration of post-trade infrastructure was nearing completion. At the end of the 1990s, the US economy was enjoying strong growth, rising productivity and a boom in 'new economy' activities linked to the spread of information technology. Academic literature suggested that the US's securities-based financial structure was superior to the bank-based financial systems of many European countries in encouraging economic development. As the trading infrastructure in the US was in large part inferior to screen-based systems adopted in Europe, the conviction grew that it was the low cost, integrated, continent-wide post-trade infrastructure which gave the US an advantage.

Talks began in the summer of 1998 on integrating the US equities CCP – the National Securities Clearing Corporation or NSCC – and the CSD – The Depository Trust Company or DTC. Nine months later, the two boards gave their approval. On 4 November 1999, The Depository Trust & Clearing Corporation (DTCC) was created to consolidate US clearing and settlement infrastructures for equities in a low cost, user-governed, regulated monopoly. As well as charging what were thought to be the lowest fees in the world, DTCC promised to speed the introduction of new products, services and technologies for its users.

The DTCC model, combining a CCP and CSD, undoubtedly had its attractions. But it was not obvious that it could be transposed to the EU. The DTCC was the product of an extraordinarily grave paperwork crisis that in the 1960s had shut US exchanges for one day every week. This crisis generated a determination in the US securities industry to solve the problem, while there was no such common purpose in the EU securities industry. The DTCC operated in a single country, with a single language, a single currency, a powerful single securities regulator, a common regulatory framework and a relatively homogeneous tax and legal system. The problem of cross-border settlement, of such importance in Europe, did not figure on the US radar screen.

The DTCC was a product of decisive legislative action and yet the process that turned the NSCC and DTC into monopoly providers had lasted some 20 years. Nor were the two companies without critics. European settlement providers would mutter that monopoly status made them slow to innovate and that they were technologically behind the curve.[25]

---

[24] Conversation with the author, 25 July 2006.
[25] A charge that is difficult to sustain in the case of DTCC since the 1999 merger.

However, André Lussi of Cedel was influenced by developments in the US. 'I remember thinking that if the euro was to come true, we needed a European infrastructure. I wanted clearing, settlement and custody all concentrated into one utility,' he said later.[26]

Cedel, which at the time saw itself as leading efforts to consolidate the post-trade sector in Europe, devised a 'European Clearing House' model. First outlined in 1997, this would link infrastructure providers at different levels of integration, ranging downwards from full mergers through technical ties such as delivery versus payment (DvP) links to looser cooperation agreements.

Although hoping ultimately to create a European DTC, the Cedel model was in fact more nuanced than the US example. Sometimes presented as a pyramid, it recognised the problems of consolidating Europe's fragmented infrastructure by acknowledging that CSDs and ICSDs could find appropriate levels of cooperation with each other short of merging.

Euroclear was developing what became known as the hub and spokes model. This sought to harness the existing infrastructure of the two ICSDs and the 30 or so national CSDs in Europe to give cross-border investors access to all clearing and settlement services through a single point of entry.

The model would cater for different types of user. It would link the 'spokes' – the national CSDs – to a single 'hub', which – although it was not clearly spelled out – would be a merged entity formed of Euroclear and Cedel. The hub and the spokes would have clearly defined roles, underpinned by agreement among the constituents on which member depository was best suited to perform certain tasks. These would be allocated according to their respective core competences, closeness to the markets or client base.

The hub would serve as the main cross-border settlement provider for globally active clients such as broker-dealers, custodians and investment managers. There would be a high concentration of assets and counterparties in the hub to guarantee the greatest possible settlement efficiency. It would be supported by integrated credit facilities, collateral management and sophisticated core custody services.

While global securities would be administered in the hub, the spokes would be responsible for the majority of securities that would still be issued in domestic markets.

The spokes would settle high volume, domestic, retail-driven securities transactions and could even settle the domestic transactions of globally active clients. They would be the system's point of contact with the various domestic markets and therefore be responsible for the supply and quality of securities information to the hub and the system as a whole. They would have an important role in securities issuance and communications with issuers, registrars and tax authorities. They would act as the primary securities depositories for domestic issuers and provide users with settlement and custody services for foreign securities through their links with the hub.

Euroclear claimed that hub and spokes, by avoiding a fragmentation of assets and counterparties, would reduce frictional costs and the inefficient use of collateral. It would avoid duplication of functions. And because it leveraged existing infrastructure, it would be cheap and quick to implement.

But hub and spokes had a great potential weakness. It was difficult to see Euroclear as an acceptable promoter of takeovers or partner in mergers with national CSDs in a process of European consolidation as long as it was operated by a large US bank.

---

[26] Interview with author, 1 December 2005.

Hub and spokes received mixed reviews when unveiled in May 1999. In general the big investment bank users, which would settle through the hub, were supportive. But it had little appeal for managers of the national CSDs or many supporters of Cedel.

Opponents saw the relationship of hub to spoke as one of master to servant, in which Euroclear would be the dominant player and the national CSDs would be left gradually to die. Lussi was dismissive. The spokes, he said,[27] 'would have to yield ground to the hub and give up their independence. This would revive the old political factionalisms that have characterised previous failed attempts to create a pan-European solution.' Chris Tupker, who had recently joined the Euroclear board, has since admitted that hub and spokes 'was badly thought through: who wants to be a spoke, when you can be a hub?'[28]

Another model doing the rounds was the 'spaghetti' model, based on links or interoperable systems among the CSDs. This was advocated by ECSDA and promoted by SIS and CREST. Like hub and spokes, the spaghetti model had the advantage of enabling local users to access just their national CSD to settle deals in both international and domestic securities. Each national settlement system would act as a hub for its users by establishing bilateral links with other national CSDs. It would be through these bilateral links that settlement, custody and collateral services would be offered for cross-border securities transactions.

Critics argued that the model would be costly and queried whether there would be sufficient business between many of the smaller national CSDs to justify the creation of 'bridges' or DvP links between them. When the ECSDA model was first mooted, there were 29 CSDs in Europe. According to the maths, more than 800 links would be required to link each bilaterally. According to Werner Seifert, even a simple bridge cost about €10 million when IT, testing and roll-out costs were taken into account.[29]

However, Iain Saville, CREST's chief executive, saw the spaghetti model as a high-tech solution in which a network of CSDs, offering real-time settlement, would be linked by detailed, standardised message protocols. Using ECSDA as a forum for discussions, he worked with the Swiss, Italian and Scandinavian CSDs, all of which either had or were developing real-time capabilities, to establish the protocols for such a system to function.

Taken together, the various models highlighted the absence of any consensus on how to reshape Europe's clearing and settlement industries. The euro's creation may have been Europe's biggest step towards integration in a generation but – in advance of its launch – it had not provided a sufficient spur to consolidation among the EU's securities settlement companies.

---

[27] As quoted in the *Financial Times* of 14 May 1999.
[28] In a conversation with the author, 27 March 2006. Tupker became chairman of Euroclear in March 2000, succeeding Sir Andrew Large.
[29] In a conversation with the author, 12 October 2005.

10

Corporate Manoeuvrings

May is a curious month in the European business calendar. Punctuated as it is by public holidays, it is well suited for the staging of corporate surprises and often for plotting.

On Friday 14 May 1999, three of Europe's leading financial infrastructure providers dropped a bombshell. At a press conference in Luxembourg, the chief executives of Deutsche Börse, Cedel International and the Paris Bourse announced the merger of their securities settlement activities.

The appearance of Werner Seifert, André Lussi and Jean-François Théodore before the press when much of Europe was in the middle of the Ascension holiday weekend followed months, if not years, of informal contacts among securities industry executives about the sector's future; some weeks of serious negotiation between Deutsche Börse and Cedel, and a whirlwind courtship of Sicovam, the French CSD, by Cedel, acting for itself and its new German partner.

Seifert and Lussi disclosed that Deutsche Börse Clearing, the CSD belonging to the German stock exchange, and Cedel would merge their clearing, settlement and custody activities to create 'new Cedel International'. At the same time, SBF Group, the holding company of the Paris Bourse, and Sicovam, the French CSD, signed a memorandum of understanding to join the new venture once it was legally established. The announcements marked the beginning of four hectic years that were dramatically to change the structure of the European settlement industry, without achieving the far reaching consolidation that most users wished.

10.1 PRESSURE FOR CHANGE

The tripartite deal surprised many because for much of the previous year market gossip had focused on the possibility of combining Euroclear and Cedel. There was a strong feeling among many users that the interests of the international bond market could be well served by a cost cutting merger of the two ICSDs.

Rolf-E. Breuer, who stepped down after nearly 14 years as chairman of Euroclear in April 1998, came to the conclusion that a merger with Cedel would make a lot of sense. 'It seemed to me – and this was my judgement based on my experience as chairman of Euroclear – that prices had hit rock bottom. There was nothing left,' Breuer recalled.[1] 'And that brought about the idea: do we really need two [ICSDs] in parallel, with high costs of IT systems up to standard, development, counterparty risks and the nightmare of the functioning and not so well functioning Bridge between the two? So that brought about the question: are two institutions really necessary? And wouldn't a merger make sense?'

There were shareholders and board members of Cedel who sympathised with Breuer. In September 1997 Cedel had tried to raise $300 million from its shareholders to finance an investment and expansion programme that included preparations for EMU. However, the

---

[1] Interview with the author, 16 December 2005.

'voluntary subscription', which was not underwritten, raised only $120.2 million in new equity, indicating a lack of enthusiasm for Lussi's ambitions.

But there were other drivers at work: notably the difficulty of developing and installing new technologies and the very different personalities and ambitions of the senior executives of leading settlement providers. After these had come into play, the end result of four years of corporate manoeuvrings would be very different to the templates proposed by the infrastructure providers at the end of the 20th century.

Platforms, and the costs and challenges of updating them, were a growing preoccupation for settlement systems as the 1990s drew to a close. Demands on IT and financial resources grew as increased pressure from regulators and users to shift towards real-time settlement coincided with the need to adapt systems for the switch to the euro and to take steps against the Y2K millennium bug.

Euroclear's decision on 5 May 1998 to delay its 'Next' real-time settlement system showed how even the most experienced operators could run into difficulties. The delay was a blow to Euroclear's pride and dented its pocket. And it came at a very sensitive time, when national CSDs and the two ICSDs were jockeying for position to exploit any move towards consolidation in the securities business following the euro's launch.

'What played in the background was the realisation that we were heading to the euro, and it would become a rat race,' Peter Sucaet, chief auditor of Euroclear, remembers. 'There would be mergers and acquisitions down the line and the strongest would win out. And they would be the ones with the best technology, in other words: a real-time settlement system. People were thinking that those who could team up successfully would be those with proven expertise who could demonstrate that they could be reliable partners. There was something of a real-time settlement bubble. That was why Euroclear's decision not to launch real-time in 1998 was a big thing. It weakened Euroclear's strategic position. It created an opportunity for Lussi to take the lead. And that became the opening gambit for merger mania.'[2]

Euroclear was not the only company experiencing platform problems. Towards the end of 1998, Deutsche Börse ran into difficulties delivering a real-time settlement platform called Trust.[3] Deutsche Börse's management was rumoured to have spent between 18 months to two years and DM100 million and DM150 million on the project only to tell the board that it was behind schedule and would require further substantial financing. The board declined to authorise the additional spending and suggested that Seifert look for a partner.

Seifert visited Euroclear in Brussels with the encouragement of Rolf-E. Breuer, the head of the Börse's supervisory board. 'I always fostered the discussions and said: why do you not talk to each other because it seemed to me to make a lot of sense,' Breuer recalls.

According to Bomans, Seifert proposed that Deutsche Börse merge its securities settlement activities with Euroclear on a 50–50 basis.[4] The Euroclear chief executive turned him down on the grounds that Seifert was putting too high a value on Deutsche Börse's settlement infrastructure. Bomans also insisted that Euroclear should take the lead in any merged entity. The two met a second time in a conference room at Frankfurt airport but again reached no agreement. Seifert concluded that Deutsche Börse would not be able to get together with Euroclear.

---

[2] Conversation with the author, 17 January 2006.
[3] TRUe SettlemenT system.
[4] As told to the author, 30 September 2005.

10.2   A EUROPEAN CLEARING HOUSE?

But another potential partner was not far away. In 1997, André Lussi visited Seifert to explore the possibility of cooperation in the context of the European Clearing House scheme. 'I went to see the Germans twice,' Lussi recalls. 'The first time, they didn't want to pursue my vision. The second time Seifert did.'[5]

Lussi met Seifert for their second meeting around the end of 1998. Deutsche Börse's management was expecting a courtesy call. But Lussi had something to offer. Cedel was developing a modern platform of its own, known as Creation. Admittedly, Creation was conceived for an ICSD, an environment where Cedel could create coherent rules for a homogeneous set of clients. There could be problems adapting it to the needs of Deutsche Börse Clearing, the German CSD, with its large scale settlement of domestic equities. But unabashed, Lussi presented Creation as the platform for Europe and Seifert seemed happy to concur.

'Trust was a good platform – at least on paper – we never built it,' Seifert said later.[6] 'Creation was a good platform too. Why finance two, if you can have one? It was definitely the platform issue that was a driving force to put the two companies together. This is a fixed cost business and the costs are to a large extent platform costs.'

On 30 January, Cedel and Deutsche Börse began exploratory talks with a view to merging Cedel International and Deutsche Börse Clearing. Two weeks later, teams from both sides got down to tackling the economic, legal and technical questions associated with the project, codenamed 'Cerberus'.

It was envisaged that the business activities, staff, shareholdings and other assets and liabilities of Cedel International and DBC would be transferred to a new Luxembourg public limited company which would be owned 50% by Deutsche Börse and 50% by Cedel International. Known variously as New Cedel International or the European Clearing House, the new company would use Cedel technology and be run by Cedel's top management, with Lussi as chief executive and Douglass as chairman. Final agreement required some difficult horse trading and was only possible after Deutsche Börse paid Cedel $103 million to offset a difference in valuation.

The link between Deutsche Börse and Cedel suited Lussi very well. Some of Cedel's users and shareholders would have liked a merger with Euroclear.[7] But in fact there was little in a combination of the two ICSDs to attract Cedel's chief executive.

Lussi was deeply disliked at Euroclear. True, he and Bomans had developed a habit of meeting roughly every six months for lunch on neutral territory between Brussels and Luxembourg to discuss issues of mutual interest. Bomans recalls Lussi making an informal proposal at one of their early meetings to put their two systems together. But the contacts did nothing to foster good relations between the two men. There was no way that Euroclear under Bomans would play second fiddle to Lussi. Nor was Lussi willing to deal with Euroclear from a position of inferiority. The first job to go in any deal in which Euroclear was the dominant partner would be Lussi's.

'They always wanted to merge, but by taking us over,' Lussi said later of Euroclear. 'My ambition was always to be better than Euroclear, to be number one. I wanted to take Euroclear over. I always said: it is not an issue of Euroclear and Cedel but one of whether we have a European institution or a European company dominated by the Americans.'

---

[5] As told to the author, 1 December 2005.

[6] Interview with the author, 12 October 2005.

[7] There have been suggestions – strongly denied by Lussi and close associates – that his board asked him to negotiate with Euroclear instead of which Lussi reportedly went to Frankfurt to meet Seifert.

In Seifert, Lussi thought he had found a partner who shared his vision of a 'European' solution for the industry. When they met for the second time, Lussi challenged Seifert about his talks with Bomans: 'I said with whom do you want to merge: an independent entity like Cedel or JP Morgan?'

Lussi outlined his European ideas to Seifert before the two sides began talks. 'I had this vision that we must have the French as well as the Germans. Europe only works if the French and Germans work together. So I agreed with Seifert that we [Cedel and Deutsche Börse Clearing] should merge in 1999. A couple of months before, I told Seifert we needed to have the French on board. And everybody agreed.'

As later became clear, that agreement – if ever it existed in formal terms – was fragile. Seifert had different priorities to Lussi. Securities settlement was only one part of a bigger business that had to be judged on economic criteria. Seifert's experience at Deutsche Börse taught him that a silo system in which the exchange also controlled clearing and settlement was the best and most cost effective way of delivering a straight-through process.

'Tell me a system that runs through an order faster than others, cheaper than others and more secure than others. The result is clear. In terms of efficiency, speed and security, nothing can match a silo,' Seifert says. 'If you can put everything on one IT platform, if you can have an IT strategy prioritised according to the whole chain; if you don't need several human resources departments but only one, for example, then silo people would be dumb and should be fired immediately if they cannot be more efficient.'

But Seifert bent these rules when he negotiated the merger of Deutsche Börse Clearing and Cedel. The 50–50 deal meant he ceded control over Deutsche Börse's settlement and custody business. Deutsche Börse was no longer certain of controlling the group's overall strategy in areas such as IT, customer segmentation or product markets. This structure appeared fine so long as the new Cedel operated successfully. But when problems surfaced, the merger of equals between DBC and Cedel proved to be built on unstable foundations.

10.3   A MEETING OF MINDS IN MARRAKECH

The 8 May anniversary of the end of the Second World War in Europe is a public holiday in France. In 1999 the date fell on a Saturday, prompting Sicovam to arrange a seminar in Morocco, mixing business and pleasure, for its consultative committee over the long weekend.

Some 20 or so members of the market advisory body – drawn from users and banks friendly to Sicovam – gathered on Friday 7 May for a working session in a guest house in Marrakech that was kept for the use of the Paris Bourse, Clearnet and the French settlement company. But as the seminar gave way to the more social agenda on Saturday and Sunday, the guests could not help noticing that three of their hosts were unaccountably absent for much of the time.

Jean François Théodore, chairman of both Sicovam and SBF Group, Joël Mérère, chief executive of Sicovam and Serge Harry, Sicovam's general secretary, were holed up in conditions of great secrecy in a specially rented villa in another part of town with a negotiating team from Cedel.

The weekend's double booking had been precipitated by a visit to Paris by André Lussi some days before.

Lussi met Théodore and Mérère for breakfast in Paris on Wednesday 5 May and told them that the following week – on Friday 14 May – he and Seifert would announce the merger between Cedel and Deutsche Börse Clearing.

He wanted Sicovam to join the party so he could announce a tripartite deal that would act as a motor of consolidation in the European securities settlement industry. It was not quite a matter of 'take it or leave it'. But the invitation left little time for Sicovam to negotiate and evaluate the offer.

Lussi's ideas found a ready audience, nonetheless. 'At this point of time, there was a strong desire in Paris to do something with Frankfurt, not least because previous attempts with stock exchanges and derivatives markets had failed,' Joël Mérère recalls.[8]

The board of Sicovam had been reviewing the prospects for national CSDs in the new environment of the single currency and mandated its management to explore cooperation with others, covering all possibilities from technical cooperation to full mergers. As Sicovam's chairman, Jean-François Théodore found considerable merit in Cedel's approach.

France's financial elite saw an opportunity to make up for a history of fruitless flirtations between Germany and France in the financial services area. There had been attempts to merge the French and German stock exchanges and futures markets in the 1990s that came to nothing. The euro had only recently been launched. Although France and Germany were no longer led by passionate Europeans of the stamp of François Mitterrand and Helmut Kohl, the two countries still saw themselves as the 'motor' of the European Union.

An important supporter was Jean-Claude Trichet, governor of the Banque de France since 1993. The Paris Bourse was effectively in control of Sicovam because Théodore chaired both entities. But the French central bank had a big interest in the settlement company. It owned 40% of Sicovam following its merger in the 1990s with Saturne, the central bank's own settlement system for Treasury bills and short-term paper. As operator of the French payments system, the Banque de France was involved with Sicovam because its real-time settlement engine – Relit à Grande Vitesse – was an integrated system that operated securities accounts and cash positions for the banks in central bank money. The French central bank was also a supervisor of Sicovam because, under a law of 1993, it had responsibility for monitoring systemic risk in the financial system.

Having conducted French monetary policy through the 1990s by linking the French franc to the D-mark through the 'franc fort' policy, Trichet himself was a strong supporter of Franco-German partnership. He was an enthusiastic European integrationist and already marked out as a future president of the European Central Bank.

But the adherence of Sicovam to the tripartite memorandum was not a foregone conclusion. 'Sicovam at the time was in very good shape, with good systems, very good technology, a strong business. If it were to consider negotiations, it took the view it was better to consider negotiations from a position of strength,' Mérère adds. The talks in Marrakech lasted a day and a half – exposing Sicovam's trio of negotiators to quizzical glances from the seminar participants at the dinner in the guest house on Saturday night. It was around midday Sunday that the Sicovam team, headed by Théodore, reached agreement on the memorandum of understanding with the Cedel negotiators led by Carlos Salvatori, Lussi's deputy. There was no representative of Deutsche Börse present.

Sicovam decided to inform Euroclear of the emerging memorandum during the weekend's discussions. The two companies were not strangers to each other. There had been some promising contacts between Euroclear and Sicovam in the second half of 1998 which, for Euroclear at least, appeared more serious than others.

---

[8] Interview with the author, 8 December 2005.

'They were not at all centred on a merger of the entities,' explains Pierre Francotte, who at the time was head of Euroclear's transaction processing division.[9] In the aftermath of Euroclear's decision to postpone the introduction of real-time settlement, the two were exploring how to create synergies from platform technology, either through a common platform or separate but compatible platforms. 'This was because Sicovam was working on its RGV platform and Euroclear was looking for a way as well to have platform improvements.'

It was in the course of his discussions with Sicovam board members at this time that Bomans learned at first hand how Trichet favoured a tie up with the Germans rather than with Euroclear. He visited the governor at the central bank and remembers being told that with the euro on the horizon, the position of the Banque de France would 'never be far removed from that of the Bundesbank'.

The ideas for a joint venture with Sicovam also caused some debate in the Euroclear board. While Bomans was very much in favour of an alliance with Sicovam, Herschel Post, who had joined the Euroclear board in the mid-1990s as a representative of the National Westminster Bank group, argued that a more strategic target for Euroclear would be CREST, the British CSD.

During the May 1999 Marrakech meeting, Sicovam told Euroclear it was receiving a proposal that could be very attractive for the French market place from a political – meaning Franco-German – standpoint. It suggested Euroclear speed up its internal consideration of links to Sicovam.

Euroclear's board responded. At an emergency meeting, it put together a proposal. It fell short of a merger – just. But, according to Bomans, it 'gave away a lot of things we never meant to give away'. The board proposed a deal that would have given Sicovam equal governance rights with Euroclear.

The two companies would be shareholders in a new holding company that would set policy for the combined Euroclear-Sicovam group. The respective shareholdings of ECSplc and Sicovam would be determined, subject to valuation and analysis. But, without waiting for this, ECS was prepared to offer Sicovam 50% voting rights in the new company and a corresponding position in its board of directors.

Mérère and Harry visited Euroclear in Brussels on Tuesday 11 May, returning to Paris later that day. The Euroclear board met in the late afternoon and early evening. Its proposal was transmitted to Paris just before midnight. When the Sicovam board met the following day, Théodore put two offers on the table: the memorandum of understanding for a European Clearing House with Cedel and DBC and the joint venture with Euroclear.

The Sicovam board opted for the trilateral solution. According to Mérère, Euroclear's proposal was 'politically too late'. Bomans remembers receiving a call from Théodore. 'He said: "I'm sorry, Luc, we have a firm proposal from Cedel and the Germans and we join that party. We looked at your proposal, but this is what it is." I remember telling Théodore in French, "Jean-François, you close the door but remember, I don't lock it".'[10]

10.4   DARK DAYS FOR EUROCLEAR

Lussi was cock-a-hoop. The announcement in Luxembourg was, he declared, 'a historic day for the integration of the capital markets of Europe'.[11] He had the added satisfaction of hearing

[9] Interview with the author, 28 September 2005.
[10] Interview with the author, 30 September 2005.
[11] Quoted in the *Financial Times*, 17 May 1999.

his German partner admit Cedel's technological superiority: 'For the first time, I don't have to claim we have the best systems,' Seifert said.[12]

The Sicovam decision was a serious blow to Euroclear and morale suffered accordingly. Its dominance of cross-border securities settlement in Europe was threatened. Its hub and spokes model was thrown into doubt. The tripartite memorandum of understanding among the three settlement systems was mould breaking: by merging CSDs with an ICSD it offered a pole of attraction that was 'European, neutral and open for others to join'[13] along the lines of Cedel's European Clearing House model.

It also held out the possibility of a more far reaching consolidation along the securities industry value chain. DBC was linked to continental Europe's most important cash market – Germany. Cedel was one of Europe's two ICSDs controlling settlement of the over-the-counter fixed income market. Sicovam had its widely admired real time settlement engine. Although the Paris bourse held only slightly more than 5% of Sicovam's equity (with the rest held by the Banque de France and French banks), trading, clearing and settlement in France – as elsewhere in Europe – operated in silo-like conditions. And sandwiched between the stock exchange's trading platform and Sicovam was Clearnet, a clearing house that was 100% owned by the Paris bourse and which at the time had the only up and running central counterparty (CCP) for a big equities cash market in Europe.

The new entity appeared poised to be a significant player vis-à-vis the alliance of eight stock exchanges that had agreed to work towards the creation of a pan-European trading system for the most liquid European stocks. There was also the partnership agreed between the Frankfurt and London exchanges in July 1998 to harmonise markets for leading UK and German securities. Infrastructure providers had already started to adapt to these manoeuvrings. Earlier in May 1999, CREST had unveiled its own plan to link with Deutsche Börse Clearing by settling trades in German equities for its own members from 2000.

10.5 THE FIGHT BACK BEGINS

But Euroclear did not stand still. Its fight back began in the early summer of 1999 when ISMA, the International Securities Market Association, began looking for a partner to develop a CCP for Coredeal, an electronic bond trading system that it planned to launch the following year.

For many, Clearnet, with an operating CCP under its belt, appeared the obvious choice. But Euroclear reasoned that a central counterparty for Eurobonds under Clearnet's control would pose a threat to its core business. It began to design and develop a system of its own called TradeGO. Despite its inexperience with CCPs, Euroclear won the support of market participants in London. The backing of the broker-dealer community – which had been so important to Euroclear's growth in the past – then ensured that TradeGO was accepted by ISMA. 'Euroclear was able to win the deal by saying it had a lot of experience in Eurobonds. It knew how to value Eurobonds, and therefore how to value an exposure. So it could build a central counterparty for ISMA rather quickly,' Ignace Combes explained.[14] Coredeal with TradeGO never grew to be a large scale business. But Euroclear's success at the expense of a combination of Clearnet, Cedel and Eurex, the Deutsche Börse subsidiary, was a setback for the new Cedel partners.

---

[12] Quoted in the *Financial Times*, 17 May 1999.
[13] Joint statement of 14 May 1999.
[14] Interview with the author, 20 February 2006.

Some of the big investment institutions that supported Euroclear over TradeGO were also casting a critical eye at the way the settlement industry was consolidating. Very soon after the announcement of the trilateral link-up between the German, French and Luxembourg settlement systems, Marcel Ospel, the group chief executive officer of UBS, and Sir David Walker, chairman of Morgan Stanley Dean Witter Europe, founded the European Securities Industry Users' Group (Esiug) with the aim of bringing the influence of the biggest users of securities services to bear on the inefficiencies of the post-trade part of the value chain.

Esiug showed how far securities settlement had become a boardroom preoccupation. Because it was organised by Walker and Ospel, the group attracted high-level participants, including Chris Tupker who represented ABN AMRO. At its foundation in May 1999, the group declared that consolidation in Europe's settlement industry should aim at reducing risks, cut running and investment costs by eliminating duplication, and also be accompanied by 'strong countervailing governance' to make up for any reduction of competition among providers.

The users were soon at odds with the emerging Cedel/DBC/Sicovam group. The press reported their fears that Deutsche Börse and the Banque de France would have excessive influence over the planned trilateral group. Some complained that Lussi was seeking the right to negotiate detailed terms of the merger without having to obtain additional backing along the way from Cedel shareholders.

Tupker and a number of others formed a working group in Esiug to develop a strategy for the securities industry. 'We came up with this idea of horizontal integration by layers of the trading, the clearing and settlement as opposed to vertical integration,' Tupker explains. 'And we started to articulate the benefits of that compared with what Seifert was doing.'

Of more immediate impact was a growing disenchantment in Paris as the negotiations to flesh out the tripartite memorandum of understanding moved forward. The problems encountered by Sicovam would, in turn, expose differing priorities and tensions between Lussi and Seifert.

'We came to what we thought could be an agreement but during the summer it looked more and more difficult,' Jean-François Théodore remembers.[15] 'Deutsche Börse took some initiatives of its own. We had negotiated more bilaterally with Cedel than trilaterally with Deutsche Börse. When Deutsche Börse came into the field, they raised new issues. These were complicated: part of the original agreement was the use of the Sicovam system on the one side and the Creation system of Cedel on the other side.'

On the Deutsche Börse side, managers felt they were being kept in the dark by Cedel about important details of the French participation. It was only in June 1999 that Deutsche Börse was brought into the negotiations between Cedel and Sicovam. By that time there was considerable mistrust in Frankfurt of the emerging ties between the Luxembourg and French partners.

Cracks in the three-way alliance appeared in public in late June when Jean-Marc Eyssautier, director of commercial relations at Sicovam, made clear it wanted to keep its real-time settlement system. 'We are very proud of RGV. We think we are market leaders in this regard,' he declared.[16]

The financial details of the deal with Cedel and DBC were a still bigger bone of contention. Differences emerged over how Clearnet fitted into the arrangement: were its links to Sicovam to be factored in or not? These problems added to valuation problems that were bubbling below the surface and were to drive a wedge between Sicovam's putative partners.

---

[15] Conversation with the author, 25 July 2006.
[16] Quoted in the *Financial Times*, 1 July 1999.

The 14 May announcement said the three participants in the deal to create New Cedel International agreed 'to become true partners'. But the level of participation of the SBF Group and Sicovam was left to 'be decided on the basis of a fair valuation, consistent with that used in the merger of Cedel International and Deutsche Börse Clearing'.

André Lussi remembers being left in no doubt as to the French position after a discussion of the MoU with Théodore. 'He said to me: "Look, André: One third, one third, one third". And I said: "No, a valuation". And he said: "Look, listen to me very carefully, André: one third". And I started to think about it and I said: "He is right. He would never give in and be at a table where he is in a minority." You see, it is still *la Grande Nation*: still today. This mentality that they rule Europe and rule Brussels is very deep in the French mentality.'

Such considerations cut no ice with Werner Seifert and his top managers, however. In discussions during the summer of 1999, Seifert insisted that Sicovam's share of the combined entity was worth less than 30%.

So, while the merger of DBC and Cedel advanced, the talks with Sicovam began to drag. Despite Esiug's objections, the banks comprising Cedel's shareholders voted for the merger of DBC and Cedel by a substantial majority on 15 July. An upbeat Lussi predicted that merger talks with Sicovam would be finished by the end of September.

It was not to be. Shortly before that year's Sibos conference, which took place in Munich between 13 and 17 September, Luc Bomans learned that Sicovam was not happy with the tripartite deal because the Germans appeared to be taking the lead.

Sicovam was concerned that RGV would be scrapped, damaging the French banks, which as Sicovam shareholders would forfeit their investment in the project. Although it was still not operational, the French were becoming increasingly sceptical about the quality of Cedel's new Creation system. In addition, the French objected that valuing Sicovam at just 30% of the combined entity took no account of the value that Clearnet would bring to the project. They had made sure Clearnet was in the memorandum of understanding with Deutsche Börse and Cedel. With its functioning cash market CCP, Clearnet justified valuing Sicovam as an equal one third partner in the venture.

Bomans followed up information he gleaned at Sibos with a visit to Paris. He met Sicovam board members to sound them out on a link with Euroclear. Although the Banque de France still favoured a link between Paris and Frankfurt, Bomans was in a far stronger position than in May when Sicovam called on Euroclear to better the Franco-German offer. On 1 September, a fortnight before the Sibos meeting, Euroclear announced it was to part company from JP Morgan, its founder and operator of the Euroclear system for more than 30 years.

Lille, in northern France close to the Belgian border, became the venue for secret talks between Euroclear and Sicovam management once the agreed period for exclusive negotiations between Sicovam and Deutsche Börse and Cedel expired in mid-October.

10.6   THE FRENCH DEFECT

On 2 November 1999 Cedel and Deutsche Börse signed the legal papers formalising the merger of Cedel International with DBC. The merged entity – New Cedel International – would, they claimed, be the largest settlement organisation in the world. Lussi, who had set out to make Cedel better than Euroclear, had, at least on his own reckoning, forged a group that was bigger. A footnote to the press notice about the signing reminded readers of the 14 May memorandum of understanding with Sicovam.

On 11 November the great and the good of Europe's political and financial establishment converged on Luxembourg. The Edmond Israel Foundation – Lussi's contrivance to sweeten the retirement of Cedel's founding chairman and boost the group's international profile – was awarding its 'Vision of Europe' award for the fifth time: to Wim Duisenberg, president of the European Central Bank.

Lussi, welcoming the guests in his role as chairman of the foundation, extolled the agreement of 14 May as emblematic of a new Europe in which economies were 'becoming so intertwined that war is no longer a political option'.

But Lussi's speech referred only to Cedel's 'common vision' and merger with Deutsche Börse Clearing. There was no mention of Sicovam when he spoke of the collapse of boundaries between the domestic and the international markets, the debt and equity markets, commercial bank money and central bank money, over-the-counter and stock exchange trading.

Later in November, negotiators from Cedel, Deutsche Börse and Sicovam met in Milan to try to resolve their differences. The divergent positions of Deutsche Börse and Sicovam over the valuation of the French partner could not be reconciled.

According to Jean-François Théodore: 'It failed in the end because looking purely at calculations, Deutsche Börse said: one third, one third, one third: no never. The maximum I can give to you – and then there was a very complicated calculation – is 28.9 or something percent. And you could have 0.97 if you want, but not more. So they had a pure analyst's calculation and not at all a political one. And at that time, we had a joint board of the Paris Bourse and Sicovam, and our conclusion was that we could not accept to be only a junior partner in something that would be driven by Deutsche Börse.'

Lussi tried to mediate. 'I pleaded with Werner not to reject the French, even if his calculations showed Sicovam was worth 28% I told him that a 5 percentage point difference was worth about $100 million. And I would provide that from the merger synergies. In the first year of the merger we made $300 million of net synergies. In this deal, you couldn't think like a statistical man from McKinsey and insist on 28% or 29%. The only way was one third, one third, one third.

I said to Werner – we were down in Milan when he rejected Théodore – that the French would go into bed with the devil, just to prove that they had an alternative – and the devil was Euroclear. I told him that if they did that, the European vision was out for a long time. I said they will take about four weeks to do an alternative deal. I was wrong. It took days. The whole situation was out of control and all down to Seifert's stubbornness.'

Werner Seifert has declined to comment on deals that have not materialised. But there is another version of events that suggests calculation on his part, rather than stubbornness. Over the summer, Seifert decided Clearnet would no longer be part of the deal with Sicovam and Cedel. The reason, according to people close to the negotiations, was that Seifert had identified the CCP as an important cash cow in the securities value chain and wanted Deutsche Börse to have control over that function. Deutsche Börse went on to develop Eurex Clearing, a CCP of its own, which began settlement netting for German equities in June 2003.

With Clearnet out of the equation, the valuation issue was decisive. One third for Deutsche Börse, one third for Cedel and one third for Sicovam 'would have destroyed value' for shareholders of both Deutsche Börse and Cedel and was therefore unacceptable, Seifert said later.

Late on Monday 22 November the news broke that Sicovam was pulling out of the tripartite agreement. Just Deutsche Börse Clearing and Cedel would merge: with effect from 1 January 2000. Clearnet and Sicovam agreed to ally with Euroclear on 23 November 1999. It was the day after the tripartite agreement collapsed.

Euroclear Transformed

11.1 EUROCLEAR SEPARATES FROM MORGAN

The Euroclear that wooed Sicovam away from Deutsche Börse and Cedel in the autumn of 1999 had very different prospects to that rejected by Sicovam in May. The announcement on 1 September that Euroclear's operations would be transferred from Morgan Guaranty to a new, user-owned Euroclear Bank transformed the Brussels-based ICSD into an attractive potential partner for other European settlement systems. It would, declared Sir Andrew Large, Euroclear's chairman, 'enable us to make Euroclear more European and move ahead with the consolidation of the European clearing industry'.[1]

Although a momentous development, Euroclear's separation from Morgan was long in preparation. The issue had been broached by senior Euroclear managers at varying times over the previous two decades. Martine Dinne remembers how: 'Well before this de-merger was dreamed of, we went several times to New York to talk to Dennis Weatherstone and, back in the 80s, to Bruce Brackenridge to explain that we would need to separate from JP Morgan if, for example, we wanted to merge with Cedel.' Rolf-E. Breuer, when chairman of Euroclear, once raised with Morgan the possibility of Euroclear seeking a new operator for the system.[2]

Morgan itself was changing. It began moving out of the securities processing business in a quest to become an investment bank. In 1995 Morgan sold its corporate trust and its global custody business to The Bank of New York. That same year, it sold its local custody business in Europe to Paribas of France, sowing seeds that would bear a bitter fruit for Euroclear some years later when BNP Paribas led a campaign challenging Euroclear's right to compete against its agent banking business. After Euroclear began merging with CSDs it was in direct competition with the business developed by Morgan to serve broker-dealers in a number of European locations. The disposals continued until Euroclear was Morgan's sole remaining infrastructure service provider of any note.

The pressures for a change in Euroclear's status multiplied as the 1990s progressed. According to Peter Sucaet, 'It also became clear that the euro was not going to be a neutral event. Looking at the emergence of real-time settlement, the move to equities, the euro project and efforts to make a European capital market, people began to question whether the relationship between Euroclear and JP Morgan was sustainable.'

In the course of the 1996–97 strategic review, Sucaet prepared a paper for the corporate office of JP Morgan, which argued that American control of Euroclear's operations could be a stumbling block if Euroclear wanted to adapt and operate in the new environment. 'It was a matter of emotions – just as you couldn't imagine the New York Stock Exchange being operated by Deutsche Bank,' Sucaet said. 'In the mid-90s there was not an urgent desire within Morgan to get rid of Euroclear. But we couldn't see a way of continuing with JP Morgan and

---

[1] As quoted in the *Financial Times* of 2 September 1999.
[2] See Chapter 5.

merging with CSDs in Europe. There was no way that ex-employees of Sicovam – coming from the Banque de France – would become employees of an American bank.'

Following completion of the review, Bomans flew to New York by Concorde with Combes to begin talks with senior Morgan executives aimed at convincing the US bank that separation was a necessity.

The 1998 discussions between Euroclear and Sicovam added to the pressure on Morgan to consider whether its position as operator of the Euroclear system was compatible with Euroclear's growing ambitions. These were fuelled by a growing confidence in Brussels that Euroclear would be able to cope without its US operator.

In the 1980s, there would have been insufficient in-house know-how in Euroclear to take over the operational and banking side of the business. But the Brussels-based ICSD had built a formidable expertise over a wide range of services by the late 1990s.

The discussions at executive level between Euroclear and Morgan were concluded in 1998. Negotiations on separation followed at board level and these accelerated after the news in May 1999 of the planned tripartite link-up between Deutsche Börse, Cedel and Sicovam.

Sir Andrew Large, as chairman, took charge of the negotiations for the Euroclear side and was heavily involved in the early stages. He handled what he called 'the big picture aspect' and recruited veteran deal-maker Sir John Craven to assist him. A 1970s Euromarkets legend who slipped smoothly into investment banking making several fortunes along the way, Craven came with a warm recommendation from Steers.

For Large, the size of Morgan's profits from Euroclear was a factor adding to pressure for a change in Euroclear's status. 'We had a situation where JP Morgan had invented Euroclear, they had been immensely successful with it, and they were making money out of it. And effectively the market said: "JP Morgan is making too much money off our back". That was the sort of script,' he said. 'JP Morgan was sensible enough and mature enough to realise that everybody did have a point and that if they would dig in and say: "We own this and it's too bad", then it would not have a happy outcome for them over time. And so, they also reached a view that this was perhaps the time to separate and it became a question of negotiation.'[3]

Leading the Morgan team was Michael Patterson, a vice chairman of the bank. A key figure in the earlier discussions with Bomans and Combes, Patterson was a Euroclear board member of many years standing and the New York-based executive with responsibility for the Euroclear Operations Centre. He was also the son of a former Morgan chairman, Ellmore Patterson.

According to Patterson, Morgan recognised that Euroclear's wish to be a big player in the consolidation of the European securities settlement industry meant the two should separate. 'Although we considered Euroclear a jewel in our crown, in terms of the quality of its people, its operation and its success, we bowed to the inevitable and decided to negotiate the withdrawal.'[4]

The negotiations have always been described as amicable. But they were also very difficult. 'There was a hell of a negotiation on price,' Steers recalls. 'We all felt we should do right by JP Morgan: probably with hindsight, excessively so,' says Chris Tupker, who, as a member of the Euroclear board since 1997, took part in the negotiations. 'So it became an idea that we should let them have three years' notice, and the banking income over that period, while we took over operations on day one.'[5]

---

[3] Conversation with the author, 29 November 2005.
[4] Conversation with the author, 16 March 2006.
[5] As told to the author, 27 March 2006.

Morgan happily pocketed the offer. But, with insights gained over years of operating the system, Morgan's team also pointed out that Euroclear would be in a position to control the banking income. They therefore demanded that Euroclear guarantee Morgan at least a minimum amount of income per year. 'That meant a cap and a collar,' Tupker says. 'Most of the negotiation was about figuring out a range.'

Large had the job of finding out how much Morgan made from the system: 'We had some independent work done to determine what the profitability of JP Morgan was. One of the first things I had to do was go to JP Morgan and say look: "We cannot do this, until and unless we know how much money you are making." I remember that we had independent advisers for the board, dealing with valuation and negotiation.' One complication for the Euroclear side was that executives in the Euroclear Operations Centre could not be directly involved in the negotiations because they were Morgan employees and there would be conflicts of interest. They had to follow events from the margins.

Life for the Morgan team was easier. 'JP Morgan didn't really need much in the way of advice because they knew the system intimately from the word go, because this had been their life blood,' Large recalls. Included in the Morgan team was Luigi de Ghenghi, head of JP Morgan's legal department for Europe, the Middle East and Africa, who had served previously as general counsel of Euroclear.

Sir John Craven set about determining the 'quantum' or sum that Euroclear should pay to separate from Morgan. But the negotiations moved slowly, despite the high level of the negotiators and their protestations of good will. 'It was quite challenging finding out what the motives of different people were, who had different points of view,' Large recalls. 'The learning curve was very, very steep, because this was a very difficult and complicated area.'

Matters were not helped by friction inside the Euroclear camp. Some Euroclear board members were less inclined to be generous to Morgan after the US bank pressed for the cap and collar. They argued that Euroclear's ownership of the system should carry greater weight than the three-year notice period in the operating agreement.

There were questions about the structure Euroclear should adopt in the future. According to Large, 'different parties, who subsequently became shareholders in the operating company, had very different starting points as to what they wanted, and why they wanted it and what they thought Euroclear should do'. Jacques-Philippe Marson, the BNP Paribas nominee on the board, represented a minority view in suggesting that Euroclear should give up its banking arm and should rely, rather like the UK's CREST or Cedel in its original form, on a banking consortium to supply credit and other services.

A further complication, according to Large, was that 'the staff were all JP Morgan employees and we had to get them bought into a process of ceasing to be JP Morgan employees. The executives in the Euroclear Operations Centre started with varying degrees of comfort about that, given that the decision being made would affect their own futures.'

With the talks moving slowly, Euroclear put more board members into the negotiations. Tom Perna, a senior executive vice president of The Bank of New York, was given a leading role because he had M&A experience, having helped negotiate BoNY's acquisition of Morgan's custody business in 1995. He spent about nine months working out the details of the separation with the support of a team that included Jeffrey Tessler, at that time the London-based head of BoNY's European operations, who a few years later would become CEO of Euroclear's arch-rival Clearstream International.

For Perna, negotiating sometimes involved no more than a short walk along Wall Street, between his and Patterson's office. At other times, he would be in London or Brussels for consultations with Large and the Euroclear board. Perna got on well with Patterson, whom he described as 'a gentleman's gentleman'.[6] But good relations did nothing to cut the cost of separation for Euroclear. The 1 September announcement specified that Morgan would continue to be paid between a minimum of $195 million and a maximum of $295 million a year for three years in addition to receiving a one-off $35 million fee for know-how transferred to Euroclear.

The annual payments were roughly equivalent to the pre-tax banking income generated by Morgan from its Euroclear related operations and at last gave an insight into Euroclear's contribution to JP Morgan profits over the years. They were made effective from 1 January 2000 under the agreement[7] that Euroclear signed with Morgan Guaranty on 10 March 2000 to terminate Morgan's operating contract before completion of its three-year notice period.

Opinions differ on whether Euroclear got a good deal. Looking back, Tupker feels that Euroclear probably overpaid Morgan. 'We were very generous. We didn't need to do the three years' notice. We were bending over backwards to be nice.' Perna, on the other hand, believes the separation was cheap for Euroclear and was a good deal for both sides at the time. In the light of prices since paid for infrastructure providers, it was a 'very, very good deal for the market,' he adds. Euroclear was able to look forward to retaining banking revenues of around €300 million a year after 2002 that would be used to lower costs for customers and finance investment.

The 10 March agreement was followed quickly by other important changes. On 13 March, Tupker was named chairman to succeed Large. Whereas Large freely admitted he was 'more a front office guy' and that securities settlement was not his area of expertise before becoming chairman, the appointment of Tupker, a senior executive vice president of ABN AMRO Bank, placed a banker with long experience of financial infrastructure issues at the helm of Euroclear.

The change of chairman was followed soon afterwards by a new chief executive and management team. Luc Bomans took early retirement following illness earlier that year. He was succeeded by Pierre Francotte on 29 June 2000.

Francotte took over as general manager of Euroclear at the comparatively tender age of 43. Whereas Bomans was an engineer by background, Francotte was a lawyer with a Masters degree in financial and economic law from the Université Libre de Bruxelles and a Masters in comparative law from the Cambridge University in the UK. He joined Euroclear as assistant general counsel in 1993, became head of the legal division the following year and later took charge of the transaction processing division before becoming chief operating officer earlier in 2000.

Before joining Euroclear, Francotte was assistant general counsel at the International Monetary Fund in Washington. In that institution, he had come across several people who would later play important roles in the securities settlement business, including Hugh Simpson, a future acting chief executive of CREST and Euroclear colleague, and Nigel Wicks, who would one day be Francotte's chairman at Euroclear. More important, the arcane international politicking of the IMF proved an ideal training ground for running a business that in Francotte's period as CEO would emerge from obscurity and jump up the EU political agenda.

Francotte was a patient and unflappable negotiator. He was a conceptual thinker, who played a vital role in developing the business model for Euroclear after it separated from Morgan. He fitted in with Tupker's vision of a CEO far more than had Bomans. Francotte and his chairman tended to complement each other as they battled on Euroclear's behalf in an increasingly

---

[6] Conversation with the author, 16 March 2006.
[7] The agreement was signed on 10 March 2000 by Euroclear Clearance System Sté Coopérative, Euroclear Clearance System plc and Calar Investments SA, Euroclear's Luxembourg holding company, on behalf of the Euroclear group.

complex world. Tupker, with a sometimes alarming tendency to drop astringent *aperçus* within earshot of negotiating partners, was the more aggressive. Francotte, with the instincts and training of a legal problem solver, would take pains to find out where the other party was coming from and manoeuvre accordingly.

None of this should detract from Bomans' achievements as Euroclear CEO. His was a period of rapid growth at a time of big external challenges, including the introduction of the euro and the Y2K millennium bug. During his time in office, Euroclear's share of the cross-border settlement business handled by the two ICSDs rose to nearly 80%. It was Bomans who initiated the approaches to the French, Belgian and Dutch CSDs in the 1990s and who pressed Morgan, on behalf of Euroclear's executives, for a separation. He paved the way for Euroclear's separation from the US bank and its subsequent acquisitions of Sicovam, CIK of Belgium and Necigef of the Netherlands.

But the Bomans years also saw their fair share of strain as Euroclear's rivalry with Cedel, later Clearstream, reached new levels of bitterness. Nor were the two years of Bomans' term that overlapped with Large's chairmanship particularly harmonious internally. Relations between the two men were difficult and these tensions sometimes spilled over into heated discussions at board level.

Bomans rose to the top of the company when it had a more pliant board with relatively little to do. The board from 1998 – charged first with negotiating the separation from Morgan and then building Euroclear anew – was far more assertive. It took itself seriously and saw its role as giving the company direction. The clashes that preceded Bomans' departure were a sign of profound change at Euroclear.

More change was to come. 'Once we had done the deal [on 10 March 2000], the enormity of what we had undertaken became apparent,' Tupker says. He already had some idea. Tupker had been appointed chairman of a transition committee some time before. Its purpose was to redesign Euroclear as a user owned, user governed securities settlement system, which included a bank.

'We were taking an incomplete appendage out of a very large bank and making it into a bank,' Tupker explains. 'We had to visualise what would be missing for the future. There was, for example, a whole JP Morgan tradition on the risk management side that was not part of Euroclear and we had to build that. We only started doing this when we knew the deal with Morgan was going to happen – really during 2000.'

Some very basic questions had to be resolved. What was the appropriate capitalisation for such a bank? There was no real guidance because Euroclear had operated off the balance sheet of JP Morgan. The creation of a Belgian-based bank meant Belgium's banking commission would take reponsibility for regulating Euroclear from the Fed, which regulated the Euroclear Operations Centre as a part of the Morgan Guaranty Brussels branch. The Euroclear board also had to obtain ratings for the new structure. 'There was a huge amount of work to be done,' Tupker says. The transition committee brought Tupker into contact with the staff of Euroclear on a weekly basis. As such, it strengthened his position to be a candidate for chairman after Large.

The signing of the 10 March agreement triggered a three-phase plan to transfer the operating and banking functions of Morgan Guaranty to the new market-owned Euroclear Bank.

In May, Euroclear Clearance System Société Coopérative, the Belgian cooperative, was converted into a Société Anonyme, a public limited company, under Belgian law. It would be the future operator of the Euroclear system under licence from Euroclear Clearance System plc, the system's owner. ECSplc was the UK registered, Swiss domiciled holding company set up in 1972 which purchased the Euroclear system from Morgan for the 120 or so individual banks and brokerages that were its users.

In July, the newly formed Euroclear Clearance System SA was granted a banking licence, becoming Euroclear Bank. The bank then proceeded to raise nearly €1 billion in capital, creating tier I capital from assets previously held by different Euroclear companies, and in October adding €500 million of tier II capital through long-term borrowings by Euroclear Finance, the bank's Luxembourg-based financing vehicle. The bank later arranged a further €1.5 billion backstop borrowing facility with a syndicate of financial institutions.

Euroclear Bank would be more than a mere operator of the system. The licence from ECSplc allowed it to determine matters of policy, admit clients, approve depositories and approve the fees to be charged to clients. It also had the right to receive fees from clients.

The bank's financial position was strong. Its capital ratio, as defined by Bank for International Settlements rules, was around 30%, of which half was tier I capital. Standard and Poor's awarded it a AA+ rating. In giving Euroclear a low risk profile, S&P cited the delivery-versus-payment character of settlement activity. Conservative credit policies and procedures meant there had been no credit loss during Morgan Guaranty's management of the system. Although the bank's intraday credit exposure could reach some €33 billion, this was more than 90% secured by collateral. S&P reported that 94% of the bank's secured credit was lent to clients of investment grade quality. The 10% of unsecured exposure was mainly intraday overdrafts, 99% of which were extended to investment grade clients.

Another report from the Fitch rating agency found that 82% of Euroclear's daily turnover was settled between participants internally, 8% over the Bridge with Cedel/Clearstream and 10% across borders with other local counterparties. Although real-time settlement had played such an important part in the company's recent history, most transactions were still settled by batch processing on a T + 3 standard. Where real-time proved an advantage was in speeding repo transactions and allowing the recycling of previous unsettled transactions.

In the third stage, client and supplier contracts, trademarks and employment agreements for Euroclear's 1400 staff were transferred to the new bank from Morgan Guaranty.

Euroclear Bank was launched on the last day of 2000 with Francotte as its first CEO. Against a background of momentous change, the Euroclear Group also managed in 2000 to upgrade its real-time settlement platform, improve its custody service, achieve its best ever financial results and pass €25 million in fee reductions to clients.

The separation from Morgan and the launch of Euroclear Bank was, Francotte reported, 'virtually seamless for clients' – a reflection of the professionalism instilled in the group over the previous 30 years by Morgan Guaranty.

And to a considerable extent, Morgan Guaranty lived on in Euroclear. 'We still have a JP Morgan culture – the old JP Morgan,' says Martine Dinne.[8] 'I still have the feeling we are very similar to JP Morgan old-style, which is amazing because we have moved on. I have realised we are quite Anglo-Saxon in our way of thinking and managing. This was a discovery from me: I'm quite an American.'

11.2   THE CREATION OF EURONEXT

While Euroclear was making itself more acceptable to potential European partners in the final months of 1999, Werner Seifert appeared set on a course of creative destruction.

---

[8] In a conversation with the author, 15 November 2005.

On 6 December 1999 he announced that Deutsche Börse would become a listed company. This decision would lead in the long term to his departure as CEO from the company. Its immediate effect was to deliver a mortal blow to the European Exchange Alliance of eight stock exchanges that had been trying since May 1998 to create a common trading system for Europe's most liquid blue chip stocks.

The alliance had been struggling for some time. But Seifert's move marked its death knell because the planned listing was seen as the start of a battle for supremacy among Europe's stock markets. A combination of Deutsche Börse with the London Stock Exchange appeared a real possibility. This was bad news for Paris and Europe's smaller exchanges. Despite a strong expansion of trading as the dot-com boom moved towards its peak, there were too many exchanges in Europe struggling to defend their turf amid a proliferation of new electronic trading platforms and a growing 'internalisation' of trading inside the big investment banks.

There was, however, manoeuvring among various bourses before Seifert acted. The Brussels and Amsterdam stock exchanges were among the first to react to Sicovam's decision to quit new Cedel.

During the summer of 1999, the Belgian exchange was working with the Amsterdam exchange, Euroclear and the London Clearing House on a possible alliance to bring the two continental exchanges' equity netting technology to LCH and link the resulting CCP to Euroclear's settlement capacity. That plan got nowhere, the Belgians said, because of a lack of interest by LCH. But the contacts between the Amsterdam and Brussels exchanges and with Euroclear proved valuable when news began to seep that Sicovam might break with Deutsche Börse and Cedel.

When it became clear that Sicovam was switching its allegiance from new Cedel to Euroclear, Olivier Lefebvre, the head of the Belgian exchange, convinced George Möller, his Amsterdam counterpart, that they should go to Paris and talk to Théodore. The three met for dinner in the Hotel Crillon on 18 November and agreed in principle to put their equity netting expertise together in Clearnet and plug the whole thing onto Euroclear for settlement services. The Belgian and Amsterdam exchanges decided to suspend working with LCH on the CCP project.

Brussels, Amsterdam and Paris were the only exchanges with equity netting at the time. The Brussels and Paris bourses also had a lot of technology in common. They shared a trading system, known in Paris as NSC – the *nouveau system de cotations* – and in Brussels as NTS – the new trading system – and also had a joint IT company, presciently called Euronext.

The three exchanges did more work over the Christmas holidays, concluding that they should also link their trading operations. Théodore, Möller and Lefebvre met on Saturday 5 February 2000 in Euroclear's Brussels headquarters for discussions on the back office arrangements of their joint venture. They asked Ignace Combes if they could borrow his office for a private meeting. There they decided to merge the Paris, Amsterdam and Brussels stock exchanges. They appointed Pierre Fleuriot, president of ABN-AMRO bank in France and a former stock exchange regulator, to advise on what became known as project IEX, standing for integrated European exchange.

The appointment of Fleuriot, a one-time director general of COB, France's Commission des Opérations de Bourse, as adviser for all three exchanges helped speed the negotiations. Six weeks later, the three were ready to announce the creation of a transnational exchange on Monday 20 March 2000, at the Savoy Hotel in London. But two days before, there was still no decision about its name. On Saturday 18 March, the three executives met in the offices of Publicis, the advertising and communications group, near the Arc de Triomphe in Paris and, after reviewing several options, agreed on the name and logo of Euronext.

The three markets had moved together at lightning speed. A major driver was a shared fear that Seifert's decision in December 1999 to sell shares in Deutsche Börse presaged a merger with the LSE. But the pieces also fell rapidly into place as soon as Sicovam separated from new Cedel and began talking to Euroclear in November 1999 because there were quick wins for each of the three exchanges and their bosses.

It was critically important for Théodore to complete an international deal after the collapse of the plan to link Sicovam to what became Clearstream. Only that way would he gain the initiative in the game of consolidating the industry. For Brussels and Amsterdam the attractions of Euronext were more practical: they were able to compensate for their small size by pooling CCP technology and linking with a bigger partner in trading. For Amsterdam, which had ageing IT platforms in need of replacement, the deal promised to avoid duplication in technology investment and so could yield big savings.

11.3   EUROCLEAR ACQUIRES SICOVAM

Sicovam resumed talks with Euroclear immediately after breaking away from Cedel and Deutsche Börse on 22 November 1999. The two companies picked up from where they had left off in 1998 with the aim of reaching a cooperation agreement. 'Having failed to link with Cedel, the vision of the shareholders and users of Sicovam at that time was that it would be a mistake to stay alone,' Théodore says.

'We realised that Sicovam had experienced big problems trying to merge with Cedel, so the first thing that Euroclear and Sicovam tried to do was negotiate a joint-venture that would share technology,' Pierre Francotte recalls.[9] The idea that competing companies in the post-trade sector could successfully share technology to reduce the cost of investment and avoid duplication was in vogue at the end of the 1990s. Euroclear and Sicovam also felt that mutualising technology would involve fewer regulatory difficulties than a merger.

However, it soon became clear that the hoped-for integrated partnership of Sicovam and Euroclear would not produce the synergies and cost savings the two sides wanted. So, early in 2000, Théodore approached Francotte, who was Euroclear's chief operating officer and acting general manager during Luc Bomans' illness. Théodore suggested that Euroclear and Sicovam should merge.

'We decided to go back to basics,' Francotte remembers. 'A joint-venture will never work if you want to be really close partners. You have to choose: either you're competitors and you do a few things together, but at the margin. Or you go beyond that and do a merger.'

The merger of DBC and Cedel at the beginning of 2000 showed it was possible to merge a CSD and ICSD. The decision of Euroclear and Sicovam to follow suit was strongly influenced by the change in client needs since the start of EMU. Investment vehicles, including mutual funds, exchange traded funds and trackers, were being created to take advantage of sector-wide investment in equities in the single currency area. This put pressure on post-trade infrastructure services to try to overcome the barriers to clearing and settling securities across borders.

Euroclear and Sicovam set out to create what Francotte called 'a new beast for the industry: a mix of ICSD and CSD' in response to these developments. 'Being a CSD alone or an ICSD alone would not have been sufficient and the reason was very, very simple,' he says. 'ICSDs manage cross-border transactions. CSDs manage domestic transactions. And yet the market

---

[9] Conversation with the author, 24 November 2006.

was being transformed to the point where the boundaries between domestic and cross-border were evaporating. So the CSDs and ICSDs would each need the features that each other had.'

The talks moved ahead quickly and on a separate track to the negotiations among the Paris, Brussels and Amsterdam stock exchanges that led to the formation of Euronext. On 24 March 2000, the two sides announced an agreement in principle for Euroclear to merge with Sicovam. The deal promised synergies 'of at least €300 million'[10] for users and Euroclear shareholders, largely through avoiding duplicated investments. Sicovam, for example, would not have to build a replacement for the RGV platform, which was nearing the end of its life.

Euroclear's planned acquisition of Sicovam demonstrated that Euroclear could shake off its American parentage and put itself at the centre of efforts to reshape Europe's financial infrastructure. Coming just a fortnight after the agreement for Euroclear to separate from Morgan and 10 days after the appointment of Chris Tupker as Euroclear's new chairman, the proposed merger opened new perspectives for the extension of the horizontal model for securities settlement across European frontiers and further consolidation among providers. It signalled the end of hub and spokes.

On 30 March, less than a week after the announcement of plans to take over Sicovam, Euroclear revealed another major coup. It took over settlement of Irish government debt from the Irish central bank, cutting settlement costs by 80% for these instruments. The move – designed to increase liquidity in the €23.6 billion market and encourage foreign investors – was the first case of a eurozone country transferring the settlement of its bonds to an ICSD.

Having agreed to merge with Sicovam, Euroclear shortly afterwards began talks with Euronext about the future of CIK and Necigef, which were the wholly owned settlement subsidiaries of the Brussels and Amsterdam bourses. Here too, discussions moved ahead quickly. On 5 September 2000, Euroclear announced memoranda of understanding for eventual mergers with the two CSDs – although the final integration of CIK into the Euroclear group would take some years.[11]

Euroclear got to know CIK and Necigef in 1999, during Bomans' time as general manager, when talking with the Belgian and Dutch exchanges about the possible alliance with LCH. Having decided to cede control of the Paris Stock Exchange's CSD to Euroclear, Théodore had few qualms – as chairman designate of Euronext – about entering negotiations for Euroclear to take over the Belgian and Dutch CSDs.

Pierre Francotte and Ignace Combes handled the negotiations for Euroclear with the support of Chris Tupker. 'In terms of business philosophy, Euroclear and Euronext got on the same wavelength,' Combes observes. It was 'very natural' for CIK and Necigef to join Euroclear. The transactions were later settled by the transfer of Euroclear shares to Euronext in all-paper deals.

Euroclear was building up an alliance with the emerging Euronext group to the mutual advantage of both sides. Another important step came when Euroclear negotiated a data feed with the Paris bourse to give big broker-dealers such as Morgan Stanley and Merrill Lynch the option of settling their French securities and equity business through book entry transactions between accounts in Euroclear Bank.

---

[10] According to the Euroclear 2000 annual report.
[11] Euroclear and Euronext agreed in July 2001 that only the book entry settlement and custody business of CIK should be transferred to Euroclear, leaving CIK to handle physical securities transactions for Belgian customers as a wholly owned subsidiary of Euronext. However, in November 2004, Euroclear and Euronext signed a letter of intent providing for Euroclear to acquire the whole of CIK from Euronext. The accord was confirmed a year later after Euroclear had checked the large number of physical securities in CIK's vault. The acquisition, which reduced fragmentation in the EU settlement market, took effect on 1 January 2006, after which CIK was known as Euroclear Belgium.

Sicovam (later Euroclear France) remained the settlement provider for the French domestic market. The feed, when it went live in July 2002, enabled Euronext to give its clients a choice between two settlement providers while allowing the big international players to stay in the international settlement loop where there was greater liquidity and more scope for collateral management. It became a model for later feeds from the London, Brussels and Amsterdam stock exchanges to Euroclear.

Ties between Euronext and Euroclear were strengthened further when Euroclear was designated as the preferred settlement partner of the new transnational exchange. The preferred partnership was aimed at ensuring straight-through processing of transactions and did not specify an exclusive arrangement between the exchange and its settlement provider. However, it contained an important safeguard for Euroclear, which was investing heavily to serve Euronext. Euroclear obtained an assurance that over the next five years Euronext would not use the settlement facilities of any competitor such as Deutsche Börse that was part of a closed silo structure, unless the alternative service provider offered better quality services or the same services at lower prices. This provided insurance against the risk of a politically inspired deal between Euronext and the German exchange.

Euroclear and Sicovam signed their agreement to merge on 21 September 2000, a fortnight after the announcement of Euroclear's plans to take over CIK and Necigef. The signing was about three months later than originally planned because time was needed for the French banking community to buy out the 40% holding of the Banque de France in Sicovam. The following day, 22 September, Euronext was formally launched as a transnational exchange.

Sicovam finally joined the Euroclear group on 10 January 2001 – just 10 days after the completion of Euroclear's separation from JP Morgan. The two events transformed Euroclear. The addition of Sicovam – by now renamed Euroclear France – hugely increased the number of transactions carried out by the group. Euroclear became the only settlement service provider to offer real-time settlement in both commercial bank and central bank money for bond and equity transactions.

As part of the merger agreement, Euroclear obtained an option to acquire up to 20% of Clearnet, the CCP owned by Euronext. Euroclear had earlier joined forces with Clearnet and other leading netting providers – LCH of London and GSCC[12] of the US – to boost the efficiency of settlement and collateral management. The alliance with Clearnet aimed at providing users with straight-through processing, including netting, from trading to settlement for transactions in French, Dutch and Belgian securities traded on Euronext or the bond settlement platform MTS France. Euroclear's Clearnet option was exercised at the end of January 2002 when the agreements to purchase Necigef[13] and the book entry settlement and custody business of CIK were finalised.

As illustrated in Figure 11.1, the acquisition of Euroclear France changed the structure of Euroclear and its share register. In a move that would later contribute to the politicisation of the European securities settlement business, Euroclear France became a subsidiary of Euroclear Bank, which as the ICSD of the group was licensed to operate the Euroclear system. Euroclear Bank was also parent to other wholly owned subsidiaries, including TradeGO and Euroclear Finance.

---

[12] Government Securities Clearing Corporation, an NSCC subsidiary which provides clearing and settlement of US government securities.

[13] On 7 February 2002, Euroclear acquired an initial 51% stake in Necigef, which became known as Euroclear Netherlands. The remaining 49% was acquired on 30 April 2002.

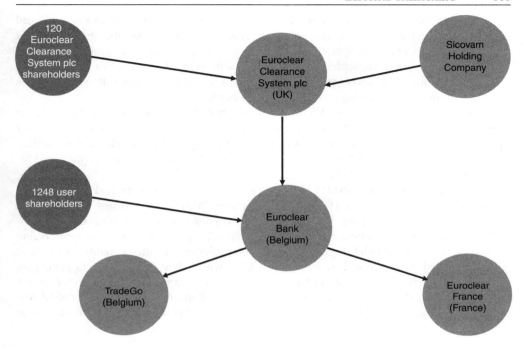

Figure 11.1   Overview of the Euroclear group (January 2001). *Source:* Euroclear group

As payment for the French CSD, the French banks which had owned Sicovam received a 16.67% stake in the enlarged share capital of Euroclear Clearance System plc, the owner of the Euroclear system. The French banks' 16.67% stake in ECSplc was held in a holding company – Sicovam Holding SA – in the form of special 'S' shares, which gave Sicovam Holding the right to appoint and remove a specified number of ECSplc directors.[14]

ECSplc changed its name to Euroclear plc on 1 June 2001. As well as licensing the right to operate the Euroclear system to Euroclear Bank, it had a direct stake of 77% in the bank with a further 20% held indirectly through Calar Investments.[15] Calar was a Luxembourg holding company created some years before to manage the investment portfolio built up from royalties paid to ECSplc. The 1248 users that held shares in the Belgian cooperative, created in the late 1980s, were minority shareholders in Euroclear Bank. They were given the opportunity to trade in their holdings and buy Euroclear plc shares.[16]

The financial details of the merger with Sicovam showed how far Euroclear had gained in strength since the dark days of May 1999. Then, in a desperate attempt to prevent Sicovam's future being entwined with those of Deutsche Börse and Cedel, Euroclear made an offer that would have given the French CSD equal voting rights with Euroclear in a joint company combining the two settlement providers. The terms of the 2001 merger gave Sicovam Holding just one sixth of ECSplc's capital.

---

[14] At this stage four.

[15] According to the Euroclear annual report for 2000.

[16] In 2003, Euroclear made a successful cash offer to the remaining minority shareholders which at that time held 1.75% of Euroclear Bank. The move unified the group's share structure, so that afterwards all the user-owners of Euroclear were shareholders of Euroclear plc, the UK registered, Swiss-domiciled holding company formerly known as ECSplc.

The impact of Euroclear France on the group's business became clear in the combined group's annual report for 2000. The volumes before and after netting also highlighted the important role of Clearnet in operations of Euroclear France and the wider group.

Whereas Euroclear Bank settled 11 million transactions in 2000, Euroclear France settled 134 million before netting and 41 million after netting. The combined group settlement volumes were 145 million before netting and 52 million afterwards.

Group turnover in 2000 was €95.5 trillion,[17] with €58 trillion accounted for by Euroclear Bank and €37.5 trillion attributed to Euroclear France. The value of securities held in custody by the Euroclear group jumped to €7.4 trillion with Euroclear France adding €3.5 trillion to Euroclear Bank's €3.9 trillion. In 1999, the previous year, the value of securities held for Euroclear participants was €3 trillion.

In the space of a year, Euroclear's strategy for consolidation in Europe had shifted from a theoretical hub and spokes model to one of merging with CSDs in a user-owned, user-governed group that linked settlement providers across borders on the basis of their function.

The greatly enlarged Euroclear group complemented Euronext, with both groups pursuing the horizontal business model. Together, the two companies broke with the tradition of vertical silos which tied most national exchanges to CCPs, where they existed, and to settlement services. Although no Euroclear staffer would relish the comparison, the group's business model had changed subtly into something akin to the European Clearing House model first proposed by André Lussi before he steered Cedel into the fateful embrace of the Deutsche Börse group.

---

[17] The key figures in the annual report for 2000 were given in euro. The report for 1999 still gave them in dollars.

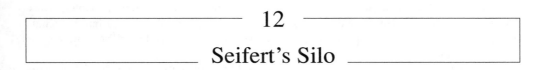

12
Seifert's Silo

As dawn rose on the new millennium, there were high hopes that the year 2000 would point the way to comprehensive consolidation and integration for Europe's financial infrastructures.

The year began hopefully enough. New Cedel International was created through the 50–50 merger of Cedel and DBC and began operating on 1 January 2000. It was rebranded 10 days later as Clearstream International, becoming the parent company for Clearstream Banking Luxembourg, the ICSD formerly known as Cedel Bank, and Clearstream Banking Frankfurt, the German CSD previously called Deutsche Börse Clearing.

It was at this point – legally backdated to 1 January – that Deutsche Börse contributed all its shares in DBC plus the euro equivalent of $103 million to Clearstream in return for 50% of Clearstream International. Cedel's employees and most, but not all, of the business and assets of the Luxembourg ICSD were transferred to the new company in return for the other half of Clearstream International's[1] shares.

This 50% stake in Clearstream became the property of Cedel International, which in the meantime had become a holding company. Cedel International had other assets, notably $118 million (€117.8 million) in cash, which it retained to ensure Clearstream's assets reflected equal contributions of its two shareholders. On 11 January, Cedel International appointed Merrill Lynch's Geneva branch to manage surplus capital totalling €160 million.

Clearstream appeared to get off to a smooth start. Cedel and DBC had established a common management team by the end of 1999 and begun to combine functions such as sales, collateral management and IT. Although the merged entity fell short of Lussi's dream of a European clearing house with French participation, he still hoped to bring more CSDs into its orbit. Cedel International's statutes were changed on 11 January 2000 to permit stock exchanges, CSDs and IT companies to join the 92 banks that were already its shareholders.

But any thought of an orderly consolidation of Europe's post-trade sector rapidly gave way to confusion as a flurry of corporate manoeuvres appeared to pull the infrastructure providers in different directions.

12.1 A FLURRY OF INITIATIVES

No sooner had Euroclear announced its plan to merge with Sicovam on 24 March 2000 than CREST of the UK and SIS of Switzerland – the two strongest advocates of the spaghetti model – announced a 'Settlement Network' of their own. The plan, to 'deliver a single integrated process for the settlement of cross-border business in Europe', was announced on 26 March 2000 and built on an integrated cross-border clearing system launched by CREST and SIS the previous August. Iain Saville, CREST's chief executive, claimed it would settle UK, Irish and Swiss stocks accounting for about 50% of the Eurotop 300 index with delivery versus payment in euros, sterling and Swiss francs.

---

[1] Clearstream International's capital comprised 1.5 million shares, each with a nominal value of € 100.

Less than 10 days later, on 4 April, there was movement among the central counterparties. The London Clearing House and Paris-based Clearnet announced plans to build a single European clearing house to operate from 2001, which would be followed by a merger 'as soon as possible'.

These back office developments were eclipsed on 3 May when the London Stock Exchange and Deutsche Börse announced their plans for a merger of equals to create an exchange called iX. This European 'mega-bourse' would be the world's third biggest stock market by turnover, with 53% of all share trading in Europe by volume. Headquartered in London, with Seifert as its chief executive, the new exchange planned to forge an alliance with Nasdaq of New York. Launched when the end of the dot-com boom was still not fully apparent, iX's promoters claimed a share of more than 80% of the trading volume of high-tech growth stocks in Europe. That would help create the 'largest pan-European growth market' alongside the biggest equity cash market in Europe and the largest derivatives market worldwide.

But, indicative of Seifert's priorities, iX had nothing to offer in terms of securities settlement. The agreement between London and Frankfurt envisaged the merger of all the divisions and holdings of the London Stock Exchange and Deutsche Börse, except for the Börse's 50% holding in Clearstream International. Perhaps ominously, Clearstream was left out of the equation because its inclusion would have given the German partner more than half of iX – a division of power unacceptable to London, which was not prepared to accept a minority stake.

CREST and Clearstream responded to the merger by promising immediately to work together 'on delivering products for the benefit for the European securities markets'. But their statement betrayed vagueness and uncertainty about the project by adding 'once details of the new trading arrangements are known'.

Clearing was another area of loose ends and doubt. The plans for iX envisaged a central counterparty but left open which company should supply it. LCH, which the month before had announced plans to merge with Clearnet, already had an agreement with the London Stock Exchange to supply CCP services from 2001. The German side had wanted to nominate Eurex Clearing to do the job. But Eurex, at this point, was a derivatives clearing house only.

Enthusiasm for iX proved short lived. The financial community in London became increasingly sceptical with doubts shared among the small brokers making up the bulk of the London exchange's 298 shareholders and the big bulge bracket investment banks. The discussions between Clearstream and CREST blew hot and cold. There was no guidance on future settlement structures forthcoming from either Seifert or from Don Cruickshank, the LSE's recently appointed chairman, a City outsider and, like Seifert, a former McKinsey consultant.

With iX in difficulty, Europe's settlement providers returned to their default mode of flirtation and courtship.

Chris Tupker, Euroclear's recently appointed chairman, met Bob Douglass, his opposite number at Clearstream International, for informal talks which touched on the pros and cons of a merger between the two ICSDs, Euroclear Bank and Clearstream Banking Luxembourg. The two chairmen asked their chief executives to hold private talks on a possible business case. Reports of contacts between the sides began to seep into the public domain in July 2000 after Francotte, by now Euroclear CEO, estimated that a Euroclear-Clearstream merger could cut users' costs by about €200 million a year, rising to €300 million if the national CSDs – Sicovam and the former Deutsche Börse Clearing – were brought into the equation.

But neither side appeared willing to move. Lussi, in particular, gave conflicting signals. Despite the weight of Deutsche Börse's 50% stake in Clearstream International, Lussi strutted his independence and appeared still to be wedded to his dream of a European Clearing House. Sometimes, he seemed to be making a serious approach to CREST – but here again, the signals were mixed. At other times, he considered an IPO for Clearstream International, in which some of the shares held by Cedel International would be offered for sale.

In July – despite the ongoing discussions between Clearstream and CREST – Euroclear forged bilateral links with CREST to allow CREST members to settle trades in Eurobonds on the books of the British CSD. It was a straw in the wind – a sign that practical, technical steps could succeed where grand alliances might fail.

In September, the iX project collapsed. The LSE pulled out of the deal. The immediate cause of the debacle was a hostile counter bid from the Scandinavian OM group. But iX had become untenable in the teeth of widespread opposition in the City of London.

12.2   LUSSI'S FORTUNES EBB

The collapse of the merger between the Frankfurt and London stock exchanges pushed Deutsche Börse's planned IPO back up Seifert's agenda.

The iX debacle also shifted Seifert's attention back towards the settlement business in which he had invested the previous year. Two years on from their initial contacts that resulted in the creation of Clearstream International, relations between Lussi and Seifert were poor. Neither man was happy with the way the ownership of the company, shared equally by Cedel International and the Deutsche Börse Group, was working out.

At first, Seifert was content to leave Lussi and Douglass as chief executive and chairman of Clearstream because they knew the business. But he was also used to controlling a vertical silo at Deutsche Börse and the independence that Lussi assumed was his right began to chafe. Having put money on the table to secure the deal with Cedel, Seifert expected a trouble-free return on that capital outlay.

Lussi in turn was accustomed to having a docile board and 90 or so shareholders at Cedel which rarely formed a coherent group. It was a culture shock to find one shareholder, holding half of Clearstream International, who expected different treatment to the banks which owned the other 50% through the Cedel International holding company. Lussi might feel a sense of security as long as the profits rolled in. But he found he was subject to constraints that conflicted with his wish to turn the Clearstream group into a motor of European integration. His one additional step towards creating a European settlement system was Clearstream's acquisition of a so-called 'strategic' 7% stake in Monte Titoli, the Italian settlement system, for €20.17 million in January 2001.

Looking back to the period following Sicovam's defection, Lussi says he realised that Seifert wanted control. 'So he threw out the French, we did the merger and made Clearstream. Then, I said to myself: Okay, it has failed with the French. But he will tell me to go with the Italians or the British. But he didn't want to do that. In my view, he wanted to do the silo. When I knew that, I always said the risk was that he is going to take over Clearstream.'

Others concluded that the shareholder structure of Clearstream International was unsustainable. Rolf-E. Breuer, chairman of Deutsche Börse's supervisory board, remembers that 'for Seifert and myself, it was clear that holding 50% of Clearstream could not be the end of the story. It was a good start.'

According to Breuer, there were two ways forward. One was to put Clearstream and Euroclear together. The other was to increase Deutsche Börse's stake in Clearstream International to 100% – the option that prevailed in the end.

In Seifert's mind there was no such choice. Winning 50% of Clearstream 'was part of a step-by-step plan,' he says today. 'Because in the meantime, we [Deutsche Börse] knew we would go public and that we would then be in a privileged position to buy the other 50%. Let me call it: the biggest bet we ever placed.'

Meanwhile, at an operational level, Clearstream pressed on with the practical integration programme agreed late in 1999. This was the responsibility of Matthias Ganz, a former McKinsey consultant recruited by Seifert when he was head of Swiss Re who had followed Seifert to Deutsche Börse in 1993. In February 2001, Ganz, who joined Clearstream's executive management at the start of 2000 from the managing board of Deutsche Börse Clearing, oversaw the successful migration of DBC's international settlement system, the former Auslandskassenverein, onto the Creation platform. During one weekend, 250 000 securities balances were transferred for a combined value of €250 billion, enabling a €50 million cut in transaction costs between the beginning of April and the end of the year.

Early in 2001, Seifert started sounding out Cedel's shareholders on a possible takeover of the rest of Clearstream International by Deutsche Börse. Towards the end of 2000, he hired Gerd Häusler, former chairman of Dresdner Bank's investment banking arm[2] and before that a member of the Central Bank Council of the Bundesbank, as a senior adviser on strategic issues at Deutsche Börse. Häusler spent much of the first quarter of 2001 visiting the Cedel International shareholders to persuade them to sell to Deutsche Börse.

Simultaneously, Seifert was building up his financial resources. Deutsche Börse's IPO, first signalled in December 1999, gave him a €1 billion war chest when completed on 5 February 2001.

These circumstances would have been sufficient to weaken Lussi's position against Seifert. But at the beginning of 2001, the CEO of Clearstream suffered a series of additional and wholly unexpected blows.

On 10 January, Clearstream announced it had overstated the value of group assets held in custody by €1000 billion (€1 trillion). It was an embarrassing admission. Deutsche Börse was in the final stages of going public. Just as serious, the problem was detected by the market participants who noticed a discrepancy between Clearstream's figures and published statistics.

When Clearstream took steps to clarify the situation, its disclosure that the overstatement was the result of wrong inputting of data by a customer did the company little good. It is generally not wise for companies to blame customers for errors. The explanation was followed by further downward revisions that left open to question whether Clearstream's reporting systems and controls were as good as they should have been. The value of securities held in custody for clients by Clearstream at the end of 2000 was finally put at €7.42 trillion, about level with Euroclear, and sharply down from the €10 trillion estimate publicised in November 2000.

Worse was to follow. A former Cedel employee, Ernest Backes, and Denis Robert, a French journalist, produced a book – *Revelation$* – which alleged that Clearstream Banking Luxembourg was at the centre of a giant money laundering operation and operated secret accounts. The two had touted the book around newspaper offices in EU countries and generally been shown the door.

Britain's *Guardian* newspaper was one that declined to print extracts. It reported later[3] that 'an English translation of the first chapter suggested that Mr Backes, or his ghost writer, had lost the plot'. The newspaper explained that 'it was clear that the author did not know what

---

[2] Häusler was chairman of Dresdner Kleinwort Benson in London from December 1997 until his resignation from the Dresdner Bank group in May 2000.
[3] On 17 May 2001.

a clearing house does – process trades – or why, for example, a central bank routinely holds banking accounts in other countries'.

The French newspaper *Le Figaro* took a different decision. On 26 February 2001, in the midst of the pre-Lenten Carnival, it printed a story based on the book's allegations. A few days later, the book was published.

Lussi and Clearstream flatly denied the allegations. But they further weakened Lussi's position. At some point during February, according to Cedel International's 2001 annual report, Deutsche Börse made its first approach to the holding company to acquire the 50% of Clearstream International it did not already own.

12.3   LUSSI'S DOWNFALL

The Luxembourg public prosecutor opened a preliminary investigation into the allegations against Clearstream and Lussi on 26 February. Carlos Zeyen, a deputy prosecutor responsible for money laundering, was given responsibility for the case. He was to prove a dogged investigator with a liking for publicity.

Across the border, in France, the allegations against Clearstream Banking Luxembourg quickly ballooned into the news story of the year. The 'Clearstream Affair' acquired all the essential ingredients of a French mega-scandal: spies; mystery witnesses; shady financial dealings, some allegedly involving a Russian bank and the Kremlin, and alleged kickbacks, linked to the sale in 1991 of frigates to Taiwan, to corrupt officials and politicians.[4]

One of the main sources of the Robert–Backes book was a witness known as 'H', who turned out to be Régis Hempel, a former employee of Cedel who left the company in 1992. The claims of 'H' to know the details of a double accounting system and concealed accounts at Clearstream were taken very seriously in France.

The apparent involvement of Luxembourg with large scale money laundering touched on a particular French political sensitivity. The Grand Duchy's prosperity, based, it was claimed, on its status as a tax haven in the heart of the European Union, rankled with French politicians and senior officials across the political spectrum. Twelve months before *Revelation$*, the French National Assembly had despatched a special committee to Luxembourg as part of an investigation into the obstacles preventing control of financial crime and money laundering. It had returned to Paris less than impressed and jumped on the Clearstream bandwagon with gusto.

Another to take up the case with enthusiasm was Carlos Zeyen. He was older than most of his peers in Luxembourg's *Palais de Justice*, having joined the public prosecutors' office relatively late in his professional life, and now in charge of a case that could transform his career. He proceeded to interview witnesses. After more than 10 years of vigorous and often abrasive management, there was no shortage of people who disliked Lussi. Some of them came forward to give statements. At the same time, Zeyen took a dim view of Clearstream's decision to appoint KPMG – its auditor for many years – as one of two companies to conduct an internal investigation of the allegations.

Although by April, Luxembourg press reports suggested there were widespread doubts about the credibility of *Revelation$*, the preliminary investigation gathered momentum. The prosecutor's researches also appeared to suggest that Lussi and his wife could have committed offences for personal gain.

---

[4] 'L'affaire Clearstream' returned to the front pages of French newspapers in May 2006. By this time it had metamorphosed into vicious infighting among politicians of the French Right and had lost all connection with Clearstream in Luxembourg – except for the name.

Seifert, meanwhile, stepped up his pursuit of Clearstream International. But he ran into opposition at Cedel International, which, like Clearstream, was chaired by Douglass. On 12 April, the Thursday before Easter, Douglass called a brainstorming session with a small group of directors and advisers in New York. Lussi participated by a telephone link from Luxembourg, where he had stayed for talks with the prime minister about Clearstream's plans for a new building.

The meeting decided to reject Deutsche Börse's approach. On being told the outcome, Seifert asked to speak with Cedel International, whereupon Douglass scheduled a meeting on 18 April, the Wednesday after Easter, in New York. Douglass made life difficult for Seifert who arrived with investment bankers and management consultants to make presentations. According to one person present, Douglass spun the proceedings out until the late afternoon by breaking off the talks and taking his team to a long lunch. Seifert, who was suffering from flu, was kept waiting and missed his flight back to Frankfurt. The message to Seifert was the same: 'No'.

Seifert was furious. But he did not give up. He tried to win Lussi's support. The two met about a week before a long-scheduled meeting of the Clearstream International board on 15 May. According to Lussi's version of events, Lussi 'spent about three hours at the airport hotel in Frankfurt, where he [Seifert] said: "André. You can have anything if you co-operate with me. Tell me what your requirements are and I will meet them." ' Lussi says he rejected the offer because 100% ownership of Clearstream by Deutsche Börse was 'not the right strategy'. He did not want to 'betray' those shareholders who approved the merger with Deutsche Börse Clearing on the premise that Deutsche Börse would not hold more than 50% of the share capital of Clearstream International.

At this point, things took a completely unexpected turn. Zeyen decided to visit Seifert in Germany to seek his cooperation with the investigation. They met, according to Zeyen, in a business centre near Frankfurt airport on Friday 11 May. The prosecutor's objective was to gain the support of Clearstream International's biggest single shareholder for searches of Clearstream Banking Luxembourg and its IT system in pursuit of the allegations of money laundering and misuse of company goods against Lussi.

Zeyen's decision to meet Seifert on German territory remains controversial in the Luxembourg legal community. But the prosecutor argues he had no other option but to turn to Seifert, and that his action was legitimate because there was no formal judicial investigation of Lussi and Clearstream at this stage.

'If we had to search Clearstream in a hostile way, we would have to close it,' Zeyen says.[5] 'It would mean going with police officers, with blue lights on the car, and closing it for some weeks and that was something we did not want to do.' On the other hand, the prosecutor could not seek the cooperation of the company's management in Luxembourg. 'We could not open our file to Mr Lussi, because he was personally implicated by so many witnesses,' Zeyen explains.

Seifert, according to Zeyen, immediately agreed to help and contacted André Roelants, a Clearstream board member and head of the audit committee, to ask him to support the prosecutor in organising the searches. Roelants, the head of Dexia BIL, the big Luxembourg bank, was a pivotal figure because he was regarded as spokesman of the Luxembourg financial community that had supported Clearstream since its creation as Cedel some 30 years before.

Zeyen returned to Luxembourg during the afternoon of 11 May. The Luxembourg authorities then launched a formal judicial investigation of the allegations against Lussi and five Clearstream colleagues that was conducted by investigating magistrate Ernest Nilles.

---

[5] Interviewed by the author, 15 May 2006.

Roelants saw Zeyen and other officials in the prosecutor's office on the following Monday. It remains a matter of some dispute whether the prosecutor's office threatened to close Clearstream's Luxembourg operation unless Lussi was no longer in situ. Zeyen denies making threats but argues that it would have been impossible to search Clearstream if Lussi were there – not least because of the furore that the 'Clearstream affair' was generating in the French press. 'In that context, it was inconceivable for us to carry out searches in the presence of Lussi,' Zeyen says.

'I think you will always have two versions of this,' says André Roelants.[6] 'It's true that you can say formally that they didn't put pressure. But they said: either we have full co-operation and full confidence, and to do that we don't want to have people [around] who can be involved.'

The Clearstream International board gathered in a Luxembourg hotel for its meeting on Tuesday 15 May. It was, Roelants recalls, 'a very particular day'. First, the board meeting was delayed because the audit committee overran. A further delay followed because Douglass, who had flown from New York to chair the Clearstream meeting, had to meet Zeyen. Later it was Roelants' turn to leave, because he had to chair another long planned meeting of the Dexia BIL board in the mid-afternoon. On his return, Roelants found the Clearstream board still in session. Eventually, it decided to suspend Lussi, Carlos Salvatori, his deputy, and Robert Massol, chief human resources officer of Clearstream, as well as three other executives – Fernand Zoller, Pierre Goffette and Richard Woodruff. One person present said Douglass was in tears afterwards.

This was not before Seifert had, in the view of many participants, attempted a coup. Gerd Häusler was an unexpected presence on the fringes of the day's meetings. According to one version of events, it was only by chance that Häusler had a bystander's role in the Clearstream boardroom drama. He had come to Luxembourg from Brussels, where he had talks with Pierre Francotte at Euroclear, with the aim of meeting Seifert to discuss matters of common interest on the car journey back to Frankfurt.

However, that is not how it looked to all those attending the Clearstream board meeting. Some board members saw Häusler as Seifert's candidate to take over from Lussi: something that Seifert has since denied.[7] Asked whether Häusler was in line to be CEO, Roelants says: 'I don't think it was really something that was discussed as a sort of decision to be made. It was put on the table, but the majority of the board members at least were not in agreement with this way of doing things.' The majority feared that Häusler, if appointed CEO of Clearstream International, would work to help Deutsche Börse acquire Cedel International's 50% stake in the company.

Instead, the board chose Roelants – the representative of the Luxembourg banks – to be Clearstream's interim chief executive. He carried out the task for two months, while continuing as chairman of the executive committee of the Dexia-BIL banking group. Roelants' appointment surprised some. He had the unenviable task of stabilising Clearstream against the background of a media frenzy in France and a prosecutor's investigation at home. But a big man, blessed with a calming personality, he succeeded.

On 10 July, the Luxembourg public prosecutor declared there was no evidence of large scale money laundering at Clearstream International. This was after having interviewed 'H' and taken him into Clearstream to assist with a search of its computers. But there was no question of Lussi returning to the company. The prosecutor's lesser accusations were still unresolved[8]

---

[6] Interviewed by the author, 15 May 2006.

[7] In correspondence with the author.

[8] The prosecutor's office later issued two statements – on 20 November 2004 and 27 April 2006 – which said there was no case for Lussi and the others suspended in May 2001 to answer.

while Clearstream's internal investigations had uncovered management irregularities. 'We discovered things that in many banks would not have been allowed,' Roelants comments. The incidents were not illegal and in each case, there was evidence that one or more board members were aware of Lussi's actions. But the practices did not conform to high standards of corporate governance. On 13 July, the Clearstream board met again. Roelants was appointed Clearstream CEO and Douglass confirmed as chairman. The Lussi era was finally over.

12.4   THE BANKS CHANGE TACK

The turmoil at Clearstream rang alarm bells among the investment banking community, and especially among the members of the European Securities Forum. The ESF had grown out of Esiug to become a more organised body of two dozen leading financial institutions campaigning for a single integrated process of clearing and settlement of equity and debt transactions in Europe. The day after Lussi's suspension, it declared that any action by Deutsche Börse to gain majority control of Clearstream would be 'a move in the wrong direction' which would increase costs for users and investors.

Two things were clear. Clearstream's 50–50 ownership structure was becoming increasingly untenable and the broker-dealer community and big investment banks were more supportive than ever of a merger between Clearstream and Euroclear. That certainly appeared to be the wish of delegates attending the annual ISMA jamboree in June 2001. But corporate politics and slumping markets pointed to a different outcome – a complete takeover by Deutsche Börse.

While Deutsche Börse was sitting on a pool of ready capital from its flotation, the banks and brokerages which owned Euroclear and the 50% of Clearstream not in Deutsche Börse's hands were becoming less inclined to dip into their coffers to finance a merger of the two ICSDs. Banks were having a miserable year following the dot-com bust of 2000 and economic downturn in the US and elsewhere.

In July 2001, the ESF sent out a clear signal of penury. Ten months earlier, the ESF had put out to tender a contract to create a single central counterparty for Europe's securities markets. The creation of a large single currency area made it even more difficult for traders to know their counterparties. The introduction of the euro, therefore, had increased the attractions of CCPs beyond the well-established benefits they already offered market participants.

The decision followed some difficult wrangling inside the ESF. Its executive chairman Pen Kent, a former Bank of England official, strongly supported the mooted merger of LCH and Clearnet and held discussions with Euronext, the owner of Clearnet, about the possibility of selling Clearnet to its users. But some of the ESF's bulge bracket members wanted their own solution for netting transactions across a range of instruments as diverse as bonds, derivatives and equities to be best able to achieve economies of scale in such back office activities as collateral management and IT resources. Their wishes prevailed.

The ESF's proposed single CCP was an ambitious project and likely to be expensive. Producing an 'hourglass' model for trading and post-trade activities, the CCP would be sandwiched between many competing platforms for trading and settlement and handle national and cross-border transactions for all types of securities.

It would cut users' risks, costs and capital requirements. And because netting through a CCP can eliminate up to 97% of settlement requirements it promised, according to Kent, 'a massive economy for the industry as a whole'.[9] Kent believed a CCP for Europe could trigger

---

[9] Conversation with the author, 1 August 2005.

consolidation among and with settlement systems and so create a pan-European utility akin to the DTCC model in the US.

The ESF, however, was manoeuvring into an increasingly crowded market where there were a number of other projects to develop CCPs for the securities industry. In February 2001, the London Stock Exchange, together with CRESTCo and LCH, launched a CCP for the LSE's electronic order book (SETS[10]). At Deutsche Börse, preliminary work had started on what would become a CCP for cash equities, operating under the Eurex brand.

In July 2001, an international group of securities clearing houses, which included LCH, Clearnet and Eurex, set up an association called CCP 12[11] with the aim of improving global clearing, netting and CCP services. The underlying message to the ESF was clear: keep your tanks off our lawn or face ruinous competition.

When the time came to finance the ESF's own CCP the funds were not forthcoming. A few days after the launch of CCP 12, Kent had to admit that his member banks were not ready to make the investment because of their need to cut costs.

Kent had to abandon the plan for a single European CCP. But the hourglass model did not disappear entirely. It would be advanced several times in future years as a possible solution to the fragmentation of the European post-trade scene. The ESF initiative also stirred the European Central Bank to lay down guidelines for the possible consolidation of CCPs in the eurozone.[12]

Published in September 2001, the ECB's conclusions were largely unexceptional. They reflected the bank's keen interest in CCPs because of their possible impact on the smooth running of monetary policy and payments and settlement systems, and their importance for the stability of financial markets. The ECB therefore specified that CCPs should have effective risk management standards. Consolidation should be driven by the private sector 'unless there are clear signs of market failure'. There should be open and fair access to facilities for trading, clearing and settlement to 'guarantee a level playing field and avoid excessive fragmentation of market liquidity'.

But, in view of what it saw as a fast growing need for CCP services in the eurozone, the ECB's statement also put on record an important principle that extended to other post-trade services and service providers.

It stated that: 'The natural geographical scope for any "domestic" market infrastructure (including central counterparty clearing) for securities and derivatives denominated in euro is the euro area. Given the potential systemic importance of securities clearing and settlement systems, this infrastructure should be located within the euro area.'

12.5   SEIFERT SECURES CLEARSTREAM

It was against the background of heavy losses among European banks that the board of Clearstream International began to explore future prospects. It drew up three scenarios: continuing on a stand-alone basis; merging with Euroclear or having Deutsche Börse take over the 50% of the company it did not already own. A special committee, headed by Andrew Bruce, the

---

[10] SETS stands for Stock Exchange Electronic Trading Service.

[11] CCP 12 followed an established tradition of international financial organisations by including an erroneous number in its title. The press release announcing CCP 12 listed 13 members. This tradition was probably started by the Group of 10 leading industrial nations, which confusingly has 11 members.

[12] 'The Eurosystem's policy line with regard to consolidation in central counterparty clearing', 27 September 2001.

Barclays Bank representative on the Clearstream board, discussed merger prospects with Euroclear.

At this stage, according to Roelants, Deutsche Börse was willing to sell its 50% stake if there was an obvious case for selling to Euroclear. Otherwise, it reserved the right to make an offer for the half of Clearstream owned indirectly by the 90 or so holders of Cedel International shares.

The Clearstream board invited both Deutsche Börse and Euroclear to put forward proposals by 31 October for the future control of the company. Deutsche Börse responded by offering to buy the remaining 50% stake in Clearstream. Euroclear offered a negotiated merger that was thought to value Clearstream at about €2.4 billion which would have entailed the shareholders in Cedel International exchanging their holdings in Clearstream for Euroclear shares.

Although the financial details were far from finalised, it seemed at first as if Cedel International's shareholders would be given the choice. Several were also users of Euroclear's services and holders of Euroclear plc shares. A merger of Clearstream with Euroclear would create a potent European settlement utility that was already plugged into important national CSDs. The merged group could act as a pole for further consolidation.

Euroclear executives estimated that savings of €1.2 billion could be achieved if the 30 or so national CSDs in Europe were consolidated. Euroclear's user governance model provided some assurance that these savings would work through into reduced settlement fees, particularly for cross-border transactions, and therefore lower back office costs year after year.

On the other hand, a sale of Cedel International to Deutsche Börse promised the banks owning Cedel access to the €1 billion war chest assembled by Seifert through the Deutsche Börse IPO and whatever extra finance the Deutsche Börse group required to complete the deal. But such short-term gains would come at the cost of strengthening an already potent silo structure, with all that could mean for limiting free competition and user access to settlement services.

Given bleak international trading conditions in 2001 it was always going to be a difficult call. Any inclination towards altruism on the part of Cedel International's owner banks was dealt a further blow by the 9/11 terrorist attacks in the US which gave a further downward push to world stock markets and bank profits.

The discussions between Cedel and Euroclear gave few grounds for optimism. Euroclear claimed it faced a handicap because Deutsche Börse refused to give it any insight into Clearstream's books. According to Roelants, Euroclear kept demanding sensitive information that would normally have been released only after a memorandum of understanding or an agreement in principle between the two companies.

The real problem was that Deutsche Börse had a right of veto over the sale of Clearstream. As the talks continued it became apparent that Werner Seifert was increasingly determined to take full control of Clearstream and was willing to pay a high price.

Cedel International's board met in the first week of December and rejected both offers. For Roelants, the Euroclear offer was 'absolutely unacceptable; too low'. He objected that the cash holdings of Cedel International's shareholders were included in the assets covered by Euroclear's bid.

Euroclear interpreted the rejection as a ploy to elicit higher bids from both sides. By this time, its negotiators were convinced Seifert would veto any deal between Clearstream and Euroclear. However, Euroclear responded by raising its offer to an indicative value of €2.65 billion. This would have given Clearstream 35% of the merged group against Euroclear's 65%. Euroclear offered Seifert about €1 billion in cash to buy out all but a small residual amount of Deutsche Börse's 50% stake in Clearstream. The investors in Cedel International would be offered a share exchange at a premium.

The Clearstream International board met on 7 December, the day after Cedel International's decision. It rejected Euroclear's revised offer and instead recommended that Cedel International should enter exclusive negotiations to sell itself, with its 50% holding in Clearstream International, to Deutsche Börse.

According to Roelants, Deutsche Börse also came forward with an unacceptable offer. 'We threatened to go back home,' he says. 'Then it was the usual game of discussing in separate rooms. The advisers were together with the lawyers. And in the end, they agreed to our valuation.'

Less than two months later Deutsche Börse and the owners of Cedel International agreed the terms for Deutsche Börse to buy Cedel International and its half share in Clearstream. The price for the stake was €1.6 billion, valuing Clearstream at €3.2 billion. In addition Cedel's shareholders would receive the holding company's surplus cash, estimated at €150 million.

Deutsche Börse predicted that its cash flow per share would rise by 50% in the first full business year after completion of the deal. That did not stop criticism that Seifert was overpaying for Clearstream.

Despite the torrid time that it had experienced as 50% owner of Clearstream during 2001, Deutsche Börse was in no mood to upset the status quo on completion of the takeover in February 2002. André Roelants not only stayed as Clearstream chief executive: he also became deputy CEO of Deutsche Börse. Bob Douglass remained Clearstream chairman, despite his efforts to block Seifert in the weeks before Lussi's fall.

Europe with Two Settlement Models

13.1 EUROCLEAR ACQUIRES CREST

Euroclear responded swiftly to the news that Cedel International was entering exclusive merger negotiations with Deutsche Börse. On 12 December 2001, it announced an agreement with the London Stock Exchange and London Clearing House to develop a data feed that would allow the LSE's international customers to use Euroclear to settle trades.

The feed from the LSE would be similar to that agreed with the Paris bourse and Clearnet. The agreement had been in preparation for some months. It amounted to far more than a 'plan B' to patch over Euroclear's failed merger with Clearstream. Together with the feed from Euronext's Paris exchange, it emphasised the commitment of the three groups – the LSE, Euronext and Euroclear – to the horizontal model of integration just days after Deutsche Börse and Cedel International, Clearstream's other shareholder, committed themselves to completing a silo structure for cross-border settlement.

The agreement with the LSE showed that Euroclear would be neutral in its relations with stock exchanges and was not simply an adjunct of the Euronext group. Euroclear's agreements with Euronext and LSE also showed how some stock exchanges were no longer as closely tied to their national CSDs as before. The LSE was prepared to look to other settlement providers besides CREST, the British CSD, to meet the needs of its customers. Although the feed from the LSE did not go live until 2004, the announcement of the agreement doubtless helped concentrate minds in CREST. Soon Euroclear and CREST were holding serious talks.

'We started discussions with CREST within a month of having our bid for buying 50% of Clearstream rejected,' Francotte says. 'We understood already several weeks, if not several months, before making the bid for Clearstream that Seifert would say "No". We understood our chances [of merging with Clearstream] were small and we were thinking what that meant strategically.'

At first glance, Euroclear and CREST made for an unlikely pairing. Iain Saville, CREST's Euro-sceptic chief executive, was fiercely independent and had habitually exuded confidence that CREST, with its efficient real-time systems, could plough its own furrow. He was often scornful of Euroclear and Clearstream Banking Luxembourg because of their heavy reliance on batch processing. And yet when Francotte met Saville in the course of 2001, Saville appeared fairly open to ideas of a link, including a merger.

Euroclear's prospects had in fact brightened considerably since May 2001. In that month, Sir Nigel Wicks, a former senior UK Treasury official, was appointed chairman of CRESTCo, which ran CREST. Wicks had been in charge of the Treasury's international division for many years and the experience had turned him into a supporter of European integration. He had played a key role in implementing the introduction of the euro as chairman of the EU monetary committee in the 1990s. He was a member of the EU-appointed Lamfalussy group of 'wise men' which earlier in 2001 produced an influential report mapping out how better to integrate Europe's financial markets. Wicks' decision to become CREST chairman was seen, rightly, as a sign that the UK might be willing to play a more prominent role in finding a European answer to the fragmentation of the EU's financial infrastructure.

One of Wicks' first acts was to institute a review of strategic options open to CREST. The board met in mid-June 2001 for a two-day session away from the bustle of the City at the Penny Hill Park Hotel at Ascot to the south-west of London. Also around mid-year, Tupker and Francotte met Wicks and Scott Dobbie, the outgoing CREST chairman, over dinner in London. 'It was a very nice general discussion with nothing specific put on the table, where a few sentences on each side suggested that, well maybe there is something we can do,' Francotte recalls.[1]

CREST did not feel under any compulsion to link with a foreign service provider. 'I was not under pressure. We could have remained independent. We were doing well financially,' Wicks says.[2] 'But looking ahead, what the customers wanted was integration into Europe and that is what I set about delivering.'

Wicks feared CREST risked being marginalised and that if it waited too long to find an EU partner it would be too late to have any influence on the merged entity. CREST was sceptical about the prospects for a merger between Euroclear and Clearstream and saw little chance of joining the Belgian and Luxembourg ICSDs in a threesome. On the other hand, Euroclear, if it failed to merge with Clearstream, might think of approaching CREST on terms favourable to the UK company. This could be an attractive option because Saville's efforts to develop the 'spaghetti' model as an answer to Europe's infrastructure requirements were running out of road.

CREST had built a link with SIS of Switzerland, which Saville considered to be a competent miniature ICSD, in a bid to develop its international capability. Late in 1999, CREST cut its custody costs for international securities to reflect economies of scale from its overseas initiatives. In April 2000 CREST opened a link with America's DTCC which enabled investors to access a wide range of Nasdaq and other US securities through the CREST system.

But SIS and DTCC provided no solution for CREST in the context of EU integration. Moreover, such links required a duplication of investment to handle corporate actions relating to foreign securities and never seemed to attract sufficient business to justify the extra outlays.

'The political reality was I couldn't get others to open up,' Saville said later.[3] 'We had run out of alternatives. We tried the Swiss. The Italians and the Spanish seemed to have gone for vertical silos. I tried to merge with the Scandinavians via the Swedes.'

Political and economic factors meant the German and French CSDs were not interested in Saville's spaghetti recipe. 'I did say to the [CREST] board that the biggest win you could get short term would be to go with the Germans,' Saville recalled. He reasoned that putting CREST together with Deutsche Börse's settlement operation, which by then had merged with Cedel to form Clearstream, would unite the infrastructure of the two significant equity markets in Europe and create 'something that delivers value directly to your firms: one settlement interface for all German and British equities'. He tried to interest Clearstream. 'I trailed my coat. But neither Werner [Seifert] nor [André] Roelants wanted to respond.'

Instead it was Euroclear that came knocking on CREST's door. 'As soon as it became official that Deutsche Börse was not going to take Euroclear's offer and was going to buy the rest of Clearstream, we approached London and said: why don't we have a real discussion now?' Francotte says. 'Deutsche Börse closed one door. Nigel opened another.'

---

[1] Conversation with the author, 24 November 2006.
[2] Conversation with the author, 20 July 2006.
[3] Conversation with the author, 20 September 2005.

Euroclear started negotiations with Saville towards the end of 2001. The group was in a good position, with past investment decisions coming on stream and stronger finances. Improvements in straight-through processing meant that more than 99% of all Euroclear transactions in 2001 settled without manual intervention. In that year, it upgraded its real-time settlement platform to be able to process 300 transactions a second and completed a three-year wholesale custody project to deliver improvements, including the real-time processing of corporate actions. This investment, against the background of a savage bear market in equities and the 9/11 terrorist attacks in the US, was made in anticipation of higher volumes. It symbolised the group's commitment to increasing settlement capacity and speed in pursuit of economies of scale.

Euroclear's improved financial muscle became public knowledge with the group's 2001 results. Shareholders' funds in Euroclear plc more than doubled to €1.26 billion from €521 million in 2000. Euroclear Bank's gross income from fees and commissions – its main source of revenues – jumped 26.5% to €901.6 million. Net interest income leaped to €244.5 million in 2001 from €18.3 million in 2000 and €9.6 million in 1999. The bank's income statement reflected for the first time its 31 December 2000 takeover of the banking and operational tasks related to the Euroclear system previously carried out by Morgan. Because of the terms of separation from Morgan, the group's banking activity did not feed into Euroclear Bank's profit until 2003. But the potential for financing future investment was evident.

The group had also entered a new area of activity – investment funds. Euroclear took a strategic decision in the 1990s that it should provide infrastructure services for Europe's investment fund industry, which depended heavily on manual transactions. In 2000, it launched Fundsettle, an internet-based platform that automated and standardised the subscription and redemption processes of investment fund transactions. It reported in 2001 that Fundsettle had reduced the average cost of processing a fund transaction by up to 60%.

In late January 2002, it was announced that Saville had resigned from CREST to take a board level post with a global share registration business. He was replaced as acting chief executive by Hugh Simpson, CREST's business development director. The discussions restarted with a new CREST team, which was assisted by Julian Leiper and Andrew Winckler from among the company's non-executive directors.

In the early stages of the talks between Euroclear and CREST, Wicks made a suggestion that steered the negotiations towards a merger with Euroclear. He proposed that the two sides leave aside until later such inevitably contentious issues as the valuation and management of the combined group. Instead they should focus on writing a business model that made sense. This, according to Francotte, was 'not to be a two page business model, but a 35–40 page business model with details.'

The two sides started far apart and the negotiations were not easy. But bit by bit, they produced a joint approach. Euroclear and CREST concluded that it would make sense to consolidate their operations. The outcome, published on 4 July 2002, was 'Delivering a domestic market for Europe.'

It was an ambitious blueprint that owed a great deal to Francotte's vision of combining Euroclear and national CSDs which he developed in the course of Euroclear's merger with Sicovam. The domestic market for Europe would be a single settlement and custody area for five countries: Belgium, France, Ireland, the Netherlands and the UK. The merged entity of Euroclear and CREST would be the CSD for 60% of the Eurotop 300 equities, 52% of domestic fixed interest securities and 62% of Eurobonds held by the common depositaries – the banks that held securities on behalf of Euroclear and Clearstream Banking Luxembourg. It invited 'other (I)CSDs to join in this programme.'

The new Euroclear group would offer customers a choice between service packages. A standard domestic service would bring together the services already being provided by the group's CSDs at prevailing costs. A full multi-market service package, through Euroclear Bank, would provide a single point of access for settlement and custody of group securities[4] and Eurobonds and securities from 27 markets.

Stressing that both Euroclear and CREST were user owned and user governed, the blueprint held out the prospect of a single platform – possibly in 2008. The merged group would first develop a 'single settlement engine' to provide core settlement and payment functions. It suggested that domestic markets might start migrating to this new system from 2005.

The blueprint promised eventually to shrink the costs of cross-border deliveries by more than 90% in some cases, as charges would be cut to domestic levels in the five nation settlement area. To show this pledge was more than words, Euroclear Bank in late June announced book entry settlement services for Euronext Paris equities with charges for large scale users as low as €0.55 per transaction.

The new group sought to reassure customers (and owners) of its good intentions through a statement of principles that included open access to all participants in the European securities markets. CREST's interests would be safeguarded by giving CRESTCo the right to nominate seven of the 26 directors of the Euroclear plc board and four of the 12 non-executive directors of Euroclear Bank. Wicks became the deputy chairman of Euroclear while Francotte became chairman of CRESTCo. Market advisory committees – along the lines established by Sicovam before it became Euroclear France – would be set up as channels of communication between the group and its user communities in each of Euroclear's domestic markets.

The merger with CREST was approved at the end of September. As with the earlier mergers with the French and Dutch CSDs, Euroclear acquired CREST by means of a share exchange. The former CRESTCo shareholders acquired 19% of the enlarged equity of Euroclear plc. According to Lazard, CRESTCo's financial adviser, the deal reflected a 'substantial strategic premium' over CRESTCo's actual contribution.[5] In 2001, CRESTCo would have contributed 13% of combined revenues and 14% of net assets.

For the second time in two years, Euroclear was transformed. Euroclear plc now had more than 200 shareholders while the stake of Sicovam Holding fell to around 13.1%. The enlarged group boasted it was 'Europe's premier securities settlement system for both equity and fixed interest transactions.' A settlement behemoth, Euroclear's group turnover, including CREST, soared to around €240 trillion in 2002, two and a half times the €95.5 trillion reported after its takeover of Euroclear France.

With hindsight, Euroclear was lucky in the timing of its approach to CREST. It coincided with a debate behind closed doors in the UK on CREST's strategic future. This was fuelled by a growing fear among UK policy makers – at a time when it still seemed possible that Britain would join the euro – that France and Germany would get together to dominate European financial markets.[6]

There were some in Britain who considered that Euroclear's bid to merge with Clearstream would, if successful, strengthen the Francophone-German camp. On the other hand, a takeover of CREST by Euroclear – with its history of serving the broker-dealer community – would tip

---

[4] Securities for which CIK, CREST, Euroclear Bank, Euroclear France and Euroclear Netherlands act as the sole 'home' CSD.

[5] From the 'Recommended proposal for the merger' as required by Section 425 of the UK Companies Act of 1985.

[6] The London markets were particularly concerned by the activities of Eurofi, a Paris-based lobbying group representing French and other European financial services companies led by Jacques de Larosière, the former IMF managing director and Banque de France governor, and Daniel Lebègue, a former director of the French Treasury.

the balance the other way by blocking continental ambitions and helping London as a financial centre. Euroclear's acquisition of CREST also had attractions for Euronext, which at the time was keen on linking up with the London Stock Exchange.

CREST itself had some hard choices to face. If it stayed independent, it risked losing the business of big international institutions to Euroclear. This, after all, was the aim of Euroclear's feed with the LSE.

Over the years, Euroclear had worked hard to make itself acceptable and well known to the London financial community. 'Euroclear has done a cracking job over the years of schmoozing top custodians, investment bankers and central bankers. It has treated its board very nicely. All the then decision makers knew Euroclear,' one infrastructure executive observed.

However, Euroclear was not able to please all the people all of the time. Shortly after its triumph in taking over CREST, it found itself subject to hostile fire from some prestigious members of the banking community.

13.2   A SUB-OPTIMAL OUTCOME

Euroclear's takeover of CREST set the seal on three and a half years of frantic change in the European securities settlement industry that began when André Lussi approached Werner Seifert with his idea of a trilateral merger of Cedel with the German and French CSDs around the time of the launch of the single currency in 1999.

Lussi's initiative changed the industry. 'If Cedel had not merged with the German CSD we would not be where we are today,' says Pierre Francotte, Euroclear's CEO. 'There was strong resistance from national CSDs to merge with anyone. All the CSDs had to pay attention when the news came out that the German CSD was merging with Cedel, and also that the French would merge with them. It is why CREST ultimately merged with us. Without those events, we would still have national CSDs.'

Francotte's analysis places considerable importance on the role of individuals. 'We are where we are today because Cedel merged with the German CSD and the reason for that was that Lussi didn't want to merge with Euroclear and Seifert realised he had a problem with his platform called Trust.'

Equally important were Seifert's actions that caused the French to defect from the tripartite merger of the CSDs in 1999 and his veto over the sale of Cedel International's 50% stake in Clearstream to Euroclear in 2001.

Lussi's announcement in May 1999 of the plan to merge Cedel, Deutsche Börse Clearing and Sicovam spurred Euroclear's management to accelerate the separation from Morgan Guaranty as operator of the Euroclear system and create, in Euroclear Bank, a successor that subscribes to the principles of being user owned and user governed. Without this step, Euroclear would never have been able to take over the CSDs serving the Euronext bourses of Paris, Brussels and Amsterdam and the UK's CREST and develop a horizontal approach to securities settlement under the heading of a domestic market for Europe.

Had Lussi's tripartite venture gone ahead in 1999, the merged entity might have developed as a horizontal settlement provider, serving the market and attracting additional members. However, Deutsche Börse's subsequent acquisition of 100% of Clearstream in 2002 meant the appearance of vertical integration as created in Germany during the 1990s in a cross-border context.

The four years between 1998 and 2002 turned the governance and ownership structures of Clearstream and Euroclear upside down. Cedel's boast that it was 'From the market, for the market' still resonated at the end of the 20th century, because Euroclear's operations were still provided by the branch of a US bank that earned a significant income from the activities of its users. By 2002 that situation was reversed. Euroclear, which had been user owned since 1972, could now also claim to be governed in the interests of its users. Cedel, now trading as Clearstream Banking Luxembourg, was an important contributor to the profits of the publicly quoted Deutsche Börse group.

The net result of years of corporate manoeuvring was a still fragmented settlement industry. There were two different models of integration: the vertical and the horizontal, which were difficult to reconcile. Corporate governance structures ranged from user owned, user governed in the case of Euroclear and its CSDs to the for-profit, stock exchange listed model adopted by Deutsche Börse, the parent of Clearstream. The changes of ownership and governance among infrastructure providers in the years that straddled the millennium swept away many old safeguards without, as we will see, the authorities in the EU putting regulation in their place. The outcome could be described as sub-optimal.

But were there other options on offer? The international banking community always said it wanted a merger of Euroclear and Cedel-Clearstream. In 2001, there appeared to be a chance of merging the two ICSDs to create a user-owned utility that would also own important CSDs.

Had Euroclear been able to buy Deutsche Börse's 50% holding in Clearstream and carry out a share exchange for the 50% owned by banks through Cedel International, it would have taken a significant step towards overcoming the fragmentation of Europe's settlement infrastructure. The merged group could have acted as a pole of attraction for other CSDs – in Spain or Italy – that were standing on the sidelines.

By late 2001, the animosity that characterised relations between Cedel's André Lussi and Euroclear's Luc Bomans in the 1990s was less in evidence. The Euroclear system was no longer operated by Morgan Guaranty. There was new leadership at both companies after André Roelants took over the reins at Clearstream International and a user-owned and user-governed Euroclear was headed by Chris Tupker as chairman with Pierre Francotte as chief executive.

There is no doubt Werner Seifert's right of veto over the sale of Cedel International's share of Clearstream to Euroclear, which he exercised in December 2001, was a difficult obstacle that would have required skill and pressure to remove. But, as events in May 2005 were to show, Seifert was not unmoveable.

There were some who hoped Rolf-E. Breuer would play a pivotal role in bringing the two settlement systems together. He had thought of merging the two ICSDs in 1998.

'One started to ask oneself, is it really so good to have that sort of deadly competition,' Breuer recalls. 'It was not just the competition which is usual in the finance industry and in other industries and quite accepted as a normal thing, it was rather emotional. It was close to hatred. The despicable expressions about the other side and its behaviour in the market, and so on and so forth, pointed to a sort of bizarre parallel living between two institutions.'[7]

Breuer had been chairman of Euroclear for nearly 14 years between June 1984 and April 1998. In 2001, he was supervisory board chairman of Deutsche Börse, a position he had held since 1993. He was also chief executive of Deutsche Bank, an important shareholder in both Euroclear and Cedel.

Sir David Walker, one of the activists behind the ESF, feels Breuer could have done more but may have been sidetracked by his obligations to the German financial sector. 'If there is a villain of the piece – well not a villain, I just don't think he either thought it through properly

---

[7] Conversation with the author, 16 December 2005.

or, if he did so, pushed hard enough – it is Rolf Breuer. Because of his central role, he could have had a really benign and powerful influence on this process. And he didn't. Was he busy at Deutsche Bank? Was it Finanzplatz Deutschland?'

Walker recalled discussing whether more could have been done to promote a merger of the two ICSDs.[8] 'I had an argument with him, in the friendliest and nicest way, when Deutsche Börse bought Clearstream and Euroclear separated from JP Morgan. All of that created inflection points when we could have done something significant. I don't want to lay it all on Rolf Breuer, but a lot of the rest of us would have pushed. But Rolf was in the event unable to change anything.'

Breuer insists he did his best. 'I tried for a long time in the sense that I always had the feeling that it was the duty of Deutsche Börse to have a very close look and talk to the people in charge of Euroclear on the management level about ways to get together. I felt that to be a duty vis-à-vis the shareholders of Deutsche Börse as well as those shareholders with a stake in Euroclear. In the end, it failed.'

There was 'a sort of intellectual divergence and dispute' between supporters of the vertical silo model, such as Seifert, and the more Anglo Saxon advocates of horizontal structures, such as Euroclear, 'which made it very difficult to talk about mergers,' he remembers.

A Euroclear-led merger with Clearstream in 2001 would have been difficult to implement even without the two companies' peculiarly acrimonious history. According to Chris Tupker, Euroclear 'spoke to the powers in Luxembourg and reassured them that we would keep operations there.'[9]

But André Roelants' memories are different. 'They were looking to have their platform only,' Roelants says of Euroclear. 'One of the problems of the whole negotiation was that the architecture was completely different, so you had to kill one of the two. That would mean everything disappearing from Luxembourg, and leaving just a very tiny small company in Luxembourg.'[10]

Ultimately, there was insufficient will among Clearstream's banking shareholders, grouped in Cedel International, to overcome these hurdles and secure a Euroclear-Clearstream merger.

This partly reflected a decoupling over the years of owners from users of Clearstream Banking Luxembourg. Cedel was founded with the boast that it was run from the market, for the market. When the banks holding Cedel International shares were faced with a choice between Deutsche Börse and Euroclear, the biggest shareholders were no longer the biggest users of Clearstream's ICSD. The biggest shareholders were French banks, Luxembourg banks and some Dutch banks with the non-Luxembourg banks often holding their Cedel shares through their Luxembourg subsidiaries.

Seifert's €1.6 billion offer was too good to turn down. It could mean €50 million to €60 million profit for a relatively small Luxembourg bank – and this at a time when banks across Europe were being hammered in a bear market, made worse by the 9/11 terrorist attacks on the US. Banks in the Grand Duchy were also hard hit by a downturn in private banking activities, which was exacerbated by plans, actual and reported, of tax amnesties in Italy, Germany and Belgium.

Throughout history, banks have tended to have 'long pockets and short arms'. Equally pronounced has been a preference for short-term gain over long-term investment considerations.

---

[8] Conversation with the author, 16 January 2006.
[9] Conversation with the author, 27 March 2006.
[10] Conversation with the author, 15 May 2006.

When Seifert vetoed a merger of Clearstream with Euroclear, the heavy losses being suffered by the banks and financial institutions with stakes in the two ICSDs meant many were relieved they did not have to invest in financial infrastructure.

Certainly, this is Seifert's view.[11] 'It was 2001–02 when every bank, including Deutsche, realised unrealised gains. Traditionally you had written off all your stakes in exchanges or settlement companies to €1. The banks all needed extraordinary profits. And this is why they sold to us in the case of Clearstream and why they sold out of Deutsche Börse as well. This was a completely understandable and rational decision.'

As Pen Kent observed: 'It's the familiar problem that what makes strategic sense at the level of the market sometimes conflicts with strategic sense – or certainly tactical advantage – at the level of the firm.'

Some now regret the outcome. Stephan Schuster, managing director and head of capital market policy at Deutsche Bank, admits that:[12] 'Looking back it might have been a mistake not to merge [Cedel and Euroclear]. What almost certainly was a mistake was that one of these providers – Clearstream Deutsche Börse – became a private company and part of a public listed company. We fixed that vertical silo structure, which left us very limited possibilities to influence services and pricing.'

13.3   EMBEDDING THE VERTICAL AND HORIZONTAL MODELS

There was one immediate casualty following Euroclear's takeover of CREST. SIS had been trying to build support among friendly CSDs for a solution to overcome the barriers to the settlement of cross-border equity trades. A blueprint was drawn up for a Central Securities Settlement Institution (CSSI), which would link existing national CSDs while avoiding the pitfalls of the spaghetti model. CSSI was to be constructed around a central message forwarder and translator that would create an interconnection between participating CSDs.

Each CSD in the CSSI system would have two roles. As an 'investor CSD' each would provide participants in its home market with a single access point for settling trades in foreign equities. The settlement would be handled by the domestic CSD for the security being traded, which for this purpose would be known as the 'issuer CSD'. To qualify as issuer CSDs, the participating institutions would have to operate segregated accounts on behalf of the other members of the scheme and provide them with custody services.

CSSI's issuer CSD model aimed to locate settlement where the liquidity of the security being traded was most concentrated: in its domestic market. SIS approached CREST, DTCC of the US, Italy's Monte Titoli and Iberclear of Spain, which at various points showed interest in the scheme. Supporters saw CSSI as having a global application. The plan envisaged stan-dardisation of custody, settlement and collateral service levels among participants, without – its advocates claimed – large scale sunk costs. CSSI was viewed sympathetically by the ESF, which saw it as a potentially attractive, interim solution so long as the fiscal and legal barriers that hindered cross-border settlement were not removed.

But it needed critical mass to work. Deutsche Börse's acquisition of all of Clearstream and Euroclear's takeover of CREST meant the two big ICSDs were pursuing very different business models. Although SIS continued to organise slide presentations of CSSI until late in 2002, there was insufficient support to launch the idea.

---

[11] Conversation with the author, 12 October 2005.
[12] Conversation with the author, 12 October 2005.

The CSSI initiative fizzled out and the claims of its supporters that it would produce a significant reduction of cross-border costs – especially in equities trading – were never put to the test. With CREST now part of the Euroclear group, the other supporters of CSSI pursued separate goals. Their choices cemented the vertical versus horizontal divide.

SIS continued to maintain an interest in London, where alongside Euroclear and CREST, it provided settlement services to virt-x, an electronic market for European blue chips that began operating in June 2001. virt-x was a member of the SWX group, the Swiss Stock Exchange operator. It had been developed out of Tradepoint, an automatic for-profit exchange founded in the mid-1990s with Stanley Ross as chairman, which had failed in its bid to challenge the supremacy of the LSE. Although small, virt-x proved to be a resilient competitor. In May 2003, SIS x-clear, a CCP of the SIS group, went live at virt-x. Uniquely for Europe, x-clear formed part of a two level horizontal model as a CCP directly integrated into the settlement system of SIS. As such, it offered simple, low cost netting. SIS remained separate in terms of ownership and legal structure from SWX and as such free to work with or compete against other infrastructure providers in Europe.

The trading and post-trade structures chosen by the Italian and Spanish securities industries in reaction to the corporate manoeuvring elsewhere in Europe followed the vertical integration model pioneered by Deutsche Börse in Germany.

The Italian stock exchange operator, Borsa Italiana, acquired Monte Titoli, the Italian settlement provider, for around €250 million with effect from 6 December 2002.[13] Borsa Italiana already controlled CC&G,[14] the Italian clearing house, through a 59% stake acquired in 2000. The acquisition of Monte Titoli was widely perceived as creating a 'poison pill' defence for the group against possible corporate predators. However, it also brought a CSD which had developed efficient real-time platforms, known as 'Express', into the Borsa Italiana group.

Borsa justified vertical integration for Italy on the grounds of greater efficiency, competitiveness and critical mass which would 'assure a higher international standing for the Italian market as a whole and a stronger negotiation power in view of the future evolution of the European Exchange Industry'.[15]

It insisted that in Italy's case vertical integration did not mean the creation of an exclusive silo structure. Instead, Borsa group companies would continue to provide services 'to other markets (even competitors) and to market participants'. Integration advanced further. CC&G extended CCP services to government securities in December 2002 and Borsa's equity markets in May 2003. In January 2004, Monte Titoli's Express II platform took over settlement tasks previously managed by the Bank of Italy.

In Spain, Iberclear became the single CSD for all financial instruments and part of BME,[16] a holding company created in 2002 to put all of Spain's financial infrastructure under one corporate umbrella. With effect from 1 April 2003, Iberclear took responsibility for settling equities and corporate bonds from SCLV[17] and the book entry system for public debt, CADE,[18] hitherto managed by the Bank of Spain.

---

[13] Borsa Italiana holds 98.77%. Other shareholders in Monte Titoli include Euroclear Bank with 1%.
[14] Cassa di Compensazione e Garanzia Spa.
[15] An Integrated System: an information leaflet published by the Borsa Italiana Group.
[16] Bolsas y Mercados Espanoles.
[17] Servicio de Compensación y Liquidación de Valores.
[18] Central de Anotaciones del Mercado de Deuda Pública.

Clearstream became a fully consolidated subsidiary of the Deutsche Börse Group on 1 July 2002. After first stabilising the company, André Roelants' priority was to cut costs. This he did by cutting the multitude of external consultants hired under Lussi. 'On average, these people were two and a half to three times more expensive than members of staff,' he recalls. Altogether, Clearstream cut its operating expenses by a fifth to €462.1 million in 2002 from €576.4 million in 2001. Under Roelants' stewardship Clearstream realised for the Deutsche Börse group a significant part of the synergies that had been identified for the event of it merging with Euroclear.

The Creation platform was also completed. But, ironically, given that its potential was the reason Lussi first approached Deutsche Börse with his idea of a European Clearing House, it was not used by Clearstream Banking Frankfurt, the German CSD. The German banks, which were the users of the former Deutsche Kassenverein, refused to accept Creation, because adapting to it would have meant extra back office costs. Instead Clearstream upgraded the existing German CSD platform – CASCADE – and linked it to its Luxembourg ICSD.

Meanwhile, the rival horizontal model of consolidation found new followers in Scandinavia. In 2003, the Swedish stock exchange operator OM successfully bid for HEX Integrated Markets, operator both of Finland's stock exchange and APK, the Finnish CSD. The following year, OM HEX,[19] the newly merged exchange operating group, sold APK to VPC, the Swedish CSD owned by four of the country's big banks, in return for a minority stake in the merged Finnish-Swedish CSD group. The Nordic Central Securities Depository, known as NCSD, later started developing a common platform to serve the Nordic capital markets.

Each of these moves was important in a local context. But collectively they contributed to the continuing division of Europe's settlement infrastructure. After Euroclear's acquisition of CREST, the next major step towards post-trade consolidation took place in the area of central counterparty clearing, where the rapid development of CCPs in several EU countries encouraged thoughts of mergers and economies of scale.

13.4   LCH AND CLEARNET MERGE

The London Clearing House and Clearnet announced on 25 June 2003 that they intended to merge. Their courtship began more than three years before, on 4 April 2000, when the two companies announced a cooperation agreement. The idea of a marriage was boosted by Euronext's takeover of Liffe in 2002 which gave the transnational exchange 17.7% of LCH in addition to the 80% of Clearnet that it already owned.

Paris-based Clearnet was a pioneer of large scale central counterparty clearing for securities in the late 1990s. By contrast, LCH, founded in 1888 to clear commodity contracts traded in London, was a relative newcomer to large scale CCP clearing of equities although it had cleared small amounts for Tradepoint from 1995. LCH launched a CCP with CREST and the London Stock Exchange for the exchange's electronic SETS market in February 2001 after which the average daily volume of trades on SETS increased from 50 000 to around 80 000 by mid-2002. LCH, LSE and CREST developed the service further in July 2002 when they introduced optional settlement netting for trades executed through SETS.

The detailed plans for the merger made clear that LCH.Clearnet, as the merged entity was called, fitted more into the horizontal pattern of integration than the vertical. The combined

---

[19] OM HEX was renamed OMX later in 2004.

group was structured to ensure independence from trading and settlement platforms. It would act as a neutral partner to each of its trading platform customers with the aim of becoming 'the CCP of choice for users as a truly international cross-asset-class CCP'.

The LCH.Clearnet group promised to clear cash equities, exchange traded derivatives and commodities from a number of exchanges, including rivals such as the LSE and virt-x, as well as interest rate swaps, bonds and repos traded on international over-the-counter markets. LCH and Clearnet said they would integrate their operations in phases so that over time users could work with a single clearing interface into multiple markets. Outlining the merger plans, the chief executives of LCH and Clearnet declared: 'No longer will users require myriad systems and interfaces, thereby helping to control costs.'[20]

The merger valued LCH and Clearnet each at €600 million giving LCH.Clearnet a total value of €1.2 billion. The new group was owned 45.1% by exchanges (including Euronext with a 41.5% stake) and 45.1% by users. The remaining 9.8% belonged to Euroclear.

This ownership structure – with its equal balance of user and exchange shareholders – was made possible by Euronext selling 7.6% of LCH.Clearnet to user shareholders. Without this step, Euronext would have been clearly the dominant shareholder in the merged company with a 49.1% stake.

Euronext split its holding into ordinary shares, which accounted for 24.9% of LCH.Clearnet capital, and redeemable convertible preference shares, which made up the remaining 16.6%. The idea was that Euronext would, if the opportunity arose, sell its preference shares to bring new shareholders in to the group. However, during at least a five-year period after the merger, shareholders (apart from Euroclear) would have to be users.

Euronext's voting rights were capped at 24.9% and further provisions ensured no single shareholder or group of shareholders could control the company. Euronext's influence was apparent in one important respect, however. The exchange shareholders in LCH.Clearnet had an interest in obtaining income from their investment, unlike the user shareholders whose interest lay in low cost services. It was therefore decided that the group should operate on a for-profit basis and seek to reach annual earnings before interest and tax (EBIT) of at least €150 million from the 2006 financial year onwards.

The merger was completed on 22 December 2003. From this date, Euronext ceased to hold a majority stake in Clearnet and no longer consolidated its balance sheet or results.

The planned merger of LCH.Clearnet was announced three months after the launch on 27 March 2003 of Eurex Clearing AG, the central counterparty for Xetra equity trades and floor trading on the Frankfurt Stock Exchange. After a few months of operation, Eurex Clearing was reporting a netting efficiency of more than 95%, reducing implicit trading costs for investors by around €20 million per month. In response the Deutsche Börse group lowered its fees on 1 January 2004.[21]

The creation of LCH.Clearnet was both a response to increased competition and a vote of confidence in the horizontal model of integration promoted by Euroclear. Elsewhere, however, Euroclear's ambitions had run into opposition. At the end of February 2003, 'Fair & Clear', a group of agent banks claiming responsibility for 80% of cross-border equity settlement volumes in Europe, launched a high profile lobbying action against Euroclear's business model.

---

[20] David Hardy, Chief Executive of LCH, and Patrice Renault, Chief Executive of Clearnet, in the foreword to *Creating the Central Counterparty of Choice*, a guide for users of the two systems.
[21] As reported in the Deutsche Börse Group annual report for 2003.

13.5   FAIR & CLEAR

Fair & Clear included agent banks from 10 European countries which came together in June 2002 to coordinate responses to regulators' consultations. Among its leading members were Citibank and BNP Paribas Securities Services.[22]

Both banking groups were significant market players with little reason to love Euroclear. Citibank was one of a select and powerful group of global custodians while BNP Paribas could plausibly claim to fulfil that function in many markets. Both banks were also active as local custodians in Europe. Citibank was a supplier, customer and rival of Euroclear: it was one of the first backers of Cedel. BNP Paribas and Euroclear were competitors, especially after 1995 when the French bank acquired JP Morgan's European clearing and custody network and became a force in European post-trade activities.

The two banks – and the others in the Fair & Clear group – saw Euroclear's domestic market for Europe as a threat to their own businesses. They opposed it on the grounds that it was anti-competitive and dangerous.

The Fair & Clear banks charged that Euroclear's plan to put its business onto one settlement platform could give it an unfair competitive advantage against its agent bank customers. Left outside the platform, they would suffer from unequal access and insufficient transparency.

Fair & Clear also argued that the Euroclear business model, in which the national CSDs were subsidiaries of Euroclear Bank, 'commingled' essential infrastructure services and 'the risk-taking role of commercial banks'. This, it claimed, increased risk, distorted competition and was not in the best interests of the securities market. The lobby group therefore urged the formal separation of CSDs, ICSDs and agent banks backed up by EU competition rules and regulation.

The Fair & Clear document did not pull its punches. It described Euroclear Bank, the group ICSD, as a 'for-profit, shareholder owned business', disregarding its claim to be user owned and user governed. It also alleged that Euroclear Bank posed a systemic risk for the financial system and that it had only 'a two-year track record'. It took no account of the almost complete transfer of staff from the Euroclear Operations Centre to Euroclear Bank in 2000 and their 30 years' experience running the Euroclear system.

In a way, the Fair & Clear offensive was a backhanded compliment to Euroclear. The agent banks had acquiesced in the disintermediation of the cross-border settlement of domestic bonds during the 1990s, not least because they had limited scope for restricting a business conducted 'over the counter'. Although the Euroclear group's market share of cross-border equity business remained small,[23] the threat posed to the agent banks' business by the Euroclear group, comprising Euroclear Bank and its French and British CSDs, was perceived to be of a different scale.

By the end of 2002, the agent banks had realised that merging Euroclear with the national CSDs of France and the UK had fundamentally changed the European settlement landscape. The data feeds from stock exchanges such as Euronext and the LSE to Euroclear could, they feared, shift the location of settlement of equity transactions from national markets to the ICSDs. The banks came to realise that Euroclear's strategy threatened their margins and a business model that profited from the fragmentation of the EU settlement market.

---

[22] Early in 2003, Fair & Clear also listed Den norske Bank, Sanpaolo IMI, Intesa BCI, Kasbank 'and others' among its members.
[23] Euroclear's annual report for 2002 said 'around 90%' of cross-border equity transactions in Europe were settled through agent banks.

Emotions also played a role. The unanimous approval of the sale of Sicovam to Euroclear by Sicovam's owners gave way quite quickly to a sense of regret among some French banks. Not only had the *Place de Paris* ceded control over a strategic and highly efficient unit of financial infrastructure, it had done so to a group with a clear market-oriented, anti-corporatist, 'Anglo-Saxon' DNA.

In October 2003, Euroclear acted to quell the criticism of the Fair & Clear alliance of banks and reassure regulators that the existence of Euroclear Bank and national CSDs in the same settlement group did not pose a systemic risk. It announced a corporate restructuring to take effect on 1 January 2005.

The restructuring entailed the creation of a new Belgian-registered company, Euroclear SA/NV, to operate the single platform and provide shared services to all members of the group. Euroclear Bank would no longer be the parent company of CREST, Euroclear France and Euroclear Nederland. Instead, it would rank alongside the national CSDs as a subsidiary of Euroclear SA/NV.

'It wasn't just Fair & Clear that made us change,' says Wicks. 'We came to the conclusion it was much better to have a holding company – Euroclear SA/NV – to run the platform because Euroclear Bank, CREST, Euroclear France, the Netherlands and so on would all use the platform. In those circumstances, to put the platform in the bank was not logical, because the bank was a user like the rest.'

The corporate restructuring of January 2005 saw a reshuffling of executive positions in the Euroclear group. Pierre Francotte became the first CEO of Euroclear SA/NV, the new intermediate company, with Ignace Combes as his deputy. Martine Dinne, formerly executive director of Euroclear Bank, replaced Francotte as the bank's CEO.

The restructuring was a complex internal administrative exercise. But it brought benefits. It offered clients and regulators greater protection against systemic risk. So long as the CSDs were subsidiaries of Euroclear Bank, there was always some concern that their utility function could be jeopardised in the unlikely event of the bankruptcy of Euroclear Bank.[24]

The move improved the transparency of cost allocations in the group, making clear there was no cross-subsidy, and taking some of the venom out of the charge that the Euroclear group unfairly commingled the businesses of the ICSD, which had banking status, and the national CSDs, which were utilities.

The restructuring helped Euroclear successfully to resist calls – such as those from Fair & Clear – to detach the Euroclear Bank from the group. The bank, as we shall see, has a crucial role to play in enabling Euroclear and the group's CSDs to implement the domestic market for Europe.

13.6   CHANGES IN STRUCTURES AND GOVERNANCE

The corporate manoeuvrings of 1998 to 2003 transformed the securities settlement industry in Europe but failed to reduce its fragmentation.

The horizontal and vertical business models developed by the Euroclear and Deutsche Börse groups produced two very different philosophies for consolidating securities settlement across borders that were not easy to reconcile.

---

[24] The Euroclear group's strong capitalisation and very low risk meant bankruptcy must be considered a very remote possibility. According to Euroclear's 2005 annual report, the group's ratio of total capital to risk-weighted assets reached 97.52% at the end of December that year, against the minimum risk-asset ratio of 8% specified in the Basel 1 framework for banking supervision.

Vertical integration was a viable strategy in the 1990s. It successfully created efficient national settlement infrastructures in Europe with economies of scale and straight-through processing.

It was difficult to make the same case for silos after three years of EMU. Academic researchers queried whether the silo was the best way of securing efficient straight-through processing in conditions of falling communication costs, increased standardisation of IT hardware, and no currency risk for cross-border trading in the euro area.[25] Economic theory suggested that horizontal integration in the much bigger market of the single currency area should produce bigger efficiency gains because of greater economies of scale.

Ownership structures were another dividing line. Demutualisation of financial infrastructures in Europe began in the 1990s when Deutsche Börse was set up as a joint stock company in 1992. Advocates of the 'for-profit' business model argued that it encouraged greater efficiency and innovation than the often dozy mutual institutions that ran stock exchanges previously.

But Deutsche Börse's IPO early in 2001 took demutualisation into largely uncharted territory. It was not the first example of a Stock Exchange listing in Europe: the Stockholm Stock Exchange was the first to list shortly after it demutualised in 1993 and was taken over later in the decade by the OM group. But Deutsche Börse's was the first significant European stock exchange listing and it immediately attracted important imitators. Euronext completed an IPO in July 2001 and listed its shares on Euronext's Paris market. In that month too, the LSE, which demutualised in 2000, was listed on the London Stock Exchange.

Listing added new dimensions to demutualisation. The 'for-profit' business models applying to Europe's financial infrastructure became subject to the disciplines and uncertainties of a stock exchange quotation, which in turn were being transformed by the forces of globalisation.

Listing paved the way for new tensions. Before its IPO, Deutsche Börse's owners were essentially the same German banks and regional stock exchanges that had owned and used the Frankfurt Stock Exchange before and after it demutualised in 1992. By the end of 2003, these so-called 'strategic shareholders' owned just 3% of the company's equity. They had been replaced by hedge funds and other institutional investors with no local allegiance.

Seifert's failure to adapt to this change ultimately cost him his job. There were other tensions. In its 2002 annual report, Deutsche Börse hailed the presence of its institutional investors (which by the end of 2002 held 76% of Deutsche Börse shares) as 'a positive sign for the group'. It also declared that its 'paramount goal . . . is and will remain the continuous improvement of the benefits to be gained by clients'. It remained unclear how these two statements could be reconciled in event of conflict.

The changes of ownership and governance among infrastructure providers in the years before and after the millennium swept away many old safeguards without the public authorities putting regulation in their place.

So long as financial infrastructure providers were mutual associations or member-owned limited companies, there was less incentive for them to pursue monopoly rents. The 'for-profit' model brought to the fore specific regulatory and competition policy issues. How, for example, could users be sure that they were not being overcharged – especially as tariff structures often lacked clarity and transparency?

Deutsche Börse's listing and its subsequent takeover of Clearstream meant a significant piece of European post-trade infrastructure became part of a publicly traded, profit focused

---

[25] 'The securities settlement industry in the EU: structure, costs and the way forward' by Karel Lannoo and Mattias Levin, CEPS Research Report, December 2001.

group. The same was true of Clearnet after Euronext completed its IPO in July 2001. Although by the end of 2003 Euronext's holding in the CCP had dropped below 50% following Clearnet's merger with LCH, the merged group adopted a for-profit policy in part to meet the needs of Euronext, which remained its biggest shareholder.

The demutualisation and stock exchange listing of financial infrastructures in Europe was a revolutionary development. It appears to have been a haphazard, ad hoc process driven and shaped by the coincidence of the executive ambitions of the managers of the companies involved with the greed and need of former owners, who remained users. Missing was any regulation to ensure open access and fair charging structures, as was usual for privatised water, electricity, gas, telecom or transport utilities. It was left to companies to fill in the gaps.

Euroclear, for example, included a statement of principles in its July 2002 document 'Delivering a domestic market for Europe' that outlined its plans to take over CREST. The statement set down briefly its commitments to customers, underpinned 'by strong user ownership and governance'. At LCH.Clearnet the company articles included accountability to users as well as shareholders.

But Euroclear's decision to restructure the group with effect from January 2005 showed how the best intentions needed reinforcement. LCH.Clearnet acted early in 2007 to take better account of users' needs.

A parallel development was the decline, from the late 1990s, in direct public sector involvement in Europe's securities infrastructure. The Banque de France started the process when it transferred its securities settlement activities to Sicovam, the national CSD, although until Euroclear's acquisition of Sicovam it retained a 40% stake in the company. The transfer to CREST of the Bank of England's securities settlement services was agreed shortly afterwards. The migration of UK government gilt edged stock and money market instruments to CREST for settlement was carried out in stages and completed in October 2003.

There was a recovery of public involvement in CSDs in the EU as a consequence of the Union's expansion to include the former Communist countries of eastern and central Europe, plus Malta and Cyprus. Many of the CSDs of the 10 countries that became EU members in 2004 are owned by their national central banks or finance ministries.

But according to the ECB, only Belgium, Greece and Portugal inside the eurozone still had central banks involved in securities settlement at the end of 2006. The central banks of Spain, Italy, Ireland, the Netherlands and Finland followed the Banque de France lead and shifted securities settlement to the private sector.

It was probably to be expected that the events between 1998 and 2003 should produce no clear answers on how best to structure Europe's post-trade services. They have yet to run their course.

The mergers and failed mergers polarised as much as consolidated the clearing and settlement industries. The division into horizontal and vertical forms of integration and the new fault line represented by the Fair & Clear campaign meant there could be no consensus among post-trade service providers on how to advance integration and consolidation in Europe.

In some important respects, the Fair & Clear campaign pointed to big underlying changes in the post-trade sector. Behind the rhetoric and philosophical argumentation was the fear among the Fair & Clear participants of disintermediation by Euroclear's domestic market for Europe. If Euroclear could create a single market in the area served by its CSDs, the Fair & Clear banks as intermediaries would no longer be able to profit so handsomely from the complexities caused by market fragmentation.

The slick and professional Fair & Clear campaign also showed how the post-trade sector had become politicised and, in so doing, marked a historic turning point.

EU institutions and national regulators became increasingly involved in the industry's affairs in the years following the start of EMU as the private sector's inability to put aside vested interests and reconfigure Europe's post-trade services became more obvious. It is now time to consider the EU's response to the challenges facing – and posed by – Europe's financial infrastructure providers.

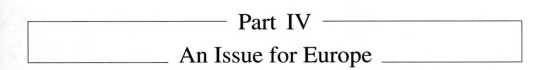

Part IV

An Issue for Europe

14

The EU Reacts

14.1 THE LISBON AGENDA

Perhaps it was the successful launch of the single currency, maybe even the manoeuvrings among post-trade service providers, but in 2000 the European Union at last recognised the policy significance of post-trade activities.

The change of heart began in Lisbon in March 2000 when EU leaders agreed a new strategy to turn Europe into 'the most competitive and dynamic knowledge-based economy in the world' by 2010.

Admittedly, there was no mention in the leaders' summit communiqué of clearing and settlement. But they backed 'efficient and transparent financial markets' to foster growth and employment. The summit, chaired by the pro-market, centre-left Portuguese leader António Guterres and strongly supported by a still popular and still effective UK prime minister Tony Blair, gave financial markets a new prominence in the EU's economic strategy and thinking.

Echoing new economic theories on both sides of the Atlantic, the leaders underlined how markets could help Europe's economy to catch up and overtake that of the US. Financial markets, by better allocating capital at lower cost, 'play an essential role in fuelling new ideas, supporting entrepreneurial culture and promoting access to and use of new technologies,' they declared.[1]

Financial services were moving up a policy agenda hitherto dominated by the need to launch EMU successfully. After 1 January 1999 there was no exchange rate risk on financial flows among 11 of the then 15 members of the EU. The time was ripe to focus on boosting Europe's competitiveness and the efficiency of its economy to cope with the new age of globalisation. In financial services policy, this became as much a priority as controlling risk.

There were some encouraging trends. The introduction of the euro led swiftly to integration of the money market with full convergence of nominal short-term interest rates for unsecured interbank deposits across the euro area. The euro-denominated bond market also integrated rapidly. By the time of the euro's launch, yield spreads for government bonds had been compressed to just 30 basis points over the 10-year German benchmark bond. During 1999, there was a big 19% jump in issuance, with a big expansion in offerings of new corporate and financial bonds.

Trading equities across borders was a different matter. The euphoria of the dot-com bubble – now on the point of bursting – could not obscure the difficulties caused by fragmentation. Equities were high profile financial instruments covered extensively in the media. When the time came for politicians to consider the problems of financial integration in Europe, it was natural that they should focus their attention on equity markets.

Words turned into deeds after France took over the Union's six-month rotating presidency at the end of June 2000 with the twin ambitions of putting its own stamp on the Lisbon agenda and promoting Paris as a European financial centre to rival London. By this time, there was a growing awareness that the Financial Services Action Plan was taking too long to get off

---

[1] Presidency Conclusions, Lisbon European Council, 23 and 24 March 2000.

the ground. For the FSAP to be effective, the EU's legislative process would have to be made more responsive if Europe were ever to meet the Lisbon goal of catching up and overtaking the US economy.

14.2   THE LAMFALUSSY COMMITTEE OF WISE MEN

Not for the first time, the EU sought out a group of 'wise men' to produce the answers. And, also not for the first time, such an initiative ran into resistance from London.

Both the UK government and the City were extremely wary of France's motives, suspecting that the real goal of the presidency in financial services was to pave the way for a single European financial regulator to be based in Paris.

Despite these difficulties, the initiative moved ahead swiftly. On 17 July 2000, the EU's Ecofin council of economics and finance ministers agreed the terms of reference for the wise men's committee and its membership.

The chairman was Baron Lamfalussy. Since retiring from the EMI in 1997, Lamfalussy had added the chairmanship of EuroMTS, an electronic wholesale market for Euro benchmark bonds, to his CV. He was joined by six committee members who brought a mix of experience and expertise to the task and who reflected the EU's diversity in terms of financial culture and geography. They were: Cornëlis Herkströter from the Netherlands, a former CEO of Shell; Luis Angel Rojo, a former governor of the Spanish central bank; Bengt Ryden, former president of the Stockholm Stock Exchange; Luigi Spaventa, the president of CONSOB, the Italian securities regulator; Norbert Walter, the chief economist of Deutsche Bank in Frankfurt and Sir Nigel Wicks, late of the UK Treasury and later to become chairman of first CREST and subsequently of Euroclear. The wise men had the backing of Frits Bolkestein, the EU internal market commissioner, who designated two of his more dynamic officials, David Wright and Pierre Delsaux, as 'rapporteur' and head of the group's secretariat respectively.

Lamfalussy and his committee were charged with finding a more effective way of adjusting, implementing and transposing EU financial regulation so that it could keep pace with rapid changes in financial markets. They were asked to look at a number of issues, including the conduct of cross-border financial operations and how regulators should respond to alliances of stock exchanges and technical innovations such as alternative trading systems. The wise men were told not to deal with prudential supervision. Nor did their brief specifically mention clearing and settlement.

They were expected to move fast, however. An interim report to 'present the state of play and initial approaches to solutions' was scheduled for November while their final report was due in the first half of 2001.

The Lamfalussy committee was strongly influenced by developments in the US, where there had been a sharp increase in the growth of labour productivity in the 1990s that went hand in hand with new jobs and falling inflation. They drew on recent academic research,[2] which suggested that the US securities-based financial system was superior to the European bank-based system in promoting growth and prosperity. This was when the long bull market of the 1980s and 1990s had only recently peaked and not yet developed clearly into the dot-com bust and equity bear market of 2000 to 2003.

---

[2] Notably 'Financial dependence and growth' by Raghuram G Rajan and Luigi Zingales, and 'Stock markets, banks and economic growth' by Ross Levine and Sara Zervos, both published in the *American Economic Review*, No. 88 of June 1998; and 'Finance and the sources of growth' by Thorsten Beck, Ross Levine and Norman Loayza in the *Journal of Financial Economics*, No. 58 of 2000.

Their initial report, published on 9 November 2000, concluded that an open European financial services and capital market was 'the major missing piece of the EU's internal market' and that action should follow without delay. As Baron Lamfalussy pointed out, the average US investment fund was six times larger than its European equivalent; venture capital per head of population in the EU was one fifth US levels and the average annual real return on US pension funds was 10.5% between 1984 and 1998 against 6.3% in the EU.

Many of the answers to Europe's problems were in the financial services action plan. The problem was that it took an average of three years to agree EU legislation with many financial laws taking much longer. The system, Lamfalussy complained, was too slow, too rigid and contained too much ambiguity and inconsistent implementation. It inhibited the development of cross-border securities business. There was, he said, 'a remarkable cocktail of Kafkaesque inefficiency that serves no one – neither consumers, nor investors, nor SMEs, nor large companies, nor governments.'

The Lamfalussy group's two reports broke new ground by outlining an improved way of passing financial legislation. They proposed using two new committees – one of national financial officials and the other of national securities regulators[3] – to give the EU a capacity for law making equivalent to secondary legislation used in the US and some EU member states, such as the UK. This constitutional innovation, Lamfalussy hoped, could halve the time needed to introduce financial market law.

The wise men included a passing reference to clearing and settlement in their first report, observing that 'major progress' was needed to reduce costs of cross-border trading to US levels as soon as possible. The brief 70 word paragraph, tucked away among 'areas for further reflection', marked the arrival of clearing and settlement on the EU's policy agenda for the single market.

The final Lamfalussy report – published on 15 February 2001 – went much further. Although it said the private sector should be mainly responsible for restructuring clearing and settlement in Europe, it insisted that important public policy issues were at stake. Moreover, public policy should show a clear lead 'if in due course it emerged that the private sector was unable to deliver an efficient pan-European clearing and settlement system for the EU'.

The report said public policy needed to focus on excessive costs of cross-border clearing and settlement compared with the US; competition issues such as open and non-discriminatory access to systems; the soundness of technical links between CSDs; the prudential implications of a single central counterparty (should one be created); and whether clearing and settlement systems should be authorised and supervised according to common European standards. The wise men suggested it might be necessary to separate clearing system issues from settlement, because (they added in parentheses) an efficient clearing system was 'a public good'.

The group urged 'serious consideration' of whether the EU needed to establish a regulatory framework for clearing and settlement activities. They floated the idea of involving the European Central Bank in this work because of the importance of clearing and settlement for the operation of monetary policy and the payment system. Finally, the wise men suggested that the European Commission's competition directorate general should examine whether EU competition rules were being properly respected in the sector.

Their ideas covered just over one page of a 109 page report. But the wise men had put clearing and settlement firmly on the EU's financial services agenda. They had acted decisively

---

[3] Later instituted as CESR – the Committee of European Securities Regulators.

and swiftly and others appeared ready to follow suit. The European Commission organised follow-up action even before Baron Lamfalussy presented his final report.

14.3   THE GIOVANNINI REPORTS

It was a Commission official of French nationality, taking the initiative during the French EU presidency of 2000, who set in motion the next stage of EU involvement with the securities settlement industry.

Hervé Carré, a quiet man with highly developed antennae for seemingly obscure matters of gathering importance, held a senior post in DG-Ecfin, the European Commission's economic and financial affairs directorate. He persuaded another quiet man, Pedro Solbes, his commissioner, to take up the issue of clearing and settlement. Together, they turned to Alberto Giovannini, an Italian financial expert and a much more extrovert character, and charged him with analysing the inefficiencies of cross-border clearing and settlement in Europe and producing solutions.

Giovannini was already well known to DG-Ecfin, as Solbes' department was called in EU shorthand. He was chairman of its 'Consultative group on the impact of the euro on European capital markets', formed in 1996 and which had provided helpful advice on the changeover to the euro and debt management in the single currency area. Having graduated in 1978 from the University of Bologna and obtained a PhD in economics from the Massachusetts Institute of Technology six years later, he had slipped back and forth in his career between the worlds of academic research and investment management, while also providing advice at various times to public authorities, including the Italian government, the IMF and the World Bank.

Giovannini reshuffled the membership of his eponymous group to bring in post-trade experts from the private and public sectors and started looking at clearing and settlement in January 2001. By now, the initiative also had the support of Frits Bolkestein and the Commission's internal market directorate. Of the 60 or so members of the group, around 25 self-selected to become enthusiastic participants.

At the time, Giovannini was working as deputy general manager of the Banco di Roma. During the course of the group's deliberations, he returned to the world of asset management, becoming chief executive and a founding shareholder of Unifortune Investment Management, which catered to institutions and high-net-worth individuals. Giovannini was earlier senior adviser and strategist at the ill-fated Long-Term Capital Management fund from 1995 to 1999. He was the first to admit to being no expert on post-trade issues. But he soon became fascinated by his new assignment.

Giovannini was determined that post-trade activities should be taken seriously. He argued with some passion that clearing and settlement, rather than trading, defined the securities market. 'They are the physical arrangement by which we can actually carry out transactions. Without that physical arrangement, we cannot carry out a transaction, so there will not be any market. It is like a square, where people meet, and one person brings the cash and the other person brings the goods. That's clearing and settlement. It's not a trading arrangement. It's not the way people negotiate price or anything like that. It is the square, where they can take the goat away and the other guy takes the money away. That is the market, and I think that intuition is very powerful.'[4]

---

[4] Conversation with the author, 23 November 2005.

Armed with this insight, he steered his group towards producing two reports. Both managed to spell out in clear – almost laymen's – language that a failure to create a single market for clearing and settlement across Europe would prevent the emergence of other benefits from financial integration.

'It is perhaps no exaggeration to conclude that inefficiencies in clearing and settlement represent the most primitive and thus the most important barrier to integrated financial markets in Europe,' declared his first report in November 2001.[5] The removal of these inefficiencies, it added, was 'a necessary condition for the development of a large and efficient financial infrastructure in Europe'.

As an individual, Giovannini was intrigued by the paradox that 'a low-profile type of thing' such as removing blockages in financial plumbing could 'change the face of Europe's financial system for the better'. Like Baron Lamfalussy and the wise men's group, he believed that 'well working financial systems tend to be strongly associated with superior economic performances'. A well-oiled financial system, which was competitive and open, could be a very important engine for unleashing Europe's unexploited economic potential, he argued. 'That's why I thought this project was a fantastically appealing project. It was one way to contribute to this.'

The first Giovannini report underlined the complexity of cross-border trading. A cross-border equity transaction typically involved 11 intermediaries (compared with just five for a domestic trade), 14 instructions between parties and as many confirmation messages. Giovannini surmised that such complexity (illustrated in Figure 14.1) added to the cost of cross-border trading. In the absence of any clear data, his report controversially claimed that per-transaction income of the two ICSDs was 'about 11 times' higher than the per-transaction income of national CSDs. It was difficult, the report added, 'to avoid the conclusion that the cost differential between ICSDs and national CSDs reflects the existence of barriers to efficient cross-border clearing and settlement within a fragmented EU infrastructure'.

The report identified 15 barriers, divided into three categories, summarised in Table 14.1. These involved: divergent technical requirements and/or market practices; differences in national tax procedures; and differences relating to legal certainty.

The Giovannini group produced a second report in April 2003.[6] This set out a strategy for removing the barriers and replacing them by technical standards, market conventions, rules, regulations and laws designed to overcome the fragmentation of the EU's post-trade services. The report set out a sequence of actions – described as a 'structured effort' – to remove the barriers within 'aggressive but realistic deadlines'. The private sector was given responsibility for removing six barriers, leaving the public sector to deal with nine. Giovannini stressed that success would depend on good cooperation between the two sides.

'The barriers, the timeline, the sequencing' were, Giovannini says, 'standard European Community tools'. But they constituted an intellectual leap forward. Instead of forcing integration, and raising the spectre of oppressive over-regulation, the concept of removing the barriers gave Giovannini and the Commission a more flexible means of boosting the efficiency of financial markets.

The second Giovannini report reshuffled the order of the barriers for the purpose of their removal. Action should start on barrier 7 to be followed by 1, 4, 6, 3, 8, 11, 12, 13, 14, 15, 2, 9, 5 and 10. The report named numbers 2, 5, 9 and 10 as 'priority barriers', which were

---

[5] 'Cross-border clearing and settlement arrangements in the European Union', The Giovannini Group, Brussels, November 2001.

[6] 'Second report on EU clearing and settlement arrangements', The Giovannini Group, Brussels, April 2003.

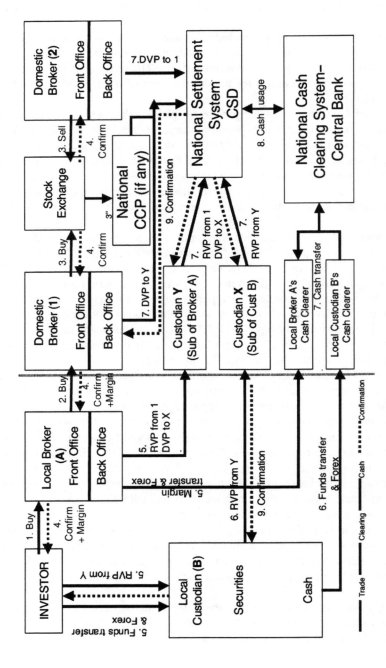

Figure 14.1 Instruction flows in cross-border equities transaction. *Source:* First report of the Giovannini group

Table 14.1 The Giovannini barriers

	Agent responsible	Deadline
Barriers related to technical requirements and/or market practice		
1 National differences in IT and computer interfaces	industry	2 years
2 National restrictions on location of C&S	governments	3 years
3 National differences for custody, corporate actions	mainly industry	$2\frac{1}{4}$ yrs
4 Differences/absence of intraday settlement finality	mainly industry	$2\frac{1}{4}$ yrs
5 Impediments to remote access of C&S systems	governments	3 years
6 National differences in settlement periods	mainly industry	$2\frac{1}{4}$ yrs
7 National differences in operating hours/deadlines	mainly industry	2 years
8 National differences in securities issuance	industry	$2\frac{1}{4}$ yrs
9 National restrictions on location of securities	governments	3 years
10 Restrictions on primary dealers and market makers, preventing centralised cross-border settlement	governments	3 years
Barriers related to taxation		
11 Withholding tax rules hurting foreign intermediaries	governments	$2\frac{1}{4}$ yrs
12 Integrated collection of taxes in local C&S systems	governments	$2\frac{1}{4}$ yrs
Barriers relating to legal certainty		
13 National differences in legal treatment of securities	governments	3 years
14 Differences in legal treatment of bilateral netting	governments	3 years
15 Uneven application of conflict of laws rules	governments	3 years

Source: Giovannini Group Reports I and II.

'related to restrictions on the location of clearing and settlement and the location of securities'. It specified that they should be removed at the end, rather than the beginning, of the 'structured effort' because removing them first would stimulate cross-border trading, and in the process increase operational and legal risk.

Giovannini left the choice of system for delivering pan-European clearing and settlement to the companies involved. But his second report noted that getting rid of the barriers would speed the consolidation of the EU's post-trade sector and this process would favour large service providers.

He therefore called for a regulatory and supervisory structure with powers 'to make clearing and settlement providers deliver fair and low cost access, respond quickly and flexibly to changes in their operating environment, and charge prices that are close to a minimised level of costs'. There should also be legal and operational safeguards to make the industry manage risk adequately and function efficiently in times of financial crisis.

The Giovannini reports recognised a difference between barriers that could be removed by market participants, working together, and those that required government intervention. The legal barriers, in particular, would be especially difficult to remove because they reflected fundamental differences in the concepts underpinning national legal systems.

The reports therefore put pressure on the private sector to work towards a market-led convergence of market practices and technical specifications. Progress in these areas would allow interoperability between national systems and give users a choice of settlement locations. To this end, Giovannini's second report allocated detailed responsibility for specific actions to individual industry groups such as SWIFT – the financial services industry's providers of messaging services worldwide – for barrier 1 and ECSDA – the European Central Securities Depositories Association – in the case of barriers 3, 4 and 7.

The Giovannini reports marked out a clear strategy for transforming Europe's financial market into an 'integrated entity' from 'a juxtaposition of domestic markets'.[7] But, as Giovannini has pointed out, they were not intended to solve all problems. The removal of the barriers would clear the ground for a reformed European post-trade environment. It would be up to others to provide the architecture and build it.

14.4   THE COST OF FRAGMENTATION

The Lamfalussy and Giovannini reports pointed to the high costs of cross-border clearing and settlement in Europe. But precise data of the actual costs was hard to come by.

At the end of 2001, a report from the Brussels-based Centre for European Policy Studies[8] went some way to plugging the gap. CEPS was the oldest think-tank in Brussels and under new leadership had recently shifted its ambitions away from trying to be a 'European Brookings Institute' to developing an expertise in financial market issues. In a spin-off from the Giovannini programme, Karel Lannoo, CEPS chief executive, and Mattias Levin, a CEPS research fellow, set out to discover whether the costs of cross-border securities settlement were as high as many assumed.

Their report concluded that operating costs of securities settlement systems in Europe were higher than in the US, but the difference was 'much lower than often claimed'. Instead of a difference of 10 to one, CEPS found that operating income per transaction after netting was 1.86 times higher in the EU than the US. If the comparison was based on pre-netted transactions, the EU costs would be 7.75 times higher.

Because there was no truly integrated infrastructure in Europe for securities settlement, it was inevitable that moving securities from one system to another would be more expensive than staying inside one system as in the US. Once ICSDs were left out of the comparison, CEPS found that on a post-netted basis the different domestic settlement organisations in Europe were as cost efficient as the DTCC. Moreover, the operational margins of Europe's domestic providers were much larger, 'meaning that they could become more efficient in response to market liberalisation'.

The CEPS study concluded that a centralised agency, like the DTCC, was not necessarily cheaper than competing organisations. But the EU authorities should take some action to encourage Europe's post-trade sector to restructure. The way forward, it suggested, lay in modifying the Investment Services Directive of 1993 to enforce direct remote access to securities settlement systems. The EU Commission had suggested such a move in a consultation paper for reforming the ISD, which was one of the measures envisaged under the FSAP. CEPS also urged the EU's competition authorities to keep a watch over clearing and settlement.

CEPS admitted that difficulties surrounded its comparative cost figures. It was 'almost impossible' to compare fees, 'since each one of the institutions involved has developed its own

---

[7] From the foreword of the second Giovannini report.
[8] The securities settlement industry in the EU: structure, costs and the way forward', by Karel Lannoo and Mattias Levin, CEPS Research Report, December 2001.

complex tariff structure that takes into account the kind of transaction, its volume and the size and nature of the client'. Other cost elements, such as cross-collateralisation, were difficult to quantify. CEPS, unlike a public body, had no authority to request data.

Similar problems plagued other efforts to assess the costs of post-trade services in Europe in the years that followed. Half a dozen other reports followed the CEPS study and sometimes produced strikingly different results.

Euroclear, for example, estimated that the aggregate excess cost of cross-border post-trade activities in Europe was about €5 billion a year. It attributed 2.5% of total costs to the ICSDs and CSDs respectively, while local agent banks accounted for 35% and additional back office costs 60%.[9]

In 2005, economists at the ECB reviewed several studies,[10] noting their different methodologies, country selections and sample periods. The ECB economists found most studies reached similar conclusions about a relatively large difference of clearing and settlement costs between the EU and the US. Those studies which used several years of data suggested possible cost savings of between one third and more than two thirds 'were Europe to adopt a single system'.

The final word for the time being comes from the European Commission.[11] In May 2006 it published an analysis of studies of European post-trading costs as part of its impact assessment of possible measures for the sector. Concluding that a cross-border equity transaction in Europe costs investors between two and six times more than a domestic transaction, it commented: 'The value of the ratio is very high and not in line with the ambitions of a single securities market in the EU.' It also reported that domestic transactions were up to eight times more expensive in EU post-trade infrastructures than in the DTCC.

The Commission found the average excess cost of cross-border equity settlement was between €15 and €20 per transaction, making aggregate excess costs of post-trading for investors of between €2 billion and €5 billion. As it estimated the total spending of investors on trading and post-trading at €28 billion a year in Europe, the elimination of €2 billion to €5 billion of excess costs would cut investors' transaction costs by between 7% and 18%, adding between 0.2% and 0.6% to the level of EU GDP in any given year. In addition, market consolidation could save a further €700 million.

These figures are the subject of dispute in the industry. The Commission has admitted that the pricing of post-trade services is complex and that 'none of the studies produced so far has been universally accepted as providing an accurate description of prices or costs incurred by investors in acquiring post-trade services in Europe'. It has commissioned Oxera, a British-based economic research consultancy, to develop a methodology to monitor the evolution of prices, costs and volumes in the sector.[12]

14.5 THE COMMISSION RESPONDS

The European Commission began working on clearing and settlement a few months after the Giovannini group. Its internal market directorate launched an internet consultation in April 2001, linking this to an ongoing review of the ISD. It promised a 'communication' or

---

[9] In 'Delivering low-cost cross-border settlement', January 2003.

[10] In 'Integration of securities market infrastructures in the Euro area', by Heiko Schmiedel and Andreas Schönenberger, ECB occasional paper No. 33, July 2005.

[11] Draft Working Document on Post-Trading, European Commission, Internal Market DG, Brussels, May 2006, plus Annex I, Analysis of studies examining European post-trading costs.

[12] Note on DG Markt website, dated 7 November 2006.

consultative document on clearing and settlement later in 2001, taking the first step in a process that might end in EU legislation.

The communication[13] was eventually published after the first Giovannini report in June 2002. It took removing Giovannini's 15 barriers as a starting point for increasing the efficiency of cross-border clearing and settlement in the EU. It also laid great stress on creating a level playing field among institutions involved in the sector with a view to encouraging open access to all systems. 'All markets, infrastructure providers and market participants should be able to access all necessary systems, regardless of their location,' it said. 'Fully integrated markets require that rights of access to systems be comprehensive, transparent and non-discriminatory and, above all, effective.' It proposed the 'parallel application of competition policy' to reinforce these measures.

Like Giovannini, the Commission refrained from defining the form of market infrastructure the EU should have. However, it did suggest that EU bodies should be heavily engaged in helping market forces create an integrated clearing and settlement industry. An annex to the report outlined how the EU should be involved in dealing with eight of the 10 market practice and technical barriers identified by Giovannini.

The Commission was concerned about the lack of a single legal regime to govern securities transactions in the EU. Referring to the multilateral treaty on the ownership of securities held in electronic form that was then being negotiated within the Hague Conference for unifying the rules of private international law, it asked whether 'further measures, beyond the adoption of the Hague Convention' were needed to resolve conflict of law. It floated one idea, put forward by Giovannini, for a 'securities code'. Based on US practice, this would detach securities from national legal systems and insolvency laws and instead establish uniform legal treatment of securities across the EU.

The Commission asked whether EU legislation should 'provide comprehensive rights of access and choice across and between all levels of the trading and settlement chain'. Noting there was no agreed common system of regulation for CCPs, settlement systems or custodians, it also mulled the possibility of an EU law containing 'some high level principles' to cover such issues as 'the authorisation, supervision, risk management techniques, default arrangements or capital treatment of such institutions'. It also wondered whether common functional definitions of clearing and settlement activities at the EU level would help achieve a level playing field.

In the space of three years, the Commission had moved from total neglect of the post-trade sector to contemplating some significant legislative initiatives. It gave interested parties three months to comment and harvested 61 responses with three quarters coming about equally from public authorities, infrastructure providers along the chain from trading to settlement, and financial institutions.

The responses identified fairly solid acceptance of Giovannini's analysis; general agreement that the market, rather than public authorities, should determine how to consolidate the post-trade sector; and general agreement on the need for open and fair access to services.

But support for EU legislation was less clear, reflecting divisions in the industry that would be a permanent feature of discussions on the pros and cons of EU intervention. The Commission, however, was sufficiently encouraged to promise a policy paper at a later date which would set out measures 'necessary to achieve the objective of integrated, competitive, safe and cost effective clearing and settlement in the EU'.

---

[13] 'Clearing and settlement in the European Union. Main policy issues and future challenges', COM(2002)257.

The intervening period would allow it to digest the responses to its communication and other reports on clearing and settlement. These would include Giovannini's second report, a European Parliament report reacting to the Commission's communication and efforts by the European Central Bank and the Committee of European Securities Regulators to draw up standards for the industry.

14.6   THE ANDRIA REPORT

Next off the production line was the European Parliament report, drafted by Generoso Andria, a centre-right Italian MEP and member of the parliament's Economic and Monetary Affairs (Econ) Committee. Andria's report, which appeared in December 2002, took a very positive view of the DTCC in the US and put forward some radical ideas to achieve similar results in Europe.

The report proposed that 'core' settlement services should be managed as user-owned services on a non-profit basis to hold down costs. So far so good. But this would be achieved through far reaching changes by which CSDs should perform national and cross-border securities settlement services 'on an exclusive basis' while value added services should be provided by a 'shared or supervised structure that should remain separate'.

Andria's report added that 'the risk-exposure of such entities should be limited to the taking of operational risks, to the exclusion of banking risk'. If implemented, the report would mean unbundling the services provided by ICSDs such as Euroclear Bank and Clearstream Banking Luxembourg and the end of their business model.

The report's ideas on CSDs bore a striking resemblance to proposals put forward by a group of agent banks earlier in 2002[14] and ideas in a 29 page paper from BNP Paribas Securities Services,[15] published in May.

Andria's suggestions were so far reaching that they stirred resistance among more market-oriented MEPs who decided to take charge of drafting the next parliamentary report that would respond to the Commission's forthcoming policy paper on clearing and settlement. This task was eventually taken up by two young female MEPs: Theresa Villiers, a UK Conservative, and, after Villiers left the European Parliament in 2005 for a seat in the UK House of Commons, Piia-Noora Kauppi, of Kokoomus, the Finnish National Coalition Party.

The Andria report was quickly overtaken by other controversies. But it was a signal to financial infrastructure providers that they neglected European politics at their peril. Because securities settlement was a single market issue, the European Parliament would have equal rights as co-legislator with the Council of Ministers (which represented the EU member states) if ever the Commission proposed an EU law to cover the sector. The one clear lesson for the industry from the Andria report was that lobbying was now a vital part of the securities settlement business.

14.7   THE ESCB/CESR STANDARDS

Once started, there was no stopping the politicisation of clearing and settlement. A battle of the brochures ensued. One among many was 'Delivering low-cost cross-border settlement',

---

[14] These included a 'Recommendation for a clear segregation between CSD (non banking) and custodian bank (banking) activities' published in April 2002 by a group of 'European Custodian Banks' based in France, Italy, the Netherlands and Scandinavia.

[15] Contribution to the joint CESR/ECB consultation in the field of clearing and settlement.

in which Euroclear set out, in January 2003, its ideas for making cross-border settlement cheaper and less risky. It was this explanation of Euroclear's domestic market for Europe which provoked the custodian banks to hit back under the 'Fair & Clear' banner.

EU policy proposals became battlefields for the prosecution of proxy wars between settlement providers. For Euroclear, the main battle lines were drawn against the agent banks rather than its old rival Clearstream.

It was in this increasingly fevered atmosphere that work on a set of standards to apply to securities settlement systems in the EU ran into controversy. The endeavour began quietly enough. In October 2001, the governing council of the ECB and CESR, the Committee of European Securities Regulators which was set up following the Lamfalussy report, announced they would work together on issues of common interest relating to securities settlement systems in the EU. Their stated aim was to establish 'standards and/or recommendations' for securities settlement systems and CCPs that would help give the industry a level playing field and overcome problems – such as regulatory arbitrage – caused by legal and legislative differences in European countries.

The quest for standards was already advanced at the G10 level. A joint task force of CPSS, the payments and settlement systems committee of the G10 central banks, and IOSCO, the International Organisation of Securities Commissions, produced 19 recommendations for minimum standards that securities settlement systems should meet[16] around the time the ECB and CESR decided to work together. These were published in November 2001. IOSCO had grown since its foundation in 1984 to become the leading international standard setter for securities markets – although its output normally took the form of non-binding recommendations. The CPSS had been an important influence on the work of the ECB and its forerunner the EMI. Another reason to expect the CPSS/IOSCO standards to be useful for EU purposes was the fact that Padoa-Schioppa was chairman of CPSS.

In March 2002, a working group of officials from CESR and the European System of Central Banks (ESCB) indicated that they planned to 'deepen and strengthen' the CPSS/IOSCO recommendations for EU purposes and called for input from the industry. It received 36 replies, including the May 2002 memo from BNP Paribas mentioned earlier. In July 2003, the group published a first draft of its ideas as a consultative report.

The report caused uproar. It upset the European Parliament which saw the ESCB/CESR standards as encroaching on its legislative prerogatives. The idea was that the EU standards should be more binding than the CPSS-IOSCO recommendations. Although the standards would not have the status of EU law, 'regulators, supervisors and overseers' were expected to adopt them and ensure their implementation by the industry.

The standards also upset the agent banks. The report followed the 'risk-based functional approach' suggested by the CPSS-IOSCO recommendations, which meant the standards would apply to 'all relevant functions' in the securities clearing and settlement business without regard to the legal status of institutions.

The ESCB/CESR approach was very different to that of the Andria report. The ESCB/CESR report proposed that several of the standards designed for CSDs and ICSDs should also apply to 'custodians operating systemically important systems'. It reasoned that the clearing and settlement activities of these major custodians were of such a scale as to harbour systemic risk that 'may affect the entire financial market of the European Union'.

---

[16] 'Recommendations for securities settlement systems', published November 2001.

The ESCB/CESR report provoked angry responses, notably from Citibank and BNP Paribas, the main backers of Fair & Clear. The European Banking Federation, which claimed to represent the interests of more than 4000 banks in the 15 EU member states, plus banks in Iceland, Norway and Switzerland, rallied to the side of the custodian banks.[17] The FBE urged that a distinction in regulation should be made between the functions of infrastructure providers, such as CSDs, and intermediaries, such as banks. The federation warned that the ESCB/CESR standards could lead to over-regulation and overlapping regulation, It pointed out that the banks were covered by the Basel rules covering capital adequacy and prudential supervision.

A year later – after two consultations and two public hearings – the ESCB/CESR working group published a new draft of the standards. The September 2004 draft appeared to deal with the banks' problems by accepting that Basel II, the revised Basel capital accord then in preparation, 'would provide banking institutions with the most appropriate instrument to address risks with their settlement activities'. But detailed issues remained, including the definition of a 'significant custodian' and the precise analysis of how far such institutions posed a risk to the financial system.

In October 2004, the ECB governing council and CESR approved the working group's report. But the standards could not be implemented because Bafin, the German securities regulator, unexpectedly raised concerns about the legal basis for their adoption in Germany. With most of the report agreed, CESR and the ESCB decided, in autumn 2005, to put the working group's activities on hold.

Eddy Wymeersch, head of Belgium's financial regulator and CESR co-chairman of the group, said the mothballing was in anticipation of a Commission position on clearing and settlement.[18] The real reason was the immoveable nature of conflicting interests, and especially Bafin's discovery of German legal problems. These, to the bemusement of fellow regulators, were not raised at the beginning of the ESCB/CESR exercise. At the time of going to press,[19] the standards remain in limbo although there is pressure from the Commission and the ECB for their revival. The industry meanwhile has had to make do with the CPSS/IOSCO recommendations.

14.8   THE G30 AND EFR REPORTS

The proxy war between Fair & Clear and Euroclear over the standards rather overshadowed two reports on the industry that appeared in 2003. In the first, published in January, the Group of 30 returned to the issue of clearing and settlement with a plan of action to overcome the risks and inefficiencies in cross-border post-trade activities worldwide.

The G30's report was produced by a steering committee chaired by Sir Andrew Large, who by now was deputy governor of the Bank of England. It put forward 20 recommendations, based substantially on those of CPSS/IOSCO, but was noteworthy for the stress that it put on interoperability among existing systems.

Interoperability for the G30 meant users along the clearing and settlement value chain should be able to work with service providers without having to make a special effort. However, this happy state of affairs would involve more than the technical compatibility of systems. It would

---

[17] In a statement dated 6 November 2003.
[18] In the CESR annual report for 2005.
[19] August 2007.

require 'like or compatible processes, business practices, controls, technologies, products, access arrangements and fee structures'.

This was a tall order. But the G30 report suggested that the rewards from such an approach could be as great as those gained from the national standardisation of railway track gauges in the US in the 19th century, or internationally from the more recent automation of air traffic control services through the standards and protocols of the International Civil Aviation Organisation.

Interoperability could offer a way of overcoming the differences between the horizontal and vertical models of integration in Europe. This, however, would depend on the owners of vertical structures allowing open access and fair tariffs for users of other stock exchanges or trading platforms and, in turn, allowing the users of their own trading platforms to clear and settle trades elsewhere.

Another elite financial ginger group put forward its ideas on clearing and settlement towards the end of 2003. Consisting of 17 chairmen and chief executives of European banks and insurance companies, the European Financial Services Round Table had set itself up in 2001 to try to give a push to the financial services action plan. Its December 2003 report, produced under the guidance of the former Euroclear chairman, Rolf-E. Breuer, the supervisory board chairman of Deutsche Bank, advocated the creation of a single European central counterparty or CCP. This should provide 'a single entry point' across securities and across markets 'for all transactions in debt securities, equity and their derivatives in Europe' as the best way to secure efficient post-trade services.

Breuer was also supervisory board chairman of Deutsche Börse at the time. The EFR report nonetheless warned that 'no trading platform should have an undue influence on any single settlement system'. It urged 'free and open access for all intermediaries' to post-trade infrastructure and suggested the regulation of clearing and settlement infrastructures should be 'a priority for future legislative activity' in the EU.

14.9   MiFID

At the end of April 2004, two important decisions affecting clearing and settlement emerged from different parts of the Brussels legislative machine. After months of intensive lobbying and often bitter infighting among EU member states, the Council of Ministers adopted a new law to open up the trading of securities in Europe to greater competition.

The law, which became known as the Markets in Financial Instruments Directive or MiFID, was one of the most important elements of the financial services action plan (FSAP). It would allow investment firms, banks and exchanges to provide their services across EU borders on the basis of their home country authorisation.

MiFID is the replacement for the 1993 Investment Services Directive (ISD), which relied heavily on the principle of mutual recognition of services by member states and proved less than effective in creating a single capital market for Europe. In the longer term one of MiFID's key aims is to create a single European 'securities rule book' by bringing more into line national rules on the provision of investment services and the operation of exchanges.

The law passed in 2004 was a so-called framework directive[20] and many details were filled in later. The entire package proved so complex that the deadline for MiFID's implementation was extended to 1 November 2007. For many, the complexity and the up-front costs of compliance made MiFID a synonym for all that is worst in EU financial legislation. But as the deadline

---

[20] A legislative innovation proposed by Baron Lamfalussy's committee of wise men.

for implementation came closer, investment companies and banks began manoeuvring to take advantage of its new rules.

Charlie McCreevy, who inherited MiFID when he became the internal market commissioner in November 2004, took a positive view. He predicted that MiFID would 'be the catalyst for significant market changes. It will dramatically increase levels of competition among and between execution venues and investment firms. It will definitely increase cross-border competition and lower costs for issuers and investors of accessing capital markets.'[21]

Articles 34 and 46 of MiFID provided some access rights to regulated markets and investment firms in the post-trade area. MiFID obliged EU member states to make sure investment firms from other member states have access to clearing, CCP and CSD services in their territory on the same conditions as local firms. It established the right of market participants to choose the settlement location (but not the CCP clearing location) for their trades so long as links were in place between the regulated market and organisation in question. Regulated markets also were given the right to choose a particular CCP and/or CSD to clear and settle their transactions.

MiFID, however, did not cover relations among post-trade infrastructures.[22] Hence, as implementation day approached, it appeared that the directive would have a greater indirect impact on Europe's post-trade sector through its provisions to allow banks and other investment institutions to compete with stock exchanges.

Since November 2007, trades no longer have to be conducted on, or reported to, local exchanges. As far as post-trade activities are concerned, one of MiFID's more important provisions could be the 'best execution' clause obliging investment firms to execute orders on terms most favourable to the client, taking into account many factors besides price. These include costs, speed, likelihood of execution and settlement, size and any other consideration relevant to the order.

14.10   THE COMMISSION'S SECOND COMMUNICATION

The other key decision of late April 2004 was the second of the promised communications on clearing and settlement[23] from the Commission. The Commission's task was not easy. It had to find a viable way forward in the absence of consensus among post-trade service providers over the industry's future and how to lower the costs and increase the efficiency of cross-border securities transactions.

In the background there was growing disenchantment in the City of London, the EU's premier financial centre, about the FSAP. Initiatives for EU-wide rules to combat market abuse, harmonise prospectuses and replace the ISD with MiFID had run into strong criticism from London financial trade associations as excessively bureaucratic and potentially costly.

The Commission put forward a carefully calibrated strategy. It endorsed the elimination of the Giovannini barriers and decided not to intervene in the structure of the industry. It therefore kept aloof from ongoing debates over whether to consolidate existing settlement systems, on the merits of user-owned against for-profit governance structures, and whether to separate the intermediary and banking functions of CSDs.

The Commission wanted investors and the intermediaries acting on investors' behalf to have all possible options for the clearing and settlement of cross-border securities transactions in

---

[21] Annual lecture at SUERF (Société Universitaire Européenne de Recherches Financière) Brussels, 30 November 2005.

[22] These became the subject of an industry code of conduct, brokered by Commissioner McCreevy in 2006 and introduced in stages from 1 January 2007. See Chapter 17.

[23] 'Clearing and settlement in the European Union – The Way Forward,' COM(2004)312 of 28 April 2004.

the EU. Its goal was for the users of clearing and settlement services to have free access to the system of their choice. It wanted a common regulatory framework covering the functions performed by the various actors in the market. This would allow mutual recognition of clearing and settlement systems across the EU, thus enhancing integration and protecting investors.

To help implement these goals, the Commission proposed a law in the form of a framework directive. The proposed legislation would be subject in advance to a regulatory impact assessment, a so-called RIA, to make sure EU intervention would benefit the sector. EU competition law would be applied effectively to clearing and settlement activities to support the initiative.

The Commission asked for responses by the end of July. By this time, its competition department had demonstrated that the promise to apply competition law to clearing and settlement was no idle threat.

On 2 June 2004, the Commission bared its teeth in support of freedom of access to national infrastructures. It decided Clearstream Banking Frankfurt and Clearstream International had abused the dominant position of Clearstream's Frankfurt operation in the German settlement market and so infringed EU competition rules.

The Commission found Clearstream had broken EU law by refusing to supply Euroclear Bank with clearing and settlement services for German registered shares. The decision, which related to infringements that ceased more than two years before, also ruled against Clearstream for discriminatory pricing. Although Clearstream was not fined, the ruling showed how EU competition rules could be applied to the clearing and settlement sector 'in the interest', competition commissioner Mario Monti said, 'of creating an integrated single market that will promote growth'.

Without waiting for the decision on a possible directive, the Commission also set up three groups of experts from the public and private sectors to provide new impetus to efforts to remove the Giovannini barriers.

The most important was Cesame, the Clearing and Settlement Advisory and Monitoring Expert Group. Cesame was charged with helping to remove the Giovannini barriers for which the industry was wholly or partly responsible and met for the first time in July 2004. A Legal Certainty Group (LCG) and a Fiscal Compliance Experts Group, or Fisco, were set up some months later. The LCG and Fisco included experts from academia and the legal and accountancy professions to look at how to remove the legal and tax barriers which were the responsibility of the public sector.

The groups operated transparently with their proceedings publicised on the Commission's website. All seemed set, after appropriate consultation and study, for new EU legislation to remove the log-jam on clearing and settlement. However, that was before the appointment, with effect from November 2004, of a new Commission and the arrival in Brussels of Charlie McCreevy, who moved from being finance minister of Ireland to become Internal Market Commissioner in succession to Frits Bolkestein.

14.11   THE ARRIVAL OF McCREEVY

With his pronounced Irish brogue, a twinkle in his eye and a fondness for the horses, Charlie McCreevy appears the archetypal Irish politician. And it was perhaps no surprise that he moved with some reluctance from Dublin and his other natural habitat – Punchestown racecourse in his home county of Kildare – to the greyness of the European quarter in Brussels. But there are other facets to Charlie McCreevy. Lurking behind the genial public persona is a trained accountant with a shrewd financial brain and a tough and wily politician, well trained in the Irish politicians' school of hard knocks.

McCreevy arrived in Brussels with a robust international reputation after seven years as finance minister in charge of the EU's best performing economy. His tax cutting, pro-business policies delivered prosperity unprecedented in Ireland's history as an independent state. The 'Celtic Tiger' economy was rooted in open markets and inward investment, making McCreevy a sound choice for the job of Commissioner in charge of the internal market under the new Commission president, José Manuel Barroso.

McCreevy took over the single market portfolio to a chorus of complaints about the burden of regulation being imposed by the financial services action plan. Bolkestein's time at the Commission saw the adoption of nearly all the 42 FSAP measures proposed in 1999, although when his term expired in late 2004, most were still waiting to be implemented in the EU member states.

Bolkestein's *tour de force* was only possible because of intensive recourse to the complex and time consuming processes of proposal, consultation, compromise, legislation and adoption that characterise all EU regulation. MiFID proved to be a particularly bruising experience for all concerned. The consequence was widespread 'regulatory fatigue' in financial markets. In the City of London, fatigue combined with disenchantment and even anger. It came as an unpleasant surprise to many market participants in the UK that other EU member states saw the FSAP as an opportunity to add to regulation, rather than simplify it, often with the aim of protecting their own financial centres.

McCreevy matched this mood perfectly. He had already demonstrated an awareness of the markets' concerns during a stint as chairman of the Ecofin council during Ireland's six-month presidency of the EU in the first half of 2004.

During this period, DG Markt, the Commission's Internal Market directorate, engaged in an extensive bout of soul searching on the future course of financial integration. In June 2004 – seven weeks before his nomination as internal market commissioner at the age of 54 – McCreevy set a high hurdle for future financial market regulation at the EU level. He told a high level 'stocktaking' conference organised by DG Markt in the Palais d'Egmont in Brussels that new legislative measures should be 'a last resort'. They should only be proposed if they passed a strict cost–benefit test and where non-legislative measures were deemed ineffective or where there was a clear case of market failure. Although McCreevy did not rule out future legislation, it would have to be carefully targeted.

Not everyone agreed with McCreevy when it came to clearing and settlement. Some permanent officials in DG Markt made no secret of their wish to start drafting legislation: this after all was what they had joined the Commission to do.

When, in March 2005, the Commission published the feedback to its consultative document of April 2004, a majority of the respondents supported an EU law. Of the 82 responses, 47 requested a directive, albeit with divergent views as to its content. A further Nine respondents were generally in favour, or not opposed to, EU legislation. Only 13 replies were categorised as being opposed, along a spectrum of 'explicitly against' to 'rather negative'. Those in favour of legislation included the Fair & Clear banks, now reduced to four members.[24] They again took the opportunity to warn against the Euroclear business model on the grounds that it bundled 'an infrastructure's core functions with credit risk-taking and competitive activities'.

---

[24] BNP Paribas, Citigroup, DnB-NOR and SEB.

Euroclear's response to the Commission was cautious.[25] Like other infrastructure providers, it underlined the need for a detailed impact analysis before any decision and urged that future legislative activity be concentrated on the legal and tax issues identified by the Giovannini group. The market, it claimed, was 'already making significant progress' removing the barriers that were the responsibility of the private sector.

Neither the EU Council of Ministers nor the European Parliament – the two bodies that would have to turn a Commission proposal into law – was particularly keen on legislation by this time. When the EU's economics and finance ministers reviewed the FSAP in November 2004, they agreed that its future focus should be convergence of supervision and implementation of measures already approved. 'Non-legislative action should be taken where possible and appropriate, and new legislation should be introduced where necessary,'[26] the ministers declared, adding a request that 'all future legislative proposals be accompanied by thorough impact assessment'.

Opinions moved in a similar direction in the European Parliament. At the end of January 2005, Theresa Villiers, the parliament's rapporteur, said in her first draft report on clearing and settlement that she was 'not convinced' of the case for a directive. Her report warned that 'even a narrowly focused proposal could eventually result in an over-burdensome directive after polarised political debate'.

The language was less strident when Piia-Noora Kauppi, Villiers' successor as rapporteur, published parliament's final report in June 2005. But it, and parliament's resolution on clearing and settlement which was passed the following month, made clear that any legislative proposal from the Commission should be based on the results of an impact assessment study and that 'principally the market should decide the structure of clearing and settlement services'.

McCreevy, meanwhile, had made clear he would not be rushed. In his first speech on financial services, the recently appointed commissioner swore off bringing forward EU legislation aimed at securities markets during 2005. Clearing and settlement might require action 'from 2006 onwards,' he told a conference early in December 2004.[27] But 2005 would be 'a year of preparation, analysis, economic impact assessment and building consensus'.

McCreevy used the time to exert pressure on the industry to regulate itself. The Cesame group took on functions additional to monitoring and reporting on the removal of the Giovannini barriers. The group, which included top level representatives from rival post-trade service providers, gave the Commission an opportunity to run broader policy issues and technical details past the industry.

Meeting three times a year under the chairmanship of David Wright of DG Markt and assisted by Alberto Giovannini, Cesame also evolved into a forum for consulting on elements of the Commission's regulatory impact assessment. The RIA was the tool which would eventually help McCreevy decide whether or not to regulate the sector. The Commissioner kept it and the attendant threat of legislation hanging like a sword of Damocles over the infrastructure providers.

On occasions, McCreevy would step up the pressure with a carefully timed public statement. On 13 September 2005, he used a speech in Luxembourg[28] to call on 'all interested actors to take their responsibilities and collectively to put their foot on the gas'. Condemning the high costs of cross-border clearing and settlement as indefensible, he warned that the Commission

---

[25] 'The way forward: Euroclear's response to the European Commission's communication', July 2004.
[26] Ecofin Council conclusions, 16 November 2004.
[27] At a CESR conference in Paris on 6 December 2004.
[28] To the 14th annual ALFI-NICSA Europe-USA Investment Funds Forum.

was taking a close look at the economic case for action. 'We will decide whether any European legislation, or other intervention, is necessary. . ... The next six months are crucial. As far as I am concerned the clock is ticking.'

Days before the six-month deadline, McCreevy and Neelie Kroes, the competition commissioner, gave the securities industry an ultimatum. A joint statement, published on 7 March 2006, told market players to come forward with effective and realistic changes to improve clearing and settlement before the EU institutions broke for the summer at the end of July.

'Where possible, we would prefer to have market-led solutions which meet effective competition and internal market concerns,' the commissioners said. But if there was no substantive move by the industry, McCreevy and Kroes would take action on the basis of EU internal market and competition rules. The two were not bluffing. The industry had four months in which to agree to draw up a viable plan for an EU-wide market for clearing and settlement.

15
Setting Parameters

15.1 ALGORITHMS AND EXCHANGES

The March 2006 statement from commissioners McCreevy and Kroes was a sign that events had not developed as anticipated in the European securities industry. McCreevy took up his post in Brussels in November 2004 at a time of great expectations of change. It was felt that securities exchanges in particular were ripe for a shake-out after limited consolidation during the term of Frits Bolkestein, his predecessor, and this would surely have an impact on Europe's post-trade structures.

These were still fragmented. An ECB study published in July 2005[1] noted that 'despite the single currency, the trading, clearing and settlement industry still shows a relatively high degree of fragmentation and insufficient harmonisation, with around 22 stock and derivatives exchanges, 8 CCPs, 18 local CSDs and 2 ICSDs active in the euro area, all operating on the basis of different technical procedures, prices, market practices and legal frameworks'. The study only looked at the 12 nation euro area rather than all 25 member states of the recently enlarged EU. The scale of fragmentation across Europe was much greater.

The exchanges themselves faced opportunities and challenges. The long bear market, which saw equity markets worldwide lose $13 trillion in capitalisation between April 2000 and March 2003,[2] gave way to a strong rally. In the 12 months to March 2004, markets worldwide recovered $10 trillion of their loss. Those in Europe outperformed the rest with the DJ Euro Stoxx index advancing by 52% in local currency terms. Although global equities were mixed in the following 12 months to March 2005, markets in the euro area continued to post moderate gains.

This revival in investors' appetite for risk coincided with rapid changes in the technology and techniques of trading. Electronic trading platforms, using ever more powerful computers, and the growing use of CCPs for settlement netting provided the perfect environment for strong growth in algorithmic trading.

Algorithms, which were first identified by an Arab mathematician in the 9th century, consist of a set of rules or steps placed in order to calculate a desired outcome. Developed first in the US, computerised algorithmic trading was a vastly more intensive version of programme trading. Complex algorithms in quantitative research systems can process huge amounts of data and provide traders with a kind of automatic pilot through increasingly complex market environments. Traders adopted algorithm-driven 'black box' techniques to beat benchmarks and conceal the scale of their activities from other market participants.

The amount of algorithmic trading is a matter of conjecture. Separate studies in the US put it at 14% and 25% of total US equity trading in the spring of 2005. What all commentators agree is that algorithmic trading is growing fast, a fact reflected in rapid growth of trading volumes on exchanges (See Table 15.1).

---

[1] 'Integration of securities market infrastructures in the Euro area' by Heiko Schmiedel and Andreas Schöenenberger. ECB occasional paper No. 33, July 2005.

[2] According to the Bank for International Settlements 74th Annual Report, June 2004.

Table 15.1   Value of electronic order-book transactions on selected European
exchanges* (euro billion)

	2000	2001	2002	2003	2004	2005	2006
Borsa Italiana	963	658	634	679	733	955	1146
Deutsche Börse	969	958	870	833	903	1125	1593
Euronext	1764	1699	1570	1359	1543	1783	2375
LSE	878	1047	1066	1034	1290	1541	2216
SWX + Virt-X	553	312	486	401	441	543	692
BME	459	440	440	494	637	848	1151

(*) Single counted
Source: FESE

By the end of 2006, market estimates suggested algorithm-driven transactions accounted for 28% of trades in London, the centre for quantitative black box trading strategies in Europe. Chris Gibson Smith, chairman of the London Stock Exchange,[3] has described algorithmic trading as part of a 'secular change in equities trading'. In the case of the LSE, it contributed to average year-on-year growth of 56% in trading volumes on the exchange's SETS electronic order book in the six months to the end of September 2006. Experts have predicted that algorithms could soon drive more than 40% of trades in London.

The surge in trading volumes reflected a specific characteristic of trading algorithms. They typically break up large orders into smaller sizes to reduce the chances of provoking adverse market movements. So while the number of trades on the LSE's SETS platform increased by 61% year-on-year to a record 8.7 million in January 2007, their value increased by a more modest 33% to £156.5 billion. Writing early in 2006, Pierre Francotte[4] noted that the average size of bargains or 'tickets' agreed on the LSE, Deutsche Börse and Euronext had fallen by 20% since 2001, with declines on SETS and Deutsche Börse's Xetra platforms amounting to 32% in that period.

The higher volumes generated by smaller ticket sizes are, at first sight, great news for exchanges and post-trade service providers. They mean more invoices and much higher revenues from fees. But such business growth has also meant much greater pressure from users, such as the big investment banks which dominate European equity trading, for lower fees and cost cutting measures on the part of infrastructure providers. Dissatisfaction with the response has encouraged users to consider strategies to disintermediate exchanges and other infrastructure providers when costs do not fall.

Adding to the urgency of the users' demands has been the high cost of their investment in high speed computer technology and the awareness that in the world of 'black box' computer trading, where instructions are executed in milliseconds thanks to high speed data transmission, there are no prizes for being second best.

Among exchanges, the high fixed costs of platform development together with the search for deeper pools of liquidity to increase the attractions for users of their respective trading platforms provided a spur for consolidation and alliances. And because Deutsche Börse and Euronext respectively owned or had an important stake in post-trade infrastructures, it seemed inevitable that any movement among the EU's big exchanges would put its clearing and settlement providers into play.

---

[3] In the introduction to the LSE's Interim Report for the six months ended 30 September 2006.
[4] In 'The view from the CEO of Euroclear', April 2006.

15.2 SEIFERT AND THE LAW OF UNINTENDED CONSEQUENCES

Europe's exchange and post-trade sectors were pitched into a new wave of corporate manoeuvring and speculation about further consolidation within days of McCreevy's announcement that 2005 would be a year for reflection and consensus building on the future of securities settlement in the EU.

On Monday 13 December 2004, the London Stock Exchange confirmed that during the preceding weekend Werner Seifert, Deutsche Börse's chief executive, had proposed buying the LSE. Seifert's indicative offer of £1.35 billion or just under €2 billion valued LSE shares at 530 pence each, about 50% up on the average of the preceding three months.

The LSE's management – unlike its predecessors at the start of the iX project in 2000 – was in no mood to accommodate him. Clara Furse, the LSE's chief executive, rebuffed the approach as too low and too vague. Although willing to talk, the LSE prepared its defences and waited for other approaches from Deutsche Börse's rivals, including – it was confidently expected – one from Euronext.

Seifert's gambit was not wholly unexpected. Deutsche Börse and the LSE came close in 2003 to agreeing an alliance that would have entailed the LSE adopting Eurex as its CCP instead of LCH.Clearnet. Seifert was a frequent visitor to London in the latter months of 2004, fuelling speculation about a new Deutsche Börse bid for the exchange. He had also been rebuffed elsewhere and was on the rebound.

Seifert has described[5] how in 2003 negotiations for a merger of Deutsche Börse with Euronext – codenamed project 'Antibes' – failed on valuation difficulties. The details have a familiar ring. According to Seifert's account, Jean-François Théodore insisted the two companies were of equal value, while in Seifert's view Deutsche Börse's value was twice that of Euronext, largely because of the German exchange's ownership of Clearstream.

Separately, talks on a takeover by Deutsche Börse of Switzerland's SWX broke down in August 2004 when the Swiss chose to stay independent. Seifert then had further negotiations with Théodore in 2004. This time, according to Seifert's book, the project – codenamed 'Edelstein' – foundered because DG Competition, the EU Commission's competition directorate, insisted that the merged group sell one of its two derivatives exchanges and part of its clearing and settlement business.

For Seifert, DG Comp's conditions meant the mooted merger with Euronext no longer made economic sense. Not only were derivatives growth markets for the future, 'Deutsche Börse's vertical integration with Clearstream was necessary for its success',[6] he noted in his book. His thoughts, he recalls, 'turned immediately towards the LSE' as soon as he heard the news from Brussels concerning Euronext.

The reappearance on the LSE's doorstep of this serial wooer, who represented a for-profit vertically integrated silo, caused concern in London's investment community. Among the first to react was APCIMS, the Association of Private Client Investment Managers and Stockbrokers, which played a big part in scuppering Seifert's iX project. Angela Knight, the APCIMS chief executive, warned in the *Financial Times*[7] that any successful merger would reduce choice in the market place. 'Users and investors will therefore require tangible benefits in return,' she said. Market users would 'want to see a reduction in the cost of trading today'.

---

[5] In his 2006 book, *Invasion der Heuschrecken*.
[6] Quoted from *Invasion der Heuschrecken*.
[7] 15 December 2004.

Seifert's initiative also triggered alarm among Deutsche Börse's competitors in the post-trade sector. In a letter to the *Financial Times*,[8] Chris Tupker, Euroclear's chairman, warned that the proposed takeover of the LSE was 'the beginning of the end game of the consolidation of all the infrastructure of financial markets in Europe – not just the equity trading platforms'.

'Issuers, securities firms, regulators and competition authorities should all be on red alert,' Tupker wrote. Seifert's move might offer these stakeholders 'their last clear opportunity to shape the model on which securities in the EU are traded, cleared and settled'.

Tupker's letter did not specifically mention Deutsche Börse. But it left readers in no doubt that, in his view, a successful takeover of the LSE by the Frankfurt exchange could lead to trades in London being cleared and settled through Deutsche Börse's own post-trade operations to the disadvantage of users. He warned that the outcome of the bid for the LSE would have a profound effect on the embedded cost of capital in European companies as well as the future efficiency and competitiveness of European capital markets.

'The question they [the stakeholders] must ask is whether it is appropriate to have any of the trading, clearing and settlement functions become a monopoly in the hands of a company driven by the goal of maximising shareholder profits,' he wrote. 'Given the ability of trading platforms to influence the choice of post-trade service provider and the driving force of economies of scale in these businesses, this could well be the outcome if the winner also owns clearing and settlement functions.'

In the event, Tupker's fears were not put to the test. This was down to the reaction of a third group of interested parties: Deutsche Börse's shareholders. Some of the institutions that had invested in Deutsche Börse since its IPO thought Seifert had overpaid for acquisitions such as Clearstream. They were not enthused at the prospect of the company engaging in a costly bidding war for a trophy asset like the LSE after two years in which Deutsche Börse shares had underperformed Germany's DAX index of blue-chip companies.

The Deutsche Börse share price gave an early hint of trouble ahead when it dropped 4% on the first news of Seifert's approach to the LSE. By the middle of January 2005, Seifert had a burgeoning shareholder revolt on his hands, when two hedge funds controlling about 7% of Deutsche Börse's equity publicly opposed the takeover. The Children's Investment Fund Management (TCI) and Atticus Capital argued that Seifert would overpay for the LSE and €600 million of cash in Deutsche Börse's balance sheet would be better spent by being returned to shareholders.

Seifert formalised his offer for the LSE on 27 January 2005 only for it to be rejected by the London exchange once again. He proved unable to curb or quell the shareholders' revolt. By the end of February, nearly 40% of shareholders opposed the LSE takeover. Deutsche Börse was obliged to shelve its offer on 6 March, although it reserved the right to return to the fray if Euronext or another third party bid for the London exchange. After weeks of mounting acrimony, Seifert resigned as chief executive on 9 May 2005 and Rolf-E. Breuer agreed to step down as Deutsche Börse's supervisory board chairman before the end of the year. It was clear they would not have the support of shareholders at the company's annual meeting, scheduled for 25 May.

The attack by Deutsche Börse's shareholders on the management of their company shocked Germany's politicians and its managerial elite. The fund managers who brought down Seifert were denounced as 'locusts' by Franz Müntefering, chairman of the ruling Social Democrat party. Seifert himself became an unlikely hero of politicians on the left and happily took up

---

[8] 7 January 2005.

the locust theme when he came to write his account of events. The title of his book – *Invasion der Heuschrecken* – translates as Invasion of the Locusts.

Seifert had fallen victim to the law of unintended consequences. He was brought down by developments that he made possible, and for a while approved. In its 2002 annual report, Deutsche Börse noted with some satisfaction how the holdings of its pre-IPO shareholders declined to 51% of equity by the end of 2001 and further to 22% by the end of 2002. By this time, the holdings of hedge funds and other institutional investors, which Deutsche Börse considered were 'focusing on sustained value growth', had reached 76% of equity.

The holdings of institutional investors reached to 93% of equity by the end of 2003. German investors, holding 41% of the company, were outnumbered by the combined strength of UK and US shareholders with 24% and 26% respectively. Deutsche Börse's annual report for 2004 disclosed a further fall in the proportion of German shareholders to 35% by the year's end.

The 2004 report was signed off on 25 February 2005 just as the shareholder revolt was becoming overwhelming. The foreign funds – led by TCI – increased their holdings in Deutsche Börse as the power struggle grew more intense. The sellers were German shareholders, who by April 2005 reportedly held only 7% of Deutsche Börse shares.

15.3 EXCHANGE CONSOLIDATION: AN UNPREDICTABLE CATALYST

The extraordinary events at Deutsche Börse upset expectations for a consolidation of Europe's post-trade sector. Until 2005, many analysts and practitioners thought, like Chris Tupker, that developments at the exchange level would trigger further changes in the post-trade area.

Instead Seifert's failed bid for the LSE and his subsequent defenestration marked the beginning of a bewildering succession of approaches, bids and manoeuvrings that enveloped the exchanges of Europe and the US during 2005 and 2006. These culminated in a transatlantic tie-up between the New York Stock Exchange and Euronext and left Deutsche Börse on the sidelines. Although Seifert's move would influence the development of post-trade activities, its effects were indirect.

During two years of turmoil:

- Euronext announced elements of a potential bid for the LSE on 9 February 2005 but held back from turning its obvious interest in the exchange into a formal bid to rival that of Deutsche Börse.
- The LSE itself became the object of other bids from Australia's Macquarie Bank in December 2005 and Nasdaq, the US exchange, in November 2006. Both bids failed. The LSE emerged triumphantly independent early in 2007, albeit with Nasdaq holding a 29% stake.

In late 2005, the focus of speculation and activity shifted to Euronext and Deutsche Börse.

- Encouraged by some of the investors that blocked Deutsche Börse's bid for the LSE and by political leaders in Berlin and Paris, Deutsche Börse and Euronext began merger discussions in mid-December 2005. The talks stalled a month later and failed in February 2006 because of differences between the two sides on substantial issues including the legal status of the proposed merged entity, its domicile and the management and ownership of technology.
- Deutsche Börse and Euronext resumed talks in the months that followed but these were thrown into doubt on 3 April 2006 when Euronext announced it was 'the preferred partner'

for a number of international securities exchanges. By early May, the incompatible nature of the two groups' vertical and horizontal business models had become a problem.

- On 19 May, Deutsche Börse outlined some details of a proposed 'merger of partners' with Euronext. While defending its 'integrated vertical model', Deutsche Börse promised to take account of different national approaches on post-trade matters, saying: 'there is no intent to change market infrastructures in markets that currently operate under a horizontal model like France'. The German group underscored its commitment to a merger by being 'prepared to contribute its cash equity clearing to a truly European cash equity clearing organisation operated as an independent, privately run service provider'.
- On 22 May 2006, the New York Stock Exchange offered nearly €8 billion in cash and shares for Euronext. The two exchanges signed an agreement on 1 June for a 'merger of equals' creating 'the first global exchange'. NYSE Euronext's European markets would be regulated by existing regulators while the SEC would continue to regulate US markets.
- The merger of NYSE and Euronext won the overwhelming support of both groups' shareholders in December 2006. This followed the collapse in November 2006 of talks on an alliance between Deutsche Börse and Borsa Italiana aimed at securing a three-way merger with Euronext.

Of all the twists and turns that followed Seifert's bid for the LSE, perhaps the least predictable in December 2004 would have been the merger of Euronext and the NYSE. This was a remarkable achievement for Théodore. He managed to neuter very strong pressure from the French political and financial establishment in favour of a merger with Deutsche Börse and secure a deal that promised him and his organisation far more independence than any offered by Seifert or Reto Francioni, Seifert's successor in Frankfurt.

As Théodore coaxed his shareholders and the French financial establishment to accept Euronext's merger with the NYSE, it was easy to believe that the succession of bruising German-led efforts to consolidate the financial infrastructures of France and Germany since the 1990s had, in the end, driven him to conclude a more congenial trans-Atlantic deal.

15.4 COMPETITION AUTHORITIES TURN AGAINST SILOS

Deutsche Börse's bid for the LSE had one significant regulatory consequence. It prompted the UK authorities to form a view on the implications for free competition of a takeover of the London exchange. The UK findings in turn helped set a benchmark for competition policy decisions at the European level. Both the UK Competition Commission and the European Commission reached judgements that were hostile to the vertical silo.

Deutsche Börse notified the UK's Office of Fair Trading about its plan to acquire the LSE on 31 January 2005, four days after it published details of its offer. Euronext confirmed its interest in making a possible cash offer for the LSE on 27 January, the day Seifert confirmed his bid, and made its submission to the OFT the following day. The OFT referred the possible acquisition of the LSE by the rival exchanges to the UK Competition Commission at the end of March.

The Competition Commission took its task seriously even though Deutsche Börse had by this time shelved its offer and Théodore was under pressure from some of Euronext's powerful hedge fund shareholders not to bid for the LSE. The UK watchdog published its provisional findings on the two potential bids on 29 July 2005. It was untroubled by the possible effects on trading or settlement in London of a takeover of the LSE by either of the two continental rivals. It nonetheless concluded that the acquisition of the London exchange by either of its erstwhile suitors might result in a 'substantial lessening of competition' in the market for the provision of on-book equity trading services in the UK. This was because 'the ownership or influence over clearing services' that Deutsche Börse and Euronext had as a result of their respective control of Eurex Clearing and holding in LCH.Clearnet would make it more difficult for other exchanges to compete with the LSE in trading UK equities.

The Competition Commission made clear that a takeover of the LSE by either Deutsche Börse or Euronext could only go ahead after measures to safeguard competition. It published provisional proposals, which in the case of Deutsche Börse included the possible sale of Eurex Clearing, a ban on its use as a provider of clearing services for the LSE and behavioural commitments such as an obligation to provide access to vital clearing services for other exchanges on fair and reasonable terms. Similarly, Euronext was presented with a menu of options ranging from divestiture of its stake in LCH.Clearnet to the provision of access to its clearing services.

In its final report of 1 November 2005, the Competition Commission stipulated that neither Deutsche Börse nor Euronext should hold more than 14.9% of the equity and voting rights of the LSE's clearing provider in the event of a takeover of the London exchange. Although by this time the attitude of the shareholders of Deutsche Börse and Euronext made the ruling appear somewhat academic, this first official judgement of a competition authority on the structure of post-trade services in Europe was a significant blow against the vertical silo.

Others followed. When the European Commission's competition department decided in June 2004 that Clearstream had infringed competition rules, Mario Monti, the competition commissioner, went out of his way to say the decision did not favour any particular business model: 'It is not directed against Deutsche Börse's business model or any other,' he said.

However, his department – known as DG Comp – was already taking a wider interest in clearing and settlement than was apparent from the Clearstream judgement. During 2003, DG Comp sent a questionnaire to the national competition authorities of the member states seeking details 'regarding exclusive arrangements relating to the trading, clearing, settlement and depository of securities'. The responses, together with replies from the industry and some EU central banks to a further consultation launched in August 2004, fed into a report commissioned by DG Comp from the consultancy London Economics that was published on 30 June 2005.

The London Economics report was trenchant. After reviewing the securities trading, clearing and settlement infrastructures of the cash equities and bond markets in the 25 EU member states as of March 2005, it concluded that 'at the present time, in the vast majority of securities cash markets in Europe, users have no choice with respect to the providers of clearing and settlement services that are to be used to clear and settle a trade in a specific security on a specific market'.

The report drew a link between restrictive practices and vertical silos. It noted that in some cases, trading or clearing membership rules prescribed just one clearing and settlement provider. In others, users were offered some choice, but this was theoretical because in practice only one service provider existed in the country concerned. These arrangements accounted for 'the vast majority of vertical arrangements between trading, clearing and settlement infrastructures in the European Union'.

DG Comp followed up the London Economics report by launching a deeper probe into vertical silos. A new batch of questionnaires went to market participants in July 2005. The swift reaction showed how Neelie Kroes, Monti's successor, was prepared to take a tougher line on clearing and settlement. The questionnaires, which were sent to exchanges, operators of alternative trading systems, clearing and settlement providers, selected broker-dealers, banks and banking associations, focused on trading and post-trade infrastructures for cash equities.

DG Comp's activism went down well with users. An alliance of four trade associations from the UK, Italy and France[9] weighed into the debate as the consultation was in progress. Timing their intervention to coincide with a meeting on 20 February 2006 of the Cesame group, they pointed to the vertically integrated systems in Germany, Italy and Spain. Warning that 'silos create potential for severe competitive distortions', the associations called on the EU Commission to impose unbundling of services on them if private stakeholders did not start the process.

At the same time, DG Comp had to admit that its powers to act were limited. EU competition rules had a narrow scope and were aimed at specific abuses between companies or the abuse of dominant positions. They were unlikely to deal with all barriers to competition. In particular, the need for the Commission to have a very high level of proof to implement competition law virtually precluded *ex-ante* actions against suspected offenders.

On 24 May 2006, the EU Commission's competition directorate published the results of its study. Its verdict on vertical silos was damning. 'Vertical integration may result in foreclosure at all levels of the value chain and therefore lead to welfare losses,' it wrote.[10] 'While there may also be efficiencies, so far the Commission has seen no convincing evidence to substantiate this.'

15.5   COMPETITION AND INTEROPERABILITY

DG Competition's condemnation of the vertical silo came in one of two Commission reports issued that day. DG Markt, the internal market directorate, also released some elements of the regulatory impact assessment (RIA) it was preparing on the desirability or otherwise of EU legislation to regulate post-trade services.

Of the two documents, the DG Comp report was the more influential. It was shorter and more complete and gave more of a steer as to how the Commission's thoughts were developing during its months of incubating the RIA. The impact assessment was notable for its estimate that eliminating excess transaction costs could add between 0.2% and 0.6% to the level of EU GDP in any given year. It kept alive a long EU tradition of underpinning policy discussions with eye-catching figures which on closer examination often turned out to be based on heroic assumptions.[11]

The DG Comp report did not mince its words. It described as 'striking' the limited degree of competition in EU securities trading and post-trading markets. Among the problems it singled out were 'lack of transparency in governance, lack of transparency in pricing and billing, disproportionate restrictions imposed on service providers and bundling of services between activities (vertically) and within activities (horizontally)'.

It took a dim view of monopoly CCPs and CSDs even when these were user owned. 'Encouraging the development of more competition would seem a more appropriate way of addressing the root issue than imposing a specific corporate structure,' was its down to earth verdict. More

---

[9] The French Association of Investment Firms (AFEI), the Italian Association of Financial Intermediaries (ASSOSIM), the French Banking Federation (FBF) and the London Investment Banking Association (LIBA).

[10] Issues Paper, 'Competition in EU securities trading and post-trading', European Commission, Competition DG, 24 May 2006.

[11] A report commissioned by the City of London later concluded that because of difficulties with the data the Commission overstated the expected costs savings. 'The European equities post-trading industry: assessing the impact of market and regulatory changes', NERA Economic Consulting, February 2007.

competition, it declared, would lower the cost of capital for Europe's businesses and 'translate ultimately into additional growth and jobs'.

The Commission's reports contained some surprises. Although of great importance to broker-dealers, post-trade infrastructure costs turned out to be only about 10% of the costs of a transaction as viewed by the final investor. The bulk of the investor's costs – about 75% – was linked to brokerage, raising the question as to whether the Commission was correct to focus so much effort on cross-border clearing and settlement as a barrier to economic growth.

Neelie Kroes, the competition commissioner, later insisted that it was. 'Any reduction in trading costs has an enormous knock-on effect on the economy and improvements in the infrastructure area would reduce the cost of broker-dealers too,' she told a group of European Parliamentarians a few weeks later.[12] 'Even if there may be imperfect competition in brokerage markets, more competition among infrastructures may bring additional players into the broker-dealer market, breathing new air into national banking communities, while at the same time driving down the cost of capital.'

DG Comp came out strongly in favour of greater interoperability among post-trade service providers. Interoperability was the 'big idea' put forward by the G30 in January 2003 to improve cross-border clearing and settlement. Rejected by many in the industry because of the risk of expensive duplication of IT equipment, the idea of linking different infrastructure providers supplying similar services to facilitate cross-border trading in securities was now gaining traction.

Buried inside the DG Competition report was the counter-intuitive assertion that all-in fees at Borsa Italiana, a silo structure, were much less per trade than at all EU rivals – whether horizontally or vertically structured.

Perhaps this was one reason why Italy suddenly appeared early in 2006 among the proponents of reform. In his first public speech, Mario Draghi, the recently appointed Bank of Italy governor, suggested that 'horizontal consolidation and federation between national markets' could boost trading and improve liquidity. Speaking in March, shortly after the trade associations' *démarche*, he commented: 'Unrestricted and equal access to settlement systems and multiple links between the various markets would foster both competition and efficiency'.[13]

When Commission officials met industry representatives on 12 June in Brussels in another Cesame meeting to discuss progress towards removing the Giovannini barriers, Monte Titoli, the settlement arm of the Borsa Italiana group, proposed interoperability as a way forward for the industry, claiming it could provide short-term solutions at minimum cost.

A few days earlier, Massimo Capuano, CEO of Borsa Italiana and president of the Federation of European Securities Exchanges, had argued that 'interoperability could lead to a higher degree of competition, ultimately reducing costs for market users'. Under Capuano's guidance, FESE proposed an industry-wide interoperability agreement with CCPs, CSDs and users.

The DG Comp report drew predictably mixed responses from the industry. Its verdict on silos went down especially badly in Germany. It drew a stinging riposte from Deutsche Börse.[14] The government in Berlin rallied to Deutsche Börse's side. Addressing the annual convention of FESE in Zurich on 8 June 2006, Jörg Asmussen, the director general of Germany's federal finance ministry, warned that the paper 'was not sufficiently detailed as to allow conclusions on how to proceed'. He noted that instruments already existed under competition law to deal

---

[12] On 11 July 2006 after Commissioner McCreevy had outlined plans for an industry code of conduct.
[13] Speech in Cagliari, 4 March 2006.
[14] Deutsche Börse AG's observations on the Commission's Issues Paper, 'Competition in EU securities trading and post-trading', June 2006.

with alleged breaches of the rules: 'To resort instead to regulatory intervention, thus favouring or discriminating against certain efficient structures, would not be the right approach.'

Asmussen also fired a shot across the bows of Commissioner McCreevy, who still had to make up his mind on whether or not to legislate on clearing and settlement. 'We cannot have integration at any price,' he said. In an obvious reference to Deutsche Börse, Asmussen added: 'Well functioning and efficient national structures which have evolved over many years may not be just simply left by the wayside. Against this background, Germany would not be able to accept a clearing and settlement directive.'

The Commission's reports suggested that action 'by a wide range of stakeholders' was needed to bring greater competition to Europe's post-trade activities. However, Asmussen's comments were one sign among many that legislation, which would require the backing of EU member states and the European Parliament, might not be the easiest way forward.

15.6   FOR AND AGAINST A SINGLE CCP

Seifert's departure from Deutsche Börse in 2005 brought home to the managers of exchanges that their job prospects depended on keeping shareholders sweet. The listed for-profit exchanges began to return surplus capital to shareholders through extra dividends and share buy-backs.[15] This – combined with soaring turnover on the back of rising share prices and algorithmic trading – helped fuel an upwards surge in the share prices of the LSE, Deutsche Börse and Euronext (see Table 15.2).

The re-rating of the listed exchanges had one serious negative side-effect, however. It raised the value attributed to Europe's post-trade infrastructure, making more difficult any project for its consolidation on a user-owned, user-governed basis. This was especially bad news for the idea of a single user-owned CCP, first proposed by the European Securities Forum in October 2000.

Although Pen Kent, as chief executive of the ESF, had to abandon his plan for a single European CCP during the summer of 2001, the idea did not die away. Sir David Walker, one of the founding fathers of the ESF and an *éminence grise* among post-trade activists, continued to promote the single CCP, arguing, like Kent, that it would act as a catalyst and trigger consolidation at the settlement level.

In December 2003, the European Financial Services Round Table had advocated the creation of a single CCP to provide 'a single entry point' across securities and across markets 'for all transactions in debt securities, equity and their derivatives in Europe'.

Table 15.2   Stock prices of Europe's main listed exchanges

	2004	2005	2006	end-June 2007
LSE	£5.82	£6.20	£13.10	£13.55
Deutsche Börse	€22.14	€43.28	€69.71	€83.75*
Euronext	€22.43	€44.00	€89.50	€93.20

*Deutsche Börse share prices have been adjusted for a one for one bonus share issue on 8 June 2007.
Source: Financial Times, 31 December 2004, 2005 and 2006 and 30 June 2007.

---

[15] At Deutsche Börse, for example, the 'payout ratio' leapt to 49% of net income for 2005 from 28% for 2004.

The idea of a single pan-European CCP caught the attention of Charlie McCreevy. In his 'ticking clock' speech to fund managers in September 2005, the Commissioner noted how 'some market participants' argued that such a consolidated structure could help the development of the European capital market. 'At face value, this is an interesting prospect. I can see that there could indeed be cost savings and improved efficiencies. If so, everyone should, of course, get a share of the benefits,' he said.[16]

Early in 2006, three private sector initiatives were tabled to coincide with the 20 February meeting of the Cesame group in Brussels and high level discussions the following day between Charlie McCreevy and CEOs and senior executives of users of clearing and settlement systems.

- The four trade associations from the UK, Italy and France,[17] which were lobbying against vertical silos, also urged more horizontal consolidation for post-trade activities. They suggested that LCH.Clearnet and Eurex Clearing on the clearing side and Euroclear and Clearstream on the settlement side should form 'the first two building blocks towards pan-European infrastructures'. However, this should not upset the status quo for settlement of Eurobonds where there was 'an apparently efficient duopoly between Clearstream International and Euroclear'.
- In a presentation to the Cesame group, Bob Wigley, chairman for Europe, the Middle East and Africa of Merrill Lynch International, called for a cross-border, user-owned, single CCP featuring cross-product clearing facilities and a choice of settlement providers.
- At the same meeting, David Hardy, chief executive of LCH.Clearnet, put forward a detailed discussion paper advocating the full consolidation of CCPs in the EU with the aim of delivering economies of scale and scope, lower fees, better risk management and greater competition at the trading levels.

Both Wigley and Hardy had to admit that the current overvaluation of CCPs put such plans in doubt. Nor did their initiatives earn unqualified approval. Indeed, several participants at the February Cesame meeting warned of potential pitfalls in a single CCP, such as the danger of monopoly power stifling innovation.

Deutsche Börse gave brief succour to supporters of the single CCP in May 2006 when, as part of its proposal to merge with Euronext, it announced it was 'prepared to contribute its cash equity clearing' to an independent European cash equity clearing organisation. However, this pledge was quickly overtaken by the successful NYSE offer for Euronext, while cynics observed that Francioni had offered only the smaller, less profitable part of its Eurex Clearing operation to the mooted independent, privately run service provider.

In truth, the official support for a single CCP was going into reverse even before Deutsche Börse's suggestion. DG Markt, the EU Commission's internal market directorate, let it be known that the Commission had no power to establish a single CCP and began to talk up the benefits of interoperability among existing CCPs instead.[18]

A similar message emerged from the 24 May report of the Commission's competition directorate. 'CCP services could – and probably should – operate in a competitive environment provided issues of interoperability are overcome,' it said.

---

[16] On 13 September 2005 in Luxembourg, at the 14th annual ALFI-NICSA Europe-USA Investment Funds Forum.

[17] The French Association of Investment Firms (AFEI), the Italian Association of Financial Intermediaries (ASSOSIM), the French Banking Federation (FBF) and the London Investment Banking Association (LIBA) included their demands for horizontal consolidation in the same statement as their critique of vertical silos, mentioned earlier.

[18] Mario Nava, a senior official in DG Markt, at the ECB Seminar: Issues related to Central Counterparty Clearing on 4 April 2006.

As if on cue, the Commission's suggestion was followed by news that the London Stock Exchange would offer its customers the choice of central counterparty clearing through Switzerland's SIS x-clear as well as LCH.Clearnet. Although virt-x, the London trading platform for Swiss and European blue chips, already offered the services of SIS x-clear and LCH.Clearnet as well as a choice of settlement location, the LSE became the first big European exchange to promise users a choice of CCP. The aim of the service, due to start from late 2007, is to cut costs. It undermined the argument that CCP services were not amenable to competition and that users stood to gain most from consolidation.

On 5 July 2006, David Hardy resigned as chief executive of LCH.Clearnet. His departure after 19 years with the group reflected anger in the board over the failure of a big IT project, the Generic Clearing System, and the group's inability to integrate the LCH and Clearnet businesses two and a half years after their merger.

LCH.Clearnet appointed a new chairman, Chris Tupker, with effect from 10 July. Tupker was due to retire after nearly seven years as Euroclear chairman at the end of 2006. But he was prevailed upon by Sir David Walker and others to accept the challenge of restoring LCH.Clearnet's fortunes. He left Euroclear earlier than planned at the end of July and was succeeded by Sir Nigel Wicks, who moved up from deputy chairman of the board.

Two weeks after taking the LCH.Clearnet chair, Tupker appointed Roger Liddell, a former Goldman Sachs managing director and Euroclear board member, as chief executive. One of the first acts of the new team was to write off the full €121.3 million cost of GCS. Hardy had 'talked the talk' on consolidation and the single CCP but in LCH.Clearnet's case, he had been unable to 'walk the walk' and deliver the benefits, in the form of lower cost and greater efficiency, which users expected from the merger.

15.7   USER DISCONTENT

Seifert's fall was the act of infuriated shareholders; Hardy's fate was sealed by angry users.

Hardy's position was untenable because of the losses on the LCH.Clearnet IT project. But in the background was a more general disenchantment among users with financial infrastructure providers. This grew in line with the recovery of stock markets after 2003.

The users felt they were being ripped off. As one investment bank representative put it: 'We don't mind people making money. We do mind people making money at our expense.'[19]

The users' main complaints were directed at the exchanges and their rising profits. But the post-trade service providers did not escape criticism. Merrill Lynch's Bob Wigley spelt out the gripes of the big investment banks at the Cesame meeting of 20 February 2006.[20] Users were not benefiting from economies of scale. Post-trade costs, in his view, had risen faster than the rise in aggregate transactions.

Trading margins meanwhile were under pressure because of heavy investment in algorithm-driven activity and fierce competition among trading desks. At Morgan Stanley, which has about 10% of the cash equity market in Europe, senior adviser Sir David Walker complained:[21] 'We do some of this business for practically nothing. In circumstances where clearing and settlement costs are either relatively the same or rising slightly, the relative significance of clearing and settlement is greatly increased.'

---

[19] Background conversation with the author.
[20] According to the synthesis report of the meeting published by the EU Commission.
[21] Conversation with the author, 16 January 2006.

In November 2006, Morgan Stanley and six other large investment banks announced plans for 'Project Turquoise', a 'multilateral trading facility' to compete directly with the exchanges. The 'G7' banks,[22] accounting for about 50% of trading in European equities, aim to exploit new MiFID rules such as the best execution requirement to muscle in on the business of exchanges. Another joint initiative[23] – Project Boat – is being set up to take advantage of the liberalisation of the trade reporting rules under MiFID.

The Turquoise announcement was not accompanied by any immediate plans to disintermediate clearing and settlement activities. But the rationale of the Turquoise and Boat projects was to reduce the frictional costs of bargains along the value chain. It was not long before ripples were felt in the post-trade sector.

In April 2007, Turquoise appointed EuroCCP, a subsidiary of DTCC, to handle its central counterparty clearing and netting. The decision was made before the choice of trading platform. EuroCCP, the European Central Counterparty Ltd, would be partnered by Citigroup's global transaction services business which would act as settlement agent and pass on positions to be settled to appropriate CSDs in Europe.

The selection of DTCC by the Turquoise consortium marks the arrival of a group with two and a half times the turnover of Euroclear in the European post-trade market. Having handled more than $1.5 quadrillion[24] of securities transactions in 2006 and with plans to run the Turquoise trades through its US facilities, DTCC could offer economies of scale and 10 years' experience of serving alternative trading systems in the US.

DTCC looks set to be a potent player. It announced that EuroCCP would be operated on an 'at cost' basis so that revenues exceeding the costs of supporting the operation would be returned to participants. It also plans to sign the European code of conduct for clearing and settlement launched in 2006.[25] It is unlikely that DTCC's ambitions in Europe will be limited to Turquoise.

The deal with Turquoise was not DTCC's first attempt to enter the European market. EuroCCP was established some six years earlier with the aim of exploiting a planned expansion of Nasdaq in the EU. The plans were shelved as exchanges retrenched during the bear market of 2000–2002. According to Don Donahue, DTCC's CEO,[26] they were revitalised before the announcement of Project Turquoise, after the NYSE and Euronext embarked on the road to their merger.

In Donahue's view, the NYSE-Euronext merger and the arrival of DTCC in Europe mark a new paradigm, a 'stitching together of markets around the globe'. The moves are a sign that the market space for post-trade activities in Europe is no longer confined by national boundaries or to continental areas such as the eurozone.

Less than two weeks after the Turquoise decision, another US infrastructure provider announced plans to create a European clearing house. The Atlanta-based Intercontinental-Exchange (ICE) said it would set up ICE Clear Europe in London to provide clearing services for its global customer base in partnership with its US clearing operation. ICE Clear Europe plans to start clearing energy futures and OTC derivatives from around the middle of 2008,

---

[22] Citigroup, Crédit Suisse, Deutsche Bank, Goldman Sachs, Merrill Lynch, Morgan Stanley and UBS. In July 2007, BNP Paribas announced it had also joined Turquoise, with a stake of 3%.

[23] Established by ABN Amro, Citigroup, Crédit Suisse, Deutsche Bank, Goldman Sachs, HSBC, Merrill Lynch, Morgan Stanley and UBS. In June 2007, Barclays Capital, BNP Paribas, Dresdner Kleinwort, JP Morgan and Royal Bank of Scotland signed up to use Boat.

[24] A quadrillion is a million billion. DTCC's annual turnover therefore is $1 500 000 000 000 000.

[25] Described in Chapter 17.

[26] Speaking on 24 May 2007 at the Exchange Forum in London.

taking business from LCH.Clearnet Ltd. According to ICE, its customers generated about $50 million in clearing fees for LCH in 2006.

The determination of ICE to build up its clearing business became obvious when it acquired the New York Board of Trade and the New York Clearing Corp (NYCC) in January 2007 and immediately began upgrading NYCC's capabilities. NYCC was renamed ICE Clear US from 1 June 2007.

Although ICE's plans for Europe pose a challenge for LCH.Clearnet, they were not unanticipated. During his last two years as Euroclear chairman, Chris Tupker became increasingly alert to the risk of disintermediation of European post-trade service providers in a tougher global competitive environment.

Under Tupker's leadership, the LCH.Clearnet board decided on radical action to safeguard the company's business. In March 2007, Euronext and LCH.Clearnet reached agreement for LCH.Clearnet to buy back most of the 41.5% stake in its capital held by Euronext. The deal, approved unanimously by LCH.Clearnet shareholders in June 2007, will leave Euronext with just 5% of the capital of LCH.Clearnet by 2009. The users' holding of ordinary shares will rise to 73.3%, with 10.9% held by exchanges and 15.8% by Euroclear, turning LCH.Clearnet into more of a user-owned, user-governed entity.

Reacting to moves such as Turquoise and ICE's acquisition of NYCC, LCH.Clearnet concluded that 'a number of recent and potential developments in the exchange and clearing markets' could pose 'significant threats to its clearing volumes and revenue streams'.[27] It therefore acted to 'minimise or remove the incentive for disintermediation, whatever its source'. The method it chose was 'by adjusting its operating model to focus more clearly on delivering benefits to users, in particular by providing an immediate financial benefit to users in the form of substantially lower fees rather than future rebates, or dividends to shareholders'.

Euronext, as a 'returns-focused' shareholder, did not fit in with these new priorities: hence the agreement to reduce its stake.

LCH.Clearnet had already announced clearing fee cuts of up to 26% for London Stock Exchange and virt-x trades and cuts averaging 15% on Euronext cash markets in October 2006. On reaching agreement to buy back the Euronext stake, it disclosed plans for tariff reductions starting in 2007 that would aggregate 'to an average of 30% of annual net revenues by 2009'.

Turquoise and the fee cuts announced by LCH.Clearnet were a sign of structural change. Market power was moving to the users, a group where power itself had become more concentrated in the hands of fewer, bigger, more global companies.

Speaking towards the end of 2006, Tupker noted how 10 companies accounted for 50% to 60% of business transacted in financial markets. 'And it isn't just 10 people in equities. Viewed from the perspective of LCH, where we handle commodities, derivatives, debt, and equity, I look at the top-10 players of those asset classes that we clear for, and it is always the same people. The biggest gold traders and biggest oil traders are now Goldman Sachs and Morgan Stanley. So a huge concentration has taken place, and that gives these people market power. So if you don't do what they want as an infrastructure service provider, you will be disintermediated. That was not possible five years ago.'[28]

The shift of power has been reinforced by technological advances, such as smart order routing systems, which include the use of algorithms to work out the whole cost of a transaction including clearing and settlement.

---

[27] Joint announcement of LCH.Clearnet and Euronext, 12 March 2007.
[28] Conversation with the author, 4 December 2006.

'There are now equity traders who have on their screen a little calculator that calculates not only the cost of trading but also the cost of clearing and settling the transaction. And they will not do certain transactions when the cost is too great,' Tupker added.

'When I heard about that, I realised that the users had finally become consistently smart. They have inculcated into their systems an awareness of the clearing and settlement costs. In the past, when times were tough, they would call for costs to come down, but they would forget about that when trading recovered and they were busy again. Now it is part of their system, which means there is pressure on all the infrastructure providers – stock exchanges, clearing houses and settlement agencies – to reduce their fees, and dramatically'.

15.8   CHANGE AT EUROCLEAR

Tupker's task at LCH.Clearnet was to transform the company. As he set out to do so, he could look back on experiences gained during six years' stewardship of Euroclear.

As Sir Nigel Wicks noted, on taking over as chairman, Euroclear changed dramatically on Tupker's watch. 'From what was in 2000 a mainly fixed-income securities settlement service provider, operated under contract by Morgan Guaranty Trust Company of New York, Euroclear has become the world's largest fully integrated, user-owned and user-governed provider of domestic and cross-border settlement and related services for bond, equity and fund transactions.'

Figure 15.1 shows how the value of securities transactions settled across the Euroclear group increased from €242 trillion in 2002, the year Wicks joined from CREST as deputy chairman, to €452 trillion four years later. The value of clients' securities held rose to €18.2 trillion by the end of 2006 from €10.9 trillion at the end of December 2002. Figure 15.2 illustrates the Euroclear group's changed structure.

In part, the soaring volumes followed from the upsurge of algorithmic trading in equities and the continued growth of repo business. The latter was reflected by the rise from €223 billion in December 2002 to €538 billion at the end of 2006 in the combined average daily value of outstanding collateral provided by Euroclear Bank and CREST.

There was also a huge increase in size and complexity of bond transactions. Since the start of the century, the plain vanilla Eurobond, which Euroclear was established to settle in the 1960s, has become a museum piece in a world of synthetic bonds and bond-based derivatives.

'The most complicated corporate actions these days are no longer with respect to equities but are with respect to Eurobonds,' says Pierre Francotte.[29] Some of the new bonds come with extremely complex rules while lacking the legal framework of equities. Payment options, including shorter payment periods and partial redemptions, make custody more labour intensive.

There is also a question of volumes. Euroclear handled two thirds of the 2005 rescheduling of Argentina's $85 billion of public debt, for example. Described as the largest single custody event in history, the rescheduling required Euroclear Bank to process more than 24 000 instructions.

'The reason people worry about bonds is that if you get it wrong, you get it wrong on a nominal value that may easily be as much as 20 to 50 times the size of an equities ticket,' Francotte explains. 'People buy very small amounts of equities, maybe €5 million to €10 million worth in the wholesale business, whereas with bonds it is as much as €250 million. Get the transfer of €250 million wrong, and the market risk is very different than on a transfer

---

[29] Conversation with the author, 24 November 2006.

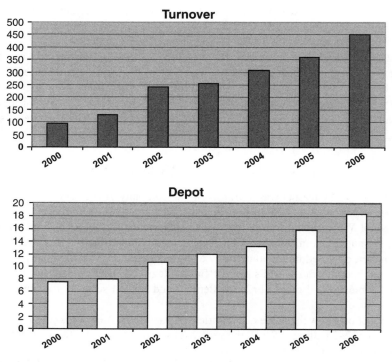

Figure 15.1 Euroclear Group – growth during the 'Tupker years' (euro trillion). *Source:* Euroclear annual reports

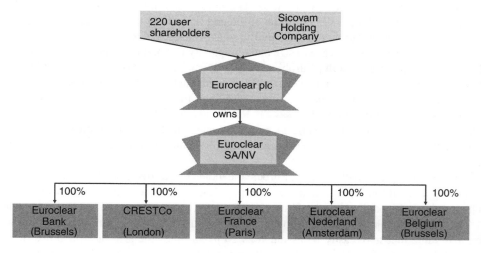

Figure 15.2 Euroclear Group – corporate structure (January 2007). *Source:* Euroclear SA/NV

of €20 million. Think of the Argentina restructuring: if we had got that wrong, the cost to us and our clients would have been a hundred times bigger than the biggest equity deal.'

Such transactions have helped Euroclear Bank to particularly strong growth. Its turnover jumped by €64 trillion or 41% to just under €219 trillion in 2006 to account for 48% of the value of securities settled by the group. The value of securities it held in custody rose by €1 trillion or 14% in the 12 months to €8.1 trillion. In part, the growth of the depository reflected net new business, worth more than €46 billion, won from Clearstream Banking Luxembourg. Euroclear estimates that, between the two ICSDs, it settled approximately 80% to 85% in terms of value of securities transactions and held 65% of assets in custody at the end of 2006.

The bank's growth was strengthened by the decision of some investment institutions – led by Merrill Lynch in November 2005 – to move their equity settlement to Euroclear Bank. The disintermediation of cross-border equity settlement, long feared by agent banks, could be under way.

The Merrill Lynch contract was made possible by strategic decisions taken in the 1990s. So too was Euroclear's diversification into providing settlement services for Europe's €6.6 trillion mutual fund market.

Euroclear's experience with equity settlement has shown how diversification in post-trade markets can be a very slow process. But after half a decade, Fundsettle, the settlement unit launched in 2000 by Euroclear, achieved critical mass. The number of transactions processed by Fundsettle's integrated order routing, settlement and custody processing platform doubled in 2005, lending credence to its managers' claims that customers could triple or quadruple transaction volumes with no increase in back office costs. By 2006, Fundsettle covered more than 33 000 offshore and domestic funds from 21 markets.

In January 2007, Euroclear acquired EMXCo, a UK provider of investment fund order routing, to supply services to the UK's £386 billion mutual fund sector. EMXCo's order routing capacity will be combined with CREST's real time settlement capabilities to cut costs and raise efficiency in a UK business sector notorious for its complex, inefficient and costly manual processing.

A policy of growth through mergers and acquisitions is one of the changes at Euroclear since the separation from Morgan. Another may be a greater willingness to cooperate with other settlement providers on projects that stand to benefit customers. Although Euroclear and Clearstream have continued to compete furiously in the ICSD market, they have also worked together, especially in cases where clients have pressed for action.

- In May 2002, Euroclear, Clearstream and DTCC launched a service to automate pre-issuance information processing and allocation of ISIN[30] for new issues of European Commercial Paper. Known as EPIM, or European Pre-Issuance Messaging, the service constituted a central messaging hub that linked banks, dealers, issuing and paying agents, numbering agencies and CSDs involved in the issuance of ECP. Euroclear France was the first European CSD to be connected to the service.
- In 2004, Euroclear Bank implemented the Automated Daytime Bridge with Clearstream Banking Luxembourg as a supplement to the electronic overnight Bridge launched in 1993. Although Bridge transactions have declined steadily as a percentage of Euroclear turnover since 1999, the move responded to the needs of clients by enabling same-day Bridge transactions between clients of the two ICSDs.

---

[30] A 12 digit code used to identify securities.

- In September 2006, and in response to requests from the market, Euroclear and Clearstream Luxembourg announced investments to improve the Automated Daytime Bridge. The ICSDs agreed to boost overall settlement efficiency and the capacity for same-day transaction settlement and securities financing across the Bridge by increasing the number of daily exchanges of information between the two systems and extending instruction input deadlines.

Early in 2007, Euroclear took what could be a significant step towards post-trade collaboration with the Clearing Corporation of India Ltd (CCIL), the institution that clears and settles Indian government securities and Treasury bills. While non-binding, a memorandum of understanding aims at building a long-term relationship in one of the world's biggest emerging market economies.

The instances of cooperation with Clearstream in part reflected changes in personnel: the departure of André Lussi from Clearstream in 2001 marked the end of more than a decade of mutual antipathy between the two ICSDs. Jeffrey Tessler, who succeeded André Roelants as CEO of Clearstream International in December 2004, has pursued a policy of having Clearstream Banking Luxembourg compete vigorously with Euroclear Bank in the ICSD market, while remaining open to opportunities for interoperability with Euroclear and other service providers.

The cooperation agreements have also coincided with an increased sensitivity at Euroclear to clients' needs. Although general managers John T. Olds and Luc Bomans placed greater emphasis on the needs of customers during the 1990s, Euroclear entered the 21st century with a reputation for treating client services as a luxury. The 2001 Agent Bank Survey conducted by Global Custodian, a trade magazine, summed up Euroclear as cruel but efficient compared with Clearstream, which it described as kind but chaotic.

In 2002, the management of Euroclear Bank instituted a detailed annual customer satisfaction survey, conducted by an independent company. Similar surveys were introduced by the group's CSDs the following year. The results for 2003 showed overall satisfaction levels ranging between 62.5% at Euroclear Nederland to 74.5% at Euroclear France.

Such results fell well short of the group's 98.5% success rate in settlement. There followed what Pierre Francotte called a 'significant soul searching'.[31] One outcome was to listen and respond to more to users, with the support of a client satisfaction programme, developed to improve the group's services.

Another outcome was the growth of fee reductions and rebates to customers. Rebating a portion of settlement fees began in 1980. The practice was suspended in 1999, despite record cross-border settlement activity, because of the need to build up the capital of Euroclear Bank.

The decision in 2002 to reinstate rebating and return €30 million of Euroclear Bank fees to customers showed that the group had successfully weathered separation from Morgan and the mergers with Sicovam and CREST. Years of strong growth since have resulted in higher rebates and fee reductions for users and, as Table 15.3 shows, increased dividends for the shareholders of Euroclear plc.

Rebates, tariff reductions and deeper sliding-scale tariff discounts amounted to cumulative savings worth €533 million for clients during the five-year period to December 2004. The Euroclear group delivered more than €115 million in tariff-related reductions, rebates and other savings to clients in 2006. Euroclear Bank has said its delivery of such savings to clients from 2005 through 2007 will amount to about €280 million. In addition, Euroclear Bank's

---

[31] In 'The view from the CEO of Euroclear', September 2005.

Table 15.3   Returning funds to customers (Euroclear Bank
rebates and Euroclear PLC dividends – euro million)

	Euroclear Bank rebates	Euroclear PLC dividends
2001	0	20.0
2002	30	27.6
2003	30	37.2
2004	40	72.5
2005	45	82.0
2006	45	93.0

Source: Euroclear annual reports.

clients should save an estimated €65 million on an annualised basis following a decision on 1 November 2006 to start paying credit interest on outstanding cash balances at market rate minus 100 basis points.

Euroclear, as Francotte explains, has sought to adapt to its customers' needs. 'You have to understand that the business model of your customers is affected by the fact that they have massively increased volumes, but they have to invest massively more in technology, so that at the same time, their margins may not be increasing at the same pace. It is natural that they will turn to their providers and look for one that allows them to generate as much profit as they can. It means Euroclear has to adapt and anticipate. In a business like ours, which is a business of economies of scale, you have to manage a large number of transactions at an increasingly low marginal cost to your clients.'[32]

'Since the volumes have increased – and invoices to clients have increased – the clients have looked at providers like Euroclear in a rather different way, as more integrated in their business model. The success of some of these firms will come from being able to manage massive increases in volume while avoiding that their cost base increases at the same pace. This is why some firms are very intent on Euroclear lowering the costs. That is what will allow some of them to maintain a positive margin.'

In the period up to 2006, the user-owned, user-governed Euroclear group has delivered savings to customers as a result of winning new business and processing record levels of transactions for existing clients.

In the years ahead, savings for Euroclear group clients will also reflect the benefits of Euroclear's 'domestic market for Europe' programme. Agreed in outline at the time of the merger with CREST, Euroclear has been pressing ahead with its programme to consolidate its securities settlement platforms and harmonise market practices in the countries served by the group as its response to the fragmentation of Europe's securities settlement sector.

---

[32] Conversation with the author, 24 October 2006.

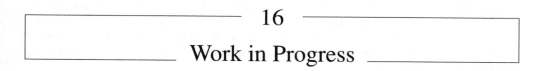

16

Work in Progress

16.1 EUROCLEAR'S DOMESTIC MARKET FOR EUROPE

Euroclear's domestic market for Europe has a straightforward objective. It is, Pierre Francotte once said,[1] 'to make cross-border activity as easy, efficient and cheap for [Euroclear's] clients as domestic activity already is in most European markets'.

For users, the domestic market for Europe holds out the promise of a one stop shop for cross-border settlement. Book entry would replace cumbersome cross-border procedures, saving on fees. There would be one single process for asset servicing, yielding back office economies. Financing costs for users would be reduced by their having one treasury and one collateral position. Systems consolidation would mean greater interoperability, lowering operating costs. When completed in 2009–10, the €500 million investment would allow a user trading equities across the markets served by Euroclear to settle at domestic rates: typically €0.50 per transaction.

The programme took Francotte's vision of a mix of ICSD and CSD that he elaborated at the time of Euroclear's takeover of Sicovam and incorporated multicurrency characteristics derived from CREST. A single multicurrency platform would settle securities in and among the euro-denominated markets of Euroclear's continental CSDs, the euro-denominated Irish market and sterling markets handled by CREST, and in Euroclear Bank, the group's ICSD serving the international bond and equities markets.

'We developed the vision starting at the beginning of 2001, and it was crystallised in 2002 at the time of the merger with CREST,' Francotte explains.[2] 'It came from one fundamental concept that I had from the beginning: that what we are building cannot be an ICSD with a few appendages called CSDs; nor can it be local CSDs, to which we add the large scale financial business of an ICSD.

This is where this concept of the dual service came from. It was always clear to me that the client would always want the option of having what is called the domestic service: cheap no-frills, essentially the infrastructure that you need to have. But they also wanted, and would never have accepted not to have, a single entry point with the more sophisticated set of services that Euroclear Bank was providing.'

Euroclear's clients would be able to choose between the domestic and full service without having to turn to another settlement provider. They would also have choice of access, through a CSD, agent bank or Euroclear Bank, and choice of jurisdiction for asset protection. Each domestic service would rely on the local laws of the Euroclear CSD while users of the full service would have recourse to Belgian Royal Decree 62 which pioneered the legal treatment of book entry settlement.

Transparent cost allocation and pricing were built into the business model from the start. The group set a cost-plus price structure for its domestic service and promised 'competitive'

[1] In *Taking Stock*, a Euroclear publication, June 2005.
[2] Conversation with the author, 24 November 2006.

rates for full service. Unlike some rivals, Euroclear declared its tariffs non-negotiable. To demonstrate that there was no cross-subsidy between the group's ICSD and CSD activities, the 2003 and subsequent annual reports included an attestation by an independent auditor that Euroclear's intercompany transaction policy complied with the OECD's transfer pricing guidelines.

The plan envisaged two types of payment mechanism. The domestic services would use central bank money provided through the national central banks in the territories of the Euroclear CSDs, while Euroclear Bank's full ICSD service would continue to operate using commercial bank money.[3]

This was the vision that the CREST board, headed by Sir Nigel Wicks, bought into. CREST contributed its experience of serving two different settlement markets – the UK and Ireland – with two different currencies, on one platform.

'Half the business model – the domestic business model – was based on what we do with Ireland,' says Wicks.[4] 'We said: we are going to have this so-called domestic platform, which was the Anglo-Irish one extended, as the domestic offering. And we are also going to have what we called the full service offering, which was Euroclear Bank.

People who said there was no cross-border settlement system operating in Europe were wrong. The UK-Irish platform was and is in CREST. It looks after Irish equities and UK equities on the same platform, even though they have different supporting law underneath. The Irish equities are settled according to Irish law, not British law.'

According to Wicks, Euroclear's domestic market for Europe generalises CREST's experience to France, Belgium and the Netherlands. 'The concept we have is effectively the Anglo-Irish concept. It's much easier with the Irish because much of the law is the same and a lot of the settlement practices are the same. That is why we have needed this enormous programme of harmonisation with France, Belgium and the Netherlands. But in essence, we demonstrated in the case of the UK and Ireland that we could put two different jurisdictions on the same platform and make it work.'

Euroclear calculates that the project will remove about €300 million annually of an estimated €1 billion of excess costs caused by infrastructure inefficiencies in the European settlement market. The savings will come through a mix of reduced fees to intermediaries (about €160 million), reduced back office complexities (€80 million) and operating cost savings at Euroclear of €60 million. The group has estimated that savings could run to between €700 million and €800 million a year if its programme of platform consolidation and harmonisation were adopted across all EU countries.

The significance of bringing CREST and the eurozone CSDs together in one system should not be underestimated, Francotte says. 'I think one of the great achievements that Euroclear should be credited for, is to have brought together France and the UK. I think very few people thought this was possible. What we have been building for a few years is a solution that makes sense across two of the three largest securities markets: the UK and France.'[5] CRESTCo's complete integration within the Euroclear group was recognised on 1 July 2007 when its legal and operating name was changed to Euroclear UK & Ireland Ltd.

Euroclear decided on a twin track approach for implementing its planned domestic market for Europe. This followed consultation with the market during 2003 in which it became clear that

---

[3] Euroclear has also contemplated making central bank money available for settlement in Euroclear Bank. However, for the time being, there does not seem to be client demand for this.
[4] Conversation with the author, 20 July 2006.
[5] Conversation with the author, 24 October 2006.

consolidation would be easier and user benefits greater the more that the settlement environment was harmonised. In consequence, it was decided that a phased consolidation of settlement platforms would go hand in hand with harmonisation of market practices.

The 'foundation stone'[6] for the domestic market is the Single Settlement Engine. Introduced progressively between May 2006 and January 2007,[7] the SSE centralises all reference data and group settlement in one system. It is the platform required to transform cross-border, intragroup settlement into book entry settlement and deliver economies of scale.

The SSE has been designed as a very high performing, high volume platform with a capability to process 400 to 500 transactions per second for the entire Euroclear group. According to Ignace Combes, Euroclear looked at the designs of CREST, RGV and Next before opting to base the SSE to a large extent on Next. The SSE's optimisation routines, needed to maximise settlement efficiency and deal with ever rising volumes, incorporate the best practices of all the legacy models.

The second phase, ESES or the Euroclear Settlement for Euronext-zone Securities platform, was inserted into Euroclear's plans to meet the specific requirements of Euronext. The transnational exchange group wanted to create a single order book for securities traded on the French, Belgian and Dutch exchanges, comprising one trading platform and one central counterparty clearer that could settle in one location. In this way it could concentrate liquidity and ensure that there was no differential price setting between the Euronext markets.

It was only after some delay, however, that Euronext realised that it would need a specialised settlement facility to achieve this goal. It persuaded Euroclear to act with the result that Euroclear developed ESES, based on the French RGV, as a harmonised platform for the straight-through processing of trades from Euronext's single order book for both local and remote Euronext members. ESES will be launched in a gradual process, scheduled for the end of 2007 and the first half of 2008. It will settle domestic and cross-border transactions involving both bonds and equities from the Belgian, Dutch and French markets.

What a single settlement platform means: the example of ESES

Joël Mérère explains how ESES will work:[8] 'ESES is the last section of the rocket that will allow Euronext to deliver a true single order book. Before Euronext, you had three stock exchanges – one in Paris, one in Brussels, and one in Amsterdam, with more or less three clearing houses, and three settlement systems. This meant that if the market user wanted to invest in Dutch securities, he had to go to the Dutch stock exchange, either directly or through a local agent. In the end, everything went through the local stock exchange, the local clearing house, and the local settlement system.

'Euronext consolidated the first two layers: trading and clearing. But this left a constraint at the level of settlement. So a market participant wishing to invest in Dutch securities had to go through Euronext Amsterdam, then the Dutch part of LCH.Clearnet. At the end of the process, the trade would still be settled in Euroclear Nederland, the Netherlands settlement system, using the Dutch technical platform.

'If a French market participant was selling Dutch securities and if the buyer was a Belgian market participant, either the two had to have direct access to Euroclear Nederland as remote

---

[6] Euroclear 2003 annual report.

[7] The SSE was launched by Euroclear France on 29 May 2006, by CRESTCo on 28 August 2006 and by Euroclear Bank at the end of January 2007.

[8] Conversation with the author, 17 January 2006.

members or they both had to settle through a local agent in Amsterdam. You still have a separate box for Dutch, Belgian and French securities.

With ESES, you will have a totally different scenario. A French market participant will be able to settle Dutch and Belgian securities through Euroclear France in exactly the same way as he would settle French domestic securities. In the case of a Belgian counterparty, who has a cash account with the National Bank of Belgium, the transaction would be settled through Euroclear France for the French participant and Euroclear Belgium for the Belgian counterparty. In this way, you create a totally open environment. The Euronext perimeter becomes the equivalent of a domestic zone.

Before ESES, France, Belgium and the Netherlands are still three different places in our perspective. With ESES, they will be one single space from a settlement standpoint. And this is the key element for Euronext.'

The third phase of platform consolidation, due for launch from 2009, comprises a Single Platform and Common Communications Interface. The Single Platform will consolidate all settlement and related functions onto one platform, offering users in Euroclear's markets a single entry point for cross-border settlement. The CCI will replace existing communications systems including Euroclear's Euclid.

Delivering Euroclear's domestic market for Europe has required – and is requiring – the intense cooperation of users. Euroclear's annual report for 2003 underlined the importance of 'meaningful harmonisation' as 'the key to accelerating, and reducing the cost of platform consolidation, as well as maximising back office benefits' for the group's clients. Without harmonisation, users' back office processes 'would remain market specific and cost savings in operations would be limited'.

A breakthrough came in July 2004 when Euroclear reached agreement with users on 'significant market practice harmonisation' as part of its agreement with Euronext to develop ESES. Only after this was the decision taken to invest in equipment and coding for new platforms. The harmonisation goals agreed by Belgian, Dutch and French banks and Irish and UK user representatives included: synchronised settlement processing times; cross-market central bank money settlement; harmonised corporate action dates, such as record, ex-dividend and dividend payment dates; simplified account structures; the use of ISO 15022 and 20022 message types for communications; and real-time settlement for equity and fixed income transactions.

Six harmonisation working groups, representing Euroclear and the users, proceeded to issue 85 proposals to harmonise market rules and practices within the five European domestic markets served by Euroclear.[9] The market practice harmonisation agenda then expanded to encompass 214 items, almost all of which were agreed by mid-2007.

The domestic market for Europe is compatible with the settlement industry's efforts to dismantle those Giovannini barriers that are the responsibility of the private sector. ECSDA, the European Central Securities Depository Association, which has been assigned a significant role in efforts to remove three of the barriers is chaired by Joël Mérère.

According to Wicks,[10] Euroclear has learned from European Union techniques to implement its harmonisation agenda. 'They [meaning Euroclear] are doing what the Commission, the Council, and the Parliament do at a much higher level with laws. They have concept discussions, refine those discussions, put them on the table, issue a concrete proposal, discuss it in each

---

[9] Belgium, France, Ireland, the Netherlands and the UK.
[10] Conversation with the author, 20 July 2006.

of the five markets with the market advisory committees and look at the interactions. If there are problems, they go to the cross-border MAC. In the end, they get agreement.' In 2005, for example, the Euroclear group published 21 formal consultation papers which generated more than 250 written responses.

Wicks stresses that Euroclear's findings are available for all. 'We do it very openly. We don't have a proprietary interest in harmonisation. Our work is reported to ECSDA,' he says. 'We are doing it for our five markets, but if another market wants to buy in or copy it, we don't hide it. Every market has its different practices and our five have decided to bring them together.'

Euroclear's harmonisation policy is not entirely altruistic. The group stands to gain from the economics of network industries. By stepping into a standard setting role Euroclear can hope to achieve economies of scale beyond the group.

'The more we harmonise our markets, the more likely it is that when we bring in new markets they will be in line with our harmonised service structure,' Ignace Combes explains.[11] 'The more we move forward, the more we have critical mass, the more we have harmonised and delivered the single platform, the more we are in a position to say: "These are the terms; that's our harmonised way of doing things in Europe, and therefore you should accept our way of working." If we integrate a market that works in exactly the same way as the settlement service already does on the single platform, it is easier to make it scalable.'

In 2006, Euroclear reported that its harmonisation programme and that of the Nordic CSD had been brought 'very close to each other' as a result of sharing ideas and experiences in ECSDA and through bilateral contacts.[12] Subsequently, in its annual report for 2006, Euroclear made clear it intends 'that the Euroclear Business Model will not be confined to the current five domestic markets of the group'.

Euroclear has been able to finance the domestic market for Europe in large part from the profits of Euroclear Bank. Without the bank 'Euroclear and settlement in Europe would never become more efficient,' Combes says. 'There is no way the CSDs could have consolidated and invested on the scale of Euroclear's €500 million programme. The whole thing hangs on Euroclear Bank', which, according to Combes, funds 60% to 70% of the total investment.

Although designed with a different purpose in mind, Euroclear's corporate restructuring, which took effect on 1 January 2005, has fitted neatly into Euroclear's domestic market programme.

Euroclear SA/NV, the Belgian registered company interposed between Euroclear plc and the (I)CSDs of the group, is destined gradually to become the locus for activities common to the group's operating subsidiaries. 'Initially it was IT,' Combes says: the single platform is already in Euroclear SA/NV for development and operation purposes. 'Gradually, we will move those parts of the operations that are exactly the same, for example, when we have a single order book in Euronext. From an operational viewpoint we lift as much as we can into it, but we are constrained by legal restraints so that we cannot yet eliminate the need for CSDs to be separate legal entities.'

Euroclear's CSDs will keep their national identities so long as the EU retains a fragmented legal environment for securities settlement. As Combes explains, 'French securities are under French law so they can only be deposited within Euroclear France. The same applies for Belgium; the same for Holland; the same for CREST. We have to have the national entities for client relationships and for depositing securities.'

---

[11] Conversation with the author, 24 October 2006.
[12] Mentioned in 'Target2-Securities: Euroclear Group's response to the ECB questionnaire', 8 September 2006.

Legal impediments to cross-border settlement are likely to be among the last of the Giovannini barriers to disappear in Europe. But Combes can see the need for the different CSDs of the Euroclear group declining over time to a point 'when the legal environment will change and we can basically eliminate the need for separate legal entities'.

'Then you will have one single entity for the whole of Europe, or possibly one entity for all the group's CSDs, plus the ICSD because that has banking activities that cannot be commingled with CSD activities. Ultimately, we may end up with two entities rather than one parent company with lots of different subsidiaries. Everything we are doing in Euroclear SA/NV points in that direction. We are just waiting for the legal changes that would allow us to rationalise the group's whole corporate structure.'

Although evidently some time in the future, the prospective migration of functions from subsidiaries to Euroclear SA/NV has prompted Combes to describe the company as Europe's settlement provider 'in embryo'.

16.2   CESAME AND DISMANTLING THE GIOVANNINI BARRIERS

Euroclear's harmonisation plans support the elimination of the Giovannini barriers. But their eventual removal depends on many other actors in both the private and public sectors.

Since July 2004, the European Commission has been attempting to steer the industry towards removing the barriers for which it has responsibility through the Cesame group.[13] Chaired usually by David Wright, director of financial services policy and financial markets in DG Markt, with Mario Nava, head of DG Markt's financial market infrastructure unit, as his alternate, Cesame has consistently managed to attract top level representatives from the industry since its first working meeting in October 2004.

The Cesame participant lists are a roll call of the movers and shakers in the post-trade sector. Euroclear's Pierre Francotte has been an assiduous participant as has Joël Mérère. The Cesame group provides a unique forum, in which senior executives from commercial rivals such as Euroclear, Deutsche Börse, Citigroup and BNP Paribas sit round the same table as the top managers of the trade associations charged with dismantling the barriers and officials from European Central Bank and the Committee of European Securities Regulators who attend as observers. The intellectually rigorous Giovannini is always present as the Commission's principal policy adviser, to keep up the pressure on the industry to do more.

Given the clout of the Cesame members, it is perhaps not surprising that there has been some disappointment that the group has not achieved more. According to the deadlines set in the second Giovannini report the maximum time envisaged for removing any of the private sector barriers was $2\frac{1}{4}$ years. Taking Cesame's first operational meeting in October 2004 as the starting point, all private sector barriers should have been lifted by January 2007.

Yet, by mid-2007, only one of the six entrusted to the industry – barrier 8 relating to differences in securities issuance – was fully dismantled. All members of ANNA, the Association of National Numbering Agencies, agreed to issue ISIN, international securities identifying numbers, on the same day as a security's issue.

There was, it is true, progress on a European protocol, drawn up by SWIFT, the banking communications organisation, to solve barrier 1 – the national differences in IT and computer interfaces. This was agreed in March 2006. But any sense of achievement was tempered by the disclosure that this would not be implemented in full until 2011.

---

[13] Clearing and Settlement Advisory and Monitoring Experts Group.

Table 16.1   An alphabet soup of trade bodies

Acronym/Initial	Full title	Barrier
Organisations with assigned responsibilities for removing the Giovannini barriers		
ANNA	Association of National Numbering Agencies	8
ECSDA	European Central Securities Depository Association	3, 4, 7
ESF	European Securities Forum	3, 6
ECSAs	European Credit Sector Associations, which includes:	3
FBE/EBF	European Banking Federation	
ESBG	European Savings Banks Group	
EACB	European Association of Cooperative Banks	
EALIC	European Association for Listed Companies	3
FESE	Federation of European Securities Exchanges	3
IPMA	International Primary Market Association[*]	8
SWIFT	Society for Worldwide Interbank Financial Telecommunication	1
Other trade organisations involved with removing the barriers		
EACH	European Association of Central Counterparty Clearing Houses	
EPDA	European Primary Dealers Association	
LIBA	London Investment Banking Association	

[*] Since merged with ISMA, the International Securities Markets Association, to form ICMA, the International Capital Market Association.

In the case of barrier 6 – removing national differences in settlement periods – there has probably been greater progress outside the Cesame framework than inside, through advances towards more straight-through processing and increased same-day confirmation and trade matching on the part of some service providers.

However, once the problems involved are examined in detail, the cup appears more half full than half empty. As Table 16.1 indicates, the complexity of the harmonisation effort is awesome.

Dealing with a barrier is a difficult three phase operation, according to Werner Frey, chief executive of the ESF. First the potential solution to the problem has to be worked out. Then approval from the various interested groups has to be obtained. Finally, implementation takes place, after gap analyses to make sure that no details are missing or misunderstood by the industry.

For example, the SWIFT solution for barrier 1 – that all market infrastructures and participants involved in clearing and settlement in the EU must support the use of ISO 15022 and ISO 20022 messaging standards – entered the phase of gap analysis and implementation at the end of 2006. When completed, this will have entailed analysis of 129 clearing activities and 234 activities in settlement and asset servicing. The results must be checked by 35 infrastructure providers from the 27 EU member states, plus Switzerland and Norway.

The handling of barrier 3, the national differences on corporate actions, has engaged an alphabet soup of trade associations: ECSDA, ESF, ECSAs (which in turn represents three banking associations), EALIC and FESE. There was one more until the Central and Eastern European Central Securities Depository Association (CEECSDA) merged into ECSDA on 1 January 2006, creating an organisation of 40 member CSDs and ICSDs from 34 European countries.

The various associations split their task of harmonising national rules on corporate actions, beneficial ownership and custody of securities into five broad issues, ranging from mandatory and optional distributions to agreeing shareholders' rights at annual meetings. The five categories were broken down for handling in 19 subgroups. In dealing with distributions, for example, different associations drew up different standards and recommendations for cash dividends, interest payment and maturity redemption, and stock distribution. These were tackled in five of the 19 subgroups.

Despite the complexity, the various associations had made progress on one set of 'common deliverables' by mid-2007 and held out the prospect of obtaining endorsement for industry standards to overcome barrier 3 before the final Cesame meeting in June 2008.

ECSDA is also responsible for achieving harmonisation of intraday settlement finality (barrier 4) and overcoming national differences in national operating hours and deadlines (barrier 7), areas where progress has been mixed.

ECSDA started work on harmonisation in these areas before the creation of the Cesame group. In its pre-merged state it agreed recommendations for 10 standards to deal with barriers 4 and 7 in April 2004. By mid-2006, it reported that four of the 10 standards were in force in all 17 of the 'old ECSDA' markets and that there was just over 85% adherence to the standards in the 17 markets, taken as a whole.

However, in the second half of 2006 ECSDA had to channel its resources into dealing with two new initiatives: the ECB's Target2-Securities settlement project and the Commission-brokered code of conduct for the industry. Another factor standing in the way of complete removal of barriers 4 and 7 was the need to make progress in overcoming legal and fiscal barriers for which the public sector has responsibility.

Harmonisation is evidently difficult to orchestrate. As with infrastructure investment, efforts tend to bear fruit only when the work is complete. However, at the end of June 2007, Commissioner McCreevy declared that progress in removing the private sector barriers was 'quite encouraging' and that the standard-setting process was 'well under way'. The performance of the public sector was slower reflecting a marked lack of action by governments to tackle the problems identified by Giovannini.

Where progress on the public sector barriers has been made, it has usually been on the back of other initiatives. The implementation of MiFID and the industry code of conduct should overcome barrier 5 – the impediments to remote access to national clearing and settlement systems.

MiFID and the code should also help remove national restrictions on the location of clearing and settlement (barrier 2). Following correspondence between the relevant trade associations and a subcommittee of national debt managers attached to the EU's Economics and Finance Committee, it was agreed that work to remove restrictions on the activity of primary dealers and market makers (barrier 10) should become part of the agenda to remove barrier 2.

Similarly, adoption and implementation of the Financial Collateral Directive has removed the main problems surrounding national differences in the legal treatment of bilateral netting (barrier 14) to the extent that the Commission, early in 2007, concluded that the barrier should no longer be considered of major importance.

By contrast, there appeared, by the end of 2006, to be no clear progress on removing barrier 9, the national restrictions on the location of securities: in late 2006, it emerged that 16 of the then 25 EU member states applied restrictive regimes of varying types.

Progress has also been very slow on the big fiscal and legal barriers, where complicated technical issues and important questions of national sovereignty are involved. The tax barriers are especially difficult to solve by EU legislation because they require the unanimous agreement of all 27 member states represented in the Ecofin Council.

In 2006 Fisco – the Fiscal Compliance Experts' Group – produced a detailed fact finding study, laying out the many different fiscal compliance procedures which raise the cost of clearing and settlement. In the group's view, none of the member states had optimal collection and relief procedures in place for withholding tax while differences in national approach added to the cost of cross-border transactions. In addition, 11 member states imposed some form of transaction tax on the transfer of securities. Transaction taxes adversely affected market liquidity and the local rules in some cases created an unlevel playing field for settlement providers.

A second Fisco report has since outlined possible solutions with the aim of stimulating debate among EU governments and the industry. Only after the Commission has evaluated its findings and produced proposals of its own are finance ministers expected to turn their attention towards lifting restrictions on foreign financial intermediaries being able to provide withholding tax agent services (barrier 11) and rules that require taxes on securities transactions to be collected by local systems (barrier 12).

During the summer of 2006, the Legal Certainty Group (LCG) advised the Commission that legislation was needed to deal with the absence of an EU-wide framework for the legal treatment of book entry securities (barrier 13). The group advised that book entries on securities accounts should become a source of rights for account holders. Otherwise it opted for a low key approach: new legislation should not upset market practices or replace existing property laws relating to securities. The group's report was praised 'as an impressive piece of work' by David Wright, not least because it was delivered within 18 months of the group starting work early in 2005. The group was asked to work out more details during the following 18 months and aims to provide full advice for the Commission at the end of 2008.

By contrast, efforts to remove the closely related barrier 15 – the uneven application of rules dealing with the conflict of laws – became mired in confusion as 2006 progressed.

The Commission proposed in December 2003 that the European Community (the part of the European Union responsible for the single market) should sign the Hague Securities Convention to solve the problem of barrier 15. The Convention is a worldwide agreement for setting ownership rights on securities held in electronic form. Negotiated in 2002, but a long way from ratification, it dealt with the difficulties of identifying in law where book entry securities were located.

Traditionally, disputes involving property and a conflict of laws were solved by the principle that the law relating to the property would be that where the property was based. Because this rule is difficult to apply to electronic records, the Convention determined that the applicable law for a security held in book entry form should be that named in the account agreement between investor and intermediary. In a cross-border transaction, the two sides could – within reason – choose any law to apply to the securities involved. The idea was similar to that put forward in 1996 by Randall D. Guynn of the London office of Davis Polk.[14]

However, the solution offered in the Hague Convention diverged in some details from existing EU directives, posing problems of alignment. The directives, which included the Financial Collateral Directive, solved the problem of the conflict of laws by adhering to a principle known as PRIMA – the Place of Relevant Intermediary Approach. PRIMA stated that the law which determined rights relating to the ownership of securities was that of the member state (or in some cases, the third country) where the securities account that recorded the existence of those rights was located. The European Parliament, when it approved the directives, took the view that PRIMA guaranteed legal certainty in an international context as regards the law applicable to the holding, disposition and collateralisation of securities credited to an account and held with intermediaries.

---

[14] See Chapter 7. Guynn said the governing law of any securities transaction should be determined by agreement among the parties involved to avoid a conflict of laws.

In July 2006, the Commission again urged member states to sign the Hague Convention. By this time, however, some EU members – all of which would have to ratify the Convention – had lost their enthusiasm for the project. Opposition was thought in some cases to reflect fears that the Convention could open the way to the use of US law in the EU. While the US and Switzerland signed the Convention in 2006, work on barrier 15 in the EU became deadlocked, partly reflecting the bad memories of some member states of the US extraterritorial imposition of Sarbanes-Oxley legislation following the Enron scandal. The ECB also expressed concerns that the Hague Convention could increase systemic risk to financial stability. In December 2006, the European Parliament kicked the Hague Convention into the long grass by passing a resolution committing itself to PRIMA and insisting that the Commission produce a comprehensive impact study, satisfactorily answering all concerns about the Hague Convention, before it could be signed on behalf of the Community.

A meeting of the Cesame group on 11 June 2007 showed that the absence of consensus among the EU member states on removing barrier 15 also applied among Europe's post-trade services providers.

Elsewhere, work is under way in Unidroit – the Rome-based International Institute for the Unification of Private Law – to produce a global 'Convention on Substantive Rules regarding Intermediated Securities'.

This has been proceeding at the level of government experts since 2001. In December 2005, the Commission was given authority to negotiate parts of the draft Unidroit convention to ensure it would be compatible with EU securities law. However, the Unidroit project, which involves more than 60 countries from five continents, is aiming for a legislative text with less harmonisation than the LCG. Even if successful, it is unlikely to solve all the legal problems identified by Giovannini.

Although Cesame, Fisco and the LCG have made slower progress on removing the Giovannini barriers than initially hoped, Cesame in particular has helped move the post-trade sector towards change.

For Alberto Giovannini, the Cesame process 'has worked well in the following sense: that sharing information and awareness is an essential ingredient of a successful reform. I think a lot of the screw-ups that occur in public policy-making, have to do with information. This is a very conscious dissemination of information that is being managed in Cesame in order to minimise public policy decisions being distorted by private interests.'[15]

The group also provided a forum for discussion between the Commission and providers and users on the regulatory impact assessment (RIA) which the Commission had to prepare in readiness for a possible directive on post-trade services. Although, in the end, Commissioner McCreevy opted in the summer of 2006 not to propose EU legislation, the group facilitated perhaps the most intensive *ex-ante* consultation on any directive affecting an industry ever conducted by the Commission.

Through a mixture of Commission cajoling and peer group pressure, Cesame has ensured that senior executives in the clearing and settlement business cannot turn their backs on efforts to overcome the sector's fragmentation. It has contributed to change in the post-trade sector in a novel and imaginative way that on balance has marked an improvement on the delays and uncertainties inherent in EU legislation.

By mid-2007, the progress achieved by the private sector – in Cesame and elsewhere – towards creating an EU-wide market for clearing and settlement had given Commissioner McCreevy some leverage to put pressure on EU governments to deliver comparable change.

---

[15] Conversation with the author, 23 November 2005.

Frameworks for the Future

17.1 TWO SOLUTIONS AT ONCE

In July 2006, Europe's providers of post-trade services suddenly learned what it was like to wait for the proverbial London bus. After being on tenterhooks for months for news of Commissioner McCreevy's ideas for the sector's future, the industry had to cope with two plans coming along at the same time.

On 11 July, McCreevy outlined an industry 'code of conduct' to enhance the efficiency and lower the cost of cross-border clearing and settlement of securities in the European Union as a whole.[1] Just a few days before his long awaited statement, the European Central Bank surprised financial infrastructure providers by announcing plans for a securities settlement service of its own for the eurozone.[2]

Although officials in Brussels and Frankfurt insisted that the two plans would complement each other, they differed fundamentally in content, philosophy and origin.

After months of keeping his counsel amid furious lobbying from backers and opponents of EU legislation, McCreevy gave infrastructure providers the option of producing an industry-led solution. He gave them until 31 October to agree a timetable to the end of 2007 for behavioural changes to overcome the barriers to cross-border clearing and settlement of equities.

McCreevy's plan was all about creating the conditions for the industry to change itself. Drawing lessons from consultations with the industry in the Cesame group and the May 2006 report from DG Competition, the Commissioner set out a road map to achieve greater efficiency in EU capital markets through price transparency and increased competition.

The approach of the ECB, by contrast, was interventionist, radical and technically unprecedented. Although the ECB was further back along the decision chain than the Commission – the ECB press release on 7 July said it was 'evaluating opportunities' with the aim of a final decision in early 2007 – it proposed to get into the business of settling securities. Its ideas promised to change completely the way the securities settlement business is structured in the eurozone

The ECB's goal was to create a new service to be named 'Target2-Securities'. This would be fully owned and operated by the Eurosystem, comprised of the ECB and the eurozone national central banks. The idea was to attach a securities settlement facility to the Target2 system for cross-border payments being developed by the Eurosystem. The outcome would be 'the processing of both securities and cash settlements on a single platform through common procedures' with the objective of allowing 'the harmonised settlement of securities transactions in euro which are settled in central bank money'.

To achieve this, the ECB proposed to take over the core securities settlement function from the CSDs of the eurozone member states, leaving them with the less pivotal but more complex jobs of issuing securities and providing custody and corporate actions services, such as paying interest and dividends to the owners of securities held in the CSD.

---

[1] 'Clearing and settlement: the way forward' – McCreevy's speech of 11 July 2006 announcing the code to the Economic and Monetary Affairs Committee of the European Parliament.

[2] ECB press release, 7 July 2006.

Both the code of conduct and T2S – as the central bank's plan became known – would require the support of Europe's infrastructure providers. Both initiatives raised many questions. Details of the ECB's plans were particularly sparse in the early days after the initial announcement. But it was clear that if implemented in anything like their draft form, the two plans – taken together and with other EU initiatives – would fundamentally change Europe's post-trade sector (see Figures 17.1 and 17.2).

17.2   THE CODE OF CONDUCT

McCreevy's preference for an industry-led solution rather than EU legislation mirrored his own deeply held free-market beliefs. It also reflected a widespread concern that, despite the reforms initiated by Baron Lamfalussy and his wise men, law making in the EU could still take far too long for fast-changing markets and lead – as with MiFID – to rules which many regarded as excessively complex.

The code outlined by McCreevy in July 2006 was designed to force the industry to reform and push down costs for users. It would be made up of three elements, to be introduced in stages:

- Price transparency in post-trade services by the end of 2006. Companies would make public the prices, specific content and conditions of each service offered, and fully disclose rebate and reduction schemes to eliminate price discrimination.
- Effective rights of access on a fair, transparent and non-discriminatory basis to service providers along the value chain: from exchanges to central counterparty clearing providers or CCPs; from CCPs to CCPs; from CCPs to CSDs; and from CSDs to CSDs by the end of June 2007. In addition, the code would set conditions for interoperability, where providers would enter more advanced relationships with the aim of producing customised services for users.
- Separate accounting for the providers' main activities and unbundling of their services by 1 January 2008.

The three elements of the code were intended to be mutually reinforcing. Intellectually, the code owed a great deal to ideas championed by Giovannini in the course of the Cesame debates. He had been a strong advocate of general remote access to, and open architecture for, post-trade services. This would foster competition to the maximum possible extent.

Another important idea was to have a clean separation of all the elements of the value chain. Giovannini's concept was not to forbid practices such as the bundling of services, but to make sure providers only offered them if unbundled services were available. This would foster price transparency.

Unbundling, fair access and price transparency would unleash a movement for simplified and reduced tariffs, especially among the providers of basic and standard services. The result would be to compress earnings among Europe's profit-oriented infrastructure providers, cut costs for users and increase the likelihood of accelerated consolidation among companies in the post-trade sector.

'What I want,' Giovannini once explained,[3] 'is a system where you can remotely access any service in any country and any part of the service in any country. Let us put in place a very simple system whereby a security is a security everywhere in Europe, where you can have the

---

[3] In a conversation with the author, 23 November 2005.

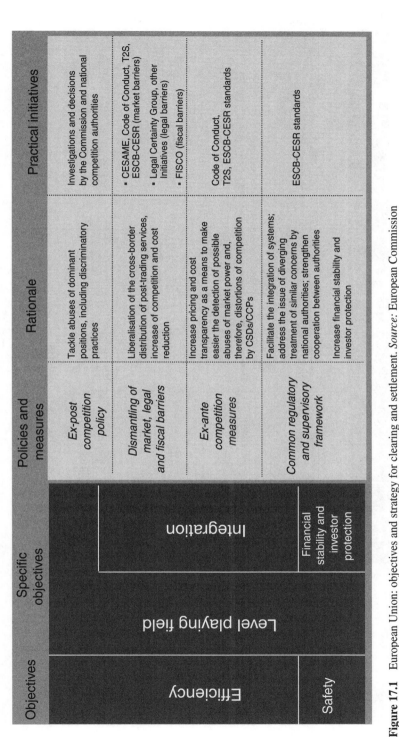

Figure 17.1 European Union: objectives and strategy for clearing and settlement. *Source:* European Commission

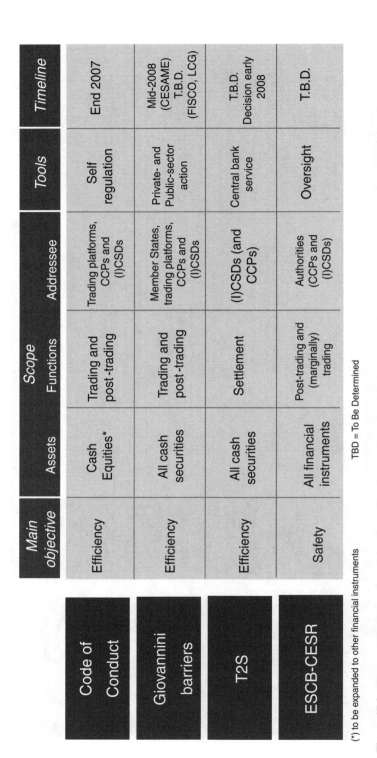

		Scope				
	Main objective	Assets	Functions	Addressee	Tools	Timeline
Code of Conduct	Efficiency	Cash Equities*	Trading and post-trading	Trading platforms, CCPs and (I)CSDs	Self regulation	End 2007
Giovannini barriers	Efficiency	All cash securities	Trading and post-trading	Member States, trading platforms, CCPs and (I)CSDs	Private- and Public-sector action	Mid-2008 (CESAME) T.B.D. (FISCO, LCG)
T2S	Efficiency	All cash securities	Settlement	(I)CSDs (and CCPs)	Central bank service	T.B.D. Decision early 2008
ESCB-CESR	Safety	All financial instruments	Post-trading and (marginally) trading	Authorities (CCPs and (I)CSDs)	Oversight	T.B.D.

(*) to be expanded to other financial instruments

TBD = To Be Determined

Figure 17.2 European Union: tools and timelines. *Source:* European Commission

title to the security in one place and the actual physical instrument in another. The concepts of generalised remote access and transparent pricing of essential basic standardised services are concepts that should be common currency in Europe in all different sectors of the securities business.'

Where Giovannini differed from McCreevy was in believing that such developments would best be directed through EU legislation.

Underlying McCreevy's preference for the code was a deep scepticism about the potential benefits of EU legislation at a time of rapid change in financial markets. In such circumstances, regulatory measures from the Commission could prove counter-productive or even slow down restructuring that was under way. On the other hand, McCreevy kept the threat of new regulations in the background to encourage the industry to adopt and comply with the code. If the signatories proved unable to implement the code 'regulators always have the range of measures at their disposal to force changes through,' he said.

The commissioner wanted bankable promises by end-October. The code, which would initially apply to cash equities, would include a verification and auditing procedure to ensure the industry met its commitments. In parallel, the Commission pledged to keep pressing the industry and governments to remove the 15 Giovannini barriers.

As before, McCreevy insisted that the Commission's role was 'not to pick winners, nor dictate a particular outcome. Nor determine the final architecture' of a clearing and settlement system for Europe. Instead, its job was to work with the grain of the market, ensure that unnecessary barriers were removed and that 'EU Treaty provisions, particularly competition policy, are applied to the full'.

The planned code was something new in EU regulation, a hybrid of self-regulation by the industry and 'soft law' where the Commission steered the process and promised to enforce compliance through strict enforcement of competition law and a strict monitoring exercise. It was, McCreevy admitted, 'not without risks'.

Successful cases of commercial rivals arriving at a cooperative solution to an industry problem as a result of Commission encouragement were rare: one of few examples cited by Commission officials was an agreement some years before among auto manufacturers to harmonise the height, off the ground, of car bumpers. Such an industry-led solution for the EU financial industry was thought to be unprecedented.

Another surprising aspect was the code's emphasis on interoperability. Although interoperability was an up-and-coming idea in 2006, there were still many with reservations about linking different infrastructure providers supplying similar services to facilitate cross-border trading. Besides requiring often expensive duplication of IT equipment, interoperability was difficult to organise because of legal and tax barriers, which governments were unable or unwilling to remove. Where links existed between CSDs, they were rarely used.

The code had to overcome other doubts. There were many – among European Parliamentarians, in member states, among officials in the Commission and in parts of the industry – who preferred legislation on clearing and settlement and who would shed no tears if the code failed.

But it passed its first hurdle on 7 November, when a smiling McCreevy appeared with senior executives of Europe's securities trading and post-trade sectors before the Brussels press corps to announce that the industry's leaders had signed up to the code.

It was, he stressed, 'a first step'. While the code would initially cover cash equities, McCreevy made clear he wanted the industry to consider extending it to other asset classes, 'specifically bonds and derivatives', and to other service providers. He invited participating companies to add other asset classes straight away. Euroclear, represented at the November press meeting by Pierre Francotte, announced that afternoon that Euroclear Bank and the CSDs in the group would apply the code from the outset to all asset classes, including fixed income.

A notable feature of the code was that it was signed by the chief executives of the EU's exchanges, CCPs, CSDs and the two ICSDs rather than their trade associations. It also attracted signatories from non-EU financial infrastructures. These included the exchanges and CCPs of Switzerland and Norway as well as the Iceland stock exchange. The CSDs of Switzerland, Norway, Iceland, Bosnia-Herzegovina, Croatia and Montenegro as well as the CCP/CSD of Serbia also signed the code.

The high profile of the signatories made more credible the one significant sanction available to the Commission to enforce compliance. This was the naming and shaming of any backsliders.

In true EU fashion, the morning of the signing ceremony was not without a minor drama. The evening before the announcement, Clearstream Banking Luxembourg signalled that it would not sign on the grounds that the code applied to equities whereas it settled bonds. Some hurried telephone calls and the threat of an extremely negative reaction from McCreevy secured compliance half way through the morning of 7 November.

Although a week later than envisaged, the code was brought to the point of signing in a remarkably short period. The negotiations took just four months compared with more than five years of debate on clearing and settlement in the EU preceding the July announcement. This reflected intensive work by David Wright, Mario Nava and officials from DG Markt and DG Comp on the side of the Commission and by three industry federations: FESE, EACH and ECSDA. Much of the coordination and preparation on the industry side was handled by FESE under the energetic leadership of Judith Hardt, its secretary general. Unlike the other federations, FESE had a small but effective office within easy walking distance of the Commission's headquarters.

The code was a compromise. The negotiation did not include the agent banks for fear that divisions within the banking community would make agreement impossible. Some difficult negotiations were left for later, notably over the details of access and interoperability where participating companies might have to adapt their business models, incurring costs in the process.

The code cleared a second hurdle on 1 January 2007 when the signatories published details of prices, discounts and rebates in line with their price transparency commitments. The code also specified publication of price examples to help users compare offers and the provision of *ex-post* information to allow customers to reconcile bills with their use of services and the price lists provided.

The Commission's code of conduct monitoring group met on 22 January for its first appraisal of the code with Wright in the chair and Nava as deputy chairman. Glorying in its acronym MOG, it consisted of 11 Commission officials plus representatives of CESR and the ECB. After separate sessions with users and infrastructure representatives, its verdict was that 'significant steps' had been taken to implement price transparency but more work was needed, on rebates, price examples, price comparability and reconciling bills. To overcome the opacity of fee schedules that sometimes ran to more than 100 pages, the group urged infrastructure providers and users to agree a standardised set of examples to facilitate price comparability.

The code cleared an even bigger hurdle at the end of June 2007 when the three industry bodies – FESE, EACH and ECSDA – agreed a guideline defining the principles and conditions for access and interoperability among providers of post-trading services for cash equities. Billed as making 'the concept of cross-border redundant for securities transactions within the

EU', the guideline was the result of complex and very difficult negotiations that also involved users and the Commission, CESR and the ECB among EU institutions. It ran to 128 paragraphs that spelled out in some detail how the different participants in the value chain from trading through CCP clearing to settlement should link, and how the different links should work.

For the purposes of the guideline, service providers were categorised as receiving and requesting organisations. The guideline defined their rights and obligations and how they applied to different levels of access to post-trade services and interoperability. It outlined in 14 different scenarios how the rules might work among very different organisations, ranging from the vertically to the horizontally structured.

The most basic form of access was standard access, where an organisation, such as a CCP or CSD, could become a participant in another organisation by opening an account. This was defined as a right in line with the rules of MiFID.

Going beyond standard access were customised access and transaction feed access where a requesting organisation could ask for special functions of a receiving organisation, subject to conditions intended to safeguard the interests of the organisation providing the services.

Interoperability was used to describe advanced forms of relationship between organisations which agreed to mutual solutions for specific issues. An example of interoperability in action is the Bridge between Euroclear Bank and Clearstream Banking Luxembourg.

The guideline laid down that access and interoperability agreements should not weaken the operational efficiency of financial markets. Its rules were hedged around with conditions in an attempt to prevent organisations gaining an unfair advantage from partners that were also competitors.

Thus, the reciprocity principle would apply so a receiving organisation could refuse a link where the requesting organisation was hindering access to its own infrastructure. Requesting organisations must comply with the local rules that applied for receiving organisations. A receiving organisation would not be obliged to change its market practices or extend its product range to accommodate another organisation: any change would require mutual agreement. On the other hand, a receiving organisation could not plead loss of market share as grounds for denying a request for a link.

Given the complexity of its content, it was no surprise that the guideline also set out a mediation process to deal with disputes arising from their application.

The outcome was welcomed by Commissioner McCreevy as a 'difficult but worthwhile result'.[4] Together with the freedom of choice for users laid down by MiFID, the guideline would form an important part of the EU's strategy for opening up clearing and settlement markets. For McCreevy the rules for access and interoperability formed the 'heart' of the code of conduct. And, as he told the annual FESE Convention on 26 June 2007, 'The ultimate aim of the code is to make the user choices enshrined by MiFID not a theoretical possibility, but a reality.'

But McCreevy's officials and infrastructure executives alike made clear that the proof of the pudding would be in the eating. After a meeting of MOG on 11 July, McCreevy wrote to the three trade associations suggesting improvements that, among other things, would bind the CSDs more tightly to the agreement. The associations, still punch drunk from the negotiations, asked that these be considered when the functioning of the guideline was assessed at the end of 2007.

McCreevy had already warned that the Commission would 'not accept any anti-competitive interpretation or application'[5] of the guideline. Promising to monitor very closely how the

---

[4] On 10 July 2007, to the coordinators of the European Parliament's ECON committee.
[5] On 26 June 2007, to the annual FESE Convention in Brussels.

signatories implemented the agreement, the commissioner underlined that he and competition commissioner Neelie Kroes wanted 'to hear immediately if there is any anticompetitive behaviour or unsavoury practices' – adding for good measure, 'I repeat: immediately'.

Nevertheless, the Commission had reason to feel quietly satisfied with progress on the code. Reporting on the price transparency provisions at the end of June 2007, McCreevy noted 'close to 80% overall compliance on discount schemes and the provision of examples and nearly 100% on fees'. He added: 'Achieving the same results with a directive would have taken many years.'

Progress on the code has entailed a major effort by the industry. Stefan Mai, head of market policy of the Deutsche Börse group, calculated that negotiations on the code involved 135 external meetings and some 165 persons at an estimated cost in terms of executive hours of €15 million up to the end of June 2007.[6]

More work lay ahead, including further meetings of the monitoring group a few weeks either side of the remaining code deadline of 1 January 2008 for unbundling and separation of accounting. A review of the code and whether to extend it to other service providers will take place once it has fully entered into force, possibly in April 2008. By then, the MOG will have had a first discussion on whether to extend the code to other asset classes: only Euroclear has clearly committed itself to such action. The Commission will also be able to judge whether the code has successfully enforced Articles 34 and 46 of MiFID stipulating the right of access for market participants across borders to CCP and settlement infrastructures.

If it has, and if it has been properly implemented in other ways, the code should have achieved the main objectives set out by the Commission in its 2004 communication on clearing and settlement for greater efficiency and lower costs in Europe's capital market.

17.3   TARGET2-SECURITIES

The code – although very much McCreevy's own policy choice – followed a lengthy and very transparent consultation with the industry, notably in the Cesame group. The ECB's plan – backed by its governing council on 6 July 2006 – came out of the blue.

Whereas McCreevy's code worked with the grain of the market, the ECB plan for a system owned and operated by the Eurosystem appeared to be a reversal of historical trends towards demutualised, for-profit infrastructures that had built up over nearly a decade.

Unlike McCreevy, the ECB was not proposing a solution for fragmentation throughout the post-trade sector. Its idea was limited to settlement services in the eurozone where it proposed to handle equities and bonds.

With the benefit of hindsight, it is possible to see how the protracted inability of Europe's post-trade providers to successfully consolidate and integrate the sector stoked frustration at the ECB.

When Tommaso Padoa-Schioppa expatiated on the importance of securities settlement at the Sibos conference in Munich in September 1999,[7] he had every reason to believe that consolidation of Europe's settlement infrastructure lay around the corner. Cedel, Deutsche Börse and Sicovam still appeared on track for a trilateral merger. He therefore outlined a non-interventionist approach for the ECB as the central bank's preferred position.

---

[6] Also at the FESE Convention.
[7] 'Payments and the Eurosystem', speech by Tommaso Padoa-Schioppa, ECB executive board member, Sibos, Munich, 13 September 1999. See also Chapter 7.4.

Padoa-Schioppa noted that the Maastricht Treaty made no explicit mention of securities settlement because 'central banks' involvement in securities settlement systems has only developed after the adoption of the Treaty'. But central banks needed to be increasingly concerned about the smooth functioning of securities settlement systems because of their statutory duties in the fields of payments systems and monetary policy.

Although the ECB would not be an exception to this rule, it was obliged by the terms of the EU Treaty[8] to act in accordance with the principle of an open market economy. This meant 'as long as market forces do not lead to unsound or inefficient solutions, the Eurosystem will not influence the trend towards consolidation of the central securities depositories in Europe'.

Fast forward 30 months and Sirkka Hämäläinen, another ECB board member, was sounding rather less sanguine. Commenting in April 2002 on the euro at the launch of a capital markets research network[9] in Frankfurt, she noted how 'no other currency area has ever had to cope with such a highly fragmented securities infrastructure'. Looking back at developments in the US, Italy, France and Britain over the 20 years to the mid-1990s, she first noted how there had been 'some form of public intervention either by the legislator, the securities regulator, or the central bank in order to effect changes in the national securities infrastructure. Second, the interventions all sought to improve the efficiency and competitiveness of the domestic securities industries.' She added: 'Given the current degree of fragmentation of the securities infrastructure for the euro, it is natural to study whether similar action might be useful or necessary today at the euro-area level.'

Move the clock forwards another four years to June 2006 and Gertrude Tumpel-Gugerell, the ECB board member in charge of financial infrastructure, seems close to the end of her tether.[10] Tumpel-Gugerell succeeded Hämäläinen on the ECB executive board in 2003 after a career in the Austrian central bank in which she rose to be vice governor.

After stating that integration of securities settlement providers should be market driven, she told a conference organised by the Spanish central bank: 'However, this does not mean that authorities should just stand back and wait and see. Action by authorities is warranted in the event of market failures. Some markets can be reluctant to change (the first step is always the hardest and old habits die hard) and the different time horizon of costs (today) and revenues (tomorrow) relating to the necessary investments may increase this reluctance. Moreover, market forces may not be able to take all the necessary steps to ensure effective competition as well as the stability of the infrastructure. It is not a coincidence that, to date, the most successful example of integrated infrastructure has been the TARGET system for settlement of large-value payments. It should be noted that TARGET was created not by the market, but by the central banks.'

Tumpel-Gugerell's comments reflected more than pride in the technical capabilities of TARGET. Among her officials, there was also a belief that the ECB could be a successful catalyst, bringing greater efficiency to the post-trade sector.

They looked back to the nine standards devised by the EMI in the late 1990s and concluded that these had fostered consolidation by forcing some settlement systems – in Spain and Italy, for example – to choose between investing to meet the standards or merging with others which were already compliant. But that process had run its course. In the eurozone, the national CSDs were usually local monopolies and disinclined to consolidate. Their number had dropped only

---

[8] Article 105(1).

[9] 'Consolidation in the European securities infrastructure – what is needed?' Sirkka Hämäläinen. Frankfurt, 20 April 2002.

[10] 'Drivers for change in payment and securities settlement systems', speech by Gertrude Tumpel-Gugerell, member of the executive board of the ECB, Madrid, 9 June 2006.

modestly from 23 in 1999 to 18 in 2004. The settlement sector needed a new catalyst to spur consolidation.

By the time Tumpel-Gugerell gave her speech in Madrid, the idea of T2S had already been discussed between the ECB and national central banks. It is possible that by July 2006 the ECB felt it had little choice but to take on the catalytic role. The ESCB-CESR standards, which might have been expected to foster change, were stalled. The possibility of a framework directive from the Commission – a measure which Tumpel-Gugerell explicitly backed in her Madrid speech – looked less likely as the end-July deadline for McCreevy to make up his mind drew nearer.

By putting forward its own solution for securities settlement in the eurozone, the central bank would be seen to take a decisive lead after years of only limited progress by the private sector towards a more efficient post-trade infrastructure in Europe. The history of clearing and settlement in the US provided a precedent of sorts. Intervention by Congress and the Securities and Exchange Commission in 1976 led, by the end of the 1990s, to a cheap and efficient, utility-model US clearing and settlement infrastructure with The Depository Trust and Clearing Corp. (DTCC) at its centre.

Another plus point claimed for ECB intervention was that it would help eliminate several Giovannini barriers – numbers 1, 2, 4 and 7 – by concentrating the securities settlement of several countries on one platform. It would therefore foster interoperability and promote the creation of a single capital market.

But there was another compelling reason for the ECB to act, which its officials chose at first not to advertise, and yet which determined the specifications of T2S.

For roughly a year, serious differences had persisted among some of the eurozone's leading national central banks over how to handle the cash leg of securities settlement using central bank money. The unprecedented technical design of T2S reflected an urgent need for the ECB leadership to overcome a split among the national central banks in its governing council.

In setting up T2S, the ECB proposed to follow what was accepted as best practice in the industry: the so-called 'integrated' model of cash and securities settlements on one platform, using for the cash leg central bank money, which is the most secure of all cash settlement methods.

Soon after announcing the project, ECB officials let it be known that T2S came with three non-negotiable elements. One was the use of the integrated model. The second was that T2S should have monopoly use of eurozone central bank money for securities settlement and there should be no 'outsourcing' of central bank money to other post-trade service providers. The third was that all the eurozone would be brought into the scheme.

The ECB's proposal to take control of the cash leg of settlement of eurozone securities using central bank money in an integrated system meant it would have to 'insource' securities settlement on a single platform of its own. This reversed the practice, approved in pre-euro days by the Banque de France when it outsourced the cash leg of the integrated settlement function to Sicovam, the French CSD that became Euroclear France in 2001.

For nearly 12 months, the German and Italian central banks, backed by the Spanish, led a determined, behind-the-scenes campaign to turn ECB policy against outsourcing the use of central bank money for securities settlement. Securities professionals were aware of the power struggle. Indeed in January 2006, Jean-Francois Théodore, the CEO and chairman of Euronext, wrote to Tumpel-Gugerell expressing concerns that the row could jeopardise investment in the ESES settlement system for Euronext.

In part, the opposition of the national central banks to outsourcing was principled. Historically, the control of central bank money was a core central banking function. No matter how rigorous the rules, they argued, ceding control through outsourcing entailed some risk for financial stability. But there were also suggestions that the national central banks had ulterior motives. They were interested in retaining business in their territories that might otherwise be lost to other providers through outsourcing.

Jean-Michel Godeffroy, the ECB's director general for payments systems and market infrastructure, later recalled how he and his team came up with the idea of T2S after being sent away 'to think the unthinkable'.[11] This was when the ECB, initially, had no intention of entering the securities settlement business.

'We were divided. The Eurosystem was divided,' he said. 'There were two schools of thought. And behind that was the market asking for harmonisation because some of them were considering that they were in an unfair situation.'

'Then my team was asked, after long discussions, to start thinking about something else: to think the unthinkable. We had to think the unthinkable, because for us it was unthinkable that we [the ECB] would get into this business.'

'But the logic was very simple. If we have to keep the efficiency of the market deriving from the integrated model, but at the same time we cannot outsource the central bank account, then the only solution is to insource the securities accounts. But don't believe T2S exists just because of this triggering event. It exists also because there was a lot of frustration in the market and among the political authorities in Europe.'

'To be very honest, when we presented this project – T2S – to the governors, I believed that they would not accept [it]. I thought the risk would be too big for the governing council: the financial risks and the reputational risks. And I was very surprised – I would say happily surprised – that they took this risk without division within the council. I could not name a governor who is against this project.'

While Godeffroy was 'happily surprised' by the T2S initiative, the reverse was true for the Euroclear group. Euroclear was a clear beneficiary of outsourcing of central bank money and seemed set to benefit more in the future. Euroclear France settled transactions using central bank money under outsourcing arrangements originally approved by Jean-Claude Trichet, the ECB president, when governor of the Banque de France. The integrated model of securities settlement, with an outsourced cash leg, was planned for ESES and the single settlement platform that would complete the group's €500 million investment in the domestic market for Europe.

T2S, if realised, would fundamentally change the business practices of national CSDs in all the eurozone countries. It would also force Euroclear, Europe's biggest securities settlement provider, to remodel a business plan that had already cost about €250 million and which promised to cut costs sharply for users.

The announcement of 7 July left many unanswered questions, including issues of cost and timing. The ECB envisaged recouping the cost of investing in T2S from fees paid for its settlement services by national CSDs. But would it also have to compensate Euroclear – and national CSDs – for investments taken over or rendered obsolete by its plans? Or would it wait to introduce T2S after these investments were amortised? If so, how long would that be?

Also unclear were the scope of the project and technical risks involved. ECB officials initially talked of T2S as a small operation, operating in daylight hours, which would leave settlement in commercial bank money to others including existing CSDs and ICSDs such as Euroclear Bank and Clearstream Banking Luxembourg.

---

[11] On 1 June 2007 in Berlin, to the annual conference of the International Capital Market Association (ICMA).

But was that what the market wanted? Would a small-scale T2S meet the demands – especially from investment banks – for sophisticated services tailored to fast changing requirements covering a wide range of asset classes? How would a daytime system fit with an industry that conducted many of its operations through the night?

On technology, the ECB could reflect with some satisfaction on past successes, including the TARGET1 payments system. But had it the know-how to deal with the securities infrastructure, where investments had so often gone wrong in the past? In the week the ECB governing council decided to go public with T2S, David Hardy resigned as CEO of LCH.Clearnet because its failed technology programme ran up losses of more than €120 million.

At a more fundamental level, there were questions whether a proper legal base existed for T2S in view of the absence of any mention of securities settlement in the EU treaties.

Nonetheless, the concept of bringing back to the central bank securities settlement with central bank money got the ECB off a difficult hook. It would allow the securities industry to benefit from the state-of-the-art integrated model using central bank money while ensuring peace inside the central bank's governing council. The central banks of France, the Netherlands and Belgium, which at that time backed outsourcing and which had Euroclear-owned CSDs in their territories, were thought to have acquiesced in the ECB solution rather than be outvoted.

17.4   T2S – the follow-up

The ECB was a central bank in a hurry. Its statement of 7 July pointed to early 2007 as the time for a 'final decision' on the project. It began consulting users and CSDs on 19 July and soon ran into controversy.

For a business sector accustomed to exhaustive consultations with the European Commission, what followed was a shock. On 19 July, the ECB held three separate slide presentations: one for banks, another for the eurozone CSDs, including Euroclear Bank and Clearstream Banking Luxembourg, and a third for the press. Only one bank per eurozone country was present and each was selected by its national central bank. The selection process made for some notable absentees. In Germany's case, the Bundesbank chose not to select Deutsche Bank.

ECB officials painted a positive picture when briefing after the meetings. The banks, they said, were 'absolutely delighted' by the initiative. Many CSDs were said to be 'happy', although they admitted Euroclear was not. One participant complained: 'Where people said "we welcome the initiative but we think there are lots of questions, uncertainties and risks surrounding the project", the ECB only took the first part into account and said everybody is enthusiastic.'

On 10 August, in the middle of Europe's peak vacation month, the ECB followed up the briefings with a document about T2S, containing more than 40 questions. It specified that responses from banks, settlement providers and stock exchanges should be channelled through the eurozone central banks and imposed a tight 11 September deadline for them to report back. The ECB document provided no outline of a T2S business plan, still less any indication of cost-effectiveness.

It was at this point that signs of discontent began to surface. Europe's financial trade associations have always been reluctant to question the motives of authority in public. But at a conference of EU custodian banks in September, Guido Ravoet, secretary general of the European Banking Federation, asked 'Is this development needed?' He criticised the ECB's August paper for assuming there was a need for public sector intervention in securities settlement and for rushing to discuss technical details. 'Before addressing these, a number of more fundamental strategic, policy and business issues need to be discussed with the market,' he said, listing: 'Motivation, governance, economic viability, duplication of investment and costs, practical feasibility.'

Ravoet was lucky enough to see the August document. The ECB did not publish it before the 11 September deadline. Indeed, apart from the initial press release, it had published nothing about T2S by that time.

There was also a breakdown of communications with London, the biggest centre for trading euro-denominated securities. The London-based trade associations complained that they were not sent copies of the 10 August document. The big London-based investment banks had to rely on information supplied by their representatives in the various eurozone countries. The ECB's handling of T2S fuelled suspicions in a somewhat Eurosceptic City that T2S was a politically inspired venture.

Even banks that supported T2S wondered whether it met their needs. The responses to the ECB's August document, when published on the central bank's website, showed that most trade associations had many questions and some doubts. The French banking federation viewed the project favourably. Euroclear did not.

Euroclear was still by habit a reticent company, not given to headline seeking. But it put its reactions to T2S on its own website while also publishing – before the ECB – the text of the central bank's August questionnaire.

Euroclear's 30-page document warned that the ECB's ideas of separating euro settlement from settlement in other currencies and delivery versus payment settlement from services such as corporate actions management would further fragment an already fragmented EU market. 'Overall, T2S could make it more difficult to achieve the Lisbon Agenda for the creation of an efficient single market in financial services.'

It asked whether T2S would be mandatory or optional for CSDs, warning this was of 'capital importance' for all CSD boards because of their legal responsibility to take decisions in their companies' best interests.

Euroclear argued that the ECB's wish to take the core settlement function for euro-denominated securities from eurozone CSDs would 'increase the technical risk profile and generate greater cost, complexity and inefficiency for users'. It pinpointed as a specific problem the threat that T2S posed to multi-currency settlement arrangements and by extension to the EU's single market. CREST provided settlement in euro for Ireland and sterling for the UK while the Nordic CSD served Finland, a euro country, and Sweden which was outside the eurozone. Claiming T2S could cripple existing momentum behind settlement infrastructure consolidation and harmonisation, it asked why the ECB was intervening when market failure was 'not evident'.

T2S had got off to a bumpy start. While users of settlement services, such as banks, were inclined to favour the project because it promised lower costs, most wanted more detail. The infrastructure providers were less enthusiastic. Members of the European Parliament's economic and monetary affairs committee were critical of the ECB's failure to inform when they met Tumpel-Gugerell in September. EU finance ministries watched developments with a wary eye.

The ECB realised that it needed to be more open and forthcoming about its plans. Godeffroy met bankers in London on 20 September with the message: 'We are willing to listen to the market before we proceed any further.' That was the beginning of a campaign to calm the City which saw Marc Bayle and Daniela Russo, both members of Godeffroy's team, also visit the

Square Mile in the months that followed. In early November, Tumpel-Gugerell met a group of City practitioners gathered under the auspices of the City Corporation.

The ECB worked hard to dispel any idea that T2S was at variance with other EU initiatives. Making a joint presentation, Russo and Nava told the October 2006 meeting of Cesame that T2S complied with the code of conduct and supported both the code and efforts to remove the Giovannini barriers. The ECB invited users and settlement providers to a series of meetings on specifications in Frankfurt in December and January. It also beefed up its technical expertise, hiring a number of outside consultants including Hugh Simpson, the former chief executive of CREST.

In mid-January 2007, the ECB declared that the project was economically feasible and legally possible under the EU treaties. It published an economic feasibility study that concluded 'even with very conservative assumptions' that the T2S fee would be lower than the lowest current CSD fee. It estimated the costs for the market of adapting to the system at €210 million, with CSDs carrying €170 million of the total and custodians €40 million. Against these one-off costs there would be annual savings of €85 million for the CSDs and between €300 million and €370 million for the custodians.

The central bank had in the meantime asked its in-house legal services to assess the legal feasibility of the project. Noting that T2S would be 'a purely technical platform providing harmonised IT facilities' rather than a new securities settlement system or CSD, the ECB's legal experts concluded that it would be permitted under the same articles in the EU Treaties that provided the legal base for establishing and operating TARGET2.[12]

There were, to be sure, mutterings among practitioners that studies of the standard presented by the ECB would not have passed muster in the private sector. Moreover, the central bank was conspicuously disinclined to seek an outside opinion on the legality of the scheme. However, all the signs were that the governing council would give T2S the go-ahead when it met in February 2007. It was clear, since autumn 2006, that the key questions relating to T2S were when and how, not whether.

At this point, Europe's finance ministers intervened. They were due to discuss T2S in the Ecofin council of 30 January but took the issue off the agenda after the ECB had failed to reassure their officials at a meeting of the EU's financial services committee on details of the scheme. Officials from the UK, Belgium and the Netherlands among others were reported afterwards to have expressed doubts about the legal base for T2S and questioned how the ECB would reconcile its proposed role as operator of the system with its duties and aspirations to regulate the settlement sector, as evidenced by the ESCB-CESR standards.

The Ecofin council met on 27 February 2007 and duly published conclusions on T2S. They were hardly enthusiastic. True, the statement welcomed the work done by the Eurosystem on T2S. But this, it transpired, reflected a late change in the draft following heavy lobbying by one member state. The statement noted that the project would have a profound impact on Europe's securities settlement infrastructure. As a result, the council urged the ECB to 'proceed step by step', examine carefully the results of consultation and take several points into account when deciding the way forward.

In particular, the business case should be 'clearly proven, based on well-defined user re-quirements and well-founded economic data' so that T2S 'should allow the settlement of cross-border and national transactions at an end-to-end cost lower than the lowest cost in the EU'.

---

[12] Articles 17, 18 and 22 of the protocol on the statutes of the ESCB and ECB annexed to the European Community Treaty.

'Participation in T2S should not be compulsory and access to central bank money should not be restricted for non-participants.' These 'should be able to continue to perform settlement in central bank money and provide related collateral'.

'The design and operation of the project should comply with EU competition policy and aim at promoting competition and innovation in post-trading services' so that efficiency gains would be passed to end users, including issuers.

The ministers went on to stress a number of principles. Among these, T2S should be open to non-euro area CSDs and currencies. Existing securities settlement systems should not be put into question during the migration phase until T2S was implemented. The migration phase should be competitively neutral.

'The governance structure, for the development and the future operation of T2S respectively, should provide solutions for the handling of potential conflicts of interest,' the ministers added. At this point their statement suggested that a separate legal entity could be considered as a way of distinguishing between the operation and supervision of the system.

The ministers also stressed that the governance structure of T2S should adequately involve all affected market participants from across the EU, ensure responsiveness to market needs and provide for accountability and transparency. They concluded by calling on the ECB to report back regularly on progress before taking a final decision.

This statement effectively precluded the ECB taking its 'final decision' when it met to consider T2S on 8 March. The governing council decided instead that the project was feasible and decided to go ahead with 'the next phase' which would be the definition of user requirements on the basis of contributions from the market. The scope of the project would take into account a public consultation. A decision on the development phase was scheduled for early 2008.

In its March statement, the ECB described T2S as a 'common technical service' for CSDs that would provide DvP for securities against central bank money. It confirmed that CSDs would maintain their relationships with intermediaries, investors and issuers and continue to handle corporate actions and other asset servicing and custody functions as well as the notary function of keeping records for issuers.

The ECB produced a clutch of studies that clarified some of the details of T2S. The CSDs would be directly connected to and communicate with T2S. The published blueprint for the system said participants could 'choose among multiple CSDs to access securities through a single entry point'. Elsewhere the documentation observed that users would normally connect to T2S through the CSD where they held their accounts. However, the ECB reported that some of the big European custodians were interested in having a direct technical link to the centralised infrastructure of T2S. This would be a single settlement engine which would combine real-time capabilities with technical netting cycles through day and night to catch and settle potential fails.[13]

After having toyed with the idea of a 'greenfield' approach to producing the system, it decided to base T2S on the TARGET2 platform. Using the platform would produce a cost saving of around 20% compared with the estimated €166 million to establish T2S from scratch. The investment period would be six years, suggesting T2S would be operating in March 2013. The investments would then be amortised over six years to 2019.

---

[13] In technical terms, the settlement engine will be a combination of RTGS DvP model 1 with continuous optimisation procedures. This, the ECB has defined as 'optimised continuous DvP settlement' rather than settlement using the standard DvP models 1, 2 or 3 described in Chapter 6.4.

All the ECB's cost estimates were heavily surrounded by caveats, not least because of the lack of transparency of existing CSD costs. But one projection caught the imagination of the users: the bank estimated that if T2S were to start operating on the basis of 2007 figures, it would charge on average €0.29 per transaction against a weighted average of European CSD prices of €0.60 to €0.70.

Because T2S would propose the same pricing for domestic and cross-border settlements, the savings on cross-border settlement would be much larger, giving investors greater opportunities to diversify their portfolios. The ECB cited external research that put existing cross-border settlement costs at €19.5 to €35.

The estimated one-off investment costs were put at €172 million for the CSDs and €37 million for users: virtually unchanged from the January estimates. As before, the ECB put the expected annual cost saving of the CSDs at €85 million. Its preliminary assessment of annual benefits for users was more cautious at between €140 million and €330 million. The wide range reflected uncertainty over how far collateral costs would be reduced – the ECB put the savings in a range between €30 million and €200 million against IT cost savings of €50 million to €70 million and staff efficiency gains of €60 million.

Marking a step away from the original concept, the ECB disclosed that T2S would be designed with an open architecture so that it could 'later on' provide settlement in other EU currencies 'where there is market demand' and where the relevant national central bank was prepared to enable settlement in its currency.

It also confirmed that membership of the system would not be mandatory. Although the ECB did not say so, this decision recognised that there was no legal base in EU law for a mandatory system. The ECB acknowledged that it must persuade Europe's CSDs to participate. 'The benefits for the market will only materialise if all CSDs, or at least a critical mass of them, join the project because of the greater competition it will introduce, even if this may run counter to their corporate interests in the short term,' it said. 'At this stage, the Eurosystem believes that the pressure of the market and the quality of the solution proposed are sufficiently strong to convince all CSDs to follow the European integration approach.'

The most powerful national central banks of the eurozone were lined up ready to develop and operate the system. The Bundesbank, the Banque de France, the Banca d'Italia – the three central banks developing TARGET2 – were joined by the Banco d'Espana in handling the project.

The division of labour for building T2S pointed to the ECB's solution for resolving the split in its governing council between 'outsourcers' and 'insourcers'. The French central bank would in effect be compensated for reversing its policy on outsourcing central bank money by being able to channel its expertise in IT into the T2S project. At the same time, the ECB indicated that the National Bank of Belgium and the Dutch National Bank, which were supporters of the outsourcing of central bank money for the cash leg of securities settlement, would have a role to play in developing a single platform, known as CCBM2, to replace the Eurosystem's collateral management procedures, based on the Correspondent Central Banking Model (CCBM).

Towards the end of April, the ECB governing council settled the governance arrangements for the user requirements phase of the T2S project. The months of consultation from 1 May 2007 until a decision, expected early in 2008, on whether to go ahead should provide an opportunity for a thorough evaluation of T2S including the features that were not clear at the beginning.

These include the plan to build the settlement engine on the TARGET2 platform. Hugh Simpson considered this possibility in a brief analysis of the project before he became a consultant to the ECB. Using the latest available figures (from 2004), he noted that there were more than 500 000 securities settlements a day in eurozone settlement systems against an average of 270 000 TARGET payments. T2S, he wrote, 'would not be a payment system that also settled securities. It would be a securities settlement system that also handled payments'.[14]

17.5   QUESTIONS AND MORE QUESTIONS

The ECB's decision to consult before embarking on the development phase of T2S in 2008 was welcomed by many participants. The project had rattled along at the speed of an express train, gaining momentum on the way and leaving a host of unanswered and half answered questions in its wake.

Not that there is any reason to suspect the ECB could seriously consider dropping T2S after the consultation. The bank had demonstrated overwhelming confidence in its top-down approach since first announcing it was 'evaluating' the project in July 2006. By early 2008 it will have invested nearly two years' work in T2S. The continental attitude towards consultation – less robust than in the City of London and characterised by a long standing subservience towards symbols of authority such as a central bank – enabled the ECB to set the agenda on T2S. Where searching questions were put, it tended to react in a prickly manner.

This was certainly the case when Joël Mérère, in his role as ECSDA chairman, wrote to Jean-Michel Godeffroy early in February 2007 to voice concerns about the project in the light of the ECB's January statements about the economic feasibility of T2S.

ECSDA highlighted the risks of a conflict of interest at the ECB, complained that rushed consultations about the project had fallen 'short of good practice', voiced concerns that T2S could have the perverse effect of rapidly promoting internalisation on the books of the large custodian banks and challenged the ECB's calculations on the level of charges to be expected from T2S and the savings to be realised from the project.

Godeffroy replied in robust form with countervailing arguments to ECSDA's points. But he ended his letter on a curious note that combined high politics with an element of peevishness.[15] 'T2S is a major step in the modernisation of the financial sector in Europe, in line with the Lisbon agenda,' he wrote. 'It will require active involvement from all relevant actors. To be very honest with you, I regret the pessimistic tone of your letter.'

Godeffroy's reply highlighted an important aspect of T2S. It is a political project, just as the euro was a political project.

Seen through this prism, it is easier to understand how Euroclear's domestic market for Europe does not feature in the ECB's calculations. When presenting T2S, Gertrude Tumpel-Gugerell invariably made the point that the market had failed adequately to create the sort of efficiency in cross-border trades that had emerged through integration of settlement systems at the national level. In a speech in Brussels on 30 November 2006, she observed how: 'At the international level, there have been several cross-border company mergers, which have resulted in bringing CSDs in different countries under common ownership (for example, Clearstream, Euroclear and the CSDs in Sweden and Finland). However, although these mergers have the objective of integrating settlement platforms, progress has been slow'.[16]

---

[14] 'The ECB steps in ...', Bourse Consult, September 2006.
[15] Mérère's letter and Godeffroy's reply were published on the ECB website.
[16] 'Target2-Securities: from vision to reality. The Eurosystem's contribution to an integrated securities market', Brussels, 30 November 2006.

What her remarks did not acknowledge was that the Euroclear domestic market for Europe is due to come on stream in 2009–10 and has been running on schedule. Then Euroclear will have something that is unique: a multicurrency settlement platform offering far more services than T2S, with the potential to increase market share while providing a significant fall in costs for users. Pierre Francotte, Euroclear's CEO, has said the group intends to reduce domestic CSD fees by about 20% between 2008 and 2012 as part of the roll-out of the single platform.[17]

True, ECB officials always noted that the Euroclear plan only applies to a limited number of markets rather than the eurozone and therefore was inferior to T2S. But Euroclear's single settlement system would be up and running well before T2S and, in the environment of transparent prices, unrestricted access to post-trade service providers, interoperability and unbundling required by the industry-led code of conduct brokered by Commissioner McCreevy, it should trigger falling prices elsewhere. Indeed, if the tariff trends anticipated by Chris Tupker[18] take hold, companies such as Euroclear could be under pressure to drop fees faster.

Why in these circumstances has the ECB been in such a hurry? This book has shown how the EU authorities only began to be concerned with the efficiency of securities settlement in 2000–01 well after the introduction of the euro. The ECB is a comparatively late entrant into the race for greater settlement effectiveness, having spent the 1990s (in its present form and previously as the EMI) worrying instead about collateral provision and financial stability. One reason for the sudden haste was the need in the ECB to solve the split in the governing council on outsourcing central bank money – an issue of central bank theology rather than securities market efficiency.

By mid-2007, it became clear that the ECB's theological split was forcing a rethink of Euroclear's platform policy. Published in June, the group's annual report for 2006 disclosed that Euroclear had started market consultations on adopting a different central bank money payment model when it launches the settlement phase of its single platform.

Although its system was efficient, Euroclear 'concluded that the outlook for the integrated model was not stable enough' because of opposition from some Eurosystem central banks. The integrated model would be retained for ESES because this was a temporary solution for the Euronext markets. For the single platform, Euroclear had 'decided to move to an alternative model, whereby central bank money accounts will be exclusively held and operated in national central banks (NCBs)'. However, clients using the single platform would still be able to consolidate their euro liquidity at their home CSD and use this pool for settlement in any Euroclear CSD.

The 2006 annual report also contained a preliminary assessment of the financial consequences of T2S for the Euroclear group, should the project go ahead. It noted that T2S would reduce the revenues of the affected CSDs but could prove beneficial to ICSDs such as Euroclear Bank.

Elaborating on this point, Pierre Francotte has pointed out that T2S would not solve the problem of a fragmented market for corporate action services in Europe. T2S, if it works, would solve settlement fragmentation across the markets of the eurozone, 'but any benefits are not going to go beyond settlement'. As a result, 'the corporate action inefficiencies and a variety of other problems that exist in post-trading today will not get sorted by T2S. We will still have 13 or 14 fragmented markets.'

---

[17] 'The view from the CEO of Euroclear', January 2007.
[18] See Chapter 15.6.

In these circumstances, 'big players and medium-sized players are going to be looking for an intermediary to give them the same type of homogeneity for the fragmentation of corporate actions that T2S will give on the settlement side,' Francotte predicted. The local custodians would find it difficult to provide these services. The winners would be the very big European players such as Citigroup, BNP Paribas and the two big ICSDs: Clearstream Banking Luxembourg and Euroclear Bank.

Paradoxically, Euroclear could gain financially from the changes produced by T2S. But Sir Nigel Wicks, writing in the Euroclear 2006 report, nonetheless took the view that the fragmentation brought by T2S 'would be a setback in Europe's effort to create truly efficient and competitive pan-European capital markets'.

The development of Euroclear's domestic market for Europe is part of this European effort. T2S could also pose further problems here. Provided all parties conform to the wishes of the EU economics and finance ministers, expressed in February 2007, this should not be the case. But the realities of the market place can be very different to Ecofin conclusions.

What if users and other CSDs, facing the need to adapt first to ESES, then the single Euroclear platform and finally to T2S, decide that it is all too much and run down their commitment to the Euroclear project and the harmonisation it involves? Then an opportunity to increase efficiency and competition in the European settlement market would be at best postponed until T2S comes on stream in 2013 or 2014 and could be lost.

On the other hand, the fact that T2S is not mandatory means the ECB and the CSDs must come to an accommodation if T2S is to work. This is particularly true of the Euroclear group, with its large CSD in France and others in Belgium and the Netherlands as well as CREST, which processes Irish securities.

Relations between the ECB and the CSDs have been quite fraught at times as work has gone forward on T2S. At the end of June 2007, another ECSDA letter, this time signed by senior executives of 14 member CSDs, challenged the technical assumptions behind the Eurosystem's economic feasibility study. It questioned, in particular, the figure of €0.29 quoted as the average cost of a settlement for T2S.[19]

The paper queried whether CSDs would be able to decommission databases, as suggested by the ECB, to achieve big cost savings through T2S. It found that decommissioning would not be possible for those CSDs that provided multi-currency settlement or settlement in both central bank and commercial bank money. According to ECSDA these CSDs accounted for 65% of European equity market capitalisation and about 53% of total European DvP settlement volumes.

The stakes are high on both sides. While T2S will require the support of the CSDs if it is to be a success, the CSDs cannot overplay their hand because the banks, which are their clients, generally support T2S and its promise of lower fees.

In his letter to ECSDA of February 2007, Godeffroy warned CSDs not to neglect the interests of their clients. 'We are following very carefully how CSDs will address possible conflicts of interest between their corporate interests and the interests of their users in this debate.' By this he meant the ECB suspected some CSDs might not join T2S because it would put them at a competitive disadvantage and, because of this, their users would suffer. For this reason, Godeffroy added, banks were strongly insisting that they should be represented alongside CSDs in the governance of the T2S project.

---

[19] 'The ECSDA view on the decommissioning of databases in a T2S environment', 29 June 2007.

The ECB's statement of March 2007 made sorting out the governance of T2S a priority and with good reason. Although the ECB has decided how to involve central banks, CSDs and users during the project stage, it needs to clarify the broader issues of the governance of T2S within the framework of the world's most independent central bank.

Sir Nigel Wicks, Euroclear's chairman, has raised the issue of who should supervise T2S and posed deeper constitutional questions. Speaking in January 2007,[20] Wicks noted that securities settlement was hitherto carried out according to law enacted by national parliaments and supervised by national regulatory authorities and law that is potentially within the power of the European Community legislator – the Council of Ministers and the European Parliament. Would, he asked, national security regulators be able to continue their function of supervising securities settlement? Was the ECB taking over a sphere of responsibility previously the preserve of the Community legislator? If the ECB justified entering the securities settlement business on the strength of Article 22 of the EU Treaty, would it have established a precedent for further initiatives relating to financial markets?

Willem Buiter, a former member of the Bank of England's monetary policy committee, has warned that T2S 'is a form of mission and mandate creep' that could ultimately weaken the ECB.[21] 'The legitimacy of central bank independence where it makes sense – in the conduct of monetary policy – is undermined when the independent central bank accumulates tasks and functions that do not require the same degree of independence.' The absence of accountability enjoyed by members of the ECB executive board is, Buiter argued, 'unnecessary and undesirable for the manager of the securities settlement and clearing system'.

Securities settlement is a commercial activity, liable to all manner of disputes among contracting parties. These can arise, for example, when systems fail and trades go astray. A common consequence in such cases would be that the offending party is sued. Would there not be a danger that operating in such an environment could diminish the justifiably high reputation of the European Central Bank?

In various presentations Gertrude Tumpel-Gugerell and her officials have pointed out that securities settlement is not a novelty for central bankers. The Belgian, Greek and Portuguese central banks have securities settlement operations, as do the US Federal Reserve and the Japanese central bank. In the eurozone, only the central banks of Germany, Austria and Luxembourg were not engaged in securities settlement in the 20 years before the announcement of T2S. In the EU, the central banks of the UK, France, Spain, Italy, Ireland and the Netherlands were all involved in securities settlement during the previous 20 years.

The ECB's case ignores the fact that neither the Federal Reserve nor the Bank of Japan has any experience of settling equities.[22] In other respects, the ECB's argument cuts both ways. The European central banks that quit the business did so partly in the belief that settlement could be more efficient in the private sector, but also to allow them to focus without distraction on their core vocation of controlling inflation through monetary policy. In the eurozone, the coming of the single currency has greatly diminished this core role for the national central banks. Could it be that T2S is a make-work policy for national central banks, harking back to the traditions of yesteryear?

---

[20] A sustainable supervisory system for Europe, at the 5th annual financial services conference, Brussels, 23 January 2007.
[21] Letter to the *Financial Times*, 19 January 2007.
[22] A point made forcefully by Clearstream's Jeffrey Tessler at the June 2007 ICMA meeting in Berlin.

If so, it is a policy that seems to go against the grain of the market. One does not have to approve the haphazard demutualisation process of securities markets infrastructure providers around the turn of the 21st century to fear that placing a securities settlement facility in public sector hands could be a prescription for bureaucracy and ossification.

Although the Commission is satisfied that T2S is compatible with the other elements of EU policy to inject more efficiency and transparency into post-trade services, it is not necessarily ideal. It is rather ironic that T2S surfaced just as the EU, through a combination of the code of conduct, the MiFID directive, and a determination by Neelie Kroes, the competition commissioner, to use EU competition law in clearing and settlement seemed to find a formula for delivering price transparency, access, interoperability and unbundling.

Although the efforts of the securities business to consolidate and integrate in the period between 1999 and 2003 and after 2005 yielded meagre results, who is to say that it will not be third time lucky for the private sector in the circumstances of 2007 and beyond?

If the first half of 2007 is any guide, there is plenty of action that may add up to a new wave of private sector restructuring. Projects Boat and Turquoise point to disintermediation of infrastructure providers at the exchange level. The plan for Euronext to cut its holding in LCH.Clearnet has been followed by a programme to cut costs for users sharply. The departure of Werner Seifert's acolytes Matthias Ganz and Mathias Hlubek from the managing board of Deutsche Börse, combined with the impatience of one of Deutsche Börse's hedge fund shareholders with the capital cost of maintaining Clearstream International as a consolidated subsidiary, signal change.

In June 2007, the London Stock Exchange announced and agreed a deal to acquire Borsa Italiana, the Italian exchange operator, which includes Monte Titoli, Italy's highly regarded CSD, among its businesses. Material presented to investors by Borsa Italiana stated that Monte Titoli's average settlement fee in 2006 was just €0.11 per transaction, well below the €0.29 fee projected by the ECB for T2S. The circular detailing terms of the merger of the two groups not only described Monte Titoli as Europe's 'lowest cost provider of post-trade services'. It said the enlarged group would be 'strongly positioned to take advantage of market opportunities presented by the future implementation of the European Code of Conduct on clearing and settlement'.[23]

The corporate kaleidoscope is being shaken again with the inevitably unpredictable results. Not for the first time in this story, US business developments and US businesses are bringing change to Europe. The NYSE's merger with Euronext may come to be perceived as a historical turning point: the moment when the securities market place became global, leaving national or even continental preoccupations and structures looking old fashioned.

The subsequent award by Project Turquoise of its clearing contract to DTCC of the US and the decision of IntercontinentalExchange (ICE) to create a European clearing house suggest that US providers of central counterparty clearing services have taken this lesson to heart. The announcement at the end April 2007 that the Eurex subsidiary of Deutsche Börse and SWX Swiss Exchange would buy the International Securities Exchange of the US, with its strong franchise in electronic options trading, for $2.8 billion showed there is a two-way investment flow across the Atlantic. The news, late in May 2007, that Nasdaq would buy OMX, the Nordic stock exchange operator, for 25.1 billion kroner or $3.7 billion in an agreed deal shifted the focus back to Europe. The combined Nasdaq OMX group sees itself as a partner for future cooperation and consolidation efforts.

---

[23] London Stock Exchange: Circular to shareholders and notice of Extraordinary General Meeting, 23 July 2007.

These developments and announcements came thick and fast in a very short time. More manoeuvrings are likely as MiFID takes effect and the code of conduct is developed further. It would be strange if the European securities settlement market remains unaffected by such developments. Could it be that Europe's policy makers and practitioners have been focusing too closely on regional solutions while a revolutionary transformation to a new global paradigm for securities markets and securities settlement has begun?

18
Conclusions and Reflections

Securities markets are only as good as the infrastructure that supports them.

Some 40 years after the launch of the pilot scheme for Eurobond settlement that became Euroclear, Europe has a huge and elaborate securities settlement infrastructure. It has developed, like the European Union itself, in a haphazard and erratic manner. The sector's technical capability to handle the needs of securities markets is not in question. The Euroclear group's €450 trillion worth of securities settled in 2006 bears witness to that. So too do ECB figures showing a 10% increase to 160 million in the volume of transactions denominated in euro that were settled by 18 national CSDs in that year.[1]

What is in question is whether the infrastructure, taken as a whole, matches up to the requirements of a European single currency area which from 1 January 2008 embraces 15 EU member states and a single market of 27 EU countries. Moreover, will measures in the pipeline, and proposed, provide necessary improvements?

Despite the many difficulties arising from comparisons of outdated and incompatible statistics, it is clear that the cost of cross-border securities transactions in Europe is higher than inside the territories of EU member states or in the US.

This is important. If the infrastructure for the cross-border trading of securities in Europe is less than optimal, somebody is losing out. That somebody is the investor, the saver, the entrepreneur and the consumer: the people who make up the European economy and shape Europe's economic prospects.

This book has described why this is. Financial services and financial infrastructures were segmented and fragmented into national units by political borders and capital controls when the European Common Market was founded 50 years ago, in 1957. The programme to create a European single market by 1992 concentrated on goods rather than services. The sensible aim of making securities markets and their infrastructures safer after the 1987 global stock market crash encouraged national rather than cross-border solutions. The 1992 Maastricht Treaty, which set out the path to economic and monetary union, was agreed in an age before policy makers were fully aware of the benefits that securities markets could generate for a continent-wide economy and before they were conscious of the importance of securities settlement. The European Monetary Institute, which prepared the ground for EMU from 1994 onwards, paid close attention to securities settlement, but from the viewpoints of financial stability and securing suitable collateral arrangements for the future European Central Bank.

The thought leadership that encouraged the gradual emergence in the US over more than 20 years of a single, low cost, user-governed clearing and settlement infrastructure for equities in the shape of The Depository Trust and Clearing Corporation was not on offer in Europe. Nor was it to be expected.

The US was and is a political union, with a common language, a single currency, a powerful securities regulator in the shape of the SEC, a common regulatory framework and relatively

---

[1] Figure cited in 'Target2-Securities – economic feasibility', ECB, 8 March 2007.

homogeneous tax and legal systems. Even so, nearly three decades passed between the start of work on the New York CSD – The Depository Trust Company – and the formation of DTCC. And at the end of this process, the US was still left with different financial infrastructures for equities, bonds and derivatives.

The US experience helps put Europe's securities settlement arrangements in perspective. The length of time required for consolidation in the US should give pause for thought to some of Europe's more impatient policy makers.

The European Union has few of the attributes of a political union. Its member states jealously guard their sovereignty in matters of taxation and law. The euro coexists with 14 non-euro currencies. Structured cooperation among national securities regulators only began late in 2001. The EU is split in terms of financial culture between states such as Germany with a traditional bias to bank finance and others such as the UK, where financial markets dominate.

Until the early 2000s, the efficient execution of cross-border financial transactions in Europe was an issue for specialists in the two big ICSDs – Euroclear and Cedel – in parts of the Swiss banking sector and among a small number of commercial and investment bankers who, through a curious process of self-selection, took an interest in such matters.

Symptomatic of the limited awareness of post-trade issues was the EU's failure in 1999 to include clearing and settlement in the Financial Services Action Plan, its ambitious programme to create a single European financial market. That omission spoke volumes for the obscurity in which providers of settlement services plied their trade. It was a world in which many service providers had – and still have – a strong interest in maintaining a fragmented infrastructure to be able to offer complex and often elegant solutions for clients – at a price.

Left to their own devices, it was little wonder that many of Europe's financial infrastructure providers shifted haphazardly from the 1990s onwards into demutualisation, for-profit business models and stock market listings. Nor should it surprise that when exchanges and securities depositories responded to the coming of the euro, their projects for alliances and mergers triggered years of corporate manoeuvring between 1999 and 2003 and again in 2005 and 2006 that resulted in continued fragmentation and little by way of consolidation.

Though the post-trade world appeared dull to the few outsiders who were aware of its existence, it was a home to some powerful personalities with well-developed egos and vested interests to protect. This book has demonstrated how at various times the best laid plans have been upset by individual caprices.

It is instructive to compare Europe's halting progress towards a single market for securities with its achievement in creating a single currency. Intuitively, one would think that creating a single currency would be the more difficult task. And indeed the creation and successful launch of the euro was an enormous undertaking.

But, as Alberto Giovannini has asked, who in advance can identify the winners and losers from a single currency? It is not easy. Take, however, a project to create a single, barrier-free market for securities settlement services. In a world of imperfect competition, it is comparatively easy for the companies and managers involved to work out who will win, and who will lose and react accordingly.

For-profit systems of corporate governance have compounded the difficulties of bridging the divide between silo-type infrastructures, such as those that tie trading to CCP clearing and settlement in Germany, Italy and Spain, with the more open, horizontal post-trade arrangements of France, Britain, Belgium, the Netherlands and Switzerland. It is the challenge of creating a single market from such incompatible components that makes the November 2006 agreement on an industry-led code of conduct for the providers of trade and post-trade services for equities such an interesting development.

The code signed by infrastructure providers along the value chain from trading to settlement could pave the way for falling fees and a more efficient capital market in Europe. Seen in conjunction with other initiatives, such as the Market in Financial Instruments Directive (MiFID), the application of EU competition law to post-trade services, Euroclear's domestic market for Europe and the private sector's efforts to remove those Giovannini barriers for which it carries responsibility, the code of conduct offers a real possibility of creating a European settlement market.

Taken together, the code's components – price transparency, open access, separate accounting and unbundling – offer some hope of more competition in the post-trade sector. The code will need tough policing to be effective. But it seems that in Neelie Kroes, the EU has a competition commissioner who is aware of the importance of financial infrastructure and not frightened of a fight.

A notable development since the EU became engaged in securing greater efficiency and lower costs in securities clearing and settlement has been the growing belief that there is room for competition in post-trade activities.

Fierce competition has always existed between Euroclear and Clearstream in settling international bonds. Traditionally, however, clearing and settlement are seen as scale economies where one big provider can become a monopoly supplier and benefit hugely from that position. Plans, such as those that are bringing competitors to the market for central counterparty clearing of equities in London, will put such orthodoxies to the test.

There are risks in these private sector solutions, in particular the danger that one or another infrastructure provider will cheat or renege on the code. To reduce this hazard, it is important that the code signatories ensure that the mechanism they have agreed to settle disputes among themselves is effective. Charlie McCreevy, the EU's internal market commissioner, is godfather to the code. But it will only work if it is genuinely an industry code with the industry taking responsibility for its success – or failure.

The public sector must also play its role in making Europe's post-trade infrastructure suitable for purpose. Look at the progress, or lack of it, towards dismantling the 15 barriers identified by the Giovannini group in its reports of 2001 and 2003. The public sector – in the shape of national governments of EU member states – is lagging behind the private sector infrastructure providers in attacking practices that are no longer appropriate for a Europe-wide capital market. As we have seen, lack of progress in dismantling some public sector barriers is holding up the removal of some of the private sector barriers.

That said, the jury is still out on the European Central Bank's proposed T2S securities settlement platform. The central bank has concluded that the project is feasible. By providing a single platform for the settlement of the cash and securities legs of all transactions carried out in Europe's CSDs, T2S 'will significantly contribute to increasing the efficiency of settlement and the integration of capital markets infrastructure'. The single platform, it says, 'will enable the settlement of all domestic and cross-border securities transactions'.[2]

At the time of writing, T2S is not yet in the development phase. The ECB has still to define the project's scope and content. A year of examination of T2S is under way. This will provide an opportunity for the ECB and the industry to answer the many questions that have arisen and fill in the many gaps in our understanding.

---

[2] 'Target2-Securities, the blueprint', European Central Bank, 8 March 2007.

As a public sector venture, T2S reverses a decade long trend towards private sector solutions for the securities settlement market in Europe. The ECB will have to explain where exactly the market failure lies to justify such radical action. Is it wise for an independent and largely unaccountable central bank to engage in an enterprise where it could be held responsible for commercial losses? Is it also prudent to embark on a development that is unprecedented in terms of technology?

The history of securities settlement has been punctuated by expensive IT failures from the UK's Taurus project in the 1990s to LCH.Clearnet's Generic Clearing System in 2006. It is precisely those failures that have resulted in the twists and turns that have characterised this history. And yet T2S, according to the ECB, will be twice as complex as TARGET2, the payments infrastructure on which it is to be based.[3]

T2S will have to be assessed against potentially significant changes elsewhere in the European post-trade environment. For example, it is unclear how it will relate to private sector efforts already under way to reduce fragmentation in Europe's settlement infrastructure or to the globalisation of securities markets.

A great deal of time and effort is being spent on harmonising market practices in Europe. And experience has shown that time is needed – to use the railway analogy – before the last rail can be hammered into place. The long lead times of successful harmonisation and infrastructure investment do not, in themselves, constitute market failure.

In its analysis of the European settlement industry, the ECB has tended to view consolidation as perhaps the most effective route to integration.[4] But if, as may be the case, the fresh breeze of competition is about to blow in the European settlement space, consolidation of infrastructures should no longer be considered the proxy for integration.

There are still many gaps in the understanding of post-trade activities in Europe, as Gertrude Tumpel-Gugerell noted some months before the plans for T2S emerged. 'The securities settlements industry is very technical,' she said. 'The economics of the settlement industry have not been written yet. We know all about the various interests in the regulation debate in banking. But here we are more at the beginning of understanding the business, writing the economics, and finding the right regulation. In this sense, it is a new business. Admittedly, there has always been settlement over hundreds of years, but it was seen as the back office. It was technical. It was the end of the process of doing business. It was not seen as a business on its own, and yet obviously it has grown into such a business.'[5]

The ECB has time to allay these and other uncertainties and demonstrate beyond doubt that T2S will bring clear advantages to European securities markets. The EU treaties set a high standard of proof for public sector intervention in private sector markets. Article 105 of the European Community treaty requires the Eurosystem to act in accordance with the principle of an open market economy with free competition. The ECB must weigh this obligation against Article 22 of the statutes of the ESCB and ECB which, without mentioning securities settlement at all, allows national central banks and the ECB to 'provide facilities', and the ECB to 'make regulations, to ensure efficient and sound clearing and payment systems' within the eurozone and with other countries.

---

[3] 'Target2-Securities – economic feasibility', released by the ECB on 8 March 2007, speaks of T2S having on average a 'complexity factor' of 2.0 compared with TARGET2.

[4] See in particular 'Integration of securities market infrastructures in the Euro area', by Heiko Schmiedel and Andreas Schönenberger, ECB occasional paper No. 33, July 2005.

[5] Conversation with the author, 11 November 2005.

As this history has demonstrated, the infrastructure for cross-border trading of securities in Europe has been less than optimal. There has been some improvement. The industry code of conduct and the business strategies of some leading securities settlement companies provide hope that the future will bring further progress.

It is important that the industry, with public sector support, uses the present opportunities to make all possible efforts towards realising the twin goals of greater efficiency and lower costs. If the industry succeeds in this endeavour, it will increase further the depth and strength of Europe's financial markets, and so add to the wealth and welfare of Europe's businesses and consumers.

Appendix A

References and Bibliography

REFERENCES

AFEI (France), ASSOSIM (Italy), FBF (France), LIBA (UK) (February 2006), European Trade Associations' call for EU action on European exchanges and market infrastructure, London and Paris: Joint statement issued through AFEI and LIBA, 20 February 2006.

Bank of England (June 1993), Task force on securities settlement, London: Report to the Governor.

Bank of England (May 1994), CREST – the first phase completed, London: *Quarterly Bulletin*.

Bank of England (September 1998), *Securities Settlement Priorities Review*, London.

Beck, Thorsten, Levine, Ross and Loayza, Norman (2000), Finance and the sources of growth, Washington DC: World Bank Policy Research Working Paper 2057, published in the *Journal of Financial Economics*, No. 58 of 2000.

BIS (November 1990), Report of the Committee on Interbank Netting Schemes of the Central Banks of the Group of Ten Countries, Basel: Bank for International Settlements. www.bis.org

BIS (September 1992), Delivery versus payment in securities settlement systems, Basel: Committee on Payment and Settlement Systems of the central banks of the Group of Ten Countries. www.bis.org

BIS (March 1995), Cross-border securities settlements, Basel: Committee on Payment and Settlement Systems of the central banks of the Group of Ten Countries, www.bis.org

BIS (November 2001), Recommendations for securities settlement systems, Basel: Committee on Payment and Settlement Systems of the central banks of the Group of Ten Countries, with the IOSCO Technical Committee. www.bis.org

BIS (April 2003), Payment and settlement systems in selected countries, Basel: Committee on Payment and Settlement Systems of the central banks of the Group of Ten Countries. www.bis.org

BIS (June 2004), 74th Annual Report, Basel: Bank for International Settlements. www.bis.org

BIS (series running since 1966), International bonds and notes by residence of user, Basel: Bank for International Settlements statistics service. www.bis.org

BIS (series running since 1989), Domestic debt securities, Basel: Bank for International Settlements statistics service. www.bis.org

Borsa Italiana (2004), An Integrated System, Milan: Gruppo Borsa Italiana.

Borsa Italiana (July 2007), An Introduction to Borsa Italiana Group, London: Gruppo Borsa Italiana.

Bourse Consult (September 2006), The ECB steps in . . . London.

BNP-Paribas Securities Services (May 2002), Contribution to the joint CESR/ECB consultation in the field of clearing and settlement, Frankfurt: www.ecb.eu

Cedel (1989), Annual report.

Cedel (1994), Annual report.

Cedel (1995), Annual report.

CEPS (March 2001), EU securities market regulation: adapting to the needs of a single capital market, Brussels: Centre for European Policy Studies, Report of a Task Force.

CEPS (December 2001), The securities settlement industry in the EU: structure, costs and the way forward, Brussels: Lannoo, Karel and Levin, Mattias, Centre for European Policy Studies Research Report.

CESR (2005), Annual report, Paris: The Committee of European Securities Regulators' annual report for 2005. www.cesr.eu

Chabrolles, Nathalie and Juvin, Hervé (1992) *Sicovam: History of France's Depository Institution*, Paris: Éditions les Djinns.

Clearstream (2005), The European Repo Market: Its Past, Present and Future, Luxembourg: Clearstream-Deutsche Börse Group.

Competition Commission (November 2005), A Report on the proposed acquisition of London Stock Exchange plc by Deutsche Börse AG or Euronext NV. London: www.competition-commission.org.uk

CRESTCo (2002), Recommended proposal for the merger of CRESTCo Ltd and Euroclear plc, London: as required by Section 425 of the UK Companies Act.

Danmarks Nationalbank (2005), Payment systems in Denmark, Copenhagen: www.nationalbanken.dk

Deutsche Börse (2003), Annual report, Frankfurt: www.deutsche-boerse.com

Deutsche Börse (June 2006), Observations on the Commission's issues paper, Competition in EU securities trading and post-trading, Frankfurt.

Ecofin Council (November 2004), Financial integration, Brussels: Council conclusions. www.consilium.europa.eu

Ecofin Council (November 2006), Clearing and settlement, Brussels: Council conclusions. www.consilium.europa.eu

Ecofin Council (February 2007), Target2-Securities, Brussels: Council conclusions. www.consilium.europa.eu

ECSDA (February 2007), Letter of 1 February to ECB on Target2-Securities, Brussels. www.ecsda.com

ECSDA (June 2007), The ECSDA view on the decommission of databases in a T2S environment, Brussels: Letter to the ECB of 29 June 2007. Posted on www.euroclear.com

Euro-clear Clearance System Ltd (1973–1980), Annual reports.

Euro-clear Clearance System plc (1981–1986), Annual reports.

Euro-clear Clearance System Société Coopérative (1987–1989), Annual reports.

Euroclear Clearance System Société Coopérative (1990–1999), Annual reports.

Euroclear and Euroclear France (2000), Annual reports.

Euroclear Group (2001–2003), Annual reports.

Euroclear plc and subsidiaries (2004), Annual report. www.euroclear.com

Euroclear (2005–2006), Annual reports. www.euroclear.com

Euroclear (1993), *Cross-border Clearance, Settlement and Custody: Beyond the G30 recommendations*, Brussels: Published by Morgan Guaranty Trust Co. as operator of the Euroclear System.

Euroclear Review (Spring 1992), John T. Olds, an interview.

Euroclear Review (Winter-Spring 1994), Euroclear turns 25, an interview with Martine Dinne.

Euroclear Review (Autumn 1994), An interview with Luc Bomans.

Euroclear Bank (July 2002), *Delivering a Domestic Market for Europe*, London-Brussels: Joint publication with CRESTCo.

Euroclear Bank (January 2003), Delivering low-cost cross-border settlement.

Euroclear (July 2004), The way forward: Euroclear's response to the European Commission's communication. www.euroclear.com

Euroclear (June 2005), Taking stock: view from the CEO of Euroclear. Brussels: www.euroclear.com

Euroclear (September 2005), The view from the CEO of Euroclear, Brussels: www.euroclear.com

Euroclear (April 2006), The view from the CEO of Euroclear, Brussels: www.euroclear.com

Euroclear Group (September 2006), Target2-Securities: Euroclear group's response to the ECB questionnaire. Brussels: www.euroclear.com

Euroclear (January 2007), The view from the CEO of Euroclear. Brussels: www.euroclear.com

European Central Bank (1998), Assessment of EU securities settlement systems against the standards for their use in ESCB credit operations, Frankfurt: ECB press release, 29 September 1998. www.ecb.eu

European Central Bank (1999), Payments and the Eurosystem, Frankfurt: Speech by Tommaso Padoa-Schioppa, ECB executive board member at Sibos, Munich, 13 September 1999. www.ecb.eu

European Central Bank (June 2001), *Payment and Securities Settlement Systems in the European Union* (*Blue Book*, third edition), Frankfurt: ECB. www.ecb.eu

European Central Bank (September 2001) The Eurosystem's policy line with regard to consolidation in central counterparty clearing, Frankfurt: ECB Policy Statement, 27 September 2001. www.ecb.eu

European Central Bank (2002) Consolidation in the European securities infrastructure – what is needed? Frankfurt: Speech by Sirkka Hämäläinen, ECB executive board member, Frankfurt, 20 April 2002. www.ecb.eu

European Central Bank (October 2004), Governance of securities clearing and settlement systems, Frankfurt: Russo, Daniela and others, ECB Occasional Paper Series No. 21. www.ecb.eu

European Central Bank (July 2005) Integration of securities market infrastructures in the Euro area, Frankfurt: Schmiedel, Heiko and Schönenberger, Andreas, ECB Occasional Paper No. 33. www.ecb.eu

European Central Bank (February 2006), The developing EU legal framework for clearing and settlement of financial services, Frankfurt: Löber, Klaus M, ECB, Legal Working Paper Series No. 1. www.ecb.eu

European Central Bank (June 2006), Drivers for change in payment and securities settlement systems. Frankfurt: Speech by Gertrude Tumpel-Gugerell, member of the executive board of the ECB, Madrid, 9 June 2006. www.ecb.eu

European Central Bank (July 2006) The Eurosystem is evaluating opportunities to provide settlement services for securities transactions. Frankfurt: ECB press release, 7 July 2006. www.ecb.eu

European Central Bank (November 2006), Target2-Securities: from vision to reality. The Eurosystem's contribution to an integrated securities market, Frankfurt: Speech by Gertrude Tumpel-Gugerell, member of the executive board of the ECB, Brussels, 30 November 2006. www.ecb.eu

European Central Bank (February 2007), Letter to ECSDA, Frankfurt: Sent by Jean-Michel Godeffroy, 12 February 2007.

European Central Bank (2007), Target2-Securities – The blueprint; Operational feasibility study; Technical feasibility study; Economic feasibility study; Legal feasibility study; Press release, Frankfurt: Published 8 March 2007 on www.ecb.eu

European Central Bank (2007), Target2-Securities – The organisation of the first phase of the Target2-Securities project, Frankfurt: 26 April 2007 on www.ecb.eu

European Central Bank (2007), Target2-Securities and the CCBM2 – Launch of a public consultation, Frankfurt: ECB press release, www.ecb.eu

ECB and CESR (July 2003), Consultative report: Standards for securities clearing and settlement systems in the European Union, Frankfurt and Paris. www.cesr-eu.org

ECB and CESR (September 2004), Standards for securities clearing and settlement systems in the European Union, Frankfurt and Paris. www.cesr-eu.org

European Commission (1989), Study on improvements in the settlement of cross-border securities transactions in the European Economic Community, Brussels.

European Commission (October 1998), Financial services: Building a framework for action, Brussels. www.ec.europa.eu

European Commission (May 1999), Financial services: Implementing the framework for financial markets – action plan, Brussels: Com (1999) 232, 11.05.99. www.ec.europa.eu

European Commission (June 1999), Economic and monetary union. Compilation of Community legislation. Brussels.

European Commission (May 2002), Clearing and settlement in the European Union. Main policy issues and future challenges. Brussels: COM(2002)257. www.ec.europa.eu

European Commission (April 2004), Clearing and settlement in the European Union – The way forward. Brussels: COM(2004)312. www.ec.europa.eu

European Commission (June 2004), Final decision in the Clearstream case, Brussels: Commission press release IP/04/705. www.ec.europa.eu

European Commission (July 2004), Cesame Group, Brussels: Synthesis report of the meeting held on 16 July 2004. www.ec.europa.eu

European Commission (December 2004), Assessment of the integration of the Single Market for financial services by the Commission, Brussels: Speech by Commissioner Charlie McCreevy at a CESR conference in Paris, 6 December 2004. www.ec.europa.eu

European Commission (2005), Commission Services Working Document on Definitions of Post-Trading Activities. Brussels: DG Markt, Working Document/MARKT/SLG/G2(2005)D15283. www.ec.europa.eu

European Commission (June 2005), Securities trading, clearing, central counterparties and settlement in EU 25 – An overview of current arrangements, Brussels: Report by London Economics commissioned by DG Competition, European Commission. www.ec.europa.eu

European Commission (September 2005), Fund management – Regulation to facilitate competitiveness, growth and change, Brussels: McCreevy speaks to the 14th annual ALFI-NICSA Europe-USA Investment Funds Forum, Luxembourg, 13 September 2005. www.ec.europa.eu

European Commission (November 2005), Stock market consolidation and securities markets regulation in Europe, Brussels: McCreevy gives annual lecture at SUERF (Société Universitaire Européenne de Recherches Financière), Brussels, 30 November 2005. www.ec.europa.eu

European Commission (February 2006), Cesame Group, Brussels: Synthesis report of the meeting held on 20 February 2006. www.ec.europa.eu

European Commission (March 2006), Clearing and settlement: Competition and internal market commissioners will act unless there is further action from industry, Brussels: Joint statement of Commissioners McCreevy and Neelie Kroes published on 7 March 2006 as Commission press release IP/06/273. www.ec.europa.eu

European Commission (May 2006), Competition in EU securities trading and post-trading, issues paper. Brussels: DG Competition, European Commission. www.ec.europa.eu

European Commission (May 2006), Draft working document on post-trading, Brussels: DG Markt, European Commission. www.ec.europa.eu

European Commission (May 2006), Analysis of studies examining European post-trading costs (Annex I), Brussels: DG Markt, European Commission. www.ec.europa.eu

European Commission (2006), Fact finding study on fiscal compliance procedures related to clearing and settlement within the EU, Brussels: First Report, Fiscal Compliance Experts Group (FISCO). www.ec.europa.eu

European Commission (July 2006), Clearing and settlement: The way forward, Brussels: McCreevy remarks to the Economic and Monetary Affairs Committee of the European Parliament, 11 July 2006. www.ec.europa.eu

European Commission (July 2006), Competition aspects of EU securities trading and post trading, Brussels: Commissioner Kroes to the Economic and Monetary Affairs Committee of the European Parliament, 11 July 2006. www.ec.europa.eu

European Commission (October 2006), Cesame Group, Brussels: Synthesis report of the meeting held on 23 October 2006. www.ec.europa.eu

European Commission (November 2006), Clearing and settlement code of conduct, Brussels: McCreevy speech at press conference, 7 November 2006. www.ec.europa.eu

European Commission (December 2006), Evaluation report on the Financial Collateral Arrangements Directive, Brussels: www.ec.europa.eu

European Commission (June 2007), Cesame Group, Brussels: Synthesis report of the meeting held on 11 June 2007. www.ec.europa.eu

European Commission (June 2007), Speech, Brussels: McCreevy to the Federation of European Securities Exchanges Convention 26 June 2007. www.ec.europa.eu

European Commission (July 2007), Update on financial services, Brussels: McCreevy remarks to the European Parliament's Open ECON Coordinators' Meeting, Strasbourg 10 July 2007. www.ec.europa.eu

European Council (March 2000), Lisbon European Council, Brussels: Presidency Conclusions. www.consilium.europa.eu

European Financial Services Round Table (December 2003), Securities clearing and settlement in Europe, Brussels: EFR. www.efr.be

European Monetary Institute (April 1996), *Payment Systems in the European Union (The Blue Book)*, Frankfurt: EMI.

European Monetary Institute (January 1997), *The Single Monetary Policy in Stage Three – Specification of the operational framework,* Frankfurt: EMI.

European Monetary Institute (February 1997), *EU Securities Settlement Systems. Issues related to Stage Three of EMU,* Frankfurt: EMI.

European Monetary Institute (January 1998), *Standards for the use of EU securities settlement systems in ESCB credit operations*, Frankfurt: EMI.

European Parliament (December 2002), Report on the communication from the Commission to the Council and the European Parliament entitled 'Clearing and settlement in the European Union. Main policy issues and future challenges', Brussels: Andria, Generoso (Rapporteur). www.europarl.europa.eu

European Parliament (January 2005), Draft report on clearing and settlement in the European Union, Brussels: Villiers, Theresa (Rapporteur). www.europarl.europa.eu

European Parliament (June 2005), Report on clearing and settlement in the European Union, Brussels: Kauppi, Piia-Noora (Rapporteur). www.europarl.europa.eu

European Parliament (July 2005), Resolution on clearing and settlement in the European Union, Strasbourg: P6_TA(2005)0301. www.europarl.europa.eu

European Union (1992), *Treaty on European Union,* Luxembourg: Office for Official Publications of the European Communities.

Fair & Clear (February 2003), A response to Euroclear's publication, Delivering low-cost cross-border settlement. Brussels.

Fair & Clear (September 2004), Contribution to the communication on clearing and settlement in the European Union – the way forward European Commission, April 2004. Brussels.

Federation of Stock Exchanges in the European Community (October 1990), Clearing and settlement in Europe: An outline view, Paper prepared for a Federation assembly in Dublin in November 1990.

Federation of Stock Exchanges in the European Community (1991), Clearing and settlement in Europe, paper prepared for a Federation General Assembly in Athens, May 1991.

FESE, EACH, ECSDA (November 2006), European Code of Conduct for Clearing and Settlement, Brussels: Federation of European Securities Exchanges. www.fese.eu

FESE, EACH, ECSDA (June 2007), Access and Interoperability Guideline, Brussels: Federation of European Securities Exchanges. www.fese.eu

Federation Internationale des Bourses de Valeurs (1989), *FIBV Recommendations.*

Financial Times (1993), Sudden death of a runaway bull. 19 March 1993.

Financial Times (1999), Challenger from the clearing shadows, 17 May 1999.

Financial Times (1999), Clearing houses come under the spotlight, 1 July 1999.

Financial Times (1999), Euroclear to sever link with US bank, 2 September 1999.

Financial Times (2004), London Stock Exchange users must be heeded, 15 December 2004.

Financial Times (2005), Bid for London Stock Exchange raises issue of possible monopoly control of the market, 7 January 2005.

Financial Times (2007), High degree of ECB independence in securities sector is undesirable, 19 January 2007.

Financial Times (2007), No grand plans, but the financial system needs fixing, 8 February 2007.

General Accounting Office (January 1988), *Preliminary Observations on the October 1987 Crash,*Washington DC: GAO.

General Accounting Office (April 1990), Clearance and settlement reform, Washington DC: GAO Report to Congressional Committees.

Giovannini Group (November 2001), Cross-border clearing and settlement arrangements in the European Union, Brussels: European Commission. www.ec.europa.eu

Giovannini Group (April 2003), Second report on EU clearing and settlement arrangements, Brussels: European Commission. www.ec.europa.eu

G30 (1989), *Clearance and Settlement Systems in the World's Securities Markets*, New York and London: Group of Thirty.

G30 (2003), *Global clearing and settlement. A plan of action.* Washington, DC: Group of Thirty. www.group30.org

Guardian, The (2001), Nutty book with a kernel of truth, London: 17 May 2001.

Guynn, Randall D. (1996), *Modernizing Securities Ownership, Transfer and Pledging Laws*, London: The Capital Markets Forum of the International Bar Association.

Hendricks, Darryll, Kambhu, John and Mosser, Patricia (May 2006), Systemic risk and the financial system, New York: Background paper commissioned by the Federal Reserve Bank of New York.

Hinton, Longstreet, Meyer, John M. Jr and Rodd, Thomas (1979), *Some Comments about the Morgan Bank,* New York: Morgan Guaranty Trust Co.

International Monetary Fund (September 2003), Global Financial Stability Report, Chapter III Appendix: Case Studies, Washington: IMF. www.imf.org

IOSCO (November 2001), *Recommendations for securities settlement systems*, Madrid: International Organization of Securities Commissions. www.iosco.org

Israel, Edmond (2006), *In Love with Life: An American dream of a Luxembourger*, Fairfield, Connecticut: Sacred Heart University Press.

Kerr, Ian M. (1984), *A History of the Eurobond Market: The first 21 years,* London: Euromoney Publications.

Lamfalussy Group (November 2000), Initial report of the committee of wise men on the regulation of European securities markets, Brussels: European Commission. www.ec.europa.eu

Lamfalussy Group (February 2001), Final report of the committee of wise men on the regulation of European securities markets, Brussels: European Commission. www.ec.europa.eu

Levine, Ross and Zervos, Sara (December 1996), Stock markets, banks and economic growth, Washington DC: World Bank Policy Research Working Paper No. 1690; A1.213 Working Paper No. 297.

London Clearing House (2002), *Market Protection*, London: LCH.

LCH.Clearnet (2003), *Creating the Central Counterparty of Choice*, London/Paris/Brussels/Amsterdam.

London Stock Exchange (July 2007), Proposed merger of London Stock Exchange Group plc and Borsa Italiana SpA, circular to shareholders, London. www.londonstockexchange-ir.com

NERA Economic Consulting (February 2007), The European equities post-trading industry: Assessing the impact of market and regulatory changes. London: Corporation of London, City Research Series, No. 11.

Petiau, Agnès (November 2003), *Histoires d'Euroclear*, Brussels: Personal recollections.

Rajan, Raghuram G. and Zingales, Luigi (September 1996), Financial dependence and growth, NBER Working Paper No. W5758, available at SSRN.

Ross, Stanley D. L. (1971), Eurobonds – the changing face of the secondary market, London: text of speech.

Ross, Stanley D. L. (February 1972), Eurobond market report, London: Article published in *Money Management*.

Ross, Stanley D. L. (March 1979), AIBD rules and regulations, London: Monograph marking the 10th anniversary of the AIBD rule book.

Ross, Stanley D. L. (May 1993), From where I stood: recollections of twenty-five AIBD meetings, London and Zurich: Article commissioned by ISMA.

Securities Industry Association (May 2005), Organisation in the US market for clearing and settlement, New York: Background note prepared by the Cross-Border Subcommittee of the SIA for the European Commission. www.ec.europa.eu

Seifert, Werner G. with Voth, Hans-Joachim (2006), *Invasion der Heuschrecken*, Berlin: Econ Verlag.

Shearlock, Peter and Ellington, William (1994), *The Eurobond Diaries,* Brussels: Euroclear Clearance System Société Coopérative.

Van Nieuwenhove, Gérard (1992) *The Euroclear Story*, Wavre, Belgium: Personal memoir.

ADDITIONAL READING

Assemblée Nationale (January 2002), Rapport d'information sur les obstacles au controle et à la repression de la délinquance financière et du blanchiment des capitaux en Europe. Volume 5 – Le Grand Duché du Luxembourg, Paris. www.assemblee-nationale.fr

Bank of England (Series from 1996 to December 1998), *Practical Issues arising from the Introduction of the Euro,* London.

Bishop, Graham (November 2006), *MiFID – An Opportunity to Profit,* London: LogicaCMG.

BNP-Paribas Securities Services (August 2002), *Clearing and Settlement in the European Union: Main Policy Issues and Future Challenges.*

Bourse Consult (December 2005), *The future of clearing and settlement in Europe*, London: Corporation of London, City Research Series Number Seven.

BTA Consulting (March 2005), *European cross-border clearing and settlement 2005–2007,* London.

Chernow, Ron (1990). *The House of Morgan*, New York: Simon & Schuster.

Citigroup (July 2004), The Optimal Market Structure for Clearing and Settlement in the EU.

Deutsche Börse (1999–2002), Annual reports. www.deutsche-boerse.com

Deutsche Börse (2004–2005), Annual reports. www.deutsche-boerse.com

Deutsche Börse Group (February 2005), *The European post-trade market: An introduction – white paper*, Frankfurt: Deutsche Börse AG.

Euroclear SA/NV (April 2005), The Euroclear banking function, Brussels. www.euroclear.com

Euroclear SA/NV (April 2005), Risk profile of the Euroclear group, Brussels. www.euroclear.com

Euroclear SA/NV (September 2005), Internalisation of settlement, Brussels. www.euroclear.com

Euroclear, Convergence: Business model and harmonisation newsletter, Brussels. www.euroclear.com

Eurofi of Paris (2000), Proceedings of conference, Paris, September 2000.

Eurofi of Paris (2002), Proceedings of conference, Brussels, November 2002.

Eurofi of Paris (2003), Proceedings of conference, Milan, November 2003.

Eurofi of Paris (2005), Proceedings of conference, Luxembourg, March 2005.

European Commission (May 2002), Report by the Economic and Financial Committee (EFC) on EU financial integration, Brussels: DG Ecfin, European Commission in the European Economy, Economic Papers series. www.ec.europa.eu

European Union (1999), *Selected Instruments taken from the Treaties,* Luxembourg: Office for Official Publications of the European Communities.

European Union (February 2003), *Consolidated Treaties,* Luxembourg: Office for Official Publications of the European Communities.

Kazarian, Elias (October 2006), Integration of the securities market infrastructure in the European Union: Policy and regulatory issues, IMF Working Paper WP/06/241, Washington DC: IMF.

Klein, Fritz and Palazzo, Guido (2003), *Kulturgeschichte des Geldflusses*, Zurich: Verlag SKV.

McKinsey & Co. and JP Morgan (February 2002), The Future of Equity Trading in Europe, London.

Meier, Richard and Sigrist, Tobias (2006), *Der Helvetische Big Bang*, Zurich: Verlag Neue Zürcher Zeitung.

Morgan Stanley and Mercer Oliver Wyman (June 2003), Structural Shifts in Securities Trading: Outlook for European Exchanges, London.

Mügge, Daniel (December 2006), Competition politics in European finance, London: *Journal of Common Market Studies*, Vol. 44, No. 5, Blackwell.

Roberts, Richard with Arnander, Christopher (2001), *Take Your Partners: Orion, the consortium banks and the transformation of the Euromarkets,* Basingstoke, UK: Palgrave.

Storck, Ekkehard (1995), *Euromarkt: Finanz-Drehscheibe der Welt*, Stuttgart, Schäffer-Poeschel Verlag.

Appendix B
Key Dates for the Securities Settlement
Industry in Europe

1963

1 July 1963. Subscription agreement signed for $15 million, internationally syndicated Autostrade bond issue, commonly regarded as the first Eurobond.

18 July 1963. US President John F. Kennedy jump-starts the Eurobond market by announcing an Interest Equalisation Tax (IET), closing the US bond market to foreign borrowers.

1965

February 1965. Administration of US President Lyndon Johnson gives a new boost to the Eurobond market by announcing voluntary limits on outflows for direct investment abroad by US corporations and discourages US commercial banks from lending to international borrowers, including subsidiaries of US companies.

April 1965. Gordon Moore, co-founder of Intel, predicts exponential growth of computing capacity. Later known as 'Moore's law'.

End-September 1965. Morgan Guaranty's Brussels office hosts its first closing: for a $20 million, 15-year borrowing by Cynamid International Development Corp.

1967

21 July 1967. Launch of Morgan Guaranty's pilot securities settlement service for the Eurobond market in Brussels. The forerunner of Euroclear.

10 November 1967. Belgian Royal Decree 62 gives investors legal rights that facilitate fungibility and holding of securities in book entry form.

November 1967. The British pound is devalued against the dollar from $2.80 to $2.40: a signal of growing turbulence in the international monetary system founded in 1944 in the New Hampshire resort of Bretton Woods.

1968

Settlement crisis in market for Eurodollar bonds and on Wall Street.

January 1968. More US restrictions: President Johnson imposes mandatory restraints on US foreign investment and creates an Office of Foreign Direct Investments to enforce the rules.

1 April 1968. Belgian Royal Decree approves establishment of CIK, a Belgian CSD.

2 December 1968. Morgan launches Euro-clear, the first International Central Securities Depository.

1969

18 April 1969. First meeting of the Association of International Bond Dealers (AIBD) in London.

August 1969. France devalues the franc: a further nail in the Bretton Woods coffin.

1970

4 June 1970. Formation of SEGA, the Swiss CSD, in Basel.

28 September 1970. Launch of Cedel (Centrale de Livraison de Valeurs Mobilières) in Luxembourg. An ICSD to rival Euro-clear.

End-1970. Moves to set up Deutscher Auslandskassenverein (AKV) to settle foreign securities in Frankfurt.

1971

VPC, a Swedish CSD, set up.

May 1971. Central banks in West Germany, the Netherlands and Switzerland cease supporting the dollar, signalling growing shift to floating exchange rates.

15 August 1971. US President Richard Nixon suspends the convertibility of the dollar into gold, effectively floating the US currency and all other exchange rates.

December 1971. Smithsonian agreement in Washington re-pegs exchange rates but proves short lived.

1972

7 July 1972. Incorporation of Euro-clear Clearance System Ltd as non-resident English company with domicile in Switzerland, to become the vehicle for selling Euroclear to its users.

1 December 1972. Completion of sale of Euroclear to its users. Morgan Guaranty continues to operate the system. Rolf Hallberg becomes chairman.

1973

Robert Wilmers is appointed general manager of Euroclear.

Establishment of The Depository Trust Co. in New York, a CSD for Wall Street.

March 1973. Floating exchange rates become general. Death of Bretton Woods after a long illness.

October 1973. Yom Kippur War between Israel and Egypt: followed by sudden, sharp rise in oil prices as OPEC, the Organisation of Petroleum Exporting Countries, raises its price and cuts supplies. The industrialised world suffers 'stagflation', a toxic combination of recession and inflation.

1974

1 January 1974. US reduces IET to zero, but the Eurobond market continues to grow.

26 June 1974. Herstatt Bank closed by the German Bundesbank. Large losses from currency speculation highlight risk of cross-border financial transactions.

US Employment Retirement Securities Act (Erisa): creates a pool of capital to be invested in the US and abroad.

1975

US passes Securities Acts Amendments, setting in train gradual consolidation of US post-trade infrastructure.

1976

11 June 1976. Georges Streichenberg of Swiss Bank Corp. succeeds Rolf Hallberg as Euroclear chairman.

1977

May 1977. SWIFT starts operations.
    September 1977. Necigef, the Dutch CSD, starts operating.

1978

Paul Caron becomes general manager of Euroclear, taking over from Robert Wilmers.
    Banca d'Italia and Italian banks set up Monte Titoli, an Italian CSD.

1979

Second oil crisis.
    March 1979. European Monetary System starts operating: intended to limit currency fluctuations among European Community member states.
    May 1979. Euroclear introduces its Euclid communications system.
    6 October 1979. Paul Volcker, chairman of the US Federal Reserve Board announces a new, anti-inflationary monetary policy based on targeting money supply: US interest rates soar.
    23 October 1979. Exchange controls suddenly abolished in the UK by the recently elected Conservative government, exposing the economy to international competition.

1980

VP Securities Services, the Danish CSD, established.
    6 June 1980. Ian Steers of Wood Gundy becomes Euroclear chairman, taking over from Georges Streichenberg.
    November 1980. Ronald Reagan elected US President.
    December 1980. Euroclear and Cedel set up the electronic Bridge.

1981

Euroclear modernises the 'chaining' of its securities settlement system.

1982

Tom Fox becomes general manager of Euroclear, taking over from Paul Caron. Sets up Euroclear Operations Centre.
    August 1982. Mexico announces it cannot meet payments due on $80 billion of foreign debt. International debt crisis follows.

1983

June 1983. Euroclear introduces computerised securities lending and borrowing.

1984

22 June 1984. Rolf-Ernst Breuer of Deutsche Bank becomes Euroclear chairman, taking over from Ian Steers.

3 November 1984. Securities in France dematerialised.

December 1984. Euroclear annual turnover exceeds $1 trillion.

1985

Peter Culver becomes general manager of Euroclear, taking over from Tom Fox.

1986

27 October 1986. 'Big Bang' deregulation of London Stock Exchange.

21 November 1986. The Belgian cooperative, Euro-clear Clearance System Société Cooperative constituted. Begins operating on 1 January 1987.

1987

May 1987. Tom Ketchum becomes Euroclear general manager following the sudden death of Peter Culver on 11 March 1987.

19 October 1987. Dow Jones average falls 23%, its largest one-day fall in history. Equity markets fall around the world, following the US lead.

1988

31 March 1988. Formation of Intersettle, the Swiss ICSD.

September 1988. Banque de France sets up Saturne to provide DvP for Treasury bills and notes.

1989

André Lussi becomes managing director of Cedel.

March 1989. Group of Thirty publishes recommendations for securities settlement business in the wake of the 1989 equity market crash.

9 November 1989. Berlin Wall falls.

December 1989. Deutscher Kassenverein, the German CSD, formed from merger of Frankfurt Kassenverein with smaller regional CSDs.

1990

Euroclear rebranded. The hyphen that was part of the company's name since launch disappears.

Edmond Israel retires as Cedel's chairman, replaced by Hans Angermueller.

Jean-François Théodore becomes chairman and chief executive of Société des Bourses Françaises (SBF).

Relit starts operating in France.

1991

1 September 1991. John T. Olds takes over as general manager of Euroclear from Tom Ketchum.

Euroclear annual turnover exceeds $5 trillion while the value of securities held for participants – the depot – tops $1 trillion.

1992

27 February 1992. The 12 members of the European Community sign the Maastricht Treaty on European Union, and pledge to create economic and monetary union (EMU).

March 1992. New Bridge agreement between Euroclear and Cedel, leading to multiple batch deliveries between the two ICSDs from September 1993.

September 1992. G10 central banks publish report urging delivery versus payment (DvP) for securities settlement.

September 1992. Cedel arranges tri-party repo with SBC Warburg and European Bank for Reconstruction and Development (EBRD).

1993

March 1993. Werner Seifert named as CEO of Deutsche Börse.

11 March 1993. UK scraps the Taurus settlement project at a cost of around £400 million. Bank of England, at the request of the LSE, sets up a securities settlement taskforce to rescue the situation.

June 1993. Euroclear Operations Centre publishes 'Beyond the G30 Recommendations' report.

September 1993. New Bridge agreement (signed March 1992) between Euroclear and Cedel takes effect.

1994

Robert Douglass becomes Cedel chairman.

1 January 1994. European Monetary Institute begins work preparing for EMU. Focuses on securities settlement in connection with payments and collateral.

20 June 1994. Luc Bomans becomes Euroclear general manager, taking over from John T. Olds.

1995

January 1995. Cedel becomes a bank.

January 1995. 'Technical consolidation' in France as Banque de France, Sicovam and French banks agree that Sicovam should take over the central bank's securities settlement business in return for the Banque de France taking a 40% stake in Sicovam.

1 June 1995. Eurobond market adopts T + 3 settlement deadline.

December 1995. Leaders of the (now 15 member) European Union agree in Madrid that the future single currency will be called the euro and that currencies of the participating member states will be irrevocably locked from 1 January 1999.

1996

Completion of the Swiss Value Chain.

Deutsche Börse merges Deutscher Kassenverein, its CSD, with the Auslandskassenverein. Combined entity renamed Deutsche Börse Clearing in 1997.

15 July 1996. CREST, the UK's CSD, inaugurated.

1997

January 1997. EMI gives details of future repo-based monetary policy for EMU area.

June 1997. The Paris markets (SBF-Bourse de Paris, Monep and Matif) adopt Clearing 21®, in a technology swap with the Chicago Mercantile Exchange.

1998

20 April 1998. Sir Andrew Large succeeds Rolf-E. Breuer as chairman of Euroclear.

2–3 May 1998. EU summit in Brussels decides 11 countries (not including the UK) will launch EMU on 1 January 1999. Wim Duisenberg named first president of the European Central Bank, which replaces the EMI from 1 June 1998.

5 May 1998. Euroclear management decides to postpone introduction of 'Next', Euroclear's real-time settlement platform, until after the start of EMU.

1999

1 January 1999. EMU: 11 EU members launch euro, with single monetary policy and European System of Central Banks, although national notes and coins remain in circulation.

French markets restructured. All regulated markets brought together and run by Société des Bourses Françaises.

May 1999. Swiss settlement providers SEGA and Intersettle merge to form SIS SegaInter-Settle.

May 1999. French clearing houses merged into Clearnet, a subsidiary of SBF.

May 1999. European Commission published Financial Services Action Plan (FSAP).

May 1999. Euroclear unveils 'Hub and Spokes' settlement plan for Europe.

May 1999. Marcel Ospel, group chief executive officer of UBS, and Sir David Walker, chairman of Morgan Stanley Dean Witter Europe, found the European Securities Industry Users' Group (Esiug) to represent the interests of the biggest users of securities services in any restructuring of the European clearing and settlement landscape.

14 May 1999. The CEOs of Deutsche Börse, Cedel International and SBF announce plans to merge their securities settlement activities. Plan foresees Deutsche Börse Clearing, Cedel International and Sicovam becoming the European Clearing House.

23 August 1999. CRESTCo of the UK and SIS of Switzerland launch integrated cross-border settlement system.

1 September 1999. Announcement of plans for the separation of Euroclear from JP Morgan.

27 September 1999. Euroclear launches real-time settlement.

2 November 1999. Cedel International and Deutsche Börse sign legal papers formalising the merger of Cedel International with DBC to form new Cedel International with plans to turn it into the European Clearing House.

4 November 1999. The Depository Trust Company and the National Securities Clearing Corporation in the US combine to form The Depository Trust & Clearing Corporation (DTCC), a consolidated clearing and settlement infrastructure for US equities.

22 November 1999. Sicovam pulls out of the tripartite agreement with Deutsche Börse and Cedel International.

23 November 1999. Clearnet and Sicovam agree to ally with Euroclear.

6 December 1999. Werner Seifert announces that Deutsche Börse plans an IPO and stock exchange listing.

2000

1 January 2000. Merger of DBC and Cedel completed to form New Cedel International with André Lussi as CEO and Robert Douglass as chairman.

10 January 2000. New Cedel International renamed Clearstream International. Cedel International, by now a holding company owned by Cedel's former shareholders, has 50% of Clearstream. Deutsche Börse is the other Clearstream shareholder with 50%.

10 March 2000. Euroclear and JP Morgan agree to terminate Morgan's operating contract for the Euroclear system before the completion of the three-year notice period.

13 March 2000. Chris Tupker becomes Euroclear chairman, succeeding Sir Andrew Large.

20 March 2000. Stock exchanges of Paris, Brussels, and Amsterdam announce plans to merge and create a transnational exchange called Euronext.

23–24 March 2000. EU summit in Lisbon accords 'efficient and integrated financial markets' an important role in making the EU the world's 'most competitive and dynamic knowledge-based economy' by 2010.

24 March 2000. Agreement in principle for Euroclear to take over Sicovam.

26 March 2000. CRESTCo of the UK and SIS of Switzerland announce the 'Settlement Network' to 'deliver a single integrated process for the settlement of cross-border business in Europe'.

30 March 2000. Euroclear is appointed as CSD for the settlement of Irish government debt from the Irish central bank.

4 April 2000. The London Clearing House and Paris-based Clearnet announce plans for a single European clearing house to operate from 2001, to be followed by a merger 'as soon as possible'.

3 May 2000. The London Stock Exchange and Deutsche Börse announce plans for a merger of equals to create a 'mega-bourse' called iX.

29 June 2000. Pierre Francotte appointed chief executive of Euroclear, succeeding Luc Bomans, who takes early retirement after illness.

Summer 2000. Inconclusive informal talks between Euroclear and Clearstream explore the pros and cons of a merger of the two ICSDs.

5 September 2000. Announcement of memoranda of understanding for Euroclear to take over the Dutch CSD, Necigef, and the book entry settlement and custody business of CIK, the Belgian CSD.

9 September 2000. iX project collapses.

21 September 2000. Euroclear and Sicovam sign agreement to merge.

22 September 2000. Euronext launched as transnational exchange.

21 October 2000. Members of European Securities Forum (formerly Esiug) plan their own CCP.

9 November 2000. First report of Lamfalussy group of 'wise men'.

29 November 2000. Daylight bridge between Euroclear and Clearstream.

31 December 2000. Launch of Euroclear Bank as user-owned, user-governed ICSD. Separation of Euroclear and Morgan completed.

2001

January 2001. Clearstream acquires 'strategic' 7% stake in Monte Titoli, the Italian settlement system, for €20.17 million.

10 January 2001. Sicovam joins Euroclear group.

10 January 2001. Clearstream announces it has overstated the value of assets held in custody by €1 trillion.

5 February 2001. Deutsche Börse completes IPO and gains a €1 billion war chest.

15 February 2001. Final Lamfalussy 'wise men's' report puts spotlight on excessive cost of cross-border clearing and settlement in the EU.

26 February 2001. Luxembourg public prosecutor launches preliminary investigation of published allegations that Clearstream is at the centre of a money laundering scandal.

February 2001. Deutsche Börse approaches Cedel International holding company about acquiring its 50% stake in Clearstream.

May 2001. Sir Nigel Wicks appointed chairman of CRESTCo, the company that runs CREST, the British CSD and CSD of Irish equities.

11 May 2001. Carlos Zeyen of the Luxembourg public prosecutor's office meets Werner Seifert near Frankfurt and gains his support for searches of Clearstream Banking Luxembourg.

15 May 2001. Clearstream Board suspends André Lussi, Clearstream CEO, Carlos Salvatori, Lussi's deputy, and four other executives. André Roelants appointed interim chief executive of Clearstream.

1 June 2001. ECSplc changes name to Euroclear plc.

10 July 2001. Luxembourg public prosecutor declares there is no evidence of large scale money laundering at Clearstream. Other investigations continue.

13 July 2001. Roelants appointed Clearstream CEO. Douglass remains chairman.

18 July 2001. ESF ends CCP project – member banks not willing to fund it.

11 September 2001. Terrorist attacks on the US.

Autumn 2001. Clearstream board invites Deutsche Börse and Euroclear to put forward proposals for future control of the company by 31 October 2001. Deutsche Börse offers to buy the 50% it does not already own. Euroclear offers to negotiate a merger with Clearstream.

Late-October 2001. Euronext wins Liffe, the London financial futures exchange.

November 2001. First Giovannini group report on clearing and settlement.

6 December 2001. Cedel International, holder of 50% of Clearstream, rejects the Deutsche Börse and Euroclear offers.

7 December 2001. Clearstream board rejects Euroclear offer and enters exclusive merger negotiations with Deutsche Börse.

12 December 2001. Euroclear announces agreement with the London Stock Exchange and London Clearing House to develop a feed to allow the LSE's international customers to use Euroclear Bank to settle trades.

End-2001. Euroclear begins negotiations with CRESTCo.

2002

1 February 2002. Deutsche Börse and Cedel International agree the sale of Cedel's 50% stake in Clearstream to Deutsche Börse for €1.6 billion.

7 February 2002. Euroclear acquires an initial 51% stake in Necigef, which becomes Euroclear Nederland.

30 April 2002. Euroclear acquires the remaining 49% of Necigef.

May 2002. Euroclear, Clearstream and DTCC launch service, known as EPIM, to automate pre-issuance information processing and allocation of ISIN codes used to identify securities for new issues of European Commercial Paper.

June 2002. Borsa Italiana announces plans to take over Monte Titoli, the Italian CSD, creating a vertical silo.

June 2002. First EU Commission communication on clearing and settlement.

1 July 2002. Clearstream becomes a fully consolidated subsidiary of the Deutsche Börse group.

4 July 2002. Euroclear and CREST agree to merge and create a 'domestic market for Europe'.

19 July 2002. Feed from Euronext Paris to Euroclear Bank goes live.

End-September 2002. Merger of Euroclear and CREST takes effect. CREST becomes a subsidiary of Euroclear Bank in November 2002.

December 2002. European Parliament (the Andria report) pronounces on clearing and settlement.

2003

23 January 2003. G30 report advocates interoperability as part of a 20 point 'plan of action' for more efficient clearing and settlement worldwide.

25 February 2003. 'Fair & Clear' banks attack Euroclear's business model.

23 March 2003. Eurex Clearing AG, the CCP for Frankfurt equity trades, launched.

April 2003. Second Giovannini group report on clearing and settlement in the EU.

25 June 2003 LCH and Clearnet announce plans to merge.

July 2003. First draft of ESCB/CESR standards for clearing and settlement.

July 2003. Agreement on automated daytime bridge between Euroclear Bank and Clearstream Banking Luxembourg: to start June 2004, phase two in November 2004.

21 October 2003. Euroclear announces corporate restructuring to take effect from 1 January 2005. Euroclear SA/NV, a new holding company, will be the parent company for Euroclear Bank and the Euroclear-owned CSDs.

14 November 2003. New settlement model at Clearstream Banking Frankfurt. Night-time link with Bundesbank allows buyers of securities to use funds in minimum reserves.

18 December 2003. European Financial Services Roundtable Report on Clearing and Settlement.

22 December 2003. LCH.Clearnet merger completes.

2004

22 April 2004. Announcement of merger of Finnish and Swedish CSDs to create Nordic CSD (NCSD).

28 April 2004. Second communication on clearing and settlement from EU Commission.

End-April 2004. MiFID, the Markets in Financial Instruments Directives, adopted as EU law. Details remain to be fleshed out. Implementation lies in the future.

2 June 2004. EU Commission finds against Clearstream in competition case.

16 July 2004. First meeting of the Cesame group to promote removal of private sector Giovannini barriers.

July 2004. Euroclear reaches agreement with its users on 'significant market practice harmonisation' as part of the agreement with Euronext to develop ESES, 'Euroclear Settlement for Euronext-zone Securities'.

October 2004. ECB governing council and CESR approve revised version of ESCB/CESR standards.

November 2004. New EU Commission takes office, with Charlie McCreevy as internal market commissioner and Neelie Kroes as competition commissioner.

November 2004. Euroclear and Euronext sign letter of intent for Euroclear to acquire all of CIK.

13 December 2004. London Stock Exchange confirms approach from Deutsche Börse to buy the LSE.

2005

9 February 2005. Euronext announces elements of a potential bid for LSE.

6 March 2005. Deutsche Börse shelves offer for LSE.

9 May 2005. Werner Seifert resigns as Deutsche Börse CEO after shareholders' revolt. Rolf-E. Breuer agrees to step down as chairman before the end of 2005.

29 July 2005. UK Competition Commission pinpoints ownership of CCP services as stumbling block in any Deutsche Börse and Euronext bids for LSE.

30 June 2005. EU Commission's competition department publishes report critical of lack of competition in EU post-trade services.

13 September 2005. Commissioner McCreevy warns that 'the clock is ticking' for a solution to high costs of cross-border clearing and settlement.

Autumn 2005. ESCB/CESR standards put on hold.

1 November 2005. UK Competition Commission limits Deutsche Börse and Euronext to holding a maximum 14.9% in CCP for LSE.

December 2005. Euronext and Deutsche Börse begin merger discussions.

2006

1 January 2006. Euroclear completes acquisition of CIK which becomes Euroclear Belgium.

February 2006. Deutsche Börse-Euronext talks fail.

March 2006. SWIFT brokers agreement to eliminate Giovannini barrier 1: the national differences in IT protocols and computer interfaces.

7 March 2006. Commissioners McCreevy and Kroes give securities industry until the end of July 2006 to find a solution for improving clearing and settlement in the EU.

19 May 2006. Deutsche Börse outlines a proposed 'merger of partners' with Euronext.

22 May 2006. NYSE offers nearly €8 billion for merger with Euronext, which rejects Deutsche Börse.

24 May 2006. EU Commission's competition department publishes study condemning vertical silos.

29 May 2006. Euroclear launches the single settlement engine (SSE) at Euroclear France.

5 July 2006. David Hardy, long-serving CEO of LCH.Clearnet, resigns because of failure of £120 million IT project.

7 July 2006. The European Central Bank says it is 'evaluating opportunities' for a settlement service to be run by the Eurosystem called Target2-Securities (T2S).

10 July 2006. Chris Tupker becomes LCH.Clearnet chairman.

11 July 2006. Commissioner McCreevy outlines plan for an industry 'code of conduct' to boost efficiency and competition in the securities business from trading to settlement.

1 August 2006. Sir Nigel Wicks becomes Euroclear chairman, succeeding Chris Tupker who leaves the Euroclear chair six months before planned retirement date.

28 August 2006. Euroclear's SSE launched by CRESTCo.

September 2006. Euroclear Bank and Clearstream Banking Luxembourg announce investments to improve the Automated Daytime Bridge.

7 November 2006. Securities industry leaders sign the Commission-brokered code of conduct.

December 2006. NYSE and Euronext shareholders approve merger.

December 2006. Euroclear group annual turnover exceeds €450 trillion.

2007

1 January 2007. Signatories to code of conduct publish details of prices, discounts and rebates to meet transparency requirements.

End-January 2007. Euroclear Bank launches SSE.

January 2007. Euroclear signs MoU to build a relationship with Clearing Corporation of India Ltd (CCIL).

27 February 2007. EU's Ecofin council publishes its views of T2S.

8 March 2007. ECB announces year long consultation to help shape user requirements of T2S.

April 2007. Euroclear signs MoU to build a relationship with the National Depository Center (NDC) of Russia.

28 June 2007. FESE, EACH and ECSDA, the European securities industry trade associations, agree Access and Interoperability Guideline as part of the code of conduct.

1 November 2007. Implementation date for MiFID.

End-2007. Launch of ESES begins.

2008

Mid-2008. Mandate of Cesame group expires with final meeting scheduled for 9 June 2008.

In 2009 and 2010. Euroclear to launch its single platform and common communications interface, delivering the 'domestic market for Europe' initiative.

Andria, Generoso – Member of the European Parliament, June 2000 to July 2004. A member of the Forza Italia party and so part of the centre-right, Andria was rapporteur for the December 2002 parliament report on clearing and settlement that advocated unbundling ICSD services.

Angermueller, Hans – Chairman of Cedel 1990 to 1994, successor to Edmond Israel. Saw Cedel's main task during his watch as adapting to the stagnation of the Eurobond market.

Asmussen, Jörg – In charge of national and international financial markets at the German finance ministry since 2003, Asmussen came to the post as a high flying official who joined the ministry in 1996 and headed the office of minister Hans Eichel between July 1999 and October 2002.

Backes, Ernest – Former Cedel employee and co-author of *Revelation\$*, the book that triggered the 'Clearstream affair' in February 2001. The Luxembourg authorities later found there was no case to pursue while various legal actions undertaken by Clearstream found against the book's authors.

Bairiot, Etienne – Representative of Belgium's Société Générale de Banque on the first Euroclear board following the sale of the system to its users in 1972. A member of the board's executive committee.

Bayle, Marc – Deputy Head of the Market Infrastructure Division of the ECB. One of the managers of the Target2-Securities project, Bayle joined the EMI, the forerunner of the ECB, in the 1990s after working for Sicovam, the French CSD, for 10 years.

Bochow, John P. (aka Jack) – Senior international credit officer of Morgan Guaranty at the time of the 1972 sale of Euroclear to its users. Bruce Brackenridge reported to Bochow, who, he said, was very actively involved in the whole process.

Bolkestein, Frits – European Commissioner for the internal market, taxation and the customs union from 1999 to 2004, Bolkestein was a Dutch free market liberal. He worked for the Shell group from 1960 to 1976 before entering Dutch national politics in 1978. Clearing and settlement became part of the Commission's financial services agenda during Bolkestein's term of office.

---

[1] The persons in this appendix appear because they have influenced the history of securities settlement in Europe as described in the main text of this book. Most are introduced in the role in which they appear in the main text with cross references, where appropriate, to the chapters in which they mainly appear. The appendix does not include profiles of personalities, such as US President John F. Kennedy or German international banker Wilfried Guth, who appear in the text occupying more general roles.

Bomans, Luc – General manager of Euroclear, 20 June 1994 to 29 June 2000. The first non-American to hold the post, Bomans oversaw introduction of real-time settlement and initiated contacts with national CSDs. Career and achievements detailed in Chapters 8.1 and 11.1.

Brackenridge, Bruce – Head of Morgan Guaranty International Finance Corp. in 1972 when given the task of selling Euroclear to its users. Brackenridge was briefly chairman of Euroclear between its first ever board meeting in New York on 30 August 1972 until December 1972, when the sale to the participants was completed. He continued to be a Euroclear director until June 1982. Brackenridge returned to the Euroclear board as a director in 1989. Throughout, Brackenridge was a sympathetic point of contact in JP Morgan's New York head office for Euroclear managers. See Chapter 4.1.

Breuer, Rolf-Ernst (usually known as Rolf-E. Breuer) – German banker and Euroclear Chairman from 22 June 1984 until 20 April 1998, Breuer was also supervisory board chairman of Deutsche Börse from 1993 until October 2005, when he resigned in a delayed response to the shareholder revolt that obliged Werner Seifert to quit earlier in the year. Breuer's power base was Deutsche Bank, where he rose to become 'spokesman' or managing board chairman from 1997 to 2002 and supervisory board chairman from 2002 to 2006. His Deutsche Bank career ended in less than happy circumstances with his resignation in 2006 after becoming embroiled in a legal dispute with Leo Kirch, a German media mogul, who blamed Breuer for the financial collapse of his business empire after remarks made by Breuer on television. Breuer's area of expertise was financial markets and as 'Mr Finanzplatz' he was a strong supporter of Werner Seifert at Deutsche Börse and a prime mover of efforts to reform German financial services in the 1990s. Breuer tended to reach decisions through compromise rather than brute force, which may explain his limited influence on post-trade consolidation efforts in Europe. His long association with Euroclear pointed to an above average interest in financial infrastructure: he first joined the Euroclear board in 1974 and was elected vice chairman in October 1982. See Chapters 5.3–5.4, 9.1 and 13.2.

Bruce, Andrew – Barclays Bank representative on the Clearstream board who in 2001 headed a committee to investigate the prospects of a merger with Euroclear. Bruce joined Barclays in 1993 after 20 years with JP Morgan.

Bruns, Georg – General counsel of the Frankfurt Stock Exchange and manager of the Frankfurt Kassenverein, was hired as a special consultant by the creators of Cedel in 1970.

Capuano, Massimo – President and CEO of Borsa Italiana from 1998. A McKinsey alumnus who graduated in electrical engineering from Rome University with a summa cum laude, Capuano's strategy for the Italian exchange has focused on investment in state of the art technology and vertical integration by taking over infrastructure providers, including Monte Titoli, the CSD. Capuano was president of FESE, the Federation of European Securities Exchanges, during the gestation period of the industry Code of Conduct until shortly after its signing in November 2006. In 2007, he steered Borsa Italiana to a merger with the London Stock Exchange.

Caron, Paul – Second of the general managers sent by Morgan Guaranty to run Euroclear. Caron's stint in Brussels, from 1978 to 1982, was a period of rapid growth and technical enhancement for the system.

Carré, Hervé – EU Commission official who, as director for the economy of the euro zone and the EU, engaged Alberto Giovannini in 2000 to investigate the problems of cross-border securities settlement in Europe. A French national and Commission official since 1973, Carré became minister in charge of economic, financial and development affairs at the EU mission in Washington between 2002 and 2005 and came back to Brussels as deputy director general of DG-Ecfin, the Commission directorate general for economic and financial affairs, in 2005.

Cattier, John – One of a team of Eurobond professionals that made White Weld for a period in the 1960s the leading company in the market. Cattier, based in Zurich, has been credited with planting the idea of a system for Eurobond 'clearances' with Jim Chandler of Morgan Guaranty's Brussels office. Cattier became one of the traders' representatives on the first board after the sale of Euroclear to its users in 1972 and also served on the board's executive committee. He retired as a Euroclear board member in 1976.

Chandler, James (Jim) – Head of the securities department at Morgan Guaranty in Brussels in the 1960s and one of the founding fathers of Euroclear. Chandler, a UK national and resident in Belgium since its liberation from German occupation in 1944, played a big part in marketing the new system to participants. Chandler left Euroclear in 1973 to take a post in London but returned as second in command when Paul Caron was Euroclear general manager. Chandler became executive secretary of Euro-clear Clearance System plc in 1981 and held the same post with the Euroclear Belgian cooperative until his retirement in 1992. See Chapters 3.1 and 3.2.

Combes, Ignace – Deputy CEO, vice chairman of the management committee and a member of the executive committee of Euroclear SA/NV, Combes joined the systems department at JP Morgan in 1976 to work on banking technology and Euroclear-related developments. He was project leader in 1979 for developing the chaining into a new Euroclear securities settlement system. He worked in JP Morgan's New York office from 1989 to 1994, first with responsibility for worldwide marketing, and from 1993 as leader of the team that developed a new support and systems architecture for Morgan's overall businesses. Combes is chairman of Euroclear Netherlands and Euroclear Belgium. He also oversees Euroclear's IT development, the business model and harmonisation division and the strategy division.

Craven, John (Sir) – Recruited by Euroclear chairman Sir Andrew Large to assist in the negotiations on the separation of Euroclear from Morgan in 1999. As group chief executive of White Weld & Co. Ltd from 1975 to 1978 and vice chairman of SG Warburg in 1979, Craven was a prominent figure in the Euromarkets of the 1970s. In the 1980s he went on to become chairman and chief executive of the Morgan Grenfell Group and a member of the managing board of Deutsche Bank after the German bank acquired Morgan Grenfell. At the time of Euroclear's separation from Morgan, he was chairman of Lonmin, the platinum producer, and holder of many other directorships.

Cruickshank, Don – Chairman of the London Stock Exchange from 25 May 2000 until July 2003, Cruickshank was a City outsider whose previous career had segued from divisional management in media companies, into being CEO of the National Health Service in Scotland to heading the UK government's telecommunications watchdog. A former McKinsey consultant, Cruickshank supported the failed 'iX' attempt of fellow alumnus Werner Seifert to merge the LSE and Deutsche Börse.

Culver, Peter – General manager of Euroclear from 1985 until his sudden death on 11 March 1987. Culver set up Euroclear's strategy department, started and headed by Martine Dinne in 1986.

De Ghenghi, Luigi – A member of the Morgan team in negotiations on Euroclear's separation. De Ghenghi joined Morgan in the late 1980s from Davis Polk & Wardwell, Euroclear's law firm, and worked for Morgan in Brussels and London as general counsel of Euroclear and head of the legal department for Europe, the Middle East and Africa. De Ghenghi was an associate at Davis Polk from 1985 to 1989 and rejoined the firm as counsel, based in London, in 2001.

Deleebeeck, Marcel – Head of operations at Morgan Guaranty in Brussels in the late 1960s, Deleebeeck was one of the team that created the Euroclear pilot scheme in 1967 and the Euroclear system in 1968. Oversaw the computerisation of Euroclear in 1970.

Delsaux, Pierre – EU Commission official and head of the secretariat of the Lamfalussy group of wise men in 2000 and 2001, Delsaux chairs the Legal Certainty Group charged with finding ways of removing the legal barriers to cross-border settlement identified in the Giovannini reports.

Dinne, Martine – Crowned a career of nearly 40 years with Euroclear as CEO of Euroclear Bank and a member of the management committee of Euroclear SA/NV before retiring in June 2007. Martine Dinne joined Euroclear in 1969. She worked in the commercial division under Herschel Post in the 1970s, was put in charge of the strategic research and product management division, reporting to Tom Ketchum, in the 1980s, and renegotiated the Bridge agreement with Cedel in the 1990s. Dinne was managing director and head of the bank's commercial division before becoming CEO of Euroclear Bank. In her final post, Dinne was responsible for overseeing Euroclear's commercial, operations, network management and product management and banking divisions. See Chapters 5.3, 8.1 and 8.2.

Dobbie, Scott – Chairman of CREST from September 1996 until 2001 when succeeded by Sir Nigel Wicks. Dobbie joined Wood Mackenzie & Co., then a small Edinburgh stockbrokerage, in 1972 and became managing director in 1984. Dobbie became chairman of NatWest Securities Ltd from 1992 after Wood Mackenzie was acquired by NatWest in 1988, and senior adviser to Deutsche Bank following the transfer of NatWest's equities business to Bankers Trust in 1998 and DB's subsequent acquisition of Bankers Trust in 1999. Holder of many non-executive appointments.

Donahue, Donald F. – When appointed CEO of The Depository Trust and Clearing Corporation (DTCC) in May 2006, Donahue could look back on a 20-year career with DTCC and DTC. In April 2007 he was elected chairman and CEO of DTCC with effect from August 2007, when he also became chairman and CEO of its core subsidiaries: NSCC, DTC and the Fixed Income Clearing Corporation (FICC).

Douglass, Robert – New York lawyer and chairman of Cedel International from 1994 to 2002 and Clearstream International between 2000 and 2004, Douglass was a supporter of André Lussi as Cedel and Clearstream CEO. Became chairman emeritus and senior adviser to Clearstream International in December 2004. See Chapters 8.2 and 12 for profile and role.

Draghi, Mario – Italian civil servant, European Union official and international banker. Appointed governor of the Bank of Italy in late December 2005 in succession to Antonio Fazio, who resigned amid complaints that he abused his position in attempting to block the takeover of Banca Antonveneta, an Italian bank, by Netherlands-based ABN AMRO. Draghi was previously vice chairman and managing director of Goldman Sachs International in London from 2002. He led Italy's privatisation programme in the 1990s as director general of the Treasury and chaired the committee that drafted legislation governing Italian financial markets, known as Draghi's law.

Duvieusart, Philippe – As second in command at Kredietbank SA Luxembourgeoise from 1965 to early 1973, Duvieusart tried unsuccessfully to rally support among Luxembourg banks for Eurobond settlement system in the late 1960s. He fared better after Morgan created Euroclear, becoming one of the founding fathers of Cedel. See Chapters 2.5 and 3.3.

Eyssautier, Jean-Marc – Director of commercial relations at Sicovam 1997 to 2000 who expressed doubts about the tripartite merger with Deutsche Börse and Cedel. Eyssautier was one of many French post-trade professionals who began his career at the Banque de France. He left Euroclear France in October 2001 to join the custody services department of French bank CDC IXIS. In November 2006, he was appointed, aged 45, to be managing director of CACEIS bank, a custodian owned equally by France's Crédit Agricole and Caisse Nationale des Caisses d'Epargne.

Flammant, Raymond – Consultant with Fiduciaire Generale de Luxembourg which in 1970 produced the feasibility study that paved the way for the launch of Cedel. Flammant was number two to René Schmitter on the project. A confidant of Edmond Israel.

Fleuriot, Pierre – President of ABN-AMRO Bank in France in 2000, Fleuriot was appointed to advise Théodore, Möller and Lefebvre on the merger of the Paris, Amsterdam and Brussels stock exchanges to form Euronext. Fleuriot was a former director general of COB, France's Commission des Opérations de Bourse.

Fox, Tom – Euroclear general manager from 1982 to 1985, Fox set up the Euroclear Operations Centre, which separated the Euroclear's activities from those of the Brussels branch of Morgan Guaranty. He represented Morgan on the Euroclear board between 1985 and 1988.

Francioni, Reto – Chief executive of Deutsche Börse in Frankfurt since November 2005, Francioni took over the place vacated by Werner Seifert after a gap of some months. Francioni's move from the SWX Swiss exchange brought the Swiss citizen and keen fly-fisher back onto familiar territory: Francioni was a member of the Deutsche Börse board in the 1990s until a parting of the ways with Seifert over strategy.

Francotte, Pierre – CEO and chairman of the management committee of Euroclear SA/NV, Francotte joined Euroclear in 1993 as assistant general counsel from the International Monetary Fund and became head of the legal division in 1994. After a spell as head of Euroclear's transaction processing division, Francotte was appointed chief operating officer with responsibility for settlement, custody and related operations in 2000. He was appointed Euroclear general manager as successor to Luc Bomans from 29 June 2000 and the first CEO of Euroclear

Bank, when it was launched at the end of 2000. See Chapter 11.1 for profile and Chapters 11.3, 13.1 and 15.7 for subsequent career.

Franssens, Constant – Managing director of Kredietbank SA Luxembourgeoise in the late 1960s, Franssens, with his deputy Philippe Duvieusart, was an early backer of a Eurobond settlement system in the Grand Dutchy. Working with Edmond Israel of Banque Internationale à Luxembourg, the Kredietbank duo won the support of the Luxembourg banking community, including big foreign banks, for what became Cedel.

Frey, Werner – CEO of the European Securities Forum, which represents big international banks with an interest in consolidation and integration of European securities infrastructure. A Swiss national, Frey became ESF chief executive in June 2002 after some years advising financial institutions. He was an executive board member of Bank Leu, a Swiss bank, between 1988 and 1997.

Furse, Clara – Chief executive of the London Stock Exchange since January 2001, Furse successfully repelled several attempts to take over the exchange, including that of Deutsche Börse in 2004/05 which ended in the resignation of Werner Seifert as Deutsche Börse's chief executive. In 2007, Furse guided the LSE into a merger with Borsa Italiana, the parent company of Italian CSD Monte Titoli. She had already opened the LSE's post-trade arrangements to competition.

Galbraith, Evan (aka Van) – A vice president of Morgan Guaranty and director of Morgan et Cie, Paris, between 1961 and 1969, Galbraith was instrumental in selling Morgan's new Euroclear settlement service to the Eurobond market in 1968. He quit Morgan shortly after Euroclear's launch to become director and chairman of Bankers Trust International in London from 1969 to 1975. Galbraith shuttled between business and public service throughout his career. After attending Yale and Harvard Law School, Galbraith was in the US Navy from 1953 to 1957 and attached to CIA counter-espionage. He was chairman of Dillon Read and Co., London, from 1975 to 1981; US Ambassador to France between 1981 and 1985, and chairman of LVMH Moet Hennessy Louis Vuitton Inc. from 1985 to 1998. He held a number of board and advisory posts until 10 September 2001, when US Defense Secretary Donald Rumsfeld appointed him as his representative in Europe and defence adviser to the US mission to NATO in Brussels. Galbraith was 73 at the time. See Chapter 2.1 for role in the Eurobond market and Chapter 3.2 in marketing Euroclear.

Ganz, Matthias – Executive at Deutsche Börse who joined the executive management of Clearstream in 2000 and was responsible for integrating the former Auslandskassenverein, the international settlement system of Deutsche Börse Clearing, with Clearstream International. Ganz was a McKinsey consultant recruited by Seifert when he was head of Swiss Re and who followed Seifert to Deutsche Börse in 1993. He was chief operating officer at Deutsche Börse from 2003 until his resignation from the group in March 2007.

Giovannini, Alberto – Italian financial expert and chairman of the eponymous group which in two reports, published in 2001 and 2003, identified 15 barriers to efficient cross-border clearing and settlement in Europe and set out a strategy for removing them. Giovannini is principal policy adviser of the European Commission's Clearing and Settlement Advisory and

Monitoring Group (Cesame), which is working to lift the barriers considered the responsibility of the private sector. See Chapter 14.2 for a profile of Giovannini and an account of the reports and Chapter 16.2 for an assessment of progress in removing the 'Giovannini barriers'.

Godeffroy, Jean-Michel – Director general for payments systems at the European Central Bank and a key figure in the Target2-Securities project. Godeffroy began his career at the Banque de France in 1982. As deputy head of the policy division of the European Monetary Institute in the 1990s, he was in charge of the oversight of work being done in the fields of payments and settlements. Godeffroy co-chaired with Eddy Wymeersch the joint ESCB/CESR clearing and settlement expert group. See Chapters 17.2, 17.3 and 17.4.

Goffette, Pierre – One of six Clearstream managers suspended in May 2001 at the request of the Luxembourg authorities to facilitate their investigation of allegations of money laundering and other offences. The Luxembourg authorities announced in statements of July 2001 and November 2004 that there was no case to pursue.

Grandquist, Dick – One of the Davis Polk & Wardwell team that helped devise the formula for selling Euroclear to its users in 1972, Grandquist was a New-York based colleague of Bruce Nichols, Morgan's *eminence grise*.

Guynn, Randall D. – A partner in Morgan's law firm Davis Polk & Wardwell, Guynn wrote an influential discussion paper in 1996 on the need for modernisation and international harmonisation of securities ownership, transfer and pledging laws. See Chapter 7.2.

Hallberg, Rolf – The first chairman of the AIBD until May 1973 and also, from December 1972 until June 11 1976, the first chairman of Euroclear after the sale of the system to its users. Hallberg was a respected banker and fluent in several languages. His appointment as Euroclear chairman reflected his wide experience in the Eurobond market and the strong support given to Euroclear by Sweden's Wallenberg group, whose interests were represented from 1972 through Skandinaviska Enskilda Banken (SEB). Hallberg represented SEB on Euroclear's board until 1995 when he was appointed director emeritus, a position he held until 2001.

Hämäläinen, Sirkka – Appointed a member of the ECB executive board for five years from 1 June 1998, Sirkka Hämäläinen was governor of the Bank of Finland between 1992 and 1998. She began her central banking career as an economist in 1961 and stayed at the national bank, except for a period in 1981/82 when she was director of the economics department in the Finnish finance ministry.

Hardt, Judith – As secretary general of FESE, the Federation of European Securities Exchanges, Hardt played an important role in coordinating the securities industry's negotiations on the November 2006 code of conduct with the European Commission. An experienced lobbyist with expertise in financial services and capital markets regulation, Hardt was secretary general of the European Mortgage Federation before taking up the FESE post on 1 July 2005.

Hardy, David – Chief executive of LCH.Clearnet who resigned in July 2006 after the costly failure of a big IT project. Hardy was at the top of his profession for 19 years, having headed the London Clearing House and its predecessor organisation before becoming CEO of the merged Anglo-French clearing house in 2003. A big man, with big ideas but implementation was not his strong suit.

Harry, Serge – As general secretary of Sicovam in charge of finance, legal affairs, human resources, general services and communication, Harry was involved in the May 1999 negotiations in Marrakech, Paris and Brussels for Sicovam to merge with Cedel and Deutsche Börse Clearing. In June 1999 and after 16 years at Sicovam, he became deputy chief executive of ParisBourse SA. Harry was appointed chief financial officer of the newly created Euronext in 2000 and became head of finance and general services. In 2007, he was made group head of corporate strategy for NYSE Euronext.

Häusler, Gerd – Hired around the end of 2000 by Werner Seifert to be senior adviser on strategic issues to Deutsche Börse and perceived by many on the Clearstream board to be Seifert's candidate to succeed Lussi in May 2001, Häusler instead moved to the International Monetary Fund to head its international capital markets department. Chairman of Dresdner Kleinwort Benson in London from December 1997 until his resignation from the Dresdner Bank group in May 2000, Häusler was previously a member of the Central Bank Council of the Bundesbank. A member of the G30 since 1996, Häusler was appointed vice chairman of Lazard International, based in Frankfurt and Paris, in October 2006.

Hempel, Régis – The witness known as 'H' and one of the main sources for the Robert-Backes book that in 2001 alleged large scale money laundering and the operation of a double accounting system and concealed accounts at Clearstream. Hempel was a former employee of Cedel who left the company in 1992. The Luxembourg public prosecutor's office found no evidence to substantiate Hempel's claims.

Hopkins, J. Wallace (aka Wally) – Head of the Paris office of Davis Polk & Wardwell, Morgan Guaranty's lawyers, in 1972 when the sale of Euroclear to its users was being arranged. Worked in Brussels with Brackenridge and others in May/June 1972 working out the various options for the future of the Euroclear system.

Hugh Smith, Andrew (Sir) – Chairman of the London Stock Exchange at the time of the presentation of the 1989 G30 report and during the Taurus débâcle. Hugh Smith joined the LSE in 1988 after being senior partner at UK brokerage Capel Cure Myers and retired from the exchange in 1994.

Imthurn, Walter – One of the prime movers behind the establishment of the AIBD in the late 1960s, Imthurn traded Eurobonds for Weeden & Co. in London in 1969 when the company had to withdraw from trading because of the settlement problems in the market. He survived that crisis and continued to work in the Eurobond market for many years.

Israel, Edmond – One of the founding fathers of Cedel and its first chairman, who held the office from 1970 for 20 years. Israel developed his interest in Eurobond settlement after discussing the 1960s paper crisis with Constant Franssens of Kredietbank Luxembourgeoise at a lunch in 1968. While advancing as an executive at Banque Internationale à Luxembourg, the Grand Duchy's oldest bank, Israel threw a great deal of energy and time into his role as non-executive chairman of the Luxembourg-based ICSD. See Chapter 3.3.

Jackson, George Harold (usually known as Hal) – Comptroller and auditor of Morgan Guaranty Brussels in the late 1960s, Jackson was one of the small group that created the Euroclear system in 1968. He later succeeded Jim Chandler as Euroclear executive secretary in 1992.

Jamar, Alfred (aka Freddy) – Euroclear's first computer manager, responsible for hiring the first analysts and programmers. Responsible for Euroclear's first computerised chaining system.

Kauppi, Piia-Noora – Member of the European Parliament since 1999. Finnish national and member of the centre-right European People's Party, Kauppi took over as rapporteur on Clearing and Settlement after Theresa Villiers quit as an MEP in May 2005 and kept parliament away from an aggressive pro-legislative stance.

Kent, Pen – As an executive director of the Bank of England from 1988 until 1997, Kent headed the 'Task Force on Securities Settlement' that created CREST after the Taurus failure. A Bank official since 1961, he became the first CREST chairman. Kent was appointed executive chairman of the European Securities Forum in 2000, a post he held until early 2002. Following the merger of CREST and Euroclear, Kent was appointed independent chairman of Euroclear's UK Market Advisory Committee in October 2002. For profile and role at CREST see Chapter 9.3.

Kessler, Jörg-Ronald – One of the G30 working committee that produced the 1989 report on clearing and settlement, Kessler was a former member of the German Kassenverein board. As a consultant on securities operations, he also produced a report in 1989 for the European Commission which suggested improvements in the settlement of cross-border securities transactions in the European Community.

Ketchum, Tom – Euroclear general manager from May 1987 until September 1991, Ketchum headed EOC at a time of rapid diversification and growth. Client focus and implementation of system improvements were priorities during Ketchum's years at Euroclear. He also had to contend with increasingly assertive competition from Cedel, headed by André Lussi. As Morgan's chief financial officer and chief administrative officer in 2000, he was one of the top managers responsible for merging the IT capabilities of JP Morgan and Chase Manhattan.

Knight, Angela – Chief executive of APCIMS, the Association of Private Client Investment Managers and Stockbrokers, and a tough defender of the small UK brokers' interests when Werner Seifert sought to take over the London Stock Exchange in 2000 and 2004. Knight was a UK Conservative MP from 1992 to 1997 and a junior Treasury minister between 1995 and 1997. She became CEO of the British Bankers' Association late in 2006.

Koller, Walter – A key figure in setting up the AIBD in the late 1960s and in shaping the Eurobond market's response to the New York settlement crisis. Koller, who worked for White Weld in Zurich at the time, teamed up with fellow Swiss-German Armin Mattle, the AIBD's first secretary, to draw up the association's rules. Koller went on to develop the AIBD's education seminars.

Kroes, Neelie – European commissioner for competition since 2004, Kroes was previously adviser to and board member of numerous international companies. Since becoming a member of the Dutch parliament in the 1970s, 'Nickel Neelie' has built a reputation for toughness. She was Netherlands deputy minister for transport, public works and telecommunications between 1977 and 1981 and cabinet minister for the same portfolio from 1982 to 1989.

Kron, Wolfgang – Senior Eurobond dealer who represented Deutsche Bank in the negotiations leading to the creation of the AIBD. Like Stanley Ross, Kron found that the best way of overcoming the 1960s Eurobond settlement crisis was to go to New York and track payments owing to his department in the vaults of US banks.

Lamfalussy, Alexandre – President of the European Monetary Institute from January 1994 until 30 June 1997 and chairman of an eponymous group of 'wise men' on the regulation of European securities markets in 2000 and 2001, Baron Lamfalussy set guidelines for EU policy on clearing and settlement during two decades. Profile and policies in Chapters 7.3 and 14.1.

Langton, John – After trading Eurobonds for Julius Strauss, Bondtrade, Orion Royal Bank and Security Pacific, Langton became chief executive and secretary general of the Association of International Bond Dealers in 1990 and continued to head the organisation after it changed its identity to the International Securities Market Association (ISMA) on 1 January 1992. Langton was due to retire in mid-2005 but continued working for another 12 months to oversee the completion of ISMA's merger with the International Primary Market Association (IPMA) to form the International Capital Market Association (ICMA).

Lannoo, Karel – Chief executive of CEPS, the Brussels-based Centre for European Policy Studies, since 2000 and responsible for shifting the focus of the think-tank to matters of financial regulation. Co-author of a December 2001 report on securities settlement, Lannoo's areas of academic expertise are financial market integration and regulation, direct taxation and corporate governance.

Large, Andrew (Sir) – Euroclear chairman 20 April 1998 to 10 March 2000, Large was also deputy chairman of Barclays plc between 1998 and 2002. Large began his working life with BP but moved into banking in 1971 when he joined Orion Bank, a consortium bank operating in the Euromarket. He moved to Swiss Bank Corporation in 1980, becoming a board member in 1988. Between 1992 and 1997, he chaired the Securities and Investments Board, a UK regulator. After leaving Euroclear and Barclays, he served as deputy governor of the Bank of England between 2002 and 2006. See Chapter 11.1.

Lefebvre, Olivier – Played an important part in the creation of Euronext in 1999 and 2000. He became a member of the Euronext managing board on the establishment of the trans-national exchange in 2000. Lefebvre was appointed head of the Brussels stock exchange in 1996 from the Belgian Ministry of Finance, where he introduced reforms of Belgium's financial markets. See Chapter 11.2.

Leiper, Julian – One of the CREST non-executive directors who assisted in the merger negotiations with Euroclear, Leiper was chairman of Computershare Investor Services plc and a member of the CREST board since May 1997.

Levin, Mattias – A research fellow with the Brussels-based Centre for European Policy Studies and, with Karel Lannoo, co-author of a December 2001 report that first tried to work out the costs of the securities settlement industry in the EU. Later joined the EU Commission and worked on clearing and settlement in DG Internal Market.

Liddell, Roger – Appointed chief executive of LCH.Clearnet by Chris Tupker in July 2006, Liddell, a UK national, was a New York-based Goldman Sachs managing director in charge of global operations until the end of 2005. He was earlier a Euroclear board member, representing Goldman Sachs.

Lussi, André – CEO of Cedel from 1989 to end-1999 and of Clearstream International from 1 January 2000 until his suspension on 15 May 2001 to facilitate the investigation by the Luxembourg authorities of allegations of money laundering and other offences. The Luxembourg authorities issued three statements (in July 2001, November 2004 and April 2006) which stated there was no case to pursue against Lussi. Profile in Chapter 8.2 and career progress in Chapters 8.2, 10 and 12.

Lutz, Alfred G. – Represented Merrill Lynch on the first Euroclear board after the sale of the system to its users. Lutz reportedly advocated a merger of Euroclear and Cedel in the early 1970s.

Mai, Stefan – Head of market policy for the Deutsche Börse group and responsible for regulatory strategy during negotiations on the industry code of conduct. An economics graduate, Mai worked in academia in Germany from the late 1990s before a stint with the International Monetary Fund in 2004. He is a member of the Cesame group.

Marson, Jacques-Philippe – President and CEO of BNP Paribas Securities Services, the post-trade services subsidiary of the BNP Paribas group. A citizen of Luxembourg, Marson's career took him from JP Morgan, where he spent 12 years including a spell at Euroclear, through SWIFT, Cedel and State Street before he joined BNP Paribas in 1998. He became a member of the Euroclear board as the representative of BNP Paribas towards the end of the 1990s. An adherent to the Fair & Clear arguments against Euroclear's acquisition of national CSDs, Marson was one of the Euroclear board members representing Sicovam Holding until February 2004.

Massol, Robert – One of six Clearstream managers suspended in May 2001 at the request of the Luxembourg authorities to facilitate their investigation of allegations of money laundering and other offences. The Luxembourg authorities announced in statements of July 2001 and November 2004 that there was no case to pursue.

Mattle, Armin – Prominent Eurobond trader in the 1960s and, with fellow Swiss-German Walter Koller, responsible for writing much of the rule book of the Association of International Bond Dealers. During the negotiations on the creation of the AIBD, Mattle represented Bondtrade, one of the specialist consortium trading houses of the time. He later joined Union Bank of Switzerland (Securities) Ltd.

McCreevy, Charlie – Internal market commissioner from November 2004 and godfather of the industry-led European Code of Conduct for clearing and settlement, agreed on 7 November 2006. For profile and policies, See Chapters 14.10 and 17.1.

McDaniels, John – Lawyer from the Paris office of Davis Polk & Wardwell, Morgan's legal firm, who helped Evan Galbraith sell the Euroclear system to participants in Europe in 1968.

McSharry, Sean – Commercial director of Euroclear, successor to Herschel Post. Travelled with Post to Japan in the late 1970s and secured agreement in 1978 for the acceptance of 'Samurais' – yen denominated foreign bonds issued in Tokyo – in the Euroclear system. Encouraged development of the electronic Bridge with Cedel.

Mérère, Joël – Member of the executive committee of Euroclear SA/NV with responsibility for International Policy Affairs, Mérère is also vice chairman of Euroclear France and chairman of ECSDA, the European Central Securities Depositories Association. Mérère was CEO of Euroclear France until March 2006 having previously been CEO of Sicovam (which became Euroclear France) since 1998. Mérère joined Sicovam in 1995 from the Banque de France, where he created and managed the Saturne system. He was responsible for France's RGV high speed settlement project as deputy CEO of Sicovam between 1995 and 1998.

Meyer, John M. Jr – Visionary Morgan banker who backed Euroclear's creation in the 1960s. As president, the second highest ranking officer of Morgan Guaranty in New York, Meyer supported the Euroclear pilot scheme in 1967 and the creation of Euroclear in 1968. Meyer was chairman of Morgan Guaranty and JP Morgan & Co. from 1969 to 1971 and used his influence to help sell Euroclear to its users in 1972. Drawing on experiences gained in the creation of Euroclear, Meyer steered the US Banking and Securities Industry Committee (BASIC) towards establishing The Depository Trust Company, the New York CSD, in 1973. Bruce Brackenridge, who worked closely with him, remembers 'Mr Meyer' as 'highly intelligent: a man who liked details but always saw the big picture, modest yet tough and thoroughly honorable – in fact, the most impressive individual I ever met in the banking business.' See Chapters 3.1, 3.2 and 3.5.

Möller, George – Chief executive of the Amsterdam Exchanges from 1 January 1997 and as such one of the founding fathers of the Euronext transnational exchanges group. Möller became chief operating officer of Euronext when the group was launched on 22 September 2000.

Monti, Mario – European Commissioner for two terms from 1995 to November 2004, Monti was in charge of the single market, financial services, taxation and customs from 1995 to 1999 and competition commissioner between 1999 and 2004. He is president of Bocconi University in Milan and chairman of the board of BRUEGEL, a Brussels-based economic think-tank.

Muller, Georges – Cedel's managing director in the second half of the 1980s. Followed by André Lussi. Muller retired at the end of 1989 after six years running the ICSD.

Nava, Mario – Italian economist and head of the Financial Market Infrastructure unit of the European Commission's Internal Market directorate under Commissioner McCreevy. Nava started working for the Commission in 1994 while continuing to be active in research and teaching.

Nichols, Bruce – A senior lawyer in the New York office of Davis Polk & Wardwell, Morgan Guaranty's lawyers, in 1972. Nichols, remembered by contemporaries for his austere character and restricted sense of humour, was perceived as JP Morgan's *eminence grise*.

Nilles, Ernest – The Luxembourg investigating magistrate who launched the formal judicial investigation of allegations against André Lussi and five Clearstream colleagues in May 2001.

Olds, John T. – Euroclear general manager from 1 September 1991 until June 1994. Olds came to Euroclear after 18 years with Morgan Guaranty, latterly as head of corporate planning at JP Morgan. He was noted for his interest in strategy and knowledge of capital markets. His period at Euroclear saw upgrades in the system's technical capabilities including the adoption of multiple-batch processing. In the late 1990s, Olds left Morgan after 24 years to become vice chairman and CEO of the Development Bank of Singapore.

Ospel, Marcel – Co-founder in May 1999 with Sir David Walker of the European Securities Industry Users' Group (ESIUG), which was relaunched as the European Securities Forum (ESF) in June 2000. At the time, Ospel was group CEO of UBS, having been president and group CEO of Swiss Bank Corporation between 1996 and 1998. Ospel began his career in the capital markets and securities industry in 1980. He was elected to the UBS board in April 2001 and appointed chairman.

Padoa-Schioppa, Tommaso – A key policy maker in European economic and financial affairs for two decades before being appointed a member of the European Central Bank executive board for seven years from June 1998. Padoa-Schioppa was director general for economic and financial affairs at the European Commission from 1979 to 1983, deputy director general of the Banca d'Italia from 1984 to 1997, and chairman of Consob, the Italian securities regulator, from 1997 to 1998. He played a leading role in formulating payments systems policies from 1991 onwards. Padoa-Schioppa was appointed economy and finance minister in the government of Romano Prodi in May 2006.

Patterson, Michael – A vice chairman of Morgan in New York and leader of the bank's team in the negotiations on the separation of Euroclear from Morgan. Patterson was a Euroclear board member for nearly a decade until 2002. As the New York-based executive with responsibility for the Euroclear Operations Centre, he discussed separation with Luc Bomans and Ignace Combes before formal negotiations began. Patterson's father was Ellmore Patterson, a former Morgan chairman.

Perna, Tom – A senior executive vice president of The Bank of New York, Perna was the New York-based negotiator for Euroclear in the negotiations over the separation from Morgan. He had helped negotiate BoNY's acquisition of Morgan's custody business in 1995. Perna joined the Euroclear board in the late 1990s and resigned in October 2004 shortly after the announcement of his decision to leave BoNY after nearly two decades with the company.

Petiau, Agnès – After joining the Brussels office of Morgan Guaranty in 1966, Agnès Petiau spent 34 years in Euroclear's commercial department with more than 20 years in client support. After retirement, wrote *Histoires d'Euroclear*, her personal reminiscences of the company.

Petersen, Albert – Main figure behind the modernisation of Euroclear's technical capability in the 1970s. Recruited talented managers including Ignace Combes and Luc Bomans. Oversaw modernisation of the chaining, introduction of Euclid communications system, automated securities lending and borrowing, and the electronic Bridge with Cedel. Left Euroclear in 1983 to follow career opportunities in the US and later represented State Street Bank & Trust on the Euroclear board from 1999 until retirement in 2001. See Chapters 4.3 to 4.6.

Piette, Georges – A key figure, with Ignace Combes, in the re-engineering of Euroclear's chaining process from 1979 to 1981. Hired as system engineer, Piette was one of many talented persons recruited by Albert Petersen in the 1970s. He stayed in charge of the Morgan bank systems after the Euroclear activities were grouped in the Euroclear Operations Centre.

Post, Herschel – As Euroclear's commercial manager from 1974 to 1979, Post helped Euroclear regain market leadership from Cedel. He left Morgan Guaranty in 1984 when based in London and went on to hold a number of high profile City positions, including deputy chairman of the London Stock Exchange and CEO and deputy chairman of Coutts & Co., before becoming International Managing Director of Christie's International, the fine art auction house. He was a member of the Euroclear board during the 1990s as a representative first of Lehman Brothers International and later the NatWest group. Post became an independent director of CRESTCo in September 2002. See Chapters 4.2 and 4.3.

Reed, John – Chairman of Citicorp who headed the 12 strong steering committee responsible for the 1989 G30 report on clearing and settlement. Reed was Citicorp's youngest CEO when appointed in 1984. He oversaw its merger with Travelers Group in the 1990s to create Citigroup. He was later chairman of the NYSE from September 2003 until April 2005. In April 2007, Reed was appointed a director of the Dutch Foundation and a trustee of the US Trust set up to deal with regulatory issues at NYSE Euronext.

Richardson, Gordon (Lord) – G30 chairman from 1985 to 1991 on whose watch the influential 1989 study on clearance and settlement was produced in response to problems revealed by the 1987 stock market crash. Governor of the Bank of England during a turbulent 10 years from 1973 to 1983. Previously chairman of merchant bank Schroders Ltd.

Robert, Denis – French journalist, co-author with Ernest Backes of the book *Revelation$* which alleged in 2001 that Clearstream was at the centre of a giant money laundering operation and operated secret accounts. The Luxembourg authorities later found there was no case to pursue against Clearstream or its officers while various legal actions undertaken by Clearstream found against the book's authors.

Roelants, André – Took over running Clearstream International in May 2001 and credited with stabilising the company after the departure of André Lussi. Roelants was confirmed as CEO in July 2001 and continued in the post after Clearstream became a wholly owned subsidiary of Deutsche Börse in 2002. Became Clearstream International chairman in December 2004. See Chapters 12.3, 12.5 and 13.3.

Ross, Stanley – Eurobond trader and, as resident managing director of Kidder Peabody Securities in London at the time of Euroclear's creation, one of the earliest supporters of the system. A member of the founding group of the Association of International Bond Dealers, Ross was also briefly a member of the first Euroclear board after the sale of the system to its users in 1972. Ross set up Ross & Partners in 1978. After a huge row with the AIBD, his firm was the first to open up the market in new issue Eurobonds for trading at a discount during the 'grey market' period between the dates of an issue's launch and its allotment. Always an innovator, Ross became chairman of Tradepoint Investment Exchange in 1994: London's first electronic, for-profit exchange which later evolved into virt-x. See Chapters 2.2, 2.3, 3.2 and 4.1

Russo, Daniela – deputy director general of the directorate for payment systems and market infrastructure at the European Central Bank and one of the ECB officials working on T2S.

Salvatori, Carlos – Manager at Cedel/Clearstream for eight years, in which he was in charge of marketing, sales and operations and later deputy to André Lussi. Salvatori led the Cedel team in the tripartite negotiations on a merger with Deutsche Börse and Paris Bourse/Sicovam in Marrakech in May 1999. In the wake of the Clearstream affair, Salvatori was suspended from duties in May 2001 with Lussi and four other managers to facilitate the investigation of allegations of money laundering and other serious offences by the Luxembourg authorities. These announced in statements of July 2001 and November 2004 that there was no case to pursue.

Saville, Iain – CEO of CREST from its inauguration in 1996 until early 2002, Saville was the leader, with Pen Kent, of the Bank of England project to create the UK CSD after the Taurus debacle. Under Saville's leadership, the settlement of UK government debt and money market instruments was brought into CREST which later, with the LSE and LCH, launched the UK CCP for equities. As chair of ECSDA in the late 1990s, Saville sought a spaghetti-type system of interoperable links among leading CSDs in Europe. He went from CREST to be managing director for Europe and Africa of Computershare and, in October 2003, to the Lloyd's insurance market as Lloyd's first Head of Business Process Reform. See Chapters 9.3 and 13.1.

Schmitter, René – Consultant with Fiduciaire Generale de Luxembourg which in 1970 produced the feasibility study that paved the way for the launch of Cedel. Schmitter was project leader and went on to be secretary to Cedel's board and executive committee, retiring from these posts in 1990, at the same time as Edmond Israel, Cedel's long serving chairman.

Schuster, Stephan – Managing director and head of capital market policy at Deutsche Bank in Frankfurt, Schuster is also co-chair of the G30 European monitoring committee for the 2003 global Plan of Action for Clearing and Settlement and a member of the EU's Clearing and Settlement Advisory and Monitoring Experts' Group (CESAME).

Seifert, Werner – Chief executive of Deutsche Börse from 1993 until ousted by a shareholders' revolt in May 2005, Seifert is credited with lifting the Frankfurt stock exchange from a dozy backwater to one of the leading European exchanges. He built a vertical silo structure in Germany and tried to extend Frankfurt's domination outside Germany, but with limited success. See Chapter 9.1 for profile and activities before the coming of the euro and Chapters 10, 12 and 15.1 for later attempts to consolidate the securities business.

Sherwood, Paul – Strauss Turnbull representative among the Eurobond traders who set up the AIBD in 1968/69. A member of the five-strong steering committee that prepared the first AIBD meeting.

Simpson, Hugh – Chief executive of CREST and an executive director of Euroclear from 2002 to 2004 during the acquisition of the British CSD by Euroclear. Simpson joined CREST from the Bank of England. A consultant since leaving Euroclear, Simpson has been advising the European Central Bank on its Target2-Securities project.

Solbes, Pedro – Member of the European Commission responsible for economic and monetary affairs between September 1999 and April 2004 and, as such, paymaster for Alberto Giovannini's 'Consultative group on the impact of the Euro on European capital markets'. Solbes left the Commission in 2004 to become Spain's minister of economy and finance.

Steers, Ian – Euroclear chairman from 6 June 1980 until 22 June 1984 and the first representative of traders' interests to chair the company. In the 1960s, Steers headed the Eurobond operation of Wood Gundy, a Canadian house and one of the leading broker-dealers at the time. Made Euroclear better known in financial circles. Continued as a board member after 1984. Became director emeritus of Euroclear in the mid-1990s until 2001. See Chapters 5.1 and 5.4.

Strauss, Julius – Legendary trader active in the foreign bond market before and after the Second World War and in 1963 one of the first in the London market to trade Eurobonds. Gave Stanley Ross his first big break in the early 1950s after discovering the young Ross reading Proust in Strauss Turnbull's basement. Ross, who was working as a sold transfer clerk, was given the opportunity to become a trader.

Streichenberg, Georges – Euroclear chairman 11 June 1976 until 6 June 1980 and representative of Swiss Bank Corporation. During Streichenberg's chairmanship there was a debate over whether Euroclear should pay higher dividends to its shareholders. He took a pro-user stance, saying Euroclear's primary obligation was to lower the cost of the use of the system to the market and the size of the dividend should be considered in the light of the company's ability to lower fees. A member of the Euroclear board for 10 years from 1972.

Studer, Ernst – A member of the first Euroclear board after the sale of the system to its users in 1972, Studer represented Crédit Suisse. He was also a member of the board's executive committee.

Studer, Robert – Swiss banker and strong supporter of an advanced post-trade infrastructure for the Swiss banking sector. Studer made his career at Union Bank of Switzerland, which he joined in 1957. He was chief executive from 1988 to 1996 when he was appointed chairman. He was chairman until the reverse takeover of UBS by Swiss Bank Corporation in 1998.

Sucaet, Peter – A member of the Euroclear group management team; head of internal audit division. Contributed in 1996/97 to the case for Euroclear's separation from Morgan.

Tessler, Jeffrey – Appointed CEO of Clearstream International in December 2004 from The Bank of New York. Tessler began his career with the Irving Trust Co. in 1979, which merged with Bank of New York in 1988. As general manager of BoNY in Europe between 1993 and 2003, Tessler presided over a rapid expansion of the bank's securities servicing operation which saw its European staff expand to 4000 from 1000 employees. At Clearstream, Tessler has invested in client-focused innovation to be able better to compete with Euroclear Bank in the ICSD market.

Théodore, Jean-François – Appointed chairman and chief executive of Société des Bourses Françaises (SBF) in 1990, later holding the same positions at Euronext, the transnational exchange created in 2000. Théodore was a pivotal figure in the modernisation and restructuring of the French financial sector before the euro's introduction and in manoeuvrings to restructure the European post-trade sector afterwards. As chairman of Sicovam, the French CSD, from 1993 to 2000 Théodore approved its merger with Euroclear, paving the way for the development of the Euroclear group as a combination of ICSD and CSDs in a horizontal post-trade system. Became deputy chief executive of Euronext NYSE after the 2007 merger of the US and European exchange groups. See Chapter 9.2 for profile and role in France and Chapters 10 and 11 for role in shaping European post-trade sector.

Tumpel-Gugerell, Gertrude – Joined the executive board of the ECB in 2003 with responsibility for payment systems, human resources, budget and organisation. Gertrude Tumpel-Gugerell was previously vice governor of the Austrian National Bank. She began her central banking career as an economist with the national bank in 1975. After a spell as economic policy adviser to the finance minister between 1981 and 1984, she held various positions in the bank before becoming deputy governor in 1998. See Chapters 17.2–17.4.

Tupker, A. Chris – As chairman of Euroclear from March 2000 to end-July 2006, Chris Tupker oversaw the ICSD's transformation from a securities settlement provider mainly serving bond markets and operated under contract by Morgan Guaranty to the world's biggest, fully integrated, user-owned and user-governed provider of domestic and cross-border settlement services for bonds, equities and funds. He joined the Euroclear board in 1997, was one of Euroclear's negotiators on separation from Morgan and became Euroclear's first chairman without a company affiliation in 2002. Previously, Tupker combined work at Euroclear with the position of senior executive vice president of ABN AMRO Bank responsible for securities processing, IT, finance, custody, risk and compliance within the investment banking division, a post he held since 1997. Tupker's ABN AMRO career started in 1988 as managing director of ABN Securities (UK) Ltd. Before 1988, Tupker, who is a Canadian citizen, worked for 20 years at Scotia Mcleod Inc., a Canadian investment bank. He resigned as Euroclear chairman following his appointment as chairman of the LCH.Clearnet group in July 2006. See Chapters 11.1, 11.3, 13.1, 15.1, 15.5 and 15.6.

D'Ursel, Charles – Head of Morgan Guaranty's Brussels office who secured the support of the New York head office for Euroclear's creation. Count Charles d'Ursel was born into a Belgian diplomatic family and studied in Switzerland before working for the Belgian government and as a banker. He was appointed head of Morgan Guaranty's Brussels office in 1960 at a time of fast growing US investment in Belgium. D'Ursel ran Morgan's Belgian offices for 15 years. When he retired from Morgan in 1981 he was senior vice president of Morgan Guaranty International Finance Corp. and international adviser to Morgan Guaranty. See Chapters 3.1 and 3.2 for role in Euroclear's creation.

Vagliano, Alexander (aka Alec) – Head of Morgan Guaranty's international banking division in the 1970s, who hired Herschel Post to become Euroclear's commercial director. Vagliano was the Morgan representative on the Euroclear board from 1982 until 1983.

Van Nieuwenhove, Gérard – In charge of the operation of Euroclear in the 1970s, until 1978. Van Nieuwenhove joined the Brussels office of Morgan Guaranty as an auditor in 1965 and moved the securities department in 1966 where he participated in the early 'closings'. He was one of the team that helped create the Euroclear system in 1968. His memoir *The Euroclear Story*, completed in 1992, is one of the few extant accounts of Euroclear's early days. See Chapters 3.1 and 3.2.

Villiers, Theresa – Member of the European Parliament 1999 to 2005. A British Conservative and so a centre-right MEP, Villiers was rapporteur on Clearing and Settlement for the parliament's report on the second Commission communication of 2004 and as such opposed EU legislation.

Von Rosen, Rüdiger – Initiated the technical modernisation of the Frankfurt Stock Exchange in the early 1990s and oversaw the creation of Deutsche Börse AG as a holding company for the exchange and related entities. After being replaced by Werner Seifert in 1993, von Rosen became managing director and a board member of the Deutsches Aktieninstitut, a body to promote share ownership in Germany. Von Rosen was a Bundesbank official from 1974 to 1986 and worked for the Federation of German Stock Exchanges from 1986 to 1993, where he was executive vice chairman.

Walker, David (Sir) – Influential figure in UK and global capital markets from 1980s onwards. Walker was executive chairman of Morgan Stanley's European operations between 1994 and 2000, when he co-founded the European Securities Industry Users' Group (Esiug), later to become the European Securities Forum (ESF). Walker began his career in the UK Treasury in 1961; became an executive director of the Bank of England; was chairman of the Securities and Investments Board, the UK securities markets regulator between 1988 and 1992; and deputy chairman of UK bank Lloyds TSB for two years before joining Morgan Stanley in 1994. A G30 member, Sir David Walker has also been chairman of Liba, the London Investment Banking Association. He became senior adviser to Morgan Stanley International Ltd in January 2001 and has been a consistent advocate of European post-trade consolidation and a strong backer of a single user-owned CCP for Europe.

Weatherstone, Dennis (Sir) – Morgan chairman and CEO 1990 to end-1994 when he retired at 64 after a life-long career at the bank. Weatherstone, who worked his way up from foreign exchange trading through a series of senior management posts, was a member of the G30 steering committee that put in train the 1989 G30 report on clearing and settlement and later, with Rolf-E. Breuer, commissioned Morgan's 'Beyond G30' report. After Weatherstone's retirement, Morgan offloaded its post-trade servicing activities in its drive to become a big investment bank.

Weguelin, Richard – Active in setting up the Association of International Bond Dealers in 1968/69, Weguelin worked for Eurotrading, a specialist Eurobond trading house owned by a consortium of banks. He was a member of the five-strong steering committee that organised the first AIBD meeting.

Wicks, Nigel (Sir) – Chairman of Euroclear plc and Euroclear SA/NV since 1 August 2006, when he moved up from being deputy chairman to succeed Chris Tupker. Wicks was non-executive chairman of CRESTCo, the UK CSD, from May 2001 until its merger with Euroclear in 2002. After beginning his career with British Petroleum, Wicks was a member of the British civil service for 32 years. He was second permanent secretary and director of international finance at the UK Treasury from 1989 until 2000. As chairman of the EU's monetary committee in the 1990s, he played an important part in managing the successful introduction of the euro. After leaving the Treasury, Wicks was one of the Lamfalussy committee of 'wise men' in 2000 and 2001 and chairman of the UK's Committee on Standards in Public Life between March 2001 and April 2004. See Chapter 13.1 for profile and role in the merger of CREST with Euroclear, Chapter 14.1 on the Lamfalussy Committee, and Chapters 15.7 and 16.1 for subsequent role at Euroclear.

Wigley, Bob – Chairman of Europe, Middle East and Africa of Merrill Lynch, Wigley articulated the complaints of London-based investment banks about high European post-trade costs to the Commission in 2006. Wigley joined Merrill Lynch in 1996 after nearly 10 years at Morgan Grenfell. He started his career at British Gas before joining Arthur Andersen, first as a chartered accountant and then as a consultant.

Wilmers, Robert – Vice president and deputy general manager of Morgan Guaranty in Brussels from 1973 to 1978 with responsibility for Euroclear. Wilmers was the first of many able young US-based managers sent by Morgan in the US to run Euroclear. He oversaw Euroclear's recovery from Cedel's competitive onslaught in the early 1970s. An energetic and ambitious man, he later became a successful banker in Buffalo, New York State. See Chapter 4.3.

Winckler, Andrew – Senior independent director of CREST and adviser in merger talks with Euroclear in 2002. Moved to the City from the UK Treasury in the early 1980s, Winckler was chairman of UK financial services regulatory practice at Ernst & Young. He became a member of the Euroclear SA/NV board. Died in January 2007.

Woodruff, Richard – Executive director for finance and administration at Cedel in the early 1990s, Woodruff was one of six Clearstream managers suspended in May 2001 at the request of the Luxembourg authorities to facilitate their investigation of allegations of money laundering and other offences. The Luxembourg authorities announced in statements of July 2001 and November 2004 that there was no case to pursue.

Wright, David – As director of financial markets in the European Commission's directorate general for Internal Markets and Services, Wright has played a key role in pushing forward the EU's clearing and settlement agenda under Commissioners Bolkestein and McCreevy. An EU official since 1977, Wright, a UK national, became responsible for the Commission's financial markets policy in April 2000 and was a key figure in negotiations on the code of conduct.

Wymeersch, Eddy – Co-chairman of the joint CESR/ESCB expert group charged with drawing up standards for clearing and settlement in the EU, Eddy Wymeersch has been chairman of the Belgian financial regulator, the Banking, Finance and Insurance Commission (CBFA), since 2001. The group's inability to reach agreement on the standards did not stand in the way of Wymeersch's election as chairman of CESR, the Committee of European Securities Regulators, for two years from 1 February 2007.

Yassukovich, Stanislas – A prominent figure in international capital markets for more than 40 years, Yassukovich helped establish London as the leading centre for Eurobond trading while working for White Weld in the 1960s. He became managing director of the European Banking Company, a consortium bank founded in London in 1973. Yassukovich was chairman of Merrill Lynch Europe from 1985 to 1991, while also morphing into a City grandee as deputy chairman of the London Stock Exchange between 1986 and 1989 and chairman of the Securities Association, a regulatory body, from 1987 to 1991. He continued to hold numerous City positions into the 21st century.

Zeyen, Carlos – The Luxembourg deputy public prosecutor who assiduously pursued allegations against Clearstream and Lussi after they were published in the French press on 26 February 2001. Controversially, Zeyen met Werner Seifert on German territory on 11 May 2001 to gain his support for searches of Clearstream and its IT system. See Chapter 12.3.

Zoller, Fernand – One of six Clearstream managers suspended in May 2001 at the request of the Luxembourg authorities to facilitate their investigation of allegations of money laundering and other offences. The Luxembourg authorities announced in statements of July 2001 and November 2004 that there was no case to pursue. Zoller was the line manager at Cedel of Régis Hempel, the witness known as 'H' in the Clearstream affair.

Appendix D
Glossary of Technical Terms

Against payment settlement – A requirement that the delivery of securities be in exchange for assets of equal value, usually cash. Transactions may also settle on a 'free of payment' basis.

Agent – The party that acts on behalf, or upon request, of another party: as in agent bank.

Asset servicing – Services provided by an (I)CSD or a custodian in connection with settlement and/or safekeeping of securities: such as corporate actions, events, redemptions, etc.

Authentication – The methods used to verify the origin of a message or to verify the identity of a participant connected to a system and to confirm that a message has not been modified or replaced in transit.

Back-to-back transactions – A chain of transactions among three or more counterparties involving the purchase and sale of a single security for settlement on a single date. The most simple back-to-back trade is a pair of transactions in which one party agrees to purchase securities from a second party and then agrees to sell them to a third party.

Back office – The part of a firm that is responsible for post-trade activities.

Bankruptcy – The legal status of the company unable to pay creditors. Bankruptcy usually involves a formal court ruling. Securities issued by this company risk losing all their value.

Batch – The processing of a set of payment orders and/or securities transfer instructions at discrete intervals of time: for example, overnight.

Bearer security – A security where the owner is not registered in the books of the issuer or the registrar.

Beneficial ownership – The entitlement to receive some or all of the benefits of ownership of the security or other financial instrument: such as income, voting rights, power to transfer. Beneficial ownership is usually distinguished from legal ownership of a security or financial instrument.

Bond – Any interest-bearing or discounted security that normally obliges the issuer to pay the bondholder a contracted sum of money within a prescribed timeframe and to repay the principal amount of the debt.

Book-entry system – An accounting system that permits the transfer of claims (for example, the electronic transfer of securities) without the physical movement of paper documents or certificates.

Bridge – The name used for the automated interface or link between the ICSDs, Euroclear Bank and Clearstream Banking Luxembourg (formerly Cedel), that permits cross-systems settlement of a trade between a customer of one ICSD and a customer of the other ICSD. As used in electronic Bridge and Automated Daytime Bridge.

Broker – A firm that communicates bid and ask levels to potential principals and otherwise arranges transactions as agent for a fee without acting as counterparty in the transactions.

Broker-dealer – A person or firm acting sometimes as broker and sometimes as principal in securities transactions.

Bunds – German government bonds.

Business day – A day on which financial markets are open for business.

Cash dividends – Distribution of cash to shareholders in proportion to their equity holding.

Central bank money – Settlement is described as being in central bank money if payment moves directly and irrevocably between accounts on the books of the central bank.

central counterparty (CCP) – An entity that is the buyer to every seller and the seller to every buyer of a specified set of contracts or obligations: for example, those executed on a particular exchange.

Central Securities Depository (CSD) – An infrastructure that holds or controls the holding of physical or dematerialised financial instruments belonging to all, or a large proportion of, the investors in a particular securities market. The CSD effects the centralised transfer of ownership of such securities by entries on its books and records.

Chaining – Method used in certain transfer systems (mostly for securities) for processing instructions. It involves the manipulation of the sequence in which transfer instructions are processed to increase the number or value of transfers that may be settled with available funds and/or securities balances or with available credit or securities borrowing lines.

Clearing house – A central location or central processing mechanism through which financial institutions agree to exchange payment and/or securities settlement instructions or other financial obligations. The instructions then settle for assets exchanged at a designated time. In some cases, the clearing house may assume significant counterparty, financial or risk management responsibilities for the clearing system.

Clearing member – A member of the clearing house. All trades must be channelled through the clearing member. A direct clearing member is able to process its own obligations, as well as those of its customers.

Clearing or clearance – The comparison of the details of a transaction between parties prior to settlement. Sometimes, mainly historically, used to mean the final exchange of securities for cash on delivery.

Clearing system – A set of procedures whereby financial institutions present and exchange data and/or documents relating to cash and/or or securities transfers to other financial institutions at a single location: the clearing house. The procedures often also include a mechanism for the calculation of participants' bilateral and/or multilateral net positions, with a view to facilitating the settlement of their obligations on a net or net-net basis.

Closing – The procedures relating to the completion of a primary market issue on the closing date.

Closing date – The date on which a new issue's proceeds are paid to the borrower by the lead manager and securities, in temporary or definitive form, are delivered to the lead manager by the borrower.

Code of conduct – Agreement brokered by the European Commission and signed on 7 November 2006 by the chief executives of European securities trading and post-trade companies with the aim of offering market participants the freedom to choose their preferred provider of services separately at each layer of the value chain, comprising trading, clearing and settlement so that the concept of cross-border trading and settlement becomes redundant for transactions between EU member states.

Collateral – Assets pledged (for example, by credit institutions with central banks) as a guarantee for the repayment of loans, as well as assets sold (for example, to central banks by credit institutions) as part of repurchase agreements or repos.

Collateral management service – A centralised service that may handle any of a variety of collateral-related functions for a client firm, including valuation of collateral, confirmation of valuations with counterparties, optimisation of collateral usage and transfer of collateral.

Collateral pool – Assets owned by members of payment and/or settlement systems that are collectively available within the system to enable the members to collateralise cash or securities movements.

Commercial bank money – Settlement is described as being commercial bank money if the payment moves between the accounts of banks (in contrast to central bank money).

Commercial paper – A short-term note or draft of a government, bank or corporation, issued at a discount or on an interest-bearing basis.

Common Communications Interface (CCI) – In the context of Euroclear's 'domestic market for Europe' initiative, the communication interface that will provide users with a single access to all Euroclear group services. It will enable clients to send instructions and receive reports in industry standard formats using a variety of networks.

Common depositories – The banks which hold securities for Euroclear Bank and Clearstream Banking Luxembourg.

Confirmation process – The procedure for verifying trade details with a counterparty.

Conflict of laws – Where two or more sets of laws that appropriately apply to a particular transaction require different results.

Convertible bonds – a bond that can be converted into other securities.

Convertible shares – common or ordinary shares that can be converted into other securities at a designated rate at the option of the holder.

Corporate action – All of the events which may occur during the life span of the security. Certain corporate actions, such as coupon payments, take place on fixed dates. Others occur on an ad-hoc basis, such as stock splits, rights issues, tender offers, etc.

Correspondent Central Banking Model (CCBM) – A mechanism established by the European System of Central Banks (ESCB) with the aim of enabling counterparties to use securities in a cross-border context. In the CCBM, national central banks act as custodians for one another. This means each national central bank holds a securities account for each of the other national central banks as well as for the ECB.

Cost plus – A tariff set at a level which covers running costs, plus a reasonable margin.

Counterparty – The opposite party to a financial transaction: for example, the other party in any transaction with the central bank.

Coupon – In its original form, a certificate attached to a bearer security, and which evidenced the interest due on a specified date. The holder had to present the coupon to a paying agent to claim payment of interest due.

More generally, the term coupon is often used interchangeably with interest, and usually refers to the nominal interest a bond pays. Expressed as a percentage of the principal value of the fixed interest security, the coupon is the interest the borrower promises to pay the holder. In the Eurobond market, the coupon was generally payable annually, semi-annually or in some cases quarterly, depending on the type of security.

Cross-border settlement – A settlement that takes place in a country other than the country in which one trade counterparty or both are located.

Cross-border trade – A trade between counterparties located in different countries.

Cross-system settlement – A settlement of a trade that is effected through a link between two separate securities settlement systems.

Custodian – The party that safekeeps and administers assets on behalf of the owner: as in custodian bank.

Custody – Safe keeping and administration of securities and financial instruments on behalf of others.

Dealer – A firm that enters into a transaction as a counterparty on both sides of the market in one or more products.

Default – Failure to complete a cash or securities transfer according to its terms for reasons that are not technical or temporary, usually as a result of bankruptcy. Default is usually distinguished from a failed transaction.

Delivery – The final transfer of a security or financial instrument.

Delivery versus payment or DvP – A mechanism in an exchange-for-value settlement system which ensures that the final transfer of assets such as securities or other financial instruments occurs if, and only if, the final transfer of the counterparty's equivalent asset, or assets, occurs. In a 1992 report, the Committee on Payment and Settlement Systems (CPSS) of the Group of 10 leading financially important countries defined three systems of DvP:

- In Model 1 DvP systems transfer instructions for both securities and cash are settled on a trade-by-trade (gross) basis, with final transfer of the securities from the seller to the buyer (delivery) occurring at the same time as final transfer of cash from the buyer to the seller (payment);
- In Model 2 DvP systems securities transfer instructions are settled on a gross basis with final transfer of securities from the seller to the buyer (delivery) occurring throughout the processing cycle, but cash transfer instructions are settled on a net basis, with final transfer of cash from the buyer to the seller (payment) occurring at the end of the processing cycle;
- In Model 3 DvP systems transfer instructions for both securities and cash are settled on a net basis, with final transfers of both securities and cash occurring at the end of the processing cycle.

Dematerialisation – The elimination of physical securities or documents of title that represent ownership of securities so that securities exist only as accounting records.

Derivative – A financial contract, the value of which depends on the value of one or more underlying reference assets, rates or indices. For analytical purposes, all derivatives contracts can be divided into basic building blocks of forward contracts, options or combinations thereof.

DG Competition or DG Comp – The directorate general of the European Commission responsible for enforcing EU competition law.

DG Markt – Brussels shorthand for the directorate general of the European Commission responsible for the Internal Market.

Directive – A European Union law applied with binding force throughout the EU but where it is left to the member state to decide the form and methods necessary to achieve the desired result.

Discount – Price expressed as the number of percentage points below par: for example, a discount price of 3% equals a price of 97 when par is 100.

Distribution – An event that occurs when the issuer of a security delivers a particular benefit or resource (for example, cash, securities or rights) to a holder of the security and where the underlying holding, which gave rise to the distribution, is unchanged by the event. The most obvious example is a cash dividend, where the shareholder receives cash or coupons but the original shareholding is unaffected.

Domestic service package – In the context of Euroclear's 'domestic market for Europe' initiative, one of the two service levels that Euroclear will offer. This package will continue to provide those services which are currently available in each CSD of the group and which are essential for meeting the basic needs of holders and traders in the securities in any of the local markets covered by the Euroclear group.

Ecofin – The formation of the European Union's Council of Ministers comprising economic and finance ministers from all the EU's member states that meets approximately once a month.

Effective date – The first date on which transactions involving a particular security may settle.

Employment Retirement Securities Act (ERISA) – US legislation of 1974 which led to the growth of defined contribution pension funds that built up a pool of capital, some of which was invested abroad. As in ERISA funds.

Equity – Ownership interest in a corporation in the form of common stock or preferred stock. The securities representing ownership of the stake can be quoted or listed shares traded on a stock exchange, unquoted or unlisted shares and other forms of equity. Equities form the risk bearing part of the company's capital. They usually produce income in the form of dividends.

Escrow account – an account holding money, securities, or other property or instruments held by a third party until the conditions for contract are met.

Euclid – Euroclear's proprietary information and communications system.

Euro – The European single currency: usually expressed in lower case as 'euro' or by the symbol €.

Eurobond – In its 1960s meaning, a bond issued by a borrower outside its own country that may be denominated in a currency foreign to the borrower or to the purchaser, or both, and is not subject to withholding tax or other legislation by the host country, in whose currency the bond is issued.

Euro certificates of deposit (ECD) – The certificate is evidence of the deposit made with the bank, which will be redeemed on the maturity date with interest. The difference between a certificate of deposit and a normal deposit with a bank is that a certificate of deposit is an instrument which can be sold on in the money markets to other investors.

Euroclear market – A market in which the local CSD is part of the Euroclear group.

Euroclear Settlement for Euronext-zone Securities (ESES) – In the context of Euroclear's 'domestic market for Europe' initiative, the intermediate solution which will provide a single system shared by the Euronext-zone CSDs: Euroclear Belgium, Euroclear France and Euroclear Nederland, and will be available to all market participants with Euroclear accounts.

Euro-commercial paper (ECP) – Borrowing in the form of short-term paper issued by companies. Usually redeemable at par value and pays no interest. Hence it is issued and traded at a discount.

Euronext-zone securities – Securities that are listed on any stock exchange(s) that is part of Euronext and are primarily deposited in the Belgian, Dutch or French CSD.

European Central Bank (ECB) – The central bank of the eurozone, in charge of monetary policy for the countries that use the euro currency. It has legal personality under European Community law. It ensures that the tasks conferred on the Eurosystem and the ESCB are implemented either by its own activities or those of the national central banks, pursuant to the Statute of the European System of Central Banks and of the European Central Bank.

European currency unit (ECU) – A composite currency, the value of which was determined on the basis of a basket of European currencies. It was designed as a unit of account for the European monetary system, which began operating in 1979. Perceived as a forerunner of the euro.

European Pre-issuance Messaging (EPIM) – Same-day security code creation and issuance services.

European System of Central Banks (ESCB) – Comprises the ECB and central banks of all EU member states, whether or not they have adopted the euro.

Eurosystem – Comprises the ECB and the central banks of those countries that have adopted the euro. The Eurosystem and the ESCB coexist as long as there are EU member states outside the euro area.

Fail – A failure to settle a securities transaction on the contractual settlement date, usually because of technical or temporary asset-delivery difficulties. Fail is usually distinguished from default. Also called a failed transaction.

Final maturity – Repayment in full of a debt security, investment trust or a preferred stock issue, at stated maturity.

Final settlement – The discharge of an obligation by a transfer of funds and a transfer of securities that become irrevocable and unconditional.

Fixed income security – An investment that provides a return in the form of fixed periodic payments and eventual return of principal at maturity. Unlike a variable income security, where payments change based on some underlying measure such as short-term interest rates, fixed income securities payments are known in advance.

Free of payment delivery or FOP – Delivery of securities with no corresponding payment of funds. The delivery of securities becomes legally effective without the transfer of cash. Transactions may also settle on an against-payment basis.

Front office – A firm's trading unit and other areas that are responsible for developing and managing relationships with counterparties.

Full service package – In the context of Euroclear's 'domestic market for Europe' initiative, this is one of the two service levels that Euroclear will offer. This package will provide the range of services currently offered by Euroclear Bank, including settlement, safe keeping, integrated collateral management, securities lending and borrowing, and money transfer and related banking services.

Fungible – A concept that characterises the method of holding securities by a CSD or other financial intermediary in which each of a number of issues of physical or dematerialised securities are held in separate fungible pools. No owner has the rights to any particular physical or dematerialised security in a particular pool, but has a right to such an amount of physical or dematerialised securities as shown in its account with a CSD or other financial intermediary. The opposite of unfungible.

Gilts or gilt edged stock – Government securities issued by the United Kingdom.

Global (as in global instrument or bond) – A certificate, often temporary, representing a whole issue. Created to control the primary market distribution of an issue of securities in compliance with selling restrictions in certain jurisdictions or else because definitive bond certificates are not immediately available.

Global custodian – A bank that provides its customers with custody services in respect of securities traded and settled not only in the country in which the custodian is located, but also in numerous other countries throughout the world.

Global Master Repurchase Agreement (GMRA) – Introduced in November 1992 by the International Securities Market Association (ISMA) in conjunction with the Public Securities Association (PSA) of the US to standardise repo documentation across fragmented financial markets.

Group securities – In the Euroclear context, securities for which a Euroclear group CSD acts as a primary or local-market CSD. The term does not relate to Euroclear Bank, the group's ICSD.

Herstatt – German bank that foundered after massive currency speculation went wrong. The German authorities shut the bank at the end of a German banking day in June 1974 while markets in the US and elsewhere were still trading, leaving the dollar leg of some of its foreign exchange contracts unpaid. The affected counterparties were unable to recover the funds owing to them, creating the concept of Herstatt or principal risk (see also: Risk categories).

Horizontal integration – Where clearing and settlement activities are separately owned and controlled from securities trading activity but where one or all of these three activities are integrated with those of other providers according to function. Horizontal integration is suited to consolidating infrastructure providers across national borders to achieve economies of scale.

Hub and Spokes – A Euroclear concept, articulated in 1999, to harness the infrastructure of Europe's two ICSDs and its 30 or so national CSDs so that cross-border investors could have access to all settlement services through a single point of entry.

(I)CSD – Short form for either an ICSD or a CSD, or both.

Immobilisation – Placement of physical certificates for securities and financial instruments in a central securities depository so that subsequent transfers can be made by book entry, that is, by debits from and credits to holders' accounts at the depository.

Infrastructure service provider – The party that provides, through common membership, services to create a fair and open process for the execution of transactions between trading parties, and the creation of clearing and/or settlement obligations.

Integrated settlement model – Securities settlement systems (SSSs) that settle transactions directly in their own system without the constant involvement of their local central bank's payments system. An interface is used at the request of participants when they want to transfer cash into the SSS or back to the payments system. An example of an integrated settlement model is the relationship between Euroclear France and the French central bank's real-time gross settlement system (RTGS). Contrasts with the interfaced model.

Interfaced settlement model – Transactions are settled using an interface between the local central bank's payments system and the SSS. As two systems are involved, they constantly communicate with each other. The securities leg is settled in the SSS, while the cash leg is settled in the central bank's RTGS. Examples of interfaced settlement models are the relationships between Monte Titoli, and New BIREL in Italy, and between Interbolsa and SPGT in Portugal.

Intermediary – The party that provides services to investors relating to financial products. These services may include some or all of provision of information and advice on products, placement of investment orders, transmission of payment, settlement, custody of assets, and the administration of rights and benefits.

Internalisation – When settlement takes place on the books of a settlement infrastructure service provider or an agent bank. Once internalised settlement has happened, the transaction is complete and final, and no other settlement providers will play any part in settling that transaction, including the home (I)CSD of the security in the transaction settled. Internalisation reduces the number of settlement intermediaries and by doing so, reduces the costs for the investor. There are no public statistics available about the level of internalisation in European markets.

International Central Securities Depository (ICSD) – An entity which settles trades in international securities and cross-border transactions in various domestic securities. ICSDs also hold and administer securities or other financial assets, are involved with the issuance of new securities and enable transactions to be processed by book entry. Europe's two large ICSDs – Euroclear Bank and Clearstream Banking Luxembourg (formerly Cedel) – were set up in 1968 and 1970 respectively to settle Eurobonds.

international securities identification number (ISIN) – A 12-digit security identification code. Its registration and maintenance authority is ANNA, the Association of National Numbering Agencies.

International Standards Organisation (ISO) – A worldwide federation of national standards bodies from more than 146 countries, one from each country. ISO is a non-governmental organisation established in 1947. Its mission is to promote development of standardisation and related activities in the world with a view to facilitating the international exchange of goods and services, and to developing cooperation in the spheres of intellectual, scientific, technological and economic activity.

Investment Services Directive (ISD) – European Union law of 1993 that was intended to create a single capital market for Europe but had a limited impact only.

Interoperability – Where one infrastructure service provider creates a business relationship with another infrastructure service provider, horizontally or between another layer of the capital market. Interoperability requires technical compatibility between systems, but can only take effect where commercial agreements have been concluded between the schemes concerned. Interoperability is different from a 'silo' structure.

Intraday – During the business day.

Intraday liquidity – Funds which can be accessed during the business day, usually to enable financial institutions to make payments in real time.

initial public offering (IPO) – The first time a company makes its shares available for sale to the public.

Irrevocable transfer – Transfer which cannot be revoked by the transferor.

Issuer – The entity, which is obligated on a security or other financial instrument. For example, a corporation or government having the authority to issue and sell a security.

Issue price – Initial issue price of a financial instrument.

issuing and paying agent (IPA) – Acts on behalf of the issuer of securities in distributing the securities and in realising the proceeds thereof for the benefit of the issuer. Also, on behalf of an issuer an IPA makes payments of dividends, coupons and the like to holders of securities.

ISO 15022 – Sets the principles necessary to provide different communities of market participants and users with the tools to design message types to support specific information flows. These tools consist of a set of syntax and message design rules, a dictionary of data fields and a catalogue for present and future messages built by the industry.

ISO 20022 financial services – A UNIversal Financial Industry message scheme (Unifi). A newly published standard, which provides the usage of a common platform for the development of messages. A successor to ISO 15022.

Jobber – a term for a market maker used on the London Stock Exchange before Big Bang in October 1986.

Legal ownership – Recognition in law as the owner of a security or financial instrument. It is usually represented by holding 'legal title' and may differ from beneficial ownership.

Links – Between two securities settlement systems, links consist of all the procedures and arrangements needed for the transfer of securities between the two SSSs through a book entry process.

Local agent or custodian – A custodian bank that provides settlement and custody services for securities traded and settled in one or more countries to counterparties and settlement intermediaries located in other countries.

London InterBank Offered Rate (LIBOR) – An interest rate at which banks can borrow funds from other banks in the London interbank market. The LIBOR is fixed on a daily basis by the British Bankers' Association and is derived from a filtered average of the world's most creditworthy banks' interbank deposit rates for larger loans with maturities between overnight and one full year.

Mandatory cash distribution – When the issuer of a security or its chosen agent delivers a cash benefit to holders. The event generally occurs without any action required on the part of the security's holder.

Mandatory corporate action – An event that occurs without any action required on the part of the security's holder. It may involve the issuance of additional lots of securities or certain payments.

Margin call – A process whereby counterparties are required to supply additional securities or cash in cases where collateral value falls below a certain level.

Market maker – Makes a market in one or more specific financial instruments and often functions within an organised market such as a stock exchange. To make a market in an instrument, a market maker must extend a continuous offer to buy or sell the financial instruments with any qualified counterparty at a price quoted by the market maker without respect to the identity of the qualified counterparty. May frequently adjust or revise the published quote depending on market conditions, but may be prohibited from withdrawing it.

Markets in Financial Instruments Directive (MiFID) – European Union legislation taking effect in November 2007, MiFID comprehensively revises the 1993 Investment Services Directive (ISD), with the aim of further integrating and boosting competition in EU financial markets.

Matching – The process for comparing the trade or settlement details provided by counterparties to ensure that they agree with respect to the terms of the transaction. Also called comparison checking.

Medium-term notes – Negotiable debt instruments offered under a programme agreement through one or more dealers, upon request of the issuer. The programme defines the terms and conditions of the notes.

Money market instruments – Financial instruments designated at issuance as such, with a short-term life, usually 12 months or less: for example, Treasury bills, commercial paper.

Net settlement system – A settlement system in which final settlement of transfer instructions occurs on a net basis at one or more discrete pre-specified times during the processing day.

Netting – An agreed offsetting of positions or obligations by trading partners or participants. Netting reduces a large number of gross positions or obligations to a smaller number of net obligations or positions and can sharply reduce settlement volumes.

Non-group securities – In the Euroclear context, all securities other than group securities. These are mainly Eurobonds deposited in the common depositories and held on the books of Euroclear Bank and other international bonds and equities held by Euroclear Bank, directly or across its subcustodian network.

Notary – The function in a CSD of keeping records for issuers. In some countries, CSDs are the public notaries for securities because the names of the account holders on their electronic systems are the definitive record of title.

Obligation Assimable de Trésor (OAT) – French government debt instrument. OATs are fungible securities issued with maturities of seven to 50 years, generally by auction, according to an annual calendar published in advance.

Open market operation – Executed on the initiative of a central bank in its financial market to implement monetary policy. Reverse transactions are the Eurosystem's main open market instrument.

Option – A contract giving the holder the right, but not the obligation, to buy (call) or sell (put) a specified underlying asset at a pre-arranged price at either a fixed point in the future (European-style options) or at a time chosen by the holder up to maturity (American-style options). The seller of the option must meet the obligations placed on him or her by the buyer: that is to deliver (call) or receive (put) the underlying asset at the buyer's instruction.

Over the counter – Market outside an organised exchange in which transactions are conducted through a telephone or computer network connecting the market participants.

Paying agent – An institution that, acting on behalf of the issuer, makes payments to holders of securities.

Plain vanilla – Colloquial expression to describe a straightforward, uncomplicated securities issue, often with reference to bonds and Eurobonds.

Premium – Price expressed as the number of percentage points above par: for example, a premium of 3% equals a price of 103 where par is 100.

Principal – A party to a transaction that acts on its own behalf. In acting as a principal, a firm is buying or selling, or lending or borrowing securities from its own account, expecting to make a profit.

Proxy – Written power of attorney given by shareholders of a corporation, authorising a specific vote on their behalf at corporate meetings.

Real time – The processing of instructions instantaneously on settlement date.

Real Time Gross Settlement system (RTGS) – Settlement system in which occurs the continuous or real-time settlement of cash or securities transfers individually on a transaction-by-transaction basis without netting.

Redenomination – Event by which the currency unit of a debt is restated.

Registrar – Institution responsible for keeping track of the owners of securities.

Registration – The listing of ownership of securities in the records of the issuer or its transfer agent or registrar.

Regulation – In the context of the European Union, a uniform EU law applied with binding force throughout the EU.

Regulator – A government agency, or a self-regulated body, that sets the rules for the regulation of the market, as well as the relationship between the different parties in the market.

Regulatory impact assessment (RIA) – A process, carried out by the European Commission, to evaluate the regulatory costs and benefits of proposed legislation. The RIA forms part of the European Union's efforts for better regulation.

Remote access (to a Securities Settlement System) – The facility for an SSS in one country (the 'home country') to become a direct participant in an SSS established in another country (the 'host country') and, for that purpose, to have a securities account in its own name with the SSS in the host country.

Remote participant – A participant in a transfer system, which has neither its head office nor any of its branches located in the country where the transfer system is based.

Repo or sale and repurchase agreement – Contract to sell and subsequently repurchase securities at a specified date and price. It involves a cash loan against a guarantee in securities, full ownership of which is transferred, with a firm commitment that the seller will repurchase the securities and reimburse the cash at an agreed price and date. At the initiation of the transaction, the seller is the securities provider and the buyer is the cash lender. At the maturity of the transaction, remuneration – the accrued interest – is usually paid to the cash lender.

Reverse transaction – In the eurozone, an operation whereby the national central bank buys or sells assets under a repurchase agreement or conducts credit operations against collateral.

Risk – Categories include:

- Credit risk: The risk that the counterparty does not settle an obligation for full value, either when due or at any time thereafter. In the former case, the risk can take the form of replacement cost risk, in the latter case it becomes principal risk (see below).
- Custody risk: The risk of loss of securities held in custody, occasioned by the insolvency, negligence or fraudulent action of the entity safekeeping the securities.
- Interest rate risk: The risk of gain or loss as a result of movements in interest rates.
- Legal risk: The risk of loss because of the unexpected application of a law or regulation, or because a contract cannot be forced.
- Liquidity risk: The risk that a counterparty does not settle an obligation for full value when due, but only at some unspecified time thereafter.
- Market price or position risk: Where losses can arise from movements in the prices of securities held for trading purposes. More usually associated with trading.
- Operational risk: The risk of human error or a breakdown of some component of the hardware, software or communication system, which is crucial to settlement.
- Pipeline liquidity risk: Identified in Euroclear's 1993 'Beyond G30' report and particularly associated with the complexity of cross-border settlement. The risk associated with delays in the settlement pipeline arising from gaps in time between the processing cycles of different CSDs and between those of CSDs and their national payment systems.
- Principal risk: The risk that a party will lose the full value involved in the transaction. In the settlement process, this term is typically associated with exchange-for-value transactions, where there is a lag between the final settlement of the various legs of a transaction. Sometimes called Herstatt risk, with reference to the impact on foreign exchange markets of the 1974 German bank collapse.
- Replacement cost risk: The risk that an investor will lose the benefit of its bargain on an executed trade if its counterparty defaults on its delivery or payment obligation and fails to cure the default. The magnitude of the credit risk is the difference at any time between the market price of the security and the contract price.

Rolling settlement – In a rolling settlement environment, trades settle on all business days of the week after a standardised delay between trade date and settlement date, such as $T + 3$. Rolling settlement, which was one of the recommendations in the 1989 G30 report, limits the number of outstanding trades, thus reducing market exposure. Contrasts with the 'account day' settlement cycle by which securities settle on or after a specified account day, as was the case with the fortnightly account period used by the London Stock Exchange until 1994.

Safe keeping – Storage of physically evidenced securities in a vault.

Securities lending and borrowing – The lending of securities in exchange for a fee. Can involve transferring full ownership of securities with or without a guarantee or a firm commitment that the seller will repurchase the securities at an agreed price and date. Offered by banks, such as custodians, and ICSDs. Securities lending is mostly facilitated by CSDs, but not offered directly by them.

Securities settlement system or SSS – A system which permits the holding and transfer of securities, either free of payment (FOP) or against payment (delivery versus payment or DvP).

Security – An instrument that signifies an ownership position in a corporation, a credit relationship with a corporation or governmental body, or other rights to ownership.

Settlement – The completion of a transaction wherein the seller transfers securities to the buyer and the buyer transfers money to the seller. The settlement may be final or provisional.

Settlement agent – The party that provides settlement, custody, and accounting services for its own or someone else's assets.

Settlement date – The date on which a transaction is settled. A settlement may either take place on the same day as the trade (same day settlement) or on one or several days after the trade – the settlement date is specified as a precise number of business days after the trade date.

Settlement interval – The amount of time that elapses between the trade date and the settlement date. Typically measured relative to the trade date: for example, if three days elapse, the settlement interval is $T + 3$.

Settlement infrastructure service provider – An ICSD or CSD.

SIBOS – An annual conference, exhibition and networking event organised by SWIFT for the financial services industry. Has long since outgrown its origins (and acronym) as the SWIFT International Banking Operations Seminar.

Silo – Result of exclusive vertical integration, often in one infrastructure service provider corporate entity, encompassing all aspects along the value chain from trading, through clearing and/or central counterparty clearing to settlement. Especially in a cross-border context, a silo or vertical silo can be anti-competitive if it refuses access to its services at competitive and transparent rates to other service providers.

Single platform – In the context of Euroclear's 'domestic market for Europe' initiative, the long-term solution which will provide a system shared by all group (I)CSDs and available to all Euroclear group participants. Also referred to as the Euroclear single platform.

Single Settlement Engine (SSE) – In the context of Euroclear's 'domestic market for Europe' initiative, the SSE is the first building block of the single platform. It concentrates on the core settlement functions: the positioning and booking of cash and security transfers.

Society for Worldwide Interbank Financial Telecommunication (SWIFT) – A co-operative organisation created and owned by banks that operates a network which facilitates the exchange of payment and other financial messages between financial institutions, including broker-dealers and securities companies, throughout the world. A SWIFT payment message is an instruction to transfer funds. The exchange of funds or settlement subsequently takes place over a payment system or through corresponding banking relationships.

Spaghetti – A system, mooted in the late 1990s, of bilateral links between CSDs and ICSDs to overcome the problems of cross-border settlement. Each national settlement system would act as a hub for its users by establishing bilateral links with other national CSDs. It would be through these bilateral links that settlement, custody and collateral services would be offered for cross-border securities transactions. The Spaghetti model would enable local users to access just their national CSD to settle deals in both international and domestic securities. Its drawback was that it would require many links to work.

Special Drawing Right (SDR) – A composite currency unit designed by the International Monetary Fund, and based upon a standard basket system of valuation.

Stamp duty or tax – A tax in the form of the cost of stamps which have to be affixed to legal documents such as certificates, receipts and the like.

Stock distribution – The issuer of the security or its chosen agent delivers a security benefit to holders of the security.

Stock exchange – A corporation or mutual organisation which provides the facilities for stockbrokers to trade company shares and other financial instruments in the secondary market. Stock exchanges also provide facilities for the issuance of new securities.

Straight-Through Processing (STP) – The capture of trade details directly from front-end trading systems and complete automated processing of confirmations and settlement instructions without the need for manual intervention in rekeying or reformatting data.

Street lending – Service offered by some agent banks which lend clients' securities to third parties with the aim of making money for them. Qualitatively different from the securities lending and borrowing programmes of the ICSDs which exist to increase settlement efficiency and prevent transactions failing.

Sub-custodian – In cases where one custodian, such as a global custodian, holds its securities through another custodian, such as a local custodian, the latter is known as a sub-custodian.

Systemic risk – The risk that the inability of one institution to meet its obligations when due will cause other institutions to be unable to meet their obligations when due. Such a failure may cause significant liquidity or credit problems, and, as a result, might threaten the stability of financial markets.

Target2-Securities (T2S) – Securities settlement service proposed by the ECB for the eurozone and the subject of a consultation with industry and users before a decision on its development phase, expected early in 2008. Described by the ECB as a 'common technical service' for CSDs providing harmonised IT facilities that would effect DvP settlement for securities against central bank money. CSDs would maintain their relationships with intermediaries, investors and issuers and continue to handle corporate actions and other asset servicing and custody functions, as well as the notary function of keeping records for issuers. T2S would be fully owned and operated by the Eurosystem.

Trade date – The date on which a trade is executed.

Transfer agent – Companies that have publicly traded securities typically use transfer agents to keep track of the individuals and entities that own their stocks and bonds. Most transfer agents are banks or trust companies, but sometimes a company acts as its own transfer agent.

Treasury bill – A short-term debt obligation backed by a government with a maturity of less than one year.

Triparty repo – A neutral, third-party service provider, such as a custodian bank or an (I)CSD, is engaged to take on all responsibilities for monitoring and administering collateral throughout the life cycle of a repo transaction that has been agreed bilaterally between two counterparties.

Value date – The day on which payment is due to be credited to the receiving participant in the payments system. The day of value for the receiving participant's customer may or may not be the same day, depending on specific arrangements and local practice.

Vault – The protected warehouse in which physical documents and/or certificates are stored.

Verification – The process of comparing and, if necessary, reconciling discrepancies in the transaction or settlement details which is commonly handled at or close to the point of trade. Verification covers issues such as price, quantity and settlement date of the trade and is preliminary to, rather than part of, clearing and settlement.

Voluntary corporate action – An event in which holders of a security need to take action if the event is to affect their holdings. The issuing company or its agent informs all holders of the event that is about to take place. If the holder takes no action, its holdings are unaffected by the event.

Warrants – Financial instruments which permit holders to purchase a specified amount of a financial instrument, commodity, currency or other asset during a specified period at a specified price.

Withholding tax – A tax on income deducted at source, which a paying agent is legally obliged to deduct from its payments of interest on deposits, securities or similar financial instruments.

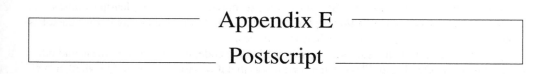

Appendix E

Postscript

No sooner was the main text of Plumbers and Visionaries despatched to the publisher in August 2007 than the world financial system was hit by a dramatic credit crunch.

Although aftershocks cannot be ruled out, the securities settlement infrastructure has been seen to cope successfully with the greatly increased volatility and massive trading volumes that at times accompanied the turbulence on financial markets.

The scale of the challenge was illustrated by trading volumes on the London Stock Exchange during August, when on three separate days more than one million trades were transacted. The record of around 1.25 million was sharply up on the previous high of 700 000 trades in February 2007. The 50 000 average daily trades conducted on the exchange's electronic market before the introduction of CCP clearing in 2001 appear tiny by comparison.

That such volumes were settled bears witness to the importance of CCPs and their role in reducing a large gross volume of trades to much smaller amounts by netting. It also vindicates the big investment by ICSDs and CSDs in real-time settlement and delivery versus payment (DvP) during the decade and a half after the global stock market crash of 1987, as well as the vigilance of supervisors and central bankers who called for these developments.

Inevitably, the financial upheavals of 2007 will have lessons for settlement providers. One of the clearest is the importance of continued investment in capacity. The volumes of August may prove to be exceptional. But the implementation of MiFID, with its promise of greater competition among trading platforms and the introduction of still faster trading systems that can handle trades in just a few milliseconds, show a potential for continued strong growth of volumes in the future.

In the European context, this is a world where cooperation and, perhaps eventually, consolidation among infrastructure providers is back on the agenda. Some of the credit goes to the industry code of conduct, brokered by the Commission.

By contrast, T2S, the European Central Bank's plan to insource the core settlement functions of the eurozone's CSDs to its own securities settlement platform from 2013, hit choppy waters during the summer and autumn of 2007. In successive meetings, the group of industry representatives providing advice on user requirements found difficulty reaching consensus on important issues. The ECB has put back until mid-2008 the point at which its governing council will decide to launch the development stage of the project. However, for reasons of prestige, if none other, it is unlikely the project will be abandoned.

The late-June agreement of the securities industry to the second part of the code has prompted action. Several requests for access and interoperability links have been made public since infrastructure providers and exchanges agreed this important element of the code.

In August, LCH.Clearnet issued formal requests to both Deutsche Börse and Borsa Italiana for full interoperability with their respective CCPs, Eurex Clearing and Cassa di Compensazione e Garanzia, to enable users of the German and Italian markets to consolidate at LCH.Clearnet in London the clearing of cash equities traded on Deutsche Börse, Borsa Italiana, the LSE and virt-x. A few weeks later, Eurex Clearing AG and Clearstream applied for access to and interoperability with the LSE and Euronext markets as well as clearing houses and settlement providers in the UK, France, the Netherlands, Belgium and Portugal. Euroclear has asked for a feed from Eurex to settle German equities.

When MOG, the Commission's group monitoring the code, met to consider these and other developments in October 2007 the general view was that it was too early to judge whether such applications presaged the successful conclusion of access and interoperability agreements.

The LCH.Clearnet and Eurex moves had a whiff of two long-standing rivals testing each others' readiness to comply with the code. By contrast, September's news that SIS x-clear and Eurex Clearing were seeking mutual access to clear equities on London's virt-x exchange and the Frankfurt stock exchange and also plan to create a mutual interoperable link will build on existing ties between their respective owners. Contacts on this specific issue started very soon after the signing of the code, at the end of 2006.

The code of conduct appears to be influencing the structure of Europe's securities trading and post-trade markets in other ways. Taken at face value, it should render obsolete the creation of exclusive vertical silos linking trading, clearing and settlement. That may prove to be the case. But paradoxically, it has also given a new lease of life to vertical integration.

Thus, in September, the banks owning Switzerland's SWX Group, SIS and Telekurs agreed to merge the companies to bring the country's exchange, clearing, settlement and payment systems under one roof in a user-owned, user-governed holding company. In insisting that the various business areas would retain their entrepreneurial independence, the companies signalled that vertical integration did not mean the creation of an exclusive silo in this case.

The merger of Borsa Italiana with the London Stock Exchange can be seen in a similar light. The Italian clearing and settlement infrastructures have become part of the LSE group with the result that the LSE, long the advocate of horizontal consolidation, joins the ranks of vertical integrators.

Developments at the LSE also underlined how far ownership changes and consolidation among securities infrastructures have become global issues. On 20 August, Nasdaq put its LSE stake – at that point 31% – up for sale to be better able to pursue the Nordic exchange group, OMX. A month later, a confusing bidding war for OMX between Nasdaq, the state-owned Borse Dubai and the Qatar Investment Authority left Borse Dubai with a deal that promised it 19.9% in the combined Nasdaq/OMX group. The wheeling and dealing left about 35% of the LSE in the hands of the two Gulf rivals.

The ICSDs have, in the meantime, extended their reach into new markets and new regions. Building on a memorandum of understanding of April 2007 between Euroclear SA/NV and the National Depository Center (NDC) of Russia, Euroclear Bank and NDC agreed in October to allow qualified members of NDC to settle transactions and safekeep international securities by way of NDC's account with the Euroclear ICSD.

Marking its entry into a new market segment, Euroclear Bank also announced it would launch an exposure-management service for over-the-counter (OTC) derivatives trades before the end of 2007. The ICSD's 'DerivManager' service, developed in close cooperation with brokers and financial intermediaries, will provide trade matching and daily portfolio reconciliations between counterparties, helping them to manage exposures arising from OTC derivatives transactions. This niche product should bring increased automation and reduced risk in a fast-growing market segment saddled with a large manual workload and matching efficiency rates as low as 60%.

Greater automation and more straight-through processing (STP) is the philosophy behind Clearstream Banking Luxembourg's Central Facility for Funds, designed to provide

DvP settlement of funds between distributors, custodians and transfer agents in markets – notably Luxembourg and Dublin - where transfer agents issue and redeem units on behalf of funds.

CFF was launched in Luxembourg in March 2007 as a 'one-stop shop' with open architecture so that different order-routing systems could connect to the platform. Schroder Investment Management (Luxembourg) and Pictet & Cie (Europe) piloted the venture. In September, 11 financial institutions, including JP Morgan, BNP Paribas Luxembourg and UBS Fund Services, joined amid projections that CFF could produce savings of up to €300 million a year in European markets where transfer agents and similar service providers handle settlement of investment funds.

Of greater significance is the joint project of Euroclear Bank and CBL to produce standards that will increase processing efficiency and straight-through processing for international securities, including Eurobonds and structured products, issued through the ICSDs. The growing complexity of bond transactions in the 21st century was described in chapter 15.8. Writing during the summer of 2007 in a Euroclear publication, Pierre Francotte, Euroclear's CEO[1], underlined how the growing complexity and expanding volume of the international securities market has not been matched by growing automation.

'Although the market has grown, it has not been standardised, and the interaction between the various players in the industry falls far short of the straight-through processing standards that exist in other securities markets,' he wrote. 'Only the processing between the ICSDs and their clients is currently straight-through, with the other links in the chain still dominated by manual intervention. As the market continues to grow and become more complex, this translates into higher costs and risks.'

Taking the Eurobond business as an example, less than 10% of corporate action information received by the ICSDs in 2006 used STP. Euroclear Bank and CBL aim to standardise issuance practices and asset servicing for international securities in a project that will take three years to complete. Working with a newly created trade body, the International Standards Market Advisory Group (ISMAG), the two ICSDs will first seek to improve new issues information through better quality and standardised documentation, and improve the quality, accuracy, transparency and timeliness of corporate action information, for example, by same-day distribution.

The project is an important development in a big and fast-growing market. The value of securities issued through Euroclear Bank and CBL amounted to €6.7 trillion in 2006. At mid-year 2007 the market was growing at an annual rate of more than 20%. During 2006, no fewer than 200 000 securities were created; about 250 000 corporate actions took place; and more than 320 000 coupon and redemption payments were managed by the two ICSDs.

Euroclear will bring to this exercise its experience of harmonisation and standardisation acquired while developing its 'domestic market for Europe'. The project is also further evidence of the two companies' willingness to cooperate in the interests of the market and contrasts with the years of often bitter rivalry that marked relations between the two ICSDs until the early years of this century.

The project may illustrate a more general tendency among European securities settlement providers towards cooperation. It is certainly an initiative with significance beyond the borders of Europe.

It therefore provides a fitting point at which to bring this account of securities settlement and Europe's financial market to an end.

---

[1] In Standardising the international securities market – the view from the CEO of Euroclear, July 2007.

However, the end of this book is not the end of the story of Europe's settlement industry. It is a business where change is always around the corner. Talks among participating firms on possible future alliances or realignments are always taking place at some level. Rumours abound. One, picked up by the UK press just as this book is going to print, tells of talks on a transatlantic merger of DTCC, LCH.Clearnet and Euroclear.

It has long been clear that not all the issues facing the European securities settlement industry and its clients have been resolved. Going forward, it is more than likely that fortune will favour those institutions and infrastructures that have an eye on global, as well as purely European developments. If this is so, it will be the job of future studies to look at securities settlement and global financial markets.

Index

Index compiled by Terry Halliday.